Report on
COMMUNION

Report on
COMMUNION

An Independent Investigation
of and Commentary on
Whitley Strieber's
COMMUNION

ED CONROY

WILLIAM MORROW AND COMPANY, INC.
New York

Permissions and acknowledgments, constituting a continuation of the copyright page, appear on page 427.

Library of Congress Cataloging-in-Publication Data

Conroy, Ed.
    Report on Communion : an independent investigation of and
commentary on Whitley Strieber's Communion / Ed Conroy.
        p.   cm.
    Bibliography: p.
    Includes index.
    ISBN 0-688-08864-3
    1. Unidentified flying objects—Sightings and encounters.
2. Strieber, Whitley.   Communion.   I. Title.
TL789.3.C66   1989
001.9'42—dc20   89-32011
                                                                                    CIP

Printed in the United States of America

First Edition

1 2 3 4 5 6 7 8 9 10

BOOK DESIGN BY KATHRYN PARISE

To Rocío Márquez,
who softened some of my hardest days
when this book was still an idea

Acknowledgments

This book requires thanks in spades for the help and attention afforded me by a great many individuals, but it would not have been possible without the complete cooperation of Whitley, Anne, and young Andrew Strieber. They opened their files to me, but they opened their lives as well.

I wish also to express my thanks to the many San Antonians who early on facilitated my initial investigations of Whitley Strieber, including Mary Strieber, his mother, Patricia Strieber, his sister, and Richard, his brother. Their willingness to give me insights into their early family life was invaluable. So, too, were my conversations with Lanette Glasscock and her son, Albert; with Milton and Elizabeth Ryan and their son, Mike; Ann Uhr Hix and her son, Guy, Jr.; and with Brother Martin McMurtrey of Central Catholic Marianist High School.

I would be remiss, too, if I neglected mention of my mother, Dolores Conroy, who not only provided me with valuable background information, but also did an extraordinary job of relating to her son's interest in a subject that might have seemed quite bizarre to another, less enlightened individual. My sister, Mary Furness, has also given me a useful perspective on "visitor" phenomena in relation to myself.

A thousand thanks to them both for tremendous love and support. Warm thanks go also to Dora Ruffner for her role in acting as a highly intelligent and objective sounding board for me during the course of writing this book, as well as for introducing me to several people who aided my investigation.

Many people with specialized interests in UFO and related phenomena made significant contributions to my book. First among them is Dennis Stacy, editor of the *MUFON UFO Journal*, who originally acquainted me with the manuscript of *Communion*, and was extraordinarily forthcoming with many items of information of use to my work. Steven Dennis, research assistant at the Mind Science Foundation in San Antonio, Texas, was also a useful source of information and contacts. Other persons who contributed to my background information are Dr. Bruce Maccabee of the Fund for UFO Research and Peter M. Rojcewicz, Ph.D., of the Juilliard School. Thanks are due, also, to Sterlin Holmesly, Paul Thompson, Roger Downing, Kristina Paledes, Dan Goddard, Tina Barneburg, Ben King, Craig Phelon, Leo Garza, and Felipe Soto, all of the *San Antonio Express-News*, for their roles in facilitating this work at various stages of its development.

My thanks also go to the numerous professional people who agreed to be interviewed for this book, with special thanks to Donald F. Klein, M.D., Nat Laurendi, Budd Hopkins, and Philip J. Klass. All of my interviewees were generous in giving me extensive information, good-sized chunks of their time, strong opinions, and good quotes.

Contents

Introduction

Late in 1986 I was handed a manuscript copy of Whitley Strieber's *Communion* by Dennis Stacy, editor of the *MUFON UFO Journal*, the monthly publication of the Mutual UFO Network. Stacy suggested I might like to take a look at it. He knew I was always on the lookout for new story material, as I was a regular contributor of feature articles to the *San Antonio Express-News*.

Although I thanked Stacy for his consideration, I pointed the manuscript back in his direction and told him it wasn't a story I wanted to touch. My journalistic bailiwick is the world of the fine arts and literature, and I wasn't sure *Communion* fit into either category. In retrospect, I now know that I wanted to take the manuscript and read it, but I had a problem.

I was—albeit subconsciously—afraid of it and the ridicule that I knew is often directed toward popular writers who deal in UFO stories.

On May 17, 1987, the *San Antonio Express-News* published a feature article headlined "CLOSE ENCOUNTERS OF AN S.A. KIND: Whitley Strieber tops non-fiction lists with story of his abduction." The byline read: "By ED CONROY, Special to the Express-News."

What happened to change my attitude toward researching the case of Whitley Strieber's "alien abduction"?

I read his books.

Initially, I had a hard time reconciling the news that Strieber was claiming firsthand contact with nonhuman beings—call them "visitors," "aliens," or what you will—with his reputation as coauthor of *Warday* and *Nature's End*, both of which he wrote with James Kunetka, a lifelong friend. Though I had not read either novel, I had followed with interest the publicity they had generated. It seemed Strieber and Kunetka were challenging readers to think both critically and imaginatively about the implications of such all-too-possible disasters as a limited nuclear war or a global environmental collapse. As artists, the documentary style in which they had written those novels (in which future scenarios are based upon existing social and environmental trends described through actual excerpts from contemporary news articles) appealed to the journalist in me, and led me to think of Strieber and Kunetka not as alarmists but as realists. I respected their work, too, because it suggested that humanity is resourceful enough to survive even the worst imaginable catastrophes.

Curious, I read *Warday*. My reaction? Jealousy. I wished *I* had written the book.

Intrigued, I embarked on a Strieber-reading project that included everything I could find. Then, having absorbed his early Gothic horror fiction as well as his more recent work, I read *Communion*.

After the first hundred pages, I had decided to interview Strieber. My decision to do so was motivated by seeing just too many similarities between qualities Strieber ascribed to the "visitors" and the characters of his own novels. The more I looked at *Communion*, the more it seemed to me that, far from being a radical departure from Strieber's previous work, the book was in some respects a continuation of the books that had preceded it. Nor was it only an extension of themes found in his Gothic horror genre alone; it included the political and environmental consciousness of *Warday* and *Nature's End*, as well as traces of the interest in nature religions one can see in *Cat Magic*.

Even before reading *Communion*, I had begun to ask myself questions about the psychological profile of the author I saw emerging through the texts of his novels. It was clear to me that Strieber was fascinated by predation, but perceived a beauty and justice in it that rarely finds literary expression in our culture. The continuity of imagery and themes that marked his books, moreover, led me to feel that his inner life had obviously been haunted by the same concerns for years. It seemed something very strange had been happening to Whitley Strieber—objectively or subjectively or perhaps even both—for a very long time. Yet after reading *Communion*, where I saw an even greater pattern of correspondence emerging with his fictional work, I had to confront the possibility that Strieber had allowed his imagination to run away with him, perhaps unconsciously—or perhaps even deliberately—constructing one of the most remarkable literary hoaxes of all time. Still, there was something compelling about his story that forced me to equally consider another possibility: that Whitley Strieber had finally stumbled upon the source of all his literary inspiration, and touched it, face-to-face—in horror, amazement, and awe.

One other thing whetted my curiosity about Whitley Strieber; his background in San Antonio. If anything could be checked in his story, I was in a position to do so, since I am a native of that same city and have worked there as a journalist for the past seven years.

I conducted a ninety-minute telephone interview with Whitley Strieber in April of 1987, and followed it up with interviews of his mother, Mary; his elder sister, Patricia; and his younger brother, Richard. I also interviewed Brother Martin McMurtrey, S.M., his high school English teacher; and friends and others in the community who knew him and his family either personally or by reputation. The feature article that resulted from that work was published just one week after *Communion* had risen to occupy the coveted number 1 position on *The New York Times* nonfiction best-seller list.

That article generated more public and professional response than any I had ever written. Encouraged, I decided to meet Strieber and pursue the possibility of a more in-depth profile.

Only two months later, on July 17, 1987, Whitley and Anne Strieber joined me and my friend, John Philip Santos, then a producer with CBS News, at a restaurant in Greenwich Village. Over an elegant nouvelle cuisine dinner, we were regaled with Strieber's "English Empire" story (which figures prominently in *Transformation*), as well as by a humorous but perfectly serious account of what Strieber described as his experience of physical levitation. Anne Strieber listened to it all with remarkable equanimity. John and I were, initially, spellbound, only to fall into an intense dialogue with Strieber that lasted well into the evening. He agreed to be interviewed further by me for a feature in *San Antonio* magazine, and responded positively to my idea of pitching a profile on him to the editors at *The New Yorker*.

John Obrecht, then editor of *San Antonio* magazine, readily agreed to a cover feature story on Strieber, but had to cancel it after a new publisher came in and scuttled the idea. I made some probes at *The New Yorker*, but the more I researched Strieber's background, the more I realized that there was a great deal more to this story than met the eye—and more than could fit into a magazine article. I became convinced that the real background and implications of Strieber's story were being missed by most journalists. Given the tremendous impact that *Communion* was having as the first UFO "abduction" story to break through "the respectability barrier," it seemed to me this story deserved a book-length examination.

As it turned out, it was extraordinarily easy for me to conduct my initial researches into Strieber's background and family in San Antonio. While discussing my plans for the book with my mother, I was surprised to hear her say that she and my father had socialized with Whitley Strieber's parents during the 1950s, prior to my family's departure for New York. Moreover, I learned that Lanette Glasscock, one of my mother's friends from girlhood, happened to be the mother of one of Strieber's closest boyhood friends. Through those and other associations, I found many a door opened to me for which I am, as we say in South Texas, much obliged. Sometimes it is said of San Antonio that it is the biggest small town in the country, and that adage certainly seemed true in this instance.

The process of learning about Strieber's life, then, was initially a relatively simple one, following standard journalistic practices of conducting interviews with people who agreed to speak on the record, attempting to avoid leading questions, and checking facts where it was possible to do so. Most of my interviews were tape-recorded, for accuracy's sake. One source led to another, with the results you will see in the first few chapters of this book.

Yet Strieber's story does not exist in a vacuum—far from it. While it has certainly become the most well-known UFO abduction story, it is only one of many that have already been thoroughly researched. In fairness to other researchers and other witnesses, it seemed to me, it would be impossible to inquire into Strieber's story without recognizing the work of researchers in the UFO community who had been looking into these matters for quite some time.

Investigating the somewhat arcane and politically convoluted world of UFO research, however, proved a difficult task. It required an immersion in the literature of UFO studies to a greater degree than I had ever previously undertaken, and took me to some gatherings of people interested in the subject. For example, I attended a major national UFO convention entitled "Angels, Aliens, and Archetypes" in San Francisco, during the weekend of November 20–21, 1987, at which time I had an opportunity to meet some of the field's leading luminaries, get a feeling for the rhetoric being used to discuss the subject, and observe Strieber's reception among people whom I regarded as the "believers." The job of trying to separate valid from spurious information in publications distributed by organizations in the UFO community was no easy task, since I found there to be a fair amount of factionalism and suspicion within its various quarters. As this book was being finished; moreover, the question of an alleged United States government UFO cover-up regained prominence, requiring me to investigate conflicting claims and assertions in that regard. While I have maintained contact with people in UFO organizations and made a point of regularly reading their publications, I have worked independently, and arrived at my own conclusions.

As tempting as it was to simply explore the mind-boggling length and breadth of the UFO world, I expanded my focus to report on how Strieber was received by various sectors of society—skeptics, mainstream intellectuals, the media, and, of course, the UFO community. Moreover, I have attempted to provide some critical background on previously published alien abduction narratives and research, so that readers left marveling at the bizarreness of Strieber's own stories might have some point of reference against which to gauge their own responses. I have even gone so far as to offer a tentative interpretative framework for understanding some of Strieber's experiences, based upon my understanding of the analytical psychology of Carl Jung and the critical thinking of Jacques Vallee.

While Jungian interpretation of UFO abductions might be regarded by some members of the psychological profession as a sort of New Age parlor game, it was appropriate to use Jung as a point of departure in discussing the content of Strieber's experiences for the reason that Strieber himself attempted to understand the visitors in Jungian terms. As he also attempted to relate them to traditional beliefs in fairies, it was necessary for me to inquire into Vallee's work, as he pioneered a historical and comparative approach to understanding human-"alien" contact in the context of UFO research. His early book, *Passport to Magonia*, startled much of the technologically oriented UFO community with his well-documented accounts of sightings and "close encounters of the third kind," which seemed to have occurred centuries ago.

Lest I be interpreted incorrectly as trying to "psychologize" Strieber's experiences, I should point out that the course of my investigation has paralleled the evolution in perspective that Strieber records in *Transformation*, his sequel to *Communion*. I began this research effort prior to the writing of *Transformation*, when it seemed imperative to find out whether there was any objective evidence to support some of the events Strieber described, and to provide the reader with a historical and psychological context for the visitor experiences he recounted. After I read the manuscript of *Transformation*, though, it appeared that Strieber was moving well beyond the psychological dimensions of his experience and was beginning to discuss the visitors as real entities with a history of social interactions with us.

That change affected the manner in which I finally sat down to write this book, which would have been drastically different had *Transformation* not been published. Since Strieber has been bold enough to move from simply wondering and speculating about the visitors to making positive comments about how they have affected his life and family, I have had to work harder to place his work in relation to the now heated debate over government secrecy. Strieber's arguments in *Transformation* challenge the reader to go beyond a personal, emotional response and require a thoughtful evaluation of the implications of his assertions. Ultimately, Strieber's work in both *Communion* and *Transformation* seriously challenges us to listen to and support those among us who report abduction or related experiences, and to develop the means by which we might all, socially, make sense of their experiences and utilize them for our benefit. Beyond that, Strieber implies, it is time we woke up to accept the fact that we as a species are already in the most intimate relation to the visitors, and have been so for as long as we can remember.

My approach to reporting on Strieber's experiences remains primarily journalistic, in that even while dealing with interpretive considerations, I draw heavily on the work of other researchers. When asked by friends and colleagues whether I was taking a skeptical approach to the subject, I have replied that I am as skeptical of the most vociferous "skeptics" as I am of the "true believers." I hope that, if I make any contribution toward a greater public understanding of Strieber's admittedly hard to accept story, it will come by means of introducing the reader to information regarding his background that may not have been previously made available. I have endeavored, as well, to juxtapose information from a variety of relatively out-of-the-way sources in such a way that it may provide a new and inviting framework suited to thinking about the implications of Whitley Strieber's reported encounters with the visitors.

As to the matter of what conclusions may ultimately be drawn from the stories of those encounters, I leave the resolution of that question to you.

In 1947, Kenneth Arnold said he saw nine disc-shaped objects flying over Mount Rainier, and the world nearly panicked at the thought of "alien invasion." Glowing discs and lighted "ships" continue to be seen, forty years later, and some of us say we've met what some call "aliens," and others call, simply, "the visitors."

Is it indeed true the human race is being visited by creatures who defy the laws of physics as we know them, sometimes flooding our homes with light that bends, whisking us away to strange places, in the middle of the night, only to return us home with odd memories, feelings of displacement, even unusual scars?

Or have the thousands of people, rich and poor, young and old, who say they've met "the visitors," suddenly all gone mad, or worse, become the victims of a sinister manipulation that would boggle even Machiavelli's mind?

Yet the reports of "visitations" continue, even proliferate, finding eloquent expression through professional communicators, talented artists, gifted healers, and just plain folks. If they are sane, and what they tell is the truth as they know it, what may we learn from them?

Report on
COMMUNION

Chapter 1

Through the Looking Glass, Darkly

How the *Communion* Story Emerged into the Light of Day

The story of *Communion* begins in the dark.

For Whitley Strieber, novelist, whose tales take place on the night side of nature, that beginning has more than its share of poetic justice. For the author of *The Wolfen, The Hunger,* and *Warday,* there could have been no better way to meet the ultimate in horror: creatures who spirited him from his bed at night and subjected him to a seemingly torturous series of tests.

Yet, as much of the English-speaking world came to learn in 1987, this was one story that Strieber says he did not set out to write as fiction. This account of "abductions" by apparently intelligent non-human beings (whom Strieber initially admitted might be mental phenomena) was, to quote the author, "a true story, as true as I know how to describe it."

In terms of the publishing industry, what was happening was simply without precedent. A successful American man of letters was coming forth with a story that, to all intents and purposes, impressed many readers as being a first-person narrative of an abduction by "aliens," the occupants of an unidentified flying object (better known as a "UFO"). Given the assumptions still prevalent in the American mind, that impression was widely interpreted to mean that Whitley Strieber

23

had actually survived an encounter with extraterrestrial beings.

In actuality, though, Strieber did not begin his tale with any direct assertion to the effect that he had been taken to meet beings whom he definitely knew to be extraterrestrials. While he admitted it was a possibility they had come from other planets, perhaps even from the future, he said he reserved judgment as to the identity of the "visitors." Even his choice of terms reflected that reservation, rejecting the common term "alien" as too charged with undesirable science fiction connotations. "I refuse to be shoehorned into the debate over whether or not UFOs are real," he told me in an interview in April 1987. He put his attention, instead, to the task of attempting to describe a series of experiences so bizarre and extraordinary in character that they provoked the full spectrum of human response, from utter fascination to disgusted disbelief.

That response, as varied as it may have been, was massive. *Communion*, released in January of 1987, quickly rose to occupy the number 1 position on *The New York Times* best-seller list and stayed on the list for nearly the entire year, making it the most successful UFO-related book in American publishing history. In a media blitz that made *Communion* a household word, Strieber set the nation abuzz with talk of his story, evoking a tidal wave of letters from people claiming similar experiences. That wave has continued as a steady stream of correspondence that received an added impetus with the publication in the fall of 1988 of *Transformation*.

Curiously enough, though, much of both *Communion* and *Transformation* remains in the dark. Although the publication of both books was accompanied by the usual spate of television and radio interviews, book reviews and commentary in both specialized and mass-media publications, a good deal of the background behind these books remained untouched by extensive critical investigation. That obscurity is understandable, for relatively few journalists would regard the field of UFO research as worthy of serious attention, given its long association with the tabloid press and the very evanescent nature of the UFO phenomenon itself. While Strieber's abduction experiences have been discussed in the journals of some North American UFO organizations, they remain far outside the mainstream of intellectual life in this country. As a result, there has been a dearth of serious reflection on the significance of Strieber's stories, and on the meaning of the obviously tremendous public response they have received.

Naturally, Strieber's tales have provoked a strong response from the community of people who make it their business to skeptically examine UFO and related paranormal stories, some of whose most prominent members have invested a fair amount of time in attempting to debunk Strieber's work. Other commentary and criticism have come, interestingly enough, from within the UFO community itself, where a fair amount of controversy has raged over the manner in which Strieber has presented the subject of UFO abductions.

Yet somehow the stories to be found in *Communion* and *Transformation* seem to be finding their way into the mass culture of North America, into its folklore, if you will. This movement should surprise no one, since both books are, after all, works of literature that evoke a personal response from the reader. Even so, Strieber is not unconcerned about the scientific implications of his story. On more than one occasion he has said he hopes to encourage increased research into the field by persons of a skeptical, scientific bent. However, it is clear that Strieber's insistence upon making his message heard derives from a form of philosophical and creative activity generally allowed only a very limited legitimacy and scope in the context of contemporary technological culture.

I refer specifically to his role as a writer, a storyteller, a poet even.

Few commentators who have ventured to express an opinion on Strieber's tales of encounters with the visitors have dared to say that his position as a novelist might serve to add credibility to his narratives. On the contrary, many commentators on *Communion* have usually said something to the effect that his story had to contend with the disadvantage that its author is a professional writer of fiction. Had the very same story, published in virtually the same words, been published by a man with a strong reputation in the physical sciences, it is fair to say there would have been much less discussion of whether or not its content was entirely the "product of the imagination" of its writer.

In the context of North American culture, the physical scientist has long ago replaced the storyteller as the chief shaman of our particular tribe. It is he or she to whom we now listen for understanding of the universe and our place in it. Instead of listening to heroic poems deliberately charged with symbolic meaning, we stand in awe of stories told by physical scientists of quarks, mesons, black holes, "wormholes," and other features of quantum physics, marvels that if we fully comprehended them might stimulate us to wonder whether time travel and telepathy might not, indeed, be possible. Of our writers, though, we only ask that they give us a good yarn. Should an "ordinary writer" shrink from his or her appointed duty to entertain us and dare to make statements regarding something as abstract as the nature of man's relationship to the cosmos—indeed, to assert that he has had direct contact with wild, untameable, magical beings—it is certainly understandable that we moderns might question his sanity, his veracity, his motivations.

That, of course, is precisely what Whitley Strieber has done in writing *Communion* and, later, *Transformation*. Not only did he make statements about "man's place in the universe," but he did something few writers ever do: He provided us with the story of his inspiration. The fact that his story was full of bizarre and unusual incidents is hardly extraordinary if one considers the lives of many creative people; few artists opt for a life of total comfort and regularity. Yet the very fact that his story was so very bizarre and that he claimed it was true caused it to be perceived by many people as disconcerting, disturbing. If one was to accept it as true, then its implications were truly "cosmic." It is no wonder that reaction to the story has been so heated.

To change once again the frame of reference, had Whitley Strieber not been born in a postindustrial society but rather among an Amazonian tribe, and had he grown up to be a shaman instead of a writer, his story of being "abducted" aboard a flying craft might have been seen as testimony that he was, indeed, fulfilling his necessary social role as the tribe's link with forces beyond its comprehension.

A vast gulf in consciousness and culture separates postindustrial populations from the world's remaining indigenous tribal peoples, but both of us share a common concern for learning how to deal with that over which we have no control, for that which is unknown. Ultimately, whether we are civilized or "savage," we would all tend to judge a story of alien abduction by a similar criterion: How can we benefit from knowledge of this story? Does it have anything to offer us besides the possibility of entertainment?

While such observations may appear to break the journalistic code against editorializing in the course of delivering a report, it is absolutely necessary to make them before beginning any examination of the story of Strieber's "visitor experiences." It is, of course, imperative to inquire into questions of Strieber's character, sanity, veracity, and so forth, but to do so without challenging even the ways in which we are accustomed to think—and especially our way of examining questions relating to that which is currently regarded as "the unknown"— would be a dereliction of my duty as an investigator. Even the scientific method as we know it is a project under gradual revision, a product, not only of the human mind, but of the culture in which we live.

I hasten to make this point at the outset of this inquiry because it has been largely forgotten in our culture that once upon a time in the story of mankind, the writer (then known simply as a poet) was held in a considerably greater degree of respect than he or she is today, although we have not totally lost our capacity to be fascinated by the well-told tale. Moreover, the stories that he narrated were regarded very differently than those that we hear today. It was expected of the poet that he should know something of that strange, dark land that lies on the border between death and life, indeed that he should have taken an initiatory journey across its length and breadth, and that he should write of his own soul's adventures for the enlightenment of those who had not yet had the courage to take that same journey.

The late Robert Graves, whose classic book *The White Goddess* explores the origins of the ancient art of poetry, well expressed the ironies contained in the contemporary world's current estimation of the poet:

> At the age of sixty-five I am still amused at the paradox of poetry's obstinate continuance in the present phase of civilization. Though recognized as a learned profession it is the only one for the study of which no academies are open and for which there is no yard-stick, however crude, by which technical proficiency is considered measurable. "Poets are born, not made." The deduction that one is expected to draw from this is that the nature of poetry is too mysterious to bear examination: is, indeed, a greater mystery even than royalty, since kings can be made as well as born and the quoted utterances of a dead king carry little weight either in the pulpit or the public bar.
>
> The paradox can be explained by the great official prestige that still somehow clings to the name of poet, as it does to the name of king, and by the feeling that poetry, since it defies scientific analysis, must be rooted in some sort of magic, and that magic is disreputable. European poetic lore is, indeed,

ultimately based on magical principles, the rudiments of which formed a closed religious sect for centuries but which were at last garbled, discredited and forgotten. Now it is only by rare accidents of spiritual regression that poets make their lines potent in the ancient sense.[1]

Did Whitley Strieber make his lines in *Communion* potent with magic, in the sense that Graves would have us understand? It would seem that indeed he did, for no story achieves such an extraordinary acceptance by the public without somehow plucking a string that resonates within the mind. True, the message of *Communion* was aided by the machinery of a modern public-relations team (something the ancient poets never had at their disposal), yet it appears that Strieber intentionally set out to strike that chord with a story that he expected would provoke both the suspicion that it was merely a work of fiction—and a great deal of wonder, as well.

Is there anything about this book's narrative that, taken at face value, would lead one to assume that it must necessarily be true or false? That question, I would submit with all due respect, has been answered by some readers according to their preexisting intellectual prejudices. No doubt persons already convinced of the "reality" of extraterrestrial life took *Communion* and *Transformation* to be confirmations of something they believed to be true. People predisposed to regard any and all literature dealing with UFOs as symptoms of a pathological mythology exploited by greedy writers who remorselessly bilk a gullible public no doubt rejected the story as a hoax. On the one hand, some readers may have read the book with an eye for passages that corroborated their own thinking on the subject of UFOs, while others doubtlessly examined it for flaws in consistency, reliability of testimony, logic, and so forth. Both believers and skeptics, however, may have missed a great deal that is to be found in *Communion* and *Transformation*, information that may be found only through comprehending Strieber's understanding of himself as a human being and as a writer. There is a great deal that is only implicit in both books. In addition to the task of examining (as much as is possible) Strieber's background, I have endeavored to make explicit that which is implicit in these works, to provide the reader with the means for understanding the manner in which Strieber makes the extraordinary statements that underlie both books.

Much of what he says is couched in metaphor and allegory, the writer's two chief tools for conveying an idea that may be difficult for the reader to accept at face value. Indeed, much of the nature of his experience may be compared to metaphors once employed in ancient times through myths now largely forgotten. Before beginning to examine Whitley Strieber the historical man, it may prove illuminating to consider whether one might make a useful correspondence between his experience and classical stories from poets of the past. I refer specifically to the epics that recount the poet's journey to the underworld.

Perhaps the most well-known story of that genre is the myth of Orpheus and Eurydice, in which the man whose music charmed savage beasts must make a journey to Hades to rescue his wife, Eurydice, who died from a snakebite while still young. In its classical form, the myth recounts the manner in which the poet braves the terrors of hell to plead his case before the thrones of Pluto and Persephone (who had herself been abducted to Hades by her consort), and moves the infernal powers to tears of pity. Allowed to return to earth with Eurydice on the condition that he not look at her until they have left the gates of Hades, Orpheus nevertheless loses his love forever through an impatient glance backward when nearing the end of their journey. Unmoved by the attentions of earthly women who attempt to soften his sadness with their charms, Orpheus is eventually torn to bits by the Bacchantes, who throw his head and lyre into a river. His shade, we are told, is happily reunited with Eurydice in eternity.[2]

The mythological motifs here are clear: The poet (whose abilities as a musician give him an innate ability to evoke sympathy from the entirety of creation) realizes he must go into the dark itself for the sake of love, not only to rescue his wife but so that he may be complete.

In its classical form, the myth of Orpheus and Eurydice seems to bear only the faintest connection to the story of Strieber's abduction in *Communion*. After all, Strieber did not lose his wife, and his story seems to involve a flight up into a craft of some sort, not descent into the bowels of the earth. Actually, though, Strieber recounts in *Communion* that he nearly did lose his wife to the emotional problems that he experienced subsequent to his first abduction. What is of correspondence to the "underworld," moreover, is that unknown other place, wherever it may be, to which his visitors took him.

In a more modern version, however, the myth of Orpheus and Eurydice takes on a number of characteristics that beg comparison with many of the elements in Strieber's abduction story. As rendered into cinematic form by the French poet Jean Cocteau in his film *Orphée* (1949), the story becomes one of a poet's own love affair with death, taking place deliberately on the borderland between light and shadow, death and life.

In Cocteau's version of the story, the brilliant but no longer young poet Orphée is abducted one day from a sidewalk café in Paris, following a fistfight that turns into a brawl. Cegéste, a young rival poet who arrives drunk in the company of an elegant young woman, referred to simply as "the princess," is run over and killed by two motorcyclists garbed entirely in black. Orphée is taken into the princess's limousine (along with Cegéste's body) and conducted to her palatial but badly dilapidated home. There, after being escorted to her bedroom, he is astonished to see her disappear by walking through a wardrobe mirror.

In this fashion, Cocteau begins the poet's tragic and haunting relationship with the underworld, from which emanate cryptic poetic messages on his car radio. Disturbed but entranced, Orphée can do virtually nothing but write down those missives from the other world, struggling to decipher their meaning. Little does he realize that they are being directed his way by the now discarnate Cegéste at the behest of the princess. Even less does he realize that he has been chosen by that royal woman (none other than Death herself) to be the object of her love.

Eurydice's death, in Cocteau's story, is engineered by the princess, who is depicted standing, wraithlike, at the foot of her bed, night after night. That event, moreover, serves only as a ruse to lure Orphée to the underworld. There, in a courtroom presided over by three impassive men in black suits, guarded by the princess's motorcyclist-henchmen, Orphée learns the truth of her love for him and confronts the fact that his love for the princess—and the dark world of the mystery of death that she personifies—compete strongly with his love for his own wife. Is it an accident that Cocteau gives us a Eurydice who is light and blond, and a princess who is dark and brunette?

In the film's extraordinary climax, the princess risks eternal punishment to make Orphée her eternal companion. She fails utterly, tragically, and resignedly walks away to banishment from the world of the living that is, by her own description, worse than an eternity in hell. Orphée and Eurydice awake to be joyously rejoined in their cottage, with just a glimmer of a dream to hint at what they nearly lost—and perhaps gained—in the underworld.

The conflict that Cocteau creates within Orphée's own soul, personified by two women who represent two utterly different kinds of experience, may perhaps also parallel the dilemma faced by anyone confronting the nature of the kind of abduction experience that Strieber describes. In order for an individual to understand this experience, Strieber would say, one must freely enter into the dark, follow its summons, and abandon the conceptions of the world, formed in the light of day, to which we have long become accustomed. One may feel tormented, living with the sense of receiving unintelligible messages from a source one cannot identify, only to find that one may be suddenly thrust into an experience that threatens to destroy whatever shred of happiness one may have known in the world.

Yet Cocteau's story of Orphée seems to suggest that one may return from the underworld, having met death and her minions face-to-face, and emerge with the seed of a new understanding of oneself, as impossible as such knowledge may be considered to be in the world in which we live. That knowledge, we are told, may only exist as the seed of a dream, but it is there nonetheless.

Cocteau's film is striking, not only for the parallel that one may draw between its plot and the outline of Strieber's experiences, but also for the striking qualities of its visual images. The three-man, dark-suited tribunal that confronts Orphée upon his entrance to the underworld is reminiscent of reports of the legendary "Men in Black" who are reported to have visited people claiming to have seen UFOs, often appearing in groups of three. The motorcyclists who guard the "princess," in addition to their close-fitting black uniforms, wear extraordinary eye goggles that, if looked at closely, have an upward-slanting design reminiscent of the eyes in the image on the cover of *Communion*.

Of course, speculation about the source of the remarkable imagery in Cocteau's film should not be overdone, since the filmmaker was also a poet fully aware of the classical tradition and deliberately seeking a way in which to convey the conflicts of the soul that animate creative life. In an interview in *Cocteau on Film: A Conversation Recorded by André Fraigneau*, Cocteau said:

> My mental life is that of a lame man, with one foot in life and the other in death. Therefore I am quite naturally drawn to a myth in which life and death meet face to face. Moreover . . . I realized that a film would serve much better to show

the incidents on the frontier separating the two worlds. . . . I had to make the magic *direct*, without ever using the laboratory, and showing only what I saw myself and wanted others to see. [Emphasis Cocteau][3]

In regard to *Communion* and *Transformation*, of course, we must deal with the question whether Whitley Strieber, to paraphrase Cocteau, made his magic direct, whether he communicated only what he saw himself and wanted others to see. This is not yet the place in which to open the question whether his accounts in both books accord with objective facts. Yet we would be remiss in beginning to view this project of examining Strieber's story were we to assume that the writing of a nonfiction book is not a creative act. First-person confessional works such as Thomas De Quincey's *Confessions of an English Opium Eater* or Núñez Cabeza de Vaca's *Relation* stand as literature, in the sense of being works of fine art, and so too, someday, may *Communion*. Both De Quincey and Cabeza de Vaca left behind remarkable stories of explorations into unknown lands; the subjective world of the mind, on the one hand, and the rugged Indian territories that were to become New Spain, on the other.

Third-person accounts of UFO abductions, however, are works of an entirely different order, especially if they purport to advance an explanatory hypothesis in relation to a body of research that the reader is asked to accept as valid. In the case of Strieber's *Communion* and *Transformation*, it should be remembered, the author makes no attempt to produce an explanation of anomalous events in his experiences in a strictly scientific sense. Both books are accounts of one man's experiences, with a fair amount of admitted speculation about their meanings. The conclusions are represented as the product of the author's experiences, not as the result of some kind of socially verifiable experimental process of research.

And yet, perhaps because Strieber initially left open a wide-ranging list of possibilities as to the nature and identity of the visitors, his readers have found themselves traveling down a multitude of pathways in the course of attempting to understand his story. We have found ourselves traversing through fairy lore, philosophical speculation, and theological meditations, perhaps even giving more of our time to those lines of reflection than to rigorous arguments from astronomers as to the possibility of life existing on other planets. Some of the best intellects in our culture may shake their heads and lament such a course in the direction of popular thought. Yet the fact remains that we are hungry for greater knowledge of who and what we are, and less and less content to allow thought about intelligent nonhuman life in the universe to be reduced to only the discourse of the physical scientists and their radio telescopes trained for interstellar communications, as important as such projects are.

Whitley Strieber fanned the flames of those desires in an extraordinary way that related, not to the cold vastness of outer space, but to the strange mystery of personal experiences so bizarre as to automatically thrust him into an extraordinary trajectory. In the course of a year, by his own account, he had gone from being a very anxious man alarmed by the intrusion of the visitors into his life to being a spokesman for a new viewpoint on the experience of alien abduction already becoming known to the public through the electronic media's talk shows. In doing so, of course, he encountered more than his share of attacks on his integrity and sanity, attacks that he had anticipated.

It was not easy for Strieber to even see *Communion* published. His publisher at the time, Warner Books, rejected his manuscript, Strieber told me, telling him that if it was published it would ruin his reputation. As he recounted in *Communion*, he dropped work on a historical novel centered about the life of a wealthy American woman who finds herself in Russia at the time of the Bolshevik revolution and throws her fortune behind it. Entitled *The Blood Eagle*, it displays the same command of rich description and sense of mystery in its plot development that made *The Wolfen* and *The Hunger* such successes. From the few chapters of it that I have read, I would hazard the opinion that it could have been a very successful novel, had it been released during the current thaw in Soviet-American relations.

That much said, it is necessary to examine how this extraordinary narrative found its way into the light of day, and whether or not the people with whom Strieber worked to check his personal sanity and veracity corroborate his story, as he told it in *Communion*, and later, *Transformation*.

In order to get some perspective on the manner in which *Communion* became a real literary property and found its way into the bookstores, I interviewed James Landis, then publisher of William Morrow and Company's Beech Tree Books, who personally handled the purchase of *Communion*. I also used the interview as an opportunity to obtain some perspective on Strieber as an author, for Landis was intimately involved with launching Strieber's literary career.

CONROY: Jim, would you describe for me the Whitley Strieber whom you met at the time you published *The Wolfen*.

LANDIS: I remember being very excited about the book when I began it, which was about ten years ago. I think it was one of those novels that you open up—at least that I did—the manuscript, and see some promise in it immediately. His agent was a guy named Charles Neighbors, with whom I was pretty close at the time, in a business way. Chuck was not a big agent; he was an independent, relatively small agent and I don't know if I had ever done any other books with him, but we came to terms pretty quickly, as I remember.

I don't know if it was out with other houses. Multiple submissions were a lot less frequent, back then. I have a vague memory that maybe someone else had seen the book and was interested in it, but I think we acted on it pretty quickly. In those days I couldn't act on my own about a book, so I undoubtedly went to one of my bosses and we decided to make an offer.

I don't remember when I met Whitley after that. You know, it was another book to buy. It's been a decade-long relationship, and it's been interrupted, now and then.

CONROY: That leads me up to the point at which you all established a business relationship. Whitley told me that he had some difficulty with his other publisher about the concept of *Communion*, that they essentially felt that it would be a disaster, so eventually the book came around to you. I wanted to ask you if you could tell me about the process of your coming to do the book. How did it come to you?

LANDIS: I didn't know there was a history with another house. I wouldn't know what house that would be. Putting aside paperback originals and YA (young adult) books, it seems we did three books: *The Wolfen*, *The Hunger*, and *Black Magic*. We made an offer on *Night Church*, I think that was the one, that was rejected, and I think he went to Simon and Schuster, and did two books there. Then *Warday* came up and by that time he was with another agent—he'd gone through a number of them—and we were invited to participate. . . . The book went to Holt, and it was Whitley's first hardcover best-seller, I believe. *Nature's End*—I don't know what happened at Holt, but it went to Warner Books, and I guess that *Communion* came next. . . .

Kirby McCauley called me and said he had a most unusual book, a book that I wouldn't be expecting at all. He wasn't going to tell me about it, he would just send it over. He asked if we were interested and I said we were interested. I believe it was a day in June when the manuscript arrived. That would be what year?

CONROY: 1986.

LANDIS: Yeah. And I took it home and I read some of it and went to work the next day. The manuscript was left in the bedroom open, where I'd stopped reading and when I came home that evening, the entire manuscript was spread all over the bedroom. Not a single page was next to a page that belonged to it, as I remember. It took two and a half hours to put the manuscript back together. It was probably the wind.

CONROY: I was just going to ask you, did you leave a window open?

LANDIS: Yeah, there was usually a window open there, but anyway, it was very strange. Rather frustrating, but in any case I put the manuscript back together, finished reading it, brought it to the office, and wrote a memo saying something like, "You may not believe this, but Whitley Strieber has written about his own experiences with alien beings, and I suggest you take this seriously. Don't scoff, and read it." I sent it around. I don't remember by what ports but it also went to Avon, our sister company, and I think that the auction was scheduled for after the Fourth of July. Then Kirby McCauley called soon thereafter, probably around June twenty-seventh . . . and said that he had an offer—a large offer, from a large company. (It turned out to be Putnam.) There was pressure to sell the book immediately, so we ended up buying it. And I've heard subsequently . . . that a lot of people were kind of put off by it.

CONROY: And as they say, the rest is history.

LANDIS: Yes. A woman at Avon, Rena Wolner was extremely helpful, because we paid a lot of money for it.

CONROY: Do you mind, for the record, talking about how much you paid for it?

LANDIS: Well, I think Whitley's always talked about it. It was a million-dollar advance. . . . Avon, particularly Rena Wolner, had a passion for it that was instrumental in our bidding efforts. Without that kind of backing on the paperback side, we couldn't have bid much more.

CONROY: There are some people out in the UFO community who are saying the deal that was originally negotiated included not just one book but two, that it was an advance that included the later *Transformation*.

LANDIS: No.

CONROY: It's not correct.

LANDIS: Mm-mm. (Negative tone)

CONROY: I wanted to ask you your estimation of the article by Claflin in *Publishers Weekly*,[4] which questioned whether or not Strieber's story should have been classified as nonfiction.

LANDIS: Claflin talked to me, and there were some errors in [his article], that I believe I wrote to *Publishers Weekly* about. There were things that I couldn't have said. Like he had me quoted as saying I went to the "pub board." Now Morrow doesn't have a "pub board." The expression doesn't exist in this house; I never would have said it.

CONROY: He seemed to be taking Morrow to task for—

LANDIS: For publishing *Communion* as nonfiction?

CONROY: Yes, exactly. Do you think the article had any effect upon your colleagues in the publishing industry? Did it cause debate or talk?

LANDIS: I don't think so. They usually don't. I don't think articles like that really— Not many articles in *Publishers Weekly* have too much effect, not because they're not serious or well done, but because people are too busy to worry about such things and they don't affect them. You know, I think a lot of houses had a chance at this book and it became an extremely visible success, as a number one hardcover best-seller *and* the number one paperback best-seller, for an enormous number of weeks in a row. That's unusual, in that volatile paperback market, for a book to stay on the list so long, and to be in top place. So it's possible that people who saw that reacted to the criticism because, one way or another, it substantiated their own supposed reasons for having rejected the book. I'm sure that most of them, had they known the sales history of *Communion*, would have been happy to have published it.

CONROY: That's the bottom line. One of the things Whitley said to me about your relationship with him was this: What struck him the most about you is that you took his book seriously. I asked him why. He said, "Well, Jim's known me for all these years." Would you say that was a pretty good estimation of it, that you knew Whitley's character, and you took it seriously because of that?

LANDIS: That's part of it, but you take a book seriously qua book, you know. You don't take the person seriously—you take the book seriously.

CONROY: So the book stood on its own, for you.

LANDIS: Well I knew the man, and that is probably an advantage over other publishers in terms of getting a submission from a guy you know. Others had never seen him, so to speak. . . .

He's a very serious man, so I took him seriously. It wasn't a joke.

CONROY: Let's move on to *Transformation*, if we may. In early discussions with Whitley, did he show any intention of writing a sequel to *Communion*?

LANDIS: No.

CONROY: Do remember at what time he came to you with the idea of a sequel?

LANDIS: I don't remember, precisely. As we were meeting and working on *Communion*, he would report further visitations. I don't believe it was to prep me for getting another contract. [But] I was certainly open to the idea—he didn't call it a sequel.

CONROY: He didn't. I wonder if you had a chance to speak with your fellow editor, Mr. Lee, about the experience that Whitley relates in regard to him in *Transformation*.

LANDIS: Yeah. I don't remember whom he told first about it, me or Whitley, but he verified it, and allowed his name to be used in relation to it. He's a very conservative guy. One of the least likely people you'd expect. . . . It's not the kind of thing he'd go around talking about. You know, I mean, for Bruce, it's not the kind of thing you'd expect from him. He's also an old reporter. He was in Washington.

CONROY: So I've heard. In regard to *Transformation*, it appears to me that the strategy that Whitley followed in terms of reviews in the print media was quite different from that for *Communion*. Whitley told me that he deliberately decided not to send out review copies to the press because he frankly didn't have much of an opinion of the print media.

LANDIS: Well, there was a sequence of events. It wasn't that we didn't send out review copies, but that we didn't send out galleys. There were no advance bound galleys. I believe that we sent out a few copies, as we normally would, only after it was published. The book would appear before the reviews would appear, and they would have a neutral presence. That's what Whitley wanted, so that's what we did. . . .

Also, with *Communion* itself, I don't know if we sent out bound galleys on that either, but we did simply drop ship it, I guess that's the expression. We didn't take orders on it. We shipped copies to bookstores, based on what we thought they might do. They'd never heard of the book before. They weren't asked to place orders on it. While some of them resented the fact that we did that (and that was very rarely), we were vindicated by the fact that it was a huge success. That book started to sell the minute it appeared on the bookshelves: no reviews, no appearances, nothing. And we had word from the bookstores that *Communion*, with this strange picture on the cover, was selling. It started right away. It was very rewarding.

CONROY: I should say. That's a pretty unusual phenomenon.

LANDIS: Well, it was unprecedented, if you consider that the book is nonfiction. His previous, coauthored book was not a success. The full strategy of *Communion* worked. Someone at Bantam said it was the most skillfully published book of the year.

CONROY: Coming from a colleague, I'm sure that's gratifying. Well, I'm wondering, how is *Transformation* doing in comparison with *Communion*?

LANDIS: It's not selling as well, but it would have been an exception if it had. Whether it was a strict sequel or not, it's perceived as such, and the rule of thumb in publishing (which there will always be exceptions to) is that a sequel does about half of what the original does. I think that the paperback will do very well. I think that the people who made *Communion* such a success in paperback may be waiting for the paperback of *Transformation*.

CONROY: You were quoted by Claflin as saying you've had a great time with *Communion*.

LANDIS: I called it a "blessed publication."

If Landis's comment seems to imply that there was something of an intervention of higher powers in the response that *Communion* received, there is already one apocryphal story that might seem to indicate that the "visitors"—whoever or whatever they are—took a particularly strong interest in the book from its outset. Bruce Lee, a former Washington journalist for *Newsweek* who is now an editor for Morrow, reported an extraordinary personal encounter in an uptown New York bookstore. Strieber reported it in *Transformation*, and stated that Lee passed a lie detector test by Nat Laurendi (the same gentleman who tested Strieber for both *Communion* and *Transformation*). It might well seem suspect to some readers that this story originated from within the publishing house of William Morrow and Company itself, so I called Lee at his office at Morrow to get the story from its source.

CONROY: I was wondering if you could tell me the story in your own words of this encounter, and also, could you place it in time.

LEE: Well, you caught me just after cutting fifty thousand words out of a manuscript. (Laughs) Well, it was wintertime, January, February, or March, terribly cold . . .

CONROY: Of '87, just after the book came out?

LEE: Yes. My wife and I went out on a weekend, it was a Saturday because Sunday the bookstores would be closed. We went up to—I think it was Womrath's on Lexington Avenue— one of the stores that had the lending library. It's no longer in existence. We went in, I had a couple of my own books, I wanted to see how they were on display, and *Communion* was more toward the rear of the store. I think there were about ten racks facing front, where they had the latest best-selling books. I showed my wife the *Communion* rack, and then I went around the store looking for some of my other books, and she went off looking for fiction to buy. And then I noticed a couple come into the store, and head directly for *Communion*. I mean, it was just, you could just see them come in—they didn't know where the book was, you couldn't see it from the street—and they came in and headed right back for where that rack was. Most unusual, if you see what I mean.

CONROY: Yes.

LEE: They were very short. My mother was five foot one, I'm six-four, so I notice these things. And they were all wrapped up. Long scarves, wool hats that you pull down, and they picked up a copy of the book and they started thumbing through it— the man was doing this. And it was obvious that they were speed-reading, too. And they would say, "Oh, he's got this wrong, he's got that wrong." And they were sort of giggling. At this point in time, particularly because they were giggling, and they were saying he's got it wrong, I thought I might as well go over and find out what's up. So I went over and introduced myself and said I'm from the publisher, and could you tell me what you think is wrong with the book. I think it was the woman that looked up. She was wearing those big sort of sunglasses that the girls keep up in their hair. And they really sort of hide the face. But by God behind those dark glasses there was a goddamn big pair of eyes. And I mean to say it was a *big* pair of eyes. And they were shaped sort of like almonds. You know how when you meet somebody the first time you can frequently get an immediate reaction? The hackles on the back of my neck just went up. I got to feeling that I was in eyeball contact with somebody who did not like me at all. In fact I got the impression that I was not wanted around there, and having been raised on a farm and seeing mad dogs I got that immediate relationship, and I went over and—I think I said "Good-bye"—and went over and got my wife and got the hell out of there. I was almost shaking. I said, "Did you see that couple?" and my wife said, "Sure I saw that couple," and I said, "Well they don't look like goddamn people!" and she said, "Well, you're crazy." So we went off and had a margarita and some nachos. It was really a very intense shock.

CONROY: I can imagine. You mentioned that your mother was five foot one. Did you mention that in reference to the fact that these people seemed to be a little shorter than normal?

LEE: Well, it's just that because I'm six-four and I say people are short, you see, and people say, "How short?" and I say, "About as tall as my mother," because they were wearing boots and it was sort of hard with those hats on, to tell what was there, underneath all the clothing. And of course, you couldn't see the hands, because they were in gloves. But you do know when somebody's reading something and comprehending it, and those pages were turning very, very fast.

CONROY: So this interaction that you had with them just lasted a minute or perhaps even less.

LEE: It was short.

CONROY: Remarkable.

LEE: You don't often get that. You know, I mean, it was complete loathing, hatred, whatever you want to call it.

CONROY: You felt this emanating generally from the woman?

LEE: Well, the man didn't look up. The man never looked up. . . . It was only she who looked up. It was almost as if I was being ignored by the guy. I'm glad he didn't look up—and he had the same eyes. That would have been too much, I think.

CONROY: I hope you don't mind my asking you what it was about the other one that gave you the impression it was a "she"?

LEE: (Long pause) That's an interesting question. (Pause) From the way they were talking, I kind of thought they were male and female. (Pause) And—I don't know, by God. That's a big question. I think possibly it was the coat. It was a longer coat and seemed to be covering a skirt.

CONROY: The glasses made you associate it with being feminine?

LEE: That was one particular. But the movement seemed feminine, the voice seemed feminine.

CONROY: Did they sound like normal human voices?

LEE: They sounded like Upper East Side Jewish.

CONROY: That's remarkable. Just the sort of cultured voice one might expect to hear in a bookstore of that sort.

I asked Lee about his wife's reaction to the event—her saying that he was "crazy."

"That's a good logical reaction from a good logical wife," he said.

According to Lee, he came back to the office the following day and told Jim Landis about his experience. "If I hadn't mentioned it to him, the thing would have disappeared," Lee said. Eventually, though, the story found its way out of the publishing house, Lee said, for before long he received a call from Strieber inquiring about the story. Not long after that, a small item appeared in *New York* magazine recounting his story. Lee wasn't entirely pleased that the story had gotten out of the house.

"By then I was had," he told me. "By then any chance of keeping the story in-house was gone. The cat was out of the bag. You don't like to go around telling stories you can get associated with—associating oneself with the 'kook factor.' Funny things happen in the course of your life. I've seen some strange things."

I had to ask Lee if he had seen anything in the UFO category.

"No," he said. "But I've seen some congressmen and senators who could probably fly."

Lee's testimony is notable for its high degree of detail and emotional punch. It is all the more remarkable in that it is being told by a veteran reporter whose experiences with "congressmen and senators who could probably fly" no doubt reinforced his professional skepticism. Still, even though his experience went well beyond the pale of the ordinary, it would be fair to say that Lee was not completely unsophisticated in matters relating to the paranormal. In the final segment of our interview, Lee casually mentioned that one of the authors whom he edits in Malachi Martin, the former Jesuit priest who wrote, among other works, *Hostage to the Devil*, an investigation of the phenomena of possession and exorcism related through several contemporary case histories. Lee said he worked on that book with Martin, and came away from it feeling "unclean."

"I went to see the exorcist for the Episcopal diocese of New York, though," he said, "and he helped me."

Lee went on to relate that one day when Malachi Martin was

visiting him in his office, he regaled him with the tale of his bookstore encounter.

"He began to get agitated and shifted in his chair as I was telling the story," he said. "Then he got up and stood behind me. When I was done he asked me, 'Does this experience disturb you?' I said, 'No.' He asked, 'Do you sleep well?' and I said, 'Yes.' He then said, 'Well, you seem all right, but they exist.' "

That anecdote, for what it is worth, is the first instance I have seen of a priest (albeit one now no longer functioning in the Roman Catholic Church) expressing concern for the welfare of someone reporting an encounter with beings matching the description of those now identified with Whitley Strieber. I must hasten to add that I do not take this story to provide any basis whatsoever for regarding the "visitor" whom Strieber describes as being necessarily demonical. I simply present it as one example of the range of response evoked by stories of these sorts of encounters, especially when delivered by credible witnesses.

The role of priest as guide through the darker areas of life, of course, has been largely replaced by that of the psychologist and psychiatrist. Though Strieber mentioned in *Communion* that he told a Catholic priest of his "visitor experiences" (and received the reply that they must, ultimately, work to the higher glory of God), what is of legitimate concern to readers is the question whether Strieber's account of his therapy with Donald F. Klein, M.D. (identified in *Communion* as director of research at the New York State Psychiatric Institute), is an accurate and valid reflection of what actually transpired. Doubt has been cast on the particulars of and motivations for Strieber's medical tests by Philip J. Klass in his book *UFO-Abductions: A Dangerous Game*[5] and in an interview with me Klass not only raised those questions again but expressed some doubt whether Dr. Klein actually wrote the letter that bears his name in Appendix I of *Communion*.

Much to his credit, although he has given no interviews regarding his therapeutic relationship with Strieber to any journalists, Dr. Klein agreed to consider four questions that I submitted in writing. I formulated those questions only after having extensively interviewed Strieber about his own testing procedures and receiving documentation on the tests that Strieber took during the period of time that he was seeking psychiatric counsel. Moreover, my questions were composed after a lengthy interview with Philip Klass and three extensive interviews with Budd Hopkins, the UFO investigator and author with whom Strieber associated during the early days of coping with his visitor experiences. In doing so, I believe that I faithfully brought up some of the principal criticisms, concerns, and suspicions that I have heard expressed, not only by Klass and Hopkins, but by some of their colleagues as well.

Because Dr. Klein chose to respond to my questions in a written manner, I have included here the verbatim texts of both my letter to him and his letter to me. His reply is informative and instructive in a number of areas. Our correspondence, then, went as follows:

December 22, 1988

Dear Dr. Klein:

Thank you for your willingness to consider a few questions regarding your patient, Whitley Strieber.

My purpose in writing you is to obtain background which may be useful for my book, *Report on* Communion, to be published in mid-1989 by Morrow. As a reporter (I am a columnist for the San Antonio Express-News) my professional interest in what you may have to say is two-fold:

1. I wish to check the accuracy of Mr. Strieber's account of the events in his therapeutic relationship with you, and;

2. I desire the benefit of your thoughts on how best to think of hypnotherapy in relation to Mr. Strieber's "visitor" experiences and those of persons reporting similar experiences.

I have formulated four questions for you, therefore, as follows:

1. Some of Mr. Strieber's critics continue to maintain that he is "emotionally unstable" and/or suffering from "temporal lobe epilepsy." Please specify what tests you administered and/or ordered administered for Mr. Strieber, explaining how you subsequently determined that (as expressed in your statement in Appendix I of *Communion*) he "is not suffering from a psychosis."

2. Budd Hopkins, in an interview with me, has asserted that, in his recollection, Mr. Strieber decided of his own volition to terminate his hypnotherapy with you. Mr. Hopkins opined he

thinks that action on Mr. Strieber's part was "premature." Please give your reasons for taking on Mr. Strieber's case, your estimation of his condition at the time therapy was brought to an end, and the reasons why therapy was concluded (if indeed it was concluded and is not now ongoing).

3. Is there any legitimate means within the parameters of professionally accepted procedures of hypnotherapy to determine whether or not events which may perhaps superficially appear to be contents of a psychotic fantasy (such as those described by Mr. Strieber in his "abduction" scenario) may in fact be event-related? If yes, how? If not, why not?

4. Philip J. Klass, in an interview with me, said he suspects that the statement in Appendix I of *Communion* which bears your name was not written by you, but rather by Whitley Strieber. Would you please clarify the circumstances under which it was written?

Please understand, sir, that none of my questions are in any way intended to question your professional competence. If some of them appear to violate the confidentiality of the doctor-patient relationship, I will of course respect your opinion. However, I hope you understand they have been specifically formulated in the interest of helping to clarify the record of what occurred in the course of Mr. Strieber's therapy with you.

In the case of Mr. Strieber, I might submit, there is an objective, social need for more information regarding his therapy with you. Allegations of insanity continue to be made against him by people who also give the appearance of wishing to socially stigmatize him in an undesirable way, and terms such as "temporal lobe epilepsy" are being bandied about in a very casual manner.

Moreover, it appears that the use of hypnosis as an investigative tool by "ufologists" exploring a phenomenon they have come to call "alien abduction" raises, as you may have observed, serious ethical and methodological questions. Many of those questions, it seems, have yet to be publicly addressed by professional therapists. One need not, of course, accept the valid-

ity of the "alien abduction" hypothesis to recognize that certain
problems may exist in the manner in which the personal crises
experienced by people who have come to be known as "UFO
abductees" are treated.

Your replies to my questions, then, would contribute greatly to
the general public's understanding of Mr. Strieber's experiences. If you wish to address any of the larger concerns I have
raised regarding "alien abduction" as a socio-psychological
phenomenon, I would be most appreciative. I am available to
speak with you on the telephone at your convenience, but would
gratefully accept a written reply to the questions, should you
prefer that option.

Sincerely,

Ed Conroy

cc Whitley Strieber

January 13, 1989

Dear Mr. Conroy:

I have recently asked Whitley Strieber to agree to my replying
to your questions and he has sent me a full consent. In that
case, I am glad to do what I can to respond accurately and
informatively to your questions.

Question 1 indicates the issue of temporal lobe epilepsy. It also
deals with the issue of psychosis.

I had raised the issue of temporal lobe epilepsy with Mr. Strieber during the course of my professional contact with him.
One reason for this was the fact that the vast majority of his
unusual experiences occurred upon being aroused from sleep.
It is a well-known phenomenon that sleep enhances the occurrence of epileptic-like phenomena. There is nothing in his experience that related specifically to the need for being aroused
from sleep. This seemed odd. I therefore suggested to Mr.
Strieber that he have neurological examinations, a CAT scan
and somewhat later an MRI. The neurological examination
was negative, the CAT scan was negative, the MRI showed

unexplained bright spots. Since MRI is a relatively new phenomenon, these unexplained bright points may be a normal variant of brain anatomy or may indeed reflect an abnormal process. Plainly it would be foolish at this point to affirm that Mr. Strieber suffers from temporal lobe epilepsy. It would also be false to claim that has been ruled out as impossible. However, I think most doctors would find it difficult to prescribe medications for temporal lobe epilepsy predicated on this level of evidence.

With regard to the definition of psychosis, it should be realized that this is a term that has had multiple definitions over the years. I enclose a copy of my chapter on "The Concept of Psychosis" that appeared in my book, *Diagnosis and Drug Treatment of Psychiatric Disorders*. As we state here, the hallmark of psychosis is that the misevaluation or misconception has the force of reality and results in unmodifiable distortion.

The Diagnostic Manual of the American Psychiatric Association states that psychotic is a term "indicating gross impairment and reality testing . . . the individual incorrectly evaluates the accuracy of his or her perception and thought; makes incorrect inferences about external reality, even in the face of contrary evidence." The point here is that the term psychotic, as used in psychiatry, refers to somebody who is really in severe difficulties with regard to their everyday functioning, ability to communicate, reason and accept criticism of their beliefs.

None of this was true of Mr. Strieber. He evidenced skepticism about his own experiences, although clearly at times he asserted varying levels of conviction. Outside of these experiences, there was no problem manifest with communication, ideation, inference, etc. To consider him psychotic on the basis of his deviant report in the context of his intact personality functioning would seem foolish to me.

The second question involves the issue of Mr. Strieber's decision to terminate hypnotherapy. Mr. Hopkins may or may not be correct that this was premature. It was not my opinion.

I saw Mr. Strieber as a psychiatrist. My main concern was restoring him to normality. He came to me in a state of marked affective distress and disorganized functioning. We were able to help him out of this and I am pleased that he has been able to maintain his gains.

I do not think that therapy has to continue indefinitely. When we seemed to reach a plateau and there were no obvious goals to pursue, termination of treatment, either permanent or temporary, made sense to me. Mr. Strieber maintains contact with me. I do not consider him to be in any sort of formal therapy, although I think that my availability to him may be of some utility.

Your third question deals with whether hypnotherapy can determine if the contents of a "psychotic fantasy" (although I do not accept that terminology) can be demonstrated as factual.

I see no way in which this can be done. My use of hypnosis was not to determine "the facts," but to help Mr. Strieber to deal with his stress inducing perceptions within a constructive framework. I am very aware of the extensive literature indicating that hypnotic reports may be entirely fantastic. I refer you to the work of Frank Pattee at the University of Kentucky back in the early 30's.

With regard to question four, I am sorry that Philip Klass still persists in the false belief that my statement was not written by myself but rather by Whitley Strieber.

I certainly accept your statement that you are not questioning my professional competence or wish to violate the confidentiality of the doctor-patient relationship. My understanding of the confidentiality of the doctor-patient relationship is that it is not the doctor's prerogative but the patient's. In so far as Mr. Strieber has specifically told me that he wishes me to reply to your questions, "fully, completely and candidly," I have no hesitation in doing so. In fact, I appreciate the opportunity to help educate the public as to the complexities of these issues.

I'm sorry if my suggestion that Mr. Strieber may suffer from temporal lobe epilepsy has been used to discount his report as "insane." I think it indicates that such a remarkable report requires the most meticulous investigation in an attempt to figure out whether it can be accepted as face valid factual or not.

With regard to the use of hypnosis as an investigative tool, I think that your question could be broadened. What about the use of ordinary interrogation or counseling? The possibility for systematic suggestion and the construction of plausible scenarios exist in all these frameworks. The idea that hypnosis has some unique ability over and above ordinary suggestion, has been denied by Theodore X. Barber and others.

In other words, if you are looking for facts, you have to be very aware of the necessity for highly sophisticated methods of objective investigation and controlled comparison. As I hope I made it clear above, that was not my intent.

With regard to alien abduction as a socio-psychological phenomenon, my initial interest stems from my interest in psychopathology. Many psychopathological states result in reports that are at substantial deviation from what seems to be objective reality. Nonetheless, these reports are often easily understood as being in the context of a severe derangement such as a toxic state, schizophrenia or a severe depression. What is really puzzling is when people report extremely unusual experiences but seem to be perfectly okay otherwise. It is possible that a better understanding of such people and their reports would cast light upon our understanding of psychopathology or might bring otherwise unsuspected aspects of reality to our attention. I confess a substantial skepticism about this latter possibility. Nonetheless, we will never learn anything unless we pay serious attention to the phenomena. Even this becomes very difficult within the context of a therapeutic relationship because these goals are not necessarily coterminous.

I hope that these remarks are of some help to you.

Sincerely,

Donald F. Klein, M.D.

cc Whitley Strieber

Dr. Klein's letter is indeed helpful in a number of ways. For one thing, it provides a documentary basis for establishing what tests Strieber did or did not take, and whether he might have omitted or invented mention of medical tests he took during his association with Dr. Klein. Importantly, Dr. Klein states that, for all the tests with which he was associated, which were ordered to determine the possibility of temporal lobe epilepsy, the results were negative. He states that this data is not finally conclusive either pro or con a diagnosis of temporal lobe epilepsy, but remarks that his colleagues would likely not prescribe medication for temporal lobe epilepsy, were they presented with the same evidence that he has seen in the case of Whitley Strieber.

His conclusion that Strieber was not psychotic, moreover, was based on his observation of what he described as Strieber's "intact personality functioning." To paraphrase him, Dr. Klein points out that psychotics do not change for the better even when confronted by facts that contradict their experiences. Strieber showed no problem in being able to question his own condition and express himself, according to Dr. Klein.

Second, this letter makes it very clear that Dr. Klein was in agreement with Strieber that his hypnotherapy was concluded at an appropriate time. Moreover, he states that, in effect, his door is always open to Strieber whenever he should wish to consult him. Most significant, he raises the point that the hypnosis performed upon Strieber was therapeutic, not investigative.

In reply to my inquiry about whether he considered hypnotherapy a useful tool for investigating whether there was any basis in fact for apparent "psychotic fantasies"—although he would not use that language—his answer is clear: no.

Strictly speaking, Dr. Klein did not explicitly state that he wrote the letter bearing his name at the back of Appendix I of *Communion*. However, he did assert that allegations to that effect are based upon belief, not fact. The implication of that statement, of course, is that he did indeed write the letter in the appendix of *Communion*, and his expression of regret over Klass's position implies that Klass is mistaken in his belief.

Considering Strieber's accounts of having had a needle inserted in his brain and having experienced the insertion of some kind of object up his nostril, perhaps into his brain, it is noteworthy that Dr. Klein spoke of an MRI (magnetic resonance imaging) test that "showed unexplained bright spots," that "may be a normal variant of brain anatomy or may indeed reflect an abnormal process." Obviously, they are of considerably less potential significance and importance to him than they are to Strieber.

Dr. Klein's comments regarding "alien abduction" as a "socio-psychological phenomenon" reveal, naturally, that he sees the problem as a psychiatrist. While he expresses some doubt that an examination of this phenomenon would "bring otherwise unsuspected aspects of reality to our attention," he nevertheless states that he believes such a study would be worthwhile.

Last, it should be noted that Klein writes in his letter that "Mr. Strieber has specifically told me that he wishes me to reply to your questions, 'fully, completely and candidly,' " a statement that speaks for itself.

In all fairness to Whitley Strieber, it must be said that he cooperated with me in providing me with the records of his medical tests, which he said were available even before I formally asked him to submit copies of them to me. In sending me his test documentation, he made it clear that there were some tests that he had received for which even he had no documentation, and proceeded to explain the circumstances pertaining to those undocumented tests. Strieber also required me not to mention the names of any of the physicians who administered tests (other than Dr. Klein), inasmuch as, he said, they had requested complete anonymity. However, I can vouch that the copies of documents that he has provided me (and which are now in my possession) correspond to the tests mentioned by Dr. Klein above, and include some additional tests not mentioned by him in his letter.

Without specifying physicians, psychologists, or laboratories, the documents confirming tests taken by Whitley Strieber sent to me by him indicate the following:

1. Psychological report for tests administered on March 7, 1986. Tests include: Bender Gestalt; WAIS-R (Wechsler Adult Intelligence Scale-Revised), House-Tree-Person (HTP), Human Figure Drawings, Rorschach, Thematic Apperception Test (TAT). The results of these tests, in brief, were as follows: Verbal IQ scores were Very Superior. Performance IQ in Average range. The report indicated that "anxiety and emotional problems account for a good deal of the irregularity in Mr. Strieber's functioning." When tested for vocabulary, general information, and numerical recall, Strieber scored "at the top of the

measuring scale." It was noted that Strieber appeared to have problems with decreased concentration and sequential thinking, and seemed to be fatigued. The Bender Gestalt found "good intelligence, absence of significant visual-motor problems, but some trouble organizing material." The psychologist observed that "at a price to his psychological well-being, he tries to repress strong emotional responses, rather than verbalize them so that he can deal more effectively. Mr. Strieber appears to be very frightened and to feel powerless." The recommendation was for psychotherapy, which would help him to "separate fantasy from reality and plan for effective action."

2. EEG (electroencephalogram) report, dated December 3, 1986. This report states: "This is a 20 channel EEG obtained when the patient was awake and asleep. Nasopharyngeal leads were used. Chloral hydrate, 1 gram was given for sedation." The final line of this report reads, under "Impression": "This EEG, which includes nasopharyngeal leads, is normal with the patient awake and asleep."

3. Report on radiologic consultation listed as "CT OF THE HEAD," dated March 14, 1988. This report is quite short and reads: "Computed tomography of the head is performed with contrast injection from the base to the vertex, showed the ventricles to be normal and symmetrical in size and shape. No mass lesion or abnormal enhancvement [sic] is seen. The posterior fossa is not remarkable. IMPRESSION: Normal contrast study of the head."

4. EEG report, dated March 14, 1988. This report is a form in which certain options for the test were marked with an "X" in the appropriate box. The boxes that are marked on this form show that the study requested was an EEG with "HV" and "Sleep." The boxes that indicated "Nasopharyngeal Leads" and "Photic" were not marked. Under the category of "CLINICAL HISTORY," the form reads: "Episodes of hallucinations." The form goes on to state that no abnormal, asymmetrical, paroxysmal, or slow activity was found in the following states: "resting," "drowsy," "sleeping," and "hyperventilation." The only state not marked is "photic stimulation." Under the category "IMPRESSION" the report reads: "Normal EEG."

5. Radiologic report, dated March 18, 1988, for magnetic resonance imaging of the brain. The report reads as follows:

TECHNIQUE:
Axial T-2 and sagittal T-1 weighted spin-echo sequences were obtained.

FINDINGS:
The ventricles and sulci are normal. There are no masses, shifts or displacements. Occasional punctate foci of high signal intensity are located in the cerebral white matter of the frontal lobes bilaterally as well as the left temporo parietal region. The extra cranial structures are within normal limits.

IMPRESSION:
Occasional punctate foci of high signal intensity in the cerebral white matter in a 43-year-old male may represent foci of demyelination of microvascular disease or other process.

The above documents, then, constitute what Strieber tells me, in what I have taken to be the best of faith, the sum total of documents in his possession detailing the tests he underwent at the time that he was seeking help. I must say that I was impressed that he had included the psychological report dated March 7, 1986, in that it contains language that some people might wish to use against him (as support for charges that his story is incredible because he is "mentally unstable") if quoted out of context or without an examination of the full record of his treatment by Dr. Klein.

Be that as it may, I asked Strieber if there were any reports that were missing. He told me that there were two reports that "didn't exist."

At this point, I quote from the interview that followed:

CONROY: There are two things that don't exist?
STRIEBER: The first is a CAT scan that was taken by Dr. (name deleted), at (name of hospital deleted). (Author's note: This was a doctor to whom Strieber was referred by Dr. Klein for testing.) That never was reported out by anybody. I inquired and Dr.——'s office also inquired about where it was and it never came out. And there's a lot of radiation involved in those things. They have to put an iodine drip in your blood, radioactive drip, and it's not something you want to take every day, because you get that heavy-duty radiation.
CONROY: So you've had two CAT scans.
STRIEBER: No, I've had three CAT scans.
When I first started seeing Dr. Klein, I was very suspicious of the whole business, because he had been recommended to

me by Budd Hopkins. . . . The result of this was that I was also, at the same time, seeing another psychiatrist. For this other psychiatrist I took a CAT scan. That was the first thing he did, was order a CAT scan. His CAT scan came back totally normal. I never saw it. He said it did. He was not the kind of psychiatrist who gives the patient the original data at all. But anyway, I had a falling-out with him because he became extremely upset when he found out that I was consulting him and Dr. Klein at the same time.

CONROY: Yes. You explained that to me.

STRIEBER: Because it was a very big embarrassment to him for some reason, or I think his ego was involved, frankly. I also think he was very wary of being publicly involved in this thing. He was nervous as hell about the whole business. But in any case, after a considerable amount of acrimony, we parted company. The net result of it was that I left his care with a promise that I would not reveal his name or anything about his practice to anyone, and I would specifically, without telling Dr. Klein who he was, tell Dr. Klein that I had been under another doctor's care for a brief period of time, but hadn't continued.

Dr. Klein's indifference to this was absolute and total. I don't think he cared one way or another whether I was in another doctor's care. Nor was he in the least interested in finding out who it was.

In any case, I took a temporal lobe EEG and a second CAT scan. The first one I had taken in March, I guess. This was about seven months later.

CONROY: Well, it says December third, 1986.

STRIEBER: . . . and I didn't want to take two CAT scans in the same year. . . . I then sent a letter to the other psychiatrist, asking him to transmit his CAT scan to [Dr. Klein], but he never did. So I was left without a CAT scan [report] from Dr. ——, meaning that he never completed his formal workup. I mean, he examined me physically and then he informed me over the telephone that he didn't think I had temporal lobe epilepsy and not to worry about it. So I never got the CAT scan [report], or what I'm sure would have been a clean bill of health, from Dr. ——

Dr. Klein said that since the temporal lobe EEG was normal, . . . he didn't think the CAT scan was important. He dropped it.

I waited until over a year later, until March of '88, to take another series like this, and this time I purposely chose another neurologist; not because I was unhappy with Dr. —— or Dr. Klein, but because I wanted someone completely different involved. So I went through my GP, Tom Silverberg,[6] and I got Dr. X (name deleted) at (institution deleted). He did an EEG with sleep but not leads, a CAT scan, and an MRI. You have the papers from all that.

The other thing that was done was that, after Dr. Klein told me that business about the temporal lobe EEG being inconclusive, I called the lab and arranged to have a temporal lobe EEG. [But] when I went to the lab, the technician involved said it hadn't been arranged with leads and sleep, apparently because it had to be done through Dr. Klein's office. Then, after a period of confusion, they gave me a regular EEG, which showed me to be completely normal. Now, whether that EEG was reported to Dr. Klein or not, I don't know. . . . It was reported to me, verbally, by the doctor.

CONROY: So there was no documentation on that second EEG?

STRIEBER: No. The only two EEGs that are documented are the one with leads and the one with sleep. The truth of the matter is that I've subsequently discovered that a regular EEG won't tell anything at all. I mean, it's absolutely useless as a diagnostic tool for temporal lobe epilepsy. The key is sleep, and if you're really going after it, the leads. But the device that was used by Dr. X, I recall them telling me, was sufficiently sensitive to where they really didn't need to use the leads with it. I think Dr. Klein might dispute that, because there's a lot of rivalry among these various neurologists as to who has the best equipment and all that. In any case, that's the whole story.

Strieber went on to say that he didn't have the report from the doctor who administered the MRI for Dr. Silverberg, his personal physician, and he wasn't sure what the legalities were about obtaining that report.

"There is one thing in the report from Dr. X to Dr. Silverberg that

I consider to be quite telling and disturbing," Strieber told me. "Dr. X told me that UBOs are seen in three to four percent of normal brains. He said 'I see them very rarely.' "

I asked Strieber if "UBO" stands for "unknown bright object."

"Yes," he said. "He [the physician who administered the MRI] then became evasive about it. He strongly stated 'I don't want my name or the name of any of my supporting physicians used.' He was very firm about it, of course, and he laughed and he said, 'These objects are exactly the last abnormality that your critics want you to have.' He was laughing about it. But in the report to Dr. Silverberg, he said these UBOs are commonplace in normal brains."

I have not been able to discover if there is any actual report from the physician who administered the MRI for Dr. Silverberg, or what it might say, because Dr. Silverberg has not returned my phone call. I made that call with Strieber's assent and cooperation. Although I made clear my intentions for an interview to Dr. Silverberg's secretary, I have not heard from the doctor.

However, Strieber has given me transparencies that he says are the result of the MRI test that was reported on March 18, 1988, and they are reproduced among the illustrations for this book.

It is important to note that the language used to describe the "unknown bright objects" in the report on the MRI dated March 18, 1988, refers to the possibility that they may represent one or another disease processes. No reference is made in the typed report to their degree of anomaly in terms of their incidence in the general population receiving MRI tests. Nor, for that matter, is any reference made in the report to Strieber's statements about having had objects inserted into his brain.

In summary, then, it may be said that the record shows Strieber took a total of three EEGs, three CAT scans, and one MRI test, in addition to the psychological tests administered to him in March of 1986.

The account of his testing that Strieber gave me in the telephone interview just cited (which transpired in December 1988, well after he had sent me documentation on his tests) accords with his account of the EEG testing in *Communion*.[7] In that passage, he says he had two tests by two different neurologists, one by a doctor recommended by Klein and another by an independent neurologist. In my interview, he pointed out that the second EEG had no leads and no sleep, because it was not recommended by Dr. Klein. The "second neurologist" involved was the doctor who supervised the test at the laboratory at Strieber's request. The third and final EEG test (which had no leads and no sleep) was arranged through Dr. Silverberg's office and occurred in March 1988, when Strieber got the second series of tests.

What was Strieber's motive for the second series of tests? He has admitted to me on more than one occasion that he was interested in seeing if anything like an "unknown bright object" might appear on his brain if examined by MRI. He also said he wanted another objective set of records regarding his condition for *Transformation*, then shortly to be published.

Considering the difficulty that many patients have in obtaining copies of their medical records from doctors, I consider it rather remarkable that Strieber was prepared to document his tests to the extent that he did so. Of course, he was certainly aware that it was in his own best interest to be able to provide documentation to reporters. What is of chief significance, I believe, in the remarks made by Dr. Klein, is that he says he could find no medical basis (given the evidence from the tests that had been performed) for treating Strieber with medication for temporal lobe epilepsy, and that he felt the termination of therapy occurred at an appropriate time.

It remains to consider the question whether Whitley Strieber faithfully recounted the story of his interaction with Nat Laurendi, the polygraphist who administered a polygraph, or "lie detector," test to Strieber on October 31, 1986. I telephoned Laurendi at his New York offices (Strieber gave me his telephone number) and proceeded to have the following interview with him:

CONROY: How did you meet Whitley Strieber?

LAURENDI: I think he was recommended by an attorney.

CONROY: Have you ever had any previous work with anyone claiming this sort of story?

LAURENDI: I had lots of people when I was a detective. I had one person who said he had some kind of message from God, that killed somebody, hit him over the head with a hammer. I tested him. I had somebody recently who says that he has people in his room at night and he plastered his walls with some kind of tape so they don't enter. He was charged with arson.

CONROY: Had Strieber gone to see Dr. Klein, therefore, before he came to see you? Were you satisfied that Whitley was certifiably sane when he came to see you?

LAURENDI: He was rational. Naturally, he found his way to my office. I had a conversation with him—I went through what we call a pretest interview, sizing up the individual. Remember, we're dealing with the human mind. If a person honestly believes what he says happened to him, just like in eyewitness identification, that person is going to come out as truthful.

CONROY: I get your point. So how did you begin to formulate how to test his story?

LAURENDI: He supplied me with a list of questions.

CONROY: He supplied the list of questions?

LAURENDI: Yeah. Actually, in a polygraph, you can't ask too many questions. You may have to reduce it to four or five, maybe, six, and zero in on those more important questions. That test took at least an hour, an hour and a quarter.

CONROY: There are eighteen questions here (in *Communion*).

LAURENDI: Which comprise the relevant questions. To establish a baseline, there are control questions . . . (tape unintelligible). And there are the relevant questions, where there are the issues.

CONROY: For the benefit of myself and the readers, maybe you could elucidate what you refer to as establishing a baseline. Maybe we could talk about how you set up the criteria for judging that.

LAURENDI: The baseline is: "Is your name so-and-so? Were you born in so-and-so?"—things we could accept as constants in the investigation. "Are you married? Do you smoke cigarettes? Were you born in such and such a place?" You also have a control question where we want to record physiological changes: Which are of concern? Which bother the person? And there is a question of uncertainty—maybe he did this, maybe he didn't do this. And the relevant questions, which pertain to the issue.

I think Strieber mentioned that he was lying a couple of times on the control questions, which he had worked out beforehand. And I think that there were other control questions where he lied, too, which he didn't talk about in his book.

CONROY: That's interesting. Were these questions something

that he might have preferred to leave out for reasons of personal privacy?

LAURENDI: I don't have my report here. Have you got the book there?

CONROY: Yeah. This is how it reads. He had a little intro here. "On October 31, 1986, I was polygraphed by Ned Laurendi, president of —

LAURENDI: It's N-a-t, Nat Laurendi. So there's an error right there.

CONROY: Okay—"by Nat Laurendi, president of the Society of Professional Investigators—

LAURENDI: At that time.

CONROY: Okay—at that time—"and vice-president of the Empire State Polygraph Society."

LAURENDI: Right.

CONROY: "The reason I carried out the polygraph was to assure readers that I honestly think that I perceived the things reported in this book. It is not fiction, and does not contain a word of fiction. My successful completion of this test in no way proves that my recollection of my experiences is correct, but it does confirm that I have described what I saw to the best of my ability."

LAURENDI: "Described what he saw." Sure. And I also grilled him about it because he lives upstate in a cabin, and there are a lot of wild mushrooms growing up there, and you mix them with wine in the supper, and in the early hours of the morning you might hear noises and things. It was disturbing him and his wife, also.

CONROY: Did you test his wife?

LAURENDI: No, no. Nobody else is in the polygraph room during the interview except an interpreter. (Laurendi explains that some clients are immigrants, etc.)

CONROY: What did you think in general about the list of questions for Communion? Did you think that the list of questions he gave you was a fair list for his experience?

LAURENDI: Well, I discarded a great many of them.

CONROY: What was your basis for discarding some of them?

LAURENDI: As I've said, you can't ask so many questions, and I zeroed in on the main ones.

CONROY: In Transformation, Strieber had the same intention, which is to provide his reader with a basis to believe what he had to say.

LAURENDI: And that's the whole issue with polygraphy: Does the speaker believe what he is saying? That's what the polygraph does: It records, anatomically, that "I saw that person on a particular day at the scene of a murder." An eyewitness— one that saw somebody and, when shown a photograph of that person, thinks he looks familiar—something is happening in that person's mind. That person is not lying.

CONROY: I see exactly what you mean; it's a subjective thing. In *Transformation*, did Whitley also supply you with a list of questions?

LAURENDI: Yeah. And I discarded some, for whatever reason.

CONROY: Did he have control questions like before?

LAURENDI: I did use control questions, yes. I think I even gave him his Miranda warning. It has a strong effect. You know, there's a concept that when somebody goes into a private examiner, that he's going to come out truthful, which is not true, you see. I was with police polygraphers for thirteen years. And everybody says, mostly private attorneys, they think it's a friendly environment, but now I'm not a friendly guy.

Getting to Whitley Strieber, personally, I don't get too many like him saying "I've seen people coming up through the ground in red forms and shapes." I have had other cases where publishers send me their clients who write out exposes, like Linda Lovelace. I had to test her before her book was published. . . . I did one for the *National Enquirer*, with the woman who claimed that she was the astrologer for Nancy Reagan. . . .

CONROY: Well the bottom line is, were you satisfied that he was telling you the truth as he knew it?

LAURENDI: As he knew it, as he envisioned it in his own mind. Here's something interesting—the control questions. I knew he was lying, I just wanted to see if he was capable of registering any emotional response. And he was. Whether that had anything to do with actual true-life situations or the control questions. If you have *Communion*, you have the other control questions—there was something about his past: did he belong to any cults? if I remember.

CONROY: Uh-huh. That's interesting. Did he belong to any cults? There are a lot of people who are accusing him of trying to start a new UFO cult. The control question was "Do you belong to any cults?" (Reading from *Communion*) "Answer: No. Evaluated true."

LAURENDI: I think I asked him "in the past, at one time," I don't know, in his early years. . . . Maybe he was dickering with me whether this particular group was a cult or not.

CONROY: Okay. This has been useful.

LAURENDI: He sounds sincere. Does he believe what he is saying? As a polygraphist, I have to say yes. He did react to the control questions that I utilized which pertain to actual life experiences. When he came in, it was Halloween, so I became suspicious right away, to see if he was going to pull—

CONROY: A prank.

LAURENDI: Yeah. . . . But I put him through the wringer.

For the record, Strieber also took a polygraph test on May 18, 1987, at the offices of Polygraph Security Services in London, England. This test, which occurred in conjunction with his promotional tour for *Communion*, was administered by Jeremy G. Barrett, the managing director of the company.

Barrett's report recounted the test's questions and replies as follows:

Do you intend to answer the questions I ask you on this test truthfully? Reply—Yes.

Are the "visitors," about whom you write in your book *Communion*, a physical reality? Reply—Yes.

Have you invented the "visitors," about whom you write, for commercial gain? Reply—No.

Whilst in the presence of your "visitors," have you actually felt them touch you? Reply—Yes.

Have you ever taken any kind of hallucinogenic drug? Reply—No.

Are the "visitors" a physical reality? Reply—Yes.

Barrett's concluding statement on the report reads as follows: "I found Mr. Whitley Strieber to be TRUTHFUL in response to all questions."

The only matter of concern in Laurendi's account of Strieber is

Laurendi's statement that there were more control questions on which Strieber was lying than were mentioned in the book. Unfortunately, Laurendi was not disposed, upon further questioning, to go into this matter in greater detail, and he began to equivocate somewhat on the "cult" question. Perhaps his memory did not serve him at the moment, or perhaps Laurendi and Strieber have diverging ideas on the definition of "cult." He said that Strieber was "dickering" with him as to whether or not a group of which he was a member was a cult, thereby indentifying this question as the one over which the men had a difference of opinion. Strieber has told me in an interview that he was a member of the Gurdjieff Foundation during his early years in New York, a group that has been suspected of being a cult by some anticult activists,[8] but which Strieber has maintained to me is by no means a cult.

Despite his statement to the effect that Strieber omitted some parts of his lie detector test, which may be interpreted by some people as a cover-up attempt on Strieber's part, Laurendi remained firm in his final professional opinion: Strieber was telling the truth as he knew it.

The record of Strieber's testing is extensive and rather complex, and no doubt represents a series of unpleasant experiences. Strieber has on more than one occasion remarked to me of the pain of having nasopharyngeal leads inserted in his nose (a pain with which, to read Communion, he should be familiar!).[9] He complained, too, that he felt as though his arm were going to fall off from lack of circulation during the polygraph tests, which he said featured an inflatable armband similar to those used to measure blood pressure. Then, too, there is the factor of having had to confront Nat Laurendi, who says himself that he's "not a friendly guy."

"He left here like a dog with his tail between his legs," Laurendi told me, referring to Strieber's second lie detector test for Transformation. Laurendi seems to be a man who enjoys his work.

Although Strieber is unwilling to provide full public disclosure of his medical records owing to confidences he has with his doctors, and despite the apparent omissions that Laurendi mentions but fails to specify from his records, I have to conclude that—to the extent that I have been able to pursue the matter—the account of Strieber's testing in Communion and Transformation checks out in its most important details.

I also have to conclude that, while Strieber has been extraordinarily forthright in opening up his life and file to me for this investigation, it does not surprise me very much that Laurendi would assert, on tape, for attribution, that his client omitted part of the content of his first polygraph test (he did not assert that anything had been omitted from the second) because of problems with some control questions. Considering that there is an "event" in Strieber's life that he himself has subjected to doubt—his much-debated presence at the Charles Whitman massacre in Austin, Texas, on August 1, 1966—it appears Strieber has suffered from some considerable doubt about events in his own past. If anything, he has been very forthright in discussing these doubts in both *Communion* and *Transformation*. Perhaps Laurendi's statements will convince some readers that Strieber may be capable of deceiving himself in certain matters in his own life, but I would urge a suspension of judgment until after a further examination of the record of the Whitman incident, to be found in Chapter 2.

I believe it is important, too, that Dr. Klein's statement regarding his "intact personality functioning" should be taken into account when considering the question whether he is a reliable witness. If he is not psychotic, as Dr. Klein believes he is not, then we find ourselves in the position of personally encountering a man who has one of the most compelling of imaginable stories to tell, an experience that could happen to anyone. We are face-to-face, one-to-one, with Whitley Strieber, journeyer through the underworld, lover of death as much as life, storyteller extraordinaire—and perhaps with his "visitors" as well.

Who is this man? He is, after all, far more than can be quantified through his medical test results. What is Whitley Strieber's personal story, and where does he come from?

Those questions can only be answered by turning to the first page in the book of his past.

Chapter 2

Will the Real Whitley
Strieber Please Stand Up?

A Profile of the Science Fiction and
Horror Novelist Who Decided to
Write Nonfiction

On June 13, 1945, Karl and Mary Strieber became the parents of their
first boy child. They named him Whitley.

Young Whitley had many decided advantages over other babies
born in San Antonio, Texas, that day. His father was a prominent
lawyer with successful investments in oil and gas. His mother was the
daughter of H. P. Drought, owner of a large construction company
and a staunch supporter of the Roman Catholic Church in San Antonio. Mary Strieber was known by her friends to be a well-read,
thoughtful woman active in local charitable organizations. Their home
was located at 630 Elizabeth Road, in the elegant suburb of Terrell
Hills; it was a street lined with large oak and pecan trees, adjoining
still-undeveloped farmland on the northern edge of town. Their
neighbors, like them, were successful people, some of whom played
leading roles in the civic life of San Antonio.

Patricia Strieber had preceded Whitley into the world by twenty
months, giving Karl and Mary a pair of toddlers to take care of as they
settled into the routines of married life. Twelve years after Whitley
was born, they were surprised to find that Mary was pregnant again,

this time with the baby they named Richard. Whitley and Patricia grew up playing together, not only in the ample space of the Strieber yard, but in the wide expanse of undeveloped land behind some of the town's still-unpaved streets. Given that the Terrell Hills police kept a close eye on security in the community (as they are still known to do), Karl and Mary Strieber had relatively few worries for the safety of their children.

The San Antonio area into which Whitley Strieber was born, in those days, had many ingenuous qualities more characteristic of rural than urban Texas. People still addressed one another with the formal southern courtesies of "sir" and "ma'am," and cowboy-style suits were occasionally seen as normal business garb. It was fitting that things were so, as the city, once the state's principal and richest metropolis, had grown from an original economic base of oil and ranching, Texas's two most traditional industries. At the end of World War II, San Antonio was only just on the verge of experiencing the dramatic surge in population that came about as a result of the expansion of the city's major Air Force bases and Fort Sam Houston, headquarters for the Fifth Army. The population base for generations had been fairly stable, consisting of a mixture of descendents of the original German, Irish, English, and Scots-Irish immigrants to Mexican Texas; the families of early Spanish and Mexican colonial settlers; more recent arrivals of middle- and upper-class Mexicans seeking to escape the Mexican revolution at the turn of the century; a very small (less than 10 percent of the city) segment of blacks, mostly employed in service jobs; and the nearly constant flow across the border of poor Mexican workers—often illegal—from the interior seeking employment in the United States.

Suburbs such as Terrell Hills and others, of course, were part of the response of the local "Anglo" community (a term meant to denote non-Mexican whites, though it is politely extended to include, whether they like it or not, persons of Greek, Irish, or other non-British descent) to a changing urban population. Like other suburbs, it was something of a conscious retreat from a social world perceived to be growing steadily darker and less familiar. Its adjoining community, Alamo Heights, to this day retains a kind of malt-shop wholesomeness now rare in many American cities. The town's main street, Broadway, could have doubled as a Hollywood lot for a southwestern version of a television show such as *Leave It to Beaver*, or *Father Knows Best*, lined as it was with fashionable storefronts and tasteful small Spanish stucco strip centers. The La Fonda restaurant, where Mexican food made bland enough for non-Mexican palates was served to Sunday-morning churchgoing families, provided (and still does) a culinary expression of much of the local ethos. Yet many people in Terrell Hills and Alamo Heights still have ties to land customarily worked by Mexican hands at ranches in outlying counties. The Strieber family was no exception, spending their summers at Droughtfels, the Drought family ranch near Comfort, north of San Antonio.

It could be fairly said, then, that Whitley Strieber grew up in one of the few communities of Texas where at least a small portion of the town was living out its own American dream. Untroubled yet by racial conflicts or demands still to be made by the growing population of "out-of-towners," the people of Terrell Hills found it easy to dream. In summer they listened to the hypnotic hum of the cicadas and waited each afternoon for the blessed relief of the cool Gulf breezes that would waft through the magnolia trees as evening drew nigh. In winter they watched the onslaught of "blue northers," walls of arctic cloud that each November would abruptly bring the heat to a close. It was a place of harsh contrasts, in nature and society, but not without con-siderable charm.

One could hardly imagine a less likely place to be visited by "aliens" of any kind, from Mexico or from Mars.

Yet was there, indeed, something truly strange going on in the Strieber neighborhood?

Whitley Strieber has recounted some aspects of his boyhood in Terrell Hills in his book, *Transformation*, partly out of information that emerged in the early phases of my research. In particular, he said that Lanette Glasscock, the mother of his best friend, Albert, at whose home he frequently slept over, remembered him being frightened of "spacemen."

As Mrs. Glasscock put it to me in an April 1987 conversation, speaking of her son, Albert, and Whitley:

"They were crazy about spaceships, aliens, and the whole idea of space travel. In fact, I remember having to take Whitley home in the middle of the night because he was afraid spacemen were going to come and get him."

Mrs. Glasscock, a well-known oil and probate attorney, remem-bered Whitley as a precocious young fellow, and spoke fondly of him. Although she had lost some of her sleep because of Strieber's fears of spacemen, she did not seem to hold it against him. At the time she made this comment to me, she had not spoken with Strieber in years, nor had she yet read *Communion*.

Given the close relations that prevailed among families on Elizabeth Road, it was not at all unusual for Strieber to spend a great deal of time with Albert, or with his other friends. "We were obsessed with each other in that neighborhood," Strieber told me in a January 1989 interview. "My parents would try to engage me more socially with the children at school, but it didn't work."

One report from Kelly Clare, an old classmate of his at Central Catholic High School in San Antonio, recounted how Strieber's parents had once rented Municipal Auditorium for a magic show, in order to host all of Whitley's classmates. When I asked Strieber about that, he said that, in fact, his parents had only gone so far as to buy tickets for all his classmates, and stopped short of renting the whole auditorium. "There were a lot of other people there, as I remember," he said. Strieber regarded that occasion as a good example of how his parents tried to encourage his socialization outside the neighborhood.

Unfortunately, it was impossible for me to interview Karl Strieber; he died in March 1977. In the course of my investigation and conversations with many people in the San Antonio community, I have found that the name of Karl Strieber immediately evokes a response of respect, particularly among people who have held or now hold responsible positions in the worlds of law and banking. In fact, when discussing the question of Strieber's "UFO abduction" story with local people who have tended to politely listen to the subject matter of my inquiry, I have found that their response changes to one of interest when they learn that Whitley was Karl's son. It is evident that Karl Strieber had extensive dealings with many people in the South Texas community, including persons in high positions of governmental authority.

Whitley Strieber has always spoken admiringly to me of his father, and once said that he showed him the importance of precise use of the English language, pointing out how his legal expertise had produced documents regulating the use of oil wells in which he invested that are still producing profits today. Yet it would be fair to say that he and his father grew apart as Whitley grew up, as is certainly reflected in Strieber's own account of the relationship in *Communion*. As a boy, Strieber said to me more than once, he was often reluctant to join his father in cutting the grass or in other activities, preferring to immerse himself in his friendships and his studies.

Strieber's father contracted cancer of the larynx, which eventually resulted in the loss of his voice. Karl Strieber's consequent inability to work at his former capabilities as an attorney resulted in difficult years for the Strieber family as Whitley was growing up, an experience that he referred to in interviews throughout his earlier career.

Strieber's "vision" of the death of his father, as related in *Communion*, is one example of the kind of experience that has led Strieber to speculate that perhaps the "visitors" have a direct relationship with the world of human souls. It was an experience that Strieber described as ultimately cathartic, enabling him to release guilt feelings about not having been present for his father's death. I asked him once if he thought the visitors might have had a role in his father's death.

"That did cross my mind and it was a terrifying and deeply disturbing thought," he said. "It also may be what I remembered under hypnosis was an expression of yet another fear of my own—and that what I saw under hypnosis was not something that happened but something I fear may have happened."

I also asked Strieber if he believed the visitors influenced families across generations.

"As far as going across generations—my sister's sense of it is that our father was involved also in the experience, but he has passed away and we can't ask him," he said. "Certainly the two of us were very much involved. Other members of the immediate family maybe were involved. My mother doesn't believe she was involved."

The question of how Whitley Strieber is remembered by his mother was relatively easy to explore, as she still lives in San Antonio. I was the first journalist to question her for attribution in regard to *Communion*, in an interview she kindly gave me in April 1987. I reproduce here the opening section of that interview verbatim. Mary Strieber's comments were casual, forthright, and delivered quickly, without hesitation.

> CONROY: As I said to Whitley, I'm an admirer of his work.
> MARY STRIEBER: It's kind of wild, isn't it?
> CONROY: Yes it is.
> MARY STRIEBER: Think of it: I raised him, I lived with him.
> CONROY: Well, that's what I wanted to ask you about, if you could give me some idea of what he was like as a boy and young man.

MARY STRIEBER: He was very smart, and had a terrifically high IQ. Did you know he took eight years of Latin? Can you believe anybody would do that? He was always interested in literature. Since the age of nine he wanted to write. He wrote poetry at first and then he started out trying to write a book. He was very popular as a kid because he had such a terrific imagination, everybody always came over to play with Whitley because he always had something that they could do.

CONROY: Some kind of new game or something?

MARY STRIEBER: Yes, that's right.

CONROY: What do you think it was that made him decide at the age of nine that he wanted to be a writer? Was there any incident that you remember?

MARY STRIEBER: No, he just always wanted to be. I always wanted to be a writer, but I never did do it, but he wanted to write.

CONROY: He certainly has. Now that he has come out with his latest book, I imagine that it was something of a surprise to people in the family to read about all that.

MARY STRIEBER: Well, you know his sister said "I don't know how Whitley said that—those things weren't true." But I said, "Patricia, people's memories are not the same." You know, the things that were important to her didn't mean anything to him, and the things that were important to him didn't mean anything to her.

CONROY: Was there anything in particular that she thought that he said that wasn't quite true?

STRIEBER: The train trip. She was the one who was sick on the train, and he said he was the one who was sick on the train. I was at home. They went with their father.

CONROY: Well, so . . . Whitley didn't seem to have any unusual interest in UFOs or anything like that?

MARY STRIEBER: Not at all, but he was very imaginative. Very.

CONROY: Did he draw or paint?

MARY STRIEBER: Yes, when he was in his teens.

CONROY: What sort of things did he paint? Anything unusual?

MARY STRIEBER: No. Mostly figures. He took lessons down the street. A man and his wife, I don't remember their names, they were both painters. We let him drive over there. He was very proud.

CONROY: You must have a lot of affectionate memories of Whitley growing up there.

MARY STRIEBER: There were some awfully funny things.

The comment that Mary Strieber made in regard to "the train trip" refers to a trip that Whitley, his sister Patricia, and their father made to Michigan to visit Karl Strieber's parents. Mentioned in *Communion*, it is of some significance because Strieber said he remembered having a "visitor experience" on that trip. When I told Strieber of what his mother said, he replied that he had indeed gotten sick, and that Patricia then got sick too, so it wasn't a case of one or the other of them. The question of who got sick, of course, is immaterial to the larger questions raised by the story of the train trip. These matters will be explored further on in the chapter.

Mary Strieber's remarks to the effect that her son had no interest in UFOs or related subjects is interesting, too, in relation to what Lanette Glasscock told me about the Whitley Strieber who spent so much time at her house with Albert Glasscock. It is all the more understandable, though, in light of Strieber having once told me that he felt his parents eventually gave up on trying to influence him. "After a while, they simply learned to ignore me," he said once. Yet Strieber's friendships with neighbors such as Albert Glasscock, Mike Ryan, Bill Mebane, and others were strong, as my encounters with these men have borne out.

It might be natural for them to look back on their boyhoods with nostalgia, but the stories of some of their antics betray a fascination with the paraphernalia of what was then being called the space age.

I met Albert Glassock, along with his wife, in August 1988, at a dinner in San Antonio. The occasion was a reunion for two old friends, and it was obvious that they took a great deal of pleasure in one another's company. Glasscock, who currently is an administrator for the Texas Highways Department, did not offer any recollections of having seen flying discs in their backyards or other anomalous phenomena.

He did, however, join Strieber in reminiscing about how they created their own nocturnal "aerial lights."

One of their favorite pastimes, it seems, was manufacturing all kinds of balloons and sending them aloft. One of Whitley's fascinations, too, was fire. Eventually, they figured out how to have the best of both worlds: incendiary balloons. As Whitley explained:

"We'd get some old plastic bags—the kind you get your clothes in from the laundry—and we'd iron them shut at one end, using a cloth to keep the iron from sticking. Then we'd go over to the maid's quarters where there was a gas nozzle sticking out of the wall and fill the bag with natural gas. We had some timed fuses, so we'd grab them and go up to the roof where we'd tie the bag shut with string and hang a fuse from the bottom and send it aloft!"

The big kick in this game, of course, came when the timed fuse ran out and ignited the gas into an exploding ball of fire. "You could see little pieces of plastic floating down from the bag, on fire," Strieber said.

One night while they were engaged in this particular diversion, Albert Glasscock said, he became convinced that the balloon they had just set off the Strieber house roof was bound for trouble.

"I just knew that it was going to fly over our house," he said, "and sure enough it did. Even worse, it went off right over a tree in the front yard."

Fortunately, Glasscock said, no damage resulted from that very risky trajectory, nor did he get into trouble with his parents.

In *Transformation*, Strieber noted Albert's father, the late Leon Glasscock, also an attorney and at one time president of the San Antonio Bar Association, once experienced an incident in which his car engine came to a stop in association with the descent of a large flying machine that landed on the highway in front of him. I was present with Strieber and Lanette Glasscock when this incident came up in conversation in Mrs. Glasscock's home in August 1988. She confirmed that the incident did in fact occur as Strieber described it in *Transformation*, although she did not remember a report being filed with the National Investigations Committee on Aerial Phenomena (NICAP). Nevertheless, Glasscock did make some attempt to communicate his experience. "I do remember he reported it to the authorities," Mrs. Glasscock said, but she could not specify to what branch of government he did so.

Mary Strieber remembers her son's revelries with Albert Glasscock, particularly one incident when the two boys were playing and young Whitley suddenly turned into a "little green man."

She told me this anecdote in an April 1987 interview:

"Well, we had a black woman working for us, Annie Bean, and she had a friend down the street, I think her name was Ethel. And she stayed with some children, both of their parents were lawyers,[1] and they weren't at home. And so Annie used to take Whitley and Patricia and go over to visit in the afternoons. Albert Glasscock painted him green one day! It was terrible! They were playing in the garage and they'd had some painting done at the house, and the paint was there, so Albert painted Whitley. Well, if you've never had a green son, you don't know what it's like."

When I asked Mrs. Strieber how Albert and Whitley reacted to this incident, she said, "Oh, they enjoyed it. They thought it was great! Oh, they were so little, they were seven or eight years old, and Annie brought home this green child that I didn't even know."

Model rockets were another fascination for Strieber and his friends, particularly Mike Ryan and Bill Mebane. They formed a club for their hobby and were adopted by scientists at the Southwest Research Institute, a San Antonio-based laboratory complex still in existence today. *San Antonio Express* columnist Paul Thompson found their activities worthy of note, and through him the boys got a fair amount of media attention.

Mike Ryan, who today owns and manages a number of San Antonio rental properties, sent me a number of clippings from the November 18, 1957, edition of the *Express* (the *Express* and *News* were joined into one paper in 1984), featuring some of the club's activities.

Thompson seemed to enjoy linguistically comparing the boys' efforts to the recent launch of the first successful artificial satellite, the Soviet Sputnik. As he wrote that day in his column, "Top of the News":

> Alamo Heights sent up the first "Frognik" recently—and the frog came back alive.
>
> Teen-age boys in an amateur science club performed the experiment. Now they're working on a rocket.
>
> The Frognik, a helium-filled balloon, went to an altitude of about 10 miles, then exploded. Back to earth came the frog, snug in a plastic container tied to a home-made parachute.
>
> Club members had attached two notes to the parachute— one in English, the other in Spanish—offering $5 for safe return of the frog.

"A Spanish-speaking man in South San Antonio phoned us the next morning," said young [Mike] Ryan.
"We went over there, collected our frog and paid the reward."

Ryan had always included mention of Strieber when he had spoken to me of his rocket-making and balloon activities. I was puzzled, then, when I didn't see any images of a young Whitley Strieber in those *San Antonio Express* clippings. I asked Strieber why he wasn't shown along with his friends.

"My father always said that a gentleman never allowed his picture to be in the paper," Strieber said, "so I wasn't allowed to participate when Mike and Bill were getting their pictures taken. I stood by the fence watching, tears streaming down my cheeks."

Mike Ryan's father had built the boys a cinder block clubhouse behind his home on Elizabeth Road, and it was there that much of the chemical mixing for the rocket—and other—experiments took place. The boys also used it to make bombs of various types, employing such tried-and-true methods as mixing weed killer and sugar, according to Strieber.

Yet it seems that the scientists at Southwest Research Institute had something of a salutary effect on this club, teaching them of the dangers of improperly mixing chemicals. They even went so far as to use them as talent for a special segment on the National Broadcasting Company's *Today* show, then hosted by Dave Garroway. Mike Ryan spoke on the show of the dangers of making rockets without proper knowledge of explosive substances, thereby beating his friend Whitley onto national television by a good many years.

Strieber had apparently forgotten about Ryan's appearance on the *Today* show. When I told him Ryan had given a small sermon promoting safe model rocketry, he said, "Little did they know he was the biggest bomb maker of us all!"

Strieber was quick to point out that there was nothing malicious in their bomb experimentation, although they did enjoy pulling pranks every now and then. One variety of bomb of which Strieber was particulary fond was the "dust bomb," made by packing plaster of paris into a pipe set into the ground along with the standard weed killer and sugar for explosive strength. When it detonated, Strieber said, "it sent a cloud of dust sailing down the street." Strieber chuckled as he remembered setting off one such bomb only to hear his mother down the street yell "Dust storm!" and set about closing all the windows in her house. He never did tell her it was just a "dust bomb," he said.

In *Communion*, Strieber mentioned that he thought his experiments with magnets toward making an antigravity device may have had a role in starting a fire that destroyed part of the roof on a second-story wing. I asked Mary Strieber about that incident.

"Oh yeah, the roof burned," she replied.

When I asked her to describe the circumstances of that fire, she said:

"Oh, I remember that. He was up in the country with my mother at Droughtfels, and he always thought he had something to do with that. I didn't know whether he did. The firemen thought a firecracker had set it. We had wood shakes for a roof, and weren't anywhere near a fireplug."

I asked Mrs. Strieber if her son played with firecrackers.

"No," she said. "He wasn't there. He was out of town when it happened. But Patricia had a girl staying with her, and they had dates, and those boys were fooling with the firecrackers. Patricia's older than Whitley, not quite two years older, and Richard was a baby."

Because of the difference in age that separated Strieber from his brother, Richard Strieber does not figure much in accounts of his youth. However, in later years, the two men became close friends, talking to one another on the telephone nearly every day.

"Whitley left home right after high school to go to college and then went to film school in London, so I didn't see him on a regular basis when I was younger," he said. "We became really close when I was in my late teens and early twenties."

Richard said that he got to know his brother during the time that he was struggling to become a published writer. He acknowledged that the early days of that struggle were fairly difficult, but added, "You have to understand how much my brother enjoys what he is doing. He never threw in the towel."

"Whitley's interests are quite broad-ranging," he said. "I think that in recent years he has become more and more concerned with the environment and essentially the ludicrous nature of international politics, where everybody is holding a gun at everybody else's head all the time. Since he was an established writer, he thought that would open a forum for him to deal with these political issues and environmental issues."

"I sent him a rather obscure book called *Science and the UFOs,* a British publication," Richard said. "Whitley had not expressed a great deal of interest in UFOs. He, by no means, is nor was a UFO buff by any stretch of the imagination. I think I probably had more interest in this subject than he did."

I asked Richard about the origin of his own interest in the UFOs.

"As a child—in my early teens and late childhood—that was a time when that subject was popular, that's where my interest stems from," he said. "The best I can remember, Whitley has never expressed much interest in UFOs."

When I asked him if he had any memory of his own "visitor experiences," Richard Strieber said he certainly had none. "Those other experiences that Whitley wrote about in the book [*Communion*] were well before my time; I don't even know if I was born then," he said.

One of the few anecdotes I have on Karl Strieber directly relates to Richard; it was told to me by Mary Strieber.

"I want to tell you the funniest thing happened one time," she said. "My husband, Karl, took Richard everywhere he went. And some friends of ours saw him and said, 'Oh that's the cutest *grand*child you have!' And he came home and he said, 'You phone Hazel and tell her that that's my son and not my grandson.' He was in his fifties when Richard was born, which was pretty funny, too."

A Christmas gift from Richard Strieber played a significant role, however, in catalyzing his brother's interest in UFOs. Whitley received it one day before the visitor experiences he recounts at the beginning of *Communion.*

If Karl Strieber was somewhat sensitive about how others saw him, it appears that his son Whitley could be fairly emotional at times, too. Strieber's account of himself as crying at not being able to join his friends being photographed surprised me somewhat, inasmuch as those of us of the male sex in our culture are generally trained not to cry, and rarely allow ourselves to do so, even in childhood, much less admit having done so. That comment is borne out by an observation his mother made of him, though, in her interview with me.

"A lot of things were funny about Whitley when he was growing up," she said. "For one thing, I never saw a kid cry like Whitley. He'd cry at everything in sight."

On the other hand, though, she described him as being very adventuresome, and taking his share of tumbles.

"We had a real tall elm tree in the front yard and he climbed all the way to the top and then he fell out," she said.

"Did he break any bones?" I asked.

"No. It didn't hurt him at all, but it scared Annie Bean half to death. She thought he was killed. But I wasn't home when that happened. She called his father at the office."

"So it turned out all right," I said.

"Sure. He never broke anything," she said. "He was terrible. Even as a little bitty boy he would climb up on the sideboard at home and things like that."

I asked Mrs. Strieber if her son was hard to keep up with, and she replied, "Yeah, he was for a fact."

Strieber may well have set a difficult pace for his mother, but that certainly wasn't the case with his friends. Years later, they spoke to me of their exploits with him as though they had happened yesterday. Mike Ryan was the first of Strieber's boyhood chums who agreed to speak with me, and we met for lunch one Saturday at a local café in July of 1987. At that time he had not spoken to Strieber in years, nor had he read *Communion*. He said he had just bought the book, but that he hadn't had a chance to read it since his daughter had gotten to it first.

I asked Ryan if he remembered Strieber going on a train trip up north when he was a boy. Ryan said he did. I then asked him if Whitley said anything odd or unusual during the period after his return from the trip. Ryan said, "I remember him telling me something about seeing soldiers."

Ryan added that Strieber had not quite seemed to be his usual, free-spirited self for a little while after his return from that trip.

Strieber mentioned this conversation with Mike Ryan in *Transformation*, and I can attest that it is an accurate representation of the facts as I gave them to him.

However, I also asked Mike Ryan if he remembered anything about seeing fireballs. He did not specifically mention to me the fireball incident Strieber describes in *Transformation* (which involved seeing a huge fireball streak across the sky, only to be followed by the appearance of a black sedan speeding down Elizabeth Road). He did say, however, that he remembered seeing burned grass in the Strieber family lawn, which at the time the children attributed to another fireball that reportedly descended and rolled around on the ground before flying away. That incident was described by Strieber in *Communion*.

An even stranger incident related to me by Ryan didn't involve Strieber directly at all, but may have some tangential relevance for its bizarreness. Ryan said, "A friend of mine and I were sitting one day beneath a big tall hedge in the neighborhood. It was like a wall of hedge, going well above our heads, when suddenly we heard a huge *whoosh* of air over our heads and were showered in leaves." Mystified, the boys stood up and brushed the hedge leaves off their clothes only to see that the top of the hedge had been sheared off in an even, straight line, Ryan said.

Ryan added that the roar wasn't like the sound of a helicopter. To this day he has no explanation for that event. I might add that Elizabeth Road lies not far from the flight paths of military helicopters servicing nearby Fort Sam Houston. Still, it would be virtually impossible for a helicopter to fly close enough to the ground to trim a hedge in a residential neighborhood!

On each occasion I met with him, Mike Ryan expressed to me a great deal of fondness for his memories of his boyhood with Strieber, whom he still calls "Whitty," using his boyhood nickname. On a visit to the home of Mr. and Mrs. Milton Ryan, Mike's parents, I found Mrs. Ryan still calling Strieber "Whitty," as well.

Bill Mebane, remarkably, summed up his feeling for his boyhood with Strieber in a slightly tongue-in-cheek letter he sent him in July of 1988. Because it was sent to his publisher in England (Mebane having been out of touch with Strieber for years), the letter did not reach him until January of 1989. It is a most extraordinary document, though, and is reproduced here with Strieber's permission:

30-7-88

Dear Whitley,

The one chosen to commune with the cosmos. Last Saturday afternoon I have mistakenly landed (flying too low) on the Matterhorn. Carefully climbing down to Zermatt, I was very shocked to find our story on sale in the local bookstore. Without my permission, and most importantly, without my point of view! And what is this *Transformation* already announced? Have you had other visitors?

Yours jealously
Slant-eyed Sally

P.S. I also visited in Zermatt a certain Signor Mebane (Italo-Texano) who claims his own version of the Elizabeth Road adventures. For example, he does confirm the sighting of a long cigar-shaped "ship" in your back lot, but he also asserts that we had previous contacts in the numerous games of night hide-and-seek around the Flowers' mansion. That was not always Patricia hiding with him! And what about that time your grandfather chased him and Mike Ryan out of the house, who was really to blame? And the old "vegetable wagon" that used to come to Elizabeth Road, who was that mysterious seller? And all the towers and treehouses that you all constructed; those in Mike's backyard, even near his pool; that wooden platform near Bill's bedroom; and all those tree outposts in your front yard. Were you all establishing, unconsciously, bridges to the sky? And all the weather balloon and rocket experiments. . . .

This Italo-Texano, a shady character, could go on and on. Perhaps you should establish a direct contact: [address in Rome, Italy listed here].

P.P.S. It's a great book. Congratulations,

                                                        Bill

So Signor Mebane (who Strieber tells me married an Italian princess—literally) confirms the "sighting of a cigar-shaped ship" in the Strieber family back lot? Hmm. While this old friend seems to have had his tongue firmly planted in cheek, he nevertheless left open the question of what was really going on during the days, as he put it, of "the Elizabeth Road adventures."

All of the response from Strieber's friends had a great influence on changing his perceptions of his youthful self. As early in my investigation as April 1987, Strieber said to me:

"I have found that the picture I paint of myself in *Communion* as being rather unconcerned with strange things and UFOs when I was a child isn't too accurate—that I was much more concerned with those things in those days when I have remembered, which is interesting to me."

Strieber's statements in *Transformation* in regard to "the children's circle"—a nocturnal gathering of children, including himself, who presumably met with the "visitors"—have been the hardest to check by means of inquiry among people who lived in his neighborhood. None of his boyhood friends has provided me with any information whatsoever regarding experiences of that kind. Yet some tangential testimony regarding the question of "alien" presence in that general area, a wooded floodplain known as the Olmos Basin, has arisen from a San Antonio man named Ron McAtee, who was anonymously mentioned by Strieber in *Transformation*. McAtee is the man who Strieber said described to him his sighting of what he perceived to be an unusual aerial craft above the Cambridge Elementary School in Alamo Heights, the suburb directly adjoining Terrell Hills and only slightly more than a mile from Strieber's neighborhood.

McAtee had originally gotten in touch with Strieber by writing to the address listed in the back of *Communion*. Strieber gave me his number and asked me to do him the favor of meeting him and seeing if he was a normal person. I agreed to do so in October of 1987, when Strieber was staying in San Antonio. McAtee came up to my office in the Casino Club Building in downtown San Antonio one afternoon, and we had a casual conversation about my work investigating Strieber. McAtee told me that ever since he had been a boy, he had felt that there was some kind of alien activity going on in the Olmos Basin. Reading *Communion*, he said, had excited him because for the first time he was encountering someone else who entertained more or less the same idea. Although he exhibited some emotion when speaking with me, he seemed to be a perfectly normal middle-aged South Texas man in every respect.

While I was speaking with McAtee, Strieber phoned me from his hotel, and I told him I thought McAtee was on the level. Within twenty minutes Strieber was in my office, listening intently to McAtee's story. After hearing him out, Strieber said he believed the story was true, not only because he felt McAtee was sincere and sane, but because of the threefold nature of the telepathic communication that McAtee said he received from the craft. Strieber details that observation in *Transformation*, and his record of what he told McAtee that day is a generally faithful account of what he actually said. The only error in the account, according to McAtee, is in what Strieber wrote regarding the direction of flight of the craft. McAtee reminded me he said the strange craft was moving north of the Olmos Basin area, not toward it (which would have been in a southerly direction), as Strieber wrote in *Transformation*.

McAtee and I later met for an extensive interview in which he showed me a package of materials dating to his elementary school days that showed a lifelong interest in the question of whether there were various alien creatures actually inhabiting—or going in and out of— Olmos Basin. Remarkably, he showed me compositions from his days at the Cambridge Elementary School that spoke of "ghosts" that came into his bedroom at night, as well as playing with a friend in the basin who had computers in an underground room. Considering the fact that computers were not the universal fascination for children in the 1950s that they are today, that mention was rather curious. The fascination manifested itself during the 1970s with a diary in which McAtee wrote dreams dealing with sightings of strange ships in the basin area, and even occasional encounters with alien beings. McAtee also bought a rather expensive aerial photograph of the Olmos Basin area on which he traced the probable route of the strange craft he saw during his first-grade year at the Cambridge school, which was, as Strieber wrote, 1957.

Strieber also relates in *Transformation* that on November 8, 1957, the *San Antonio Express* reported a sighting of a UFO over north San Antonio that occurred on November 7, 1957. That story, headlined "Round Ball 'Whatnik' Seen Over Alamo City," was indeed printed as Strieber wrote. However, to be accurate, while the report cited sightings of bright lights in the sky in the towns of New Braunfels and Boerne, which lie to the north of the city, the actual 'Whatnik" reported in the *Express* was primarily visible from downtown and south San Antonio. The story reads:

Whatnik hovered over San Antonio shortly after 7:30 p.m. Sunday night.

Fifteen hard boiled (and sober) newspapermen—all staff members of the San Antonio Express—saw the object.

They said:

—It wasn't an airplane, balloon or meteor.

—It wasn't a star, searchlight or helicopter.

—It wasn't the moon, Venus, Jupiter, or the sun.

—It also wasn't a hallucination (as Air Force representatives have assured reporters).

The story cited one Don Lively as having called the newspaper's attention to the object, which at that time was "hovering in the sky south-southwest over San Antonio."

"It was bright and glowing," Lively said, "and it was green and blue. The back of it was red—at least from my angle of vision. Two stick-like objects were thrust out from each side and they were green and blue."

San Antonio Express staff members opened third floor windows to view the object.

It had an eerie appearance and hovered at an angle of 30 to 40 degrees above the south-southwest horizon.

The object—"Whatnik"—appeared stationary, and after ten minutes slowly settled from view behind downtown buildings.

I attempted to contact Lively, but the only Don Lively listed in the San Antonio telephone book is not the same man who made the call to the newspaper. I did speak, however, with another eyewitness cited in that story, Elliot Moore, who at that time was a security guard at Stinson Field, then the airport for San Antonio, located in the southern part of the city.

Moore was quoted in that same San Antonio Express story as saying: "I think it was definitely not an airplane. It didn't have red and green lights like airplanes have, and it was too bright and too close to be a star."

In a telephone interview with me on January 6, 1989, Moore confirmed that he was quoted accurately in the Express story.

"I know damn well I wasn't drinking," he told me. "I saw whatever the object was—I didn't know—I didn't have time. I got scared of it and got out of the way so I could watch it from underneath the porch part of the airport there."

No byline appeared on the "Whatnik" story, and attempts by both myself and San Antonio Express-News staff writer Craig Phelon to determine who wrote it have been unsuccessful, so it has been impossible to check the accuracy of the other elements of the report.

It is worth pointing out, however, that this "Whatnik" story ran in the very center of the front page of that day's paper, which happened to be full of news relating in one way or another to the "space age." November 7, 1957, as it turns out, was the day the United States formally entered into competition with the Soviet Union for domination of outer space with the naming of Dr. James R. Killian of the Massachusetts Institute of Technology as special adviser on science and technology to President Dwight D. Eisenhower. The banner headline on that day's *Express* read; "IKE PICKS M.I.T.'S KILLIAN BOSS OF U.S. SPACE RACE."

Interestingly, too, November 7, 1957, was the fortieth anniversary of the Bolshevik revolution. Another front-page article was titled "Russia Displays Mighty Rockets in Arms Parade." The United Press wire story that followed read, "Russia today unveiled an arsenal of mighty rocket weapons, including a big 'mystery' rocket that an American source said may be the Soviet intercontinental ballistic missile." On that same page, another story, bearing the headline "Spacedog May be Parachuted Back to Earth," stated "Reports circulate in Moscow tonight that the Russians may be trying to parachute spacedog Laika back to earth from Sputnik II."

The appearance of these stories on November 8, 1957, is made all the more interesting in regard to the stories of experimentation with rockets and the balloon flight of a "Frognik" by Strieber and his friends when one looks again at the date on the clippings from their appearance on the pages of the *San Antonio Express*. Their exploits were reported November 18, 1957—only eleven days after "Whatnik" was reportedly seen.

That coincidence proves nothing at all about alien influence in Terrell Hill and Alamo Heights, of course, but it is certainly curious. Anyone who was a boy in those days, as I was, can remember the contagious public excitement about the beginning of the "space race," and it is likely Strieber and his friends were affected by it, too. Perhaps their "Frognik" balloon flight was even inspired by the story of Laika the Soviet spacedog in the previous week's *Express*.

The UFO—or "Whatnik"—described in the November 7 story may or may not have been the same phenomenon seen by McAtee, but the manner in which it came to light (not mentioned by Strieber in *Transformation*), is nevertheless strange, given the coincidence that Strieber's friends were in the same paper only a week later. Strieber learned of that news story in a telephone conversation with me after McAtee had shown me a copy of the original story. I found it of interest for the mere fact that it reported one very prominent sighting of a UFO over San Antonio in 1957, the same year Strieber reported what he considers to be many visitor-related phenomena in his neighborhood. It was the first documentation of a UFO sighting that could possibly have had some relationship with Strieber's stories. Yet McAtee surprised me when I asked him how he had gotten hold of the "Whatnik" report.

"I wanted to see if I could remember more about the craft I saw over Cambridge Elementary School," he said, "so I went to see a hypnotist. While I was under hypnosis, the date November 7, 1957, came up. I went down to the public library and checked in the microfilm, and this is what I found. This was in 1977 when I did all this."

McAtee later inquired further using the Freedom of Information Act to see if there was any governmental record of this sighting over San Antonio on that date. His labor paid off with his receipt from the U.S. Air Force of old Project Blue Book records of a document headed "Project 10073 Record Card," a form that documented a sighting in San Antonio, Texas, on November 7, 1957.

As reproduced in this book, the form shows that the report differs somewhat in its particulars from the eyewitness testimonies of Don Lively and Elliot Moore. Under the category of "Brief Summary of Sighting," the form reads: "Round object, size of head of pin, pale yellow, level flight, moved into cloud bank." Under "Comments" it reads: "Very limited data. However, if object moved in easterly direction could have been weather balloon which was launched at San Antonio just prior to time of sighting. If westerly—possible astronomical sighting. No evaluation made without positional information. Insufficient data."

Of course, it is possible that this report was not even of the same object as that described by Moore or Lively. Yet the possibility of there being more than one UFO report from San Antonio on that date seems rather remote, as the town was not having a UFO "flap," as far as can be told from newspaper records. Moreover, it is interesting that the Project Blue Book report reads "30 minutes" under the category "Length of Observation." In the *San Antonio Express* story of November 8, 1957, Elliot Moore was reported to say that he first observed the strange light in the sky about 7:30 P.M., and that it disappeared at 8:00 P.M.—thirty minutes' time.

McAtee relates another intriguing story, which may have some relevance to Strieber's memories about the "children's circle" in the light of an incident that he says occurred at a site in the Olmos Basin in either 1957 or 1958. According to McAtee, he saw what appeared to be a "naked man" running through a wooded area of the basin. This event occurred, McAtee said, while he was taking a walk with his father and brother, Robert.

My colleague, Craig Phelon, interviewed McAtee on this point at my request. McAtee's account of the sighting, as printed in a *San*

Antonio Express-News Sunday Magazine story on October 30, 1987,[2] read as follows:

> "It was probably the middle of winter," he says. "You could see into the trees, because they didn't have any foliage. I would say he was a good 50 feet into the woods.
>
> "We all sort of crouched down—and I don't know why we were afraid of him because there were three of us and obviously he wasn't carrying a concealed weapon. We had the dog with us and we were trying to hold the dog back.
>
> "He was light-colored, that's why we thought he was naked, but he was a ways away, too. I don't remember if he had hair on his head or any pubic hair. I just can't remember. Maybe he was just too far away to make something like that out. Why we thought it was a man, I'm not sure. I don't remember any breasts, so I guess it wasn't a woman. He was maybe about five feet tall. He wasn't really big."

This sighting may have been simply a local nudist, of course, but it would have been a very hardy one. I asked McAtee's brother, Robert, who lives in Tustin, California, if he remembered the sighting. He said he did, and described the "man" in much the same terms as his brother. He pointed out that it was a relatively cold day, with the temperature being between 40 and 50 degrees Fahrenheit, making the sighting all the more unusual.

"We were all wearing caps and jackets," he said. "What was strange about him, as I remember it, was that under one arm he was carrying something that had the shape of a surfboard. I've never figured that out. It was so bizarre to see a person naked running through the woods that we were all dumbfounded."

Robert McAtee said that he believes the incident occurred in 1957 or 1958, and that he was eleven or twelve years old at the time. He is five years senior to Ron. The bizarreness of the incident has kept it fresh in his memory over the years, he said.

"You forget the day-in, day-out humdrum things," he said. "But my mind has returned to that experience many times since then."

The extraordinary aspect of this story, especially as told by Ron McAtee, may lie in the mention of a small object resembling a "surfboard" that the "naked man" was reportedly carrying. Aliens or visitors are often described by "abductees" as wearing a close-fitting jumpsuit that appears to be made of a single piece of fabric—which could perhaps give an impression of nakedness at a distance. Yet the "surfboard" is interesting in the light of Strieber's descriptions of floating up in a kind of "raft," and his son Andrew's descriptions of being floated up in a sort of "cot" that was just his size.

Robert McAtee made no reference to these possible parallels with stories in *Communion* and *Transformation*. He simply described for me what he remembered seeing.

My association with Ron McAtee led me into discovering a number of people in the Alamo Heights area who had also had extraordinary experiences relating to UFO phenomena, some of whom lived and even continue to reside in the general neighborhood of Strieber's old house on Elizabeth Road (since torn down and replaced with a Mediterranean-style structure). My investigatory journeys down those paths are described in the epilogue to this book.

McAtee's experiences, the November 7, 1957, "Whatnik" sighting and the stories told by people whom he has met in Alamo Heights do not, naturally, add up to anything remotely resembling proof that Strieber was involved in meeting with visitors or aliens in a "children's circle" in the Olmos Basin. Whether or not the "naked man" incident of which McAtee speaks has anything to do with Strieber remains very much open to question. Yet there was an extraordinary amount of serendipity in the manner in which Ron McAtee literally plucked the date of November 7, 1957, out of his subconscious mind. Serendipity, for investigators of UFO-related phenomena, sometimes seems to crop up when least expected.

That was certainly my own experience when, while serving as a consultant to the staff of the *San Antonio Express-News Sunday Magazine*, I interviewed Ann Hix for a story on the U.S. Air Force and UFOs with a heavily local angle. Craig Phelon joined me and participated in the interview, taping it on his recorder. Mrs. Hix was of particular interest to us because her late husband, Colonel Guy Hix, was commander of Godman Air Force Base, near Fort Knox, Kentucky, on January 7, 1947, the date of the U.S. Air Force's first UFO-related fatality. We were interested in seeing if Mrs. Hix could throw some light onto the death of Captain Thomas Mantell, a young National Guard pilot whose last words were reportedly "It appears to be a metallic object . . . tremendous in size . . . directly ahead and slightly above. . . . I am trying to close for a better look."[3]

According to Timothy Good, author of *Above Top Secret: The Worldwide UFO Coverup,* that quote was obtained from a top-secret Air Force and Naval Intelligence report declassified in 1985, which may throw into some doubt earlier official reports that Mantell was chasing Venus or a weather balloon. According to Mrs. Hix, much of the general population of the area around Godman Field was electrified with excitement by the sighting of an enormous silvery disc observed flying in the sky. Apparently, the trajectory of that object intersected with the path of four National Guard P-51 Mustang aircraft, led by Mantell. In the official summary of events that Good reports in his book, Mantell is described as climbing toward the object while his companions continued on to their destination of Standiford Field, Kentucky, due to lack of oxygen. Nearly one hour later, the Wright Field Service Center was informed that Mantell had crashed some two miles south of Franklin, Kentucky. The official report read: "Accident fatal to pilot, major damage to aircraft."[4]

When I came to visit her, Mrs. Hix showed me a paperback copy of the late Major Donald Keyhoe's book, *The Flying Saucers Are Real,*[5] which begins with an account of the Mantell case. She held it in her lap during the interview and referred to it a few times while speaking. I asked her to tell me what she remembered of the details of the incident.

"As you know, as we all know, a CO is responsible for everything that happens on his base, good or bad," she said. "Colonel Hix must have been busy, and the sergeant received the wire from the officer up there, and he gave permission to pursue it. He should not have done it, but he did it, so the boy went on. As the plot developed, the boy never returned—the pilot."

I asked Mrs. Hix if she knew whether or not Mantell's body was ever recovered.

"I don't know. They say here [pointing to Keyhoe's book] it never was.[6] At that time there was a competition between the Army and the Air Force. The first I knew was that Colonel Hix told me he did not give permission for them to pursue the object. The sergeant in the office did. Now the book doesn't state that. The book states they got together and looked through binoculars. Later they did. Colonel Hix of course started looking for the boy then, you know, but they never found him. And this book said his body was never found. But the mother of the boy sued the government and, of course, that involved Colonel Hix. Right after that he got a transfer. It left him with a mild heart attack, too."

Where did Colonel Hix and his family then go? They moved to San Antonio, Texas, where the colonel was assigned to Lackland Air Force Base. The fact that Colonel Hix did not give the order for Mantell to pursue the silvery object may be of some interest to flying saucer buffs. It is at this point, though, that the story takes a twist in the direction of Strieber. As fate would have it, Colonel and Mrs. Hix bought a house only a few blocks away from the Strieber neighborhood on Elizabeth Road. It was a natural enough choice for them, as many young families were moving into the area, and Ann Hix must have enjoyed the thought of residing close to the home of her lifelong friend, Lanette Glasscock. Mrs. Hix had two boys, moreover, and before long they were playing with their new friends, Albert Glasscock and—that's right—Whitley Strieber.

"They were always in the swimming pool," Mrs. Hix said, "just like little fish. I had to always keep an eye on them."

A hack writer of science fiction could have invented no more banal and implausible scenario than this one: UFO scandal sends Air Force colonel held responsible for tragic death of flier to San Antonio; boy destined to become "Mr. UFO" grows up in his shadow. It may certainly sound like an implausible plot, but it is nevertheless true that Whitley Strieber spent a fair amount of time playing in the house of an officer whose career had been directly affected by the furor of Mantell's fatal brush with a UFO, in a family where UFOs were regarded as real indeed.

Just for the record, since we are lingering momentarily in the serendipity department, it is also rather curious that Ann Hix, Lanette Glasscock, and my mother, Dolores Conroy, are friends from girlhood. Ann and my mother were dubbed "the giggle sisters" by Leon Glasscock, who insisted on bringing them along in the backseat of his car on dates while he was courting Lanette. While I had known Mrs. Hix socially, I had no idea that she was the widow of Colonel Guy Hix until my mother casually mentioned that fact one day.

Ann Hix is a very credible witness, and the fact that she had given no previous interviews convinced me of her trustworthiness and veracity. One particular anecdote Mrs. Hix related to me, however, served to verify the accuracy of her statements regarding Strieber. She pointed out that her house happens to have a brick facade. As she put it: "Well, when Whitley first came over here he looked at the brick and said, 'Who do they think they're fooling?' "

That certainly sounded to me like Whitley Strieber.

Needless to say, Mrs. Hix has followed Strieber's recent literary career with a great deal of interest.

It was during his high school years in the later 1950s and early 1960s that Whitley Strieber began to seriously consider making such a career a reality. By all accounts, one person figures prominently in that choice: Brother Martin McMurtrey, S.M. (nicknamed Brother Mac), his English teacher at Central Catholic Marianist High School.

I asked Strieber about important early influences when I first interviewed him, and he immediately mentioned Brother Mac.

"I guess that what was the most formative experience I had in my career was at Central Catholic High School under Brother Martin McMurtrey, who's still very much alive," he said. "Brother McMurtrey believed in me as a writer and took me seriously, and as a result of that I really did expect to become a writer, and the intellectual atmosphere at Central in those days was very, very intense. I don't know what it's like now. But it was an extremely strong experience for me, a good experience for me, more important, by far more important than my college years."

I asked Mary Strieber if she had known Brother Martin McMurtrey. Indeed she did. As she put it:

"Yes, he used to call me and say, 'Now make him read the life of Abraham Lincoln,' and he'd want me to make him do all this stuff. Whitley was very impatient with him, but Brother McMurtrey was proud of him when *The Wolfen* came out. Oh, and you know, Whitley was so bad at school, it's a wonder they graduated him. You know, he made a tape and hid it in the locker of one of the brothers. And in the middle of the class this tape started talking. It was awful. We went to a parents' night and I said to this teacher, 'Don't let Whitley throw you,' and he said, 'Mrs. Strieber, he already has.' He was a terrible practical joker, just awful. Well, Brother Mac always had a lot of faith in him."

Mary Strieber also mentioned that she believed that Brother McMurtrey introduced Whitley to Oliver Heard while they were both students at Central. Heard is now a prominent attorney in San Antonio with a massive business collecting taxes for a number of large counties and school districts in Texas. It was at Central, too, that Strieber got to know Henry Cisneros, later to become the first Hispanic mayor of San Antonio in modern times. Many of Strieber's classmates went on to other very responsible positions in the local community and elsewhere.

I interviewed Brother McMurtrey in April of 1987 shortly after first interviewing Strieber. My first question asked him to describe his memory of the young Strieber's interests, particularly with a view to the young man's sense of spirituality.

"Well, he was always interested in the occult," he said. "In fact, what surprised me was that, for a boy that age, when he talked about vampires he didn't talk about some movie, he talked about the historical vampire. I don't know where he got it, but in his sophomore year, when I started teaching him—I taught him two years, I'm sure about that—and he wrote about that.

"Also his group used to ask me—the atom bomb was coming up then and they had that sense of— They used to say to me, 'You grew up in a generation that didn't have this hanging over your head, you know, like a sort of an evil.' I said, 'Yes, we did, we grew up in a kind of an Adam-and-Eve paradise situation.' I can't remember him saying that specifically, but it was sort of a group mentality."

I commented that it probably came as no surprise when his former student expressed those fears in a book like *Warday*.

"No," McMurtrey said. "You know there was a book, *Childhood's End*, by Arthur C. Clarke—that group was very interested in it. They tried to get me to read it, and I started it, but at that time I couldn't touch science fiction. I never finished it, but *Nature's End* reminds me a lot of it.

I pointed out to McMurtrey that Strieber made some comments very critical of institutional Catholicism in my original interview with him.

"That group never would accept anything on faith," he said. "They were critical, highly so, and I'm not surprised at how he's developed. That he should be criticizing the institutional Church—it needs some criticizing."

I asked McMurtrey about Strieber's sense of humor and his love of pranks, particularly a report I'd heard that Whitley may have been involved in the production of a literary anthology that lampooned a number of students and teachers at Central. I had heard this underground missive was based on an actual official school publication.

"I know that he was involved in it," he said. "They did put it out—well the school's book is still called *The Anthology*—and they put out a sort of a para-*Anthology*. They just showed me, so I never did have one. . . . They had parodied my writings, they had parodied the principal's work and he didn't like that at all. And they had parodied each others' work; made some of them very angry. I just ran into it by accident because the principal called me in. I think, in fact, some family was threatening a lawsuit or something, because he had questioned their son's virility, you know, that always happens. So it did calm down.

"He always sort of had a tongue in cheek, you know, he's still got that," McMurtrey told me. "Critical, too, his humor is critical, also. . . . [I remember] he came to me and said, 'What college should I go to? I want to be a writer.' You don't hear that often. . . . Already, at that time, he was intent on that, and I've only had one other student tell me that."

Did Brother McMurtrey have any criticisms of his former student?

"At that time, he had a very rambling style," he said. "I remember critically saying to him, 'Whitley, if you ever learn to write in sentences, you'll write.' But it was abstruse. He had a command of vocabulary, he had read deeply, but he hadn't put it all together yet."

Another important influence in Strieber's trajectory toward becoming a writer was a job in the newsroom of the *San Antonio Express*.

"Sterlin Holmesly gets a lot of the credit for giving me the break of allowing me to work at the *Express*," he told me. "I was a copy boy, I landed the copy boy job. I was around seventeen, I think, it was around 1962 or '63, somewhere in there. I worked there for a year—a full year. I didn't do a lot of writing while I was there, but I did do a lot of reading, and a lot of talking to people who did write, and I learned a lot about the rhythm of the news—what kind of things you selected to go on the front page of a newspaper, what was important to people, what wasn't, in the life of the community. I read a lot of the old papers. They had microfilm of the *Express* there, and I spent a lot of time on my breaks looking at the old papers, learning about San Antonio and the experience of trying to make a city out of what started as a little collection of houses."

Shortly after *Communion* came out, I questioned Holmesly (now editorial director of the *San Antonio Express-News*) about his association with Strieber. He said that the last he had seen of him was after *Warday* was published, when Whitley and his wife, Anne, paid him and his wife a visit at their home in San Antonio. Holmesly was not terribly impressed with *Communion*, commenting that it didn't have enough real documentation in it to convince him that anything paranormal actually occurred in Strieber's life.

There remain many questions, of course, about Strieber's childhood and youth. Some of his critics might take his penchant for exploding "dust bombs" and other pranks as evidence of a deceitfulness that simply cannot be trusted. Yet, oddly enough, the trick element of his personality is precisely what endears him to some of his oldest friends, some of whom had a good streak of the trickster, it seems, in their own personalities. Albert Glasscock, although he today occupies a very respectable position, admitted to me that he and Whitley were such mischief-makers that when younger he almost dreaded the thought of having a boy child, lest a son of his should follow in his father's footsteps. Yet did this legacy of tricksterism carry over into Strieber's youth and adulthood? Is he prone to make up stories about himself in a deliberate effort to deceive others—or had he simply lost the ability to tell reality from fantasy?

These questions form the background to the debate over Strieber's personal credibility. For what it is worth, that debate revolves around the matter of whether or not Strieber actually was present on the University of Texas at Austin campus on August 1, 1966, during the massacre of students committed by sniper Charles Whitman. (Whitman went to the top of the University of Texas clock tower, barred the door, and began shooting people with a high-powered, telescope-equipped rifle.) Strieber wrote in *Communion* that he believed his memories of that incident were "screen memories," not real memories, and that he therefore wasn't there. (Strieber had previously given interviews in which he has spoken of himself as having actually been at the massacre.) Later, as he chronicled in *Transformation*, he couldn't accept the idea that his screen memories were such painful ones, so he conducted his own investigation of the matter of whether or not he was on campus at the time. His account in *Transformation* of that investigation is not substantially different from the account of it that he gave me in an interview in April 1987:

"The Charles Whitman incident. I found after the most careful research in the past six or seven months that I definitely was there, but that illustrates the problem of trying to understand. If one asks questions about one's memories—are they true or not?—one really opens up a Pandora's box. Because you can't know. In *Communion*, I questioned my presence at the Charles Whitman massacre, along with a lot of other things I did, for two reasons. One was that Jim Kunetka, the person I thought I was with, didn't remember my being there. Number two was that I couldn't think of a motive for being on campus that August 1, 1966. I was not in any summer school classes on campus, and home was in San Antonio. So I thought, 'Why would I have been there?' See, so those two things led me to question it.

"However, the bothersome thing about it was that the memory is so much more vivid than the other three memories that I thought to myself it must be that I was there, I had to have been there, and I set about trying to place myself there, like a policeman would, trying to place someone at a scene. Did I remember seeing anyone besides Jim whom I knew? No, I didn't, except for one person, and I only saw him briefly, and I didn't know him well at the time. I saw him in a very specific situation, and I saw him dart out of the student union building and called to him.

"I called him up and asked him to describe his movements on that day, and it turns out he remembers it vividly because his girlfriend was one of the people shot, and he has a vivid memory of everything he did, and damned if he did not linger back in the doorway of the student union building and step out once or twice. I must have been there. I never would have known that.

"What would my motive have been? Why would I have been on campus that day? I finally found out from another friend, who said, 'You know, Whitley, there were a lot of us on campus that day. Scholz's Beer Garden was celebrating its one-hundredth anniversary that night.' That's why I was there.

I questioned Jim Kunetka, who has known Strieber since their earliest years at Mount Sacred Heart Elementary School in San Antonio, whether he had any recollection of Strieber having been in Austin on August 1, 1966.

"Whitley and I have talked about this several times," Kunetka said. "He called me and specifically asked me if I was sure, one way or the other. I told him and I tell you that I have no recollection of his being in Austin. . . . My involvement, which was extremely minor, was this: The day that Whitman killed all those people from the tower also happened to coincide with the one-hundredth anniversary of a place here called Scholz's Beer Garden, a watering hole for older students, graduate students, a lot of politicos, and a lot of legislators if the legislature was in session. As I recall it was nickel beer. I was working in San Antonio, Whitley was in San Antonio that summer, but I came up with someone else.

"There were other people there and we just sat around drinking and at a certain point somebody came running in, this was well into the business that somebody was shooting from the tower, and students were running out into the streets where they were obviously putting themselves in danger—Whitman actually tried to shoot some of them, because there were bullet holes from his high-powered rifle in the walls of Scholz's. Thank God he missed everybody. All I remember is that somewhat later, I don't know if it was later that evening or the next day, I was talking with Whitley about the experience and about how awful it was."

I asked Kunetka if he was in Austin or San Antonio that next day, and he said that he was in San Antonio. "I definitely got back later that night. There was no reason to stay over," he said.

When I further asked Kunetka if he remembered Strieber having been in Scholz's Beer Garden, he replied, "No, I don't. I understand, from what he says, that he believes that he was on campus."

When I pointed out that Strieber has said that he believes he had gone to Austin that day to be at Scholz's Beer Garden, he replied, "Well, you know, he may well have been. I just don't remember. I can't confirm it one way or another. He and I have talked about this. I'm not sure why it's such a big thing for him."

I mentioned that Budd Hopkins, the UFO investigator who at one time was associated with Strieber, had maintained to me that he doubted whether Strieber ever was actually at the site. I also noted that he was not convinced by the story that Strieber has told regarding the Whitman incident as a "screen memory." It was too violent and complex, in his opinion, to qualify as such. Moreover, I said, some book reviewers had used the fact that Strieber had changed his story as evidence of what they took as a lack of credibility in his personal character.

To those observations, Kunetka replied: "Well, I do know that over the years, well before *Communion* was a book, you know, Whitley would sort of alternately say that he was there, and then admit that he wasn't sure, or then say that he wasn't sure. I mean it was an issue even before then. I know he talked with Jim Bryce, our mutual friend in Austin. He was here, in fact he was on campus and couldn't get out of the building and literally saw people being shot and felled by Whitman, and Whitley has asked him if he remembers Whitley, and he said no. But, same thing, that doesn't prove that Whitley wasn't there."

Kunetka closed his remarks by pointing out that there were between 20,000 and 30,000 people on campus, and that even more people were attracted to the scene during the shooting. He emphasized that the situation was far from being a quiet affair affecting only a few people. On the contrary, it was a scene of mass panic.

There is one person who maintains that Strieber was actually in Austin during the Whitman incident: Mary Strieber. When I asked her in April of 1987 whether she remembered if Whitley had gone to Austin on that day she said; "Well, yeah, he was over there then, but he was not right on the scene. He was adjacent to it. I mean he didn't get shot at."

That comment bears some additional relevance here in that it directly contradicts Strieber's initial assertion in *Communion* that he was not at the scene of the Whitman massacre. While the rigorous investigator would tend to discount testimony from a mother who might be expected to back up whatever her son might say, this testimony indicates that Mary Strieber was not afraid to contradict her son.

I asked Mary Strieber, "Have you talked to Whitley about his experiences in *Communion*? Have you exchanged views?"

"No, I really haven't," she said. "I've read the book. I thought it was very interesting, but it did point out that people's memories are so different."

Mary Strieber's memory of the Whitman event is apparently somewhat different from her son's. Strieber now says he was right on campus at the time of the shooting, near the student union building, which lies at the base of the tower. Mary Strieber is definite about her son, Whitley, having been in Austin on that day, but she does not confirm that he was at the scene of the massacre.

My investigation has failed to turn up an eyewitness who actually saw Strieber in Austin on August 1, 1966. In the opinion of some of his friends, it is curious that this particular incident has been seized upon by some Strieber-watchers as an example of what they regard as his deceitfulness about his past. Kunetka expressed to me his puzzlement that the question of Strieber's presence at the shooting should matter so much to some people in the UFO community. From a strict, evidential point of view, the most that can actually be said about the conflicting stories that Strieber has given regarding the incident is that actually retrieving information from memory is a very difficult proposition, even under the best of conditions. To infer from the record that Strieber's confusion about the incident is a sign of his untrustworthiness seems to imply an extraordinary—if not paranormal—ability to objectively ascertain the man's intentions.

Hopkins's position regarding Strieber's questionable presence at the shooting, moreover, appears to contain severe logical problems. On the one hand, Hopkins has asserted to me, he believes that Strieber's memory of the incident could not have been a screen memory, because screen memories (he asserts) are usually simple and nonviolent. Hopkins said he could accept an image of an owl as a screen memory of an "alien," for example, because it is simple, nonviolent in nature, and has some visual similarity to reported images of alien faces. He rejects the idea of Strieber's story of being at the shooting as a screen memory, therefore, because it is too complex and painful. It could not be covering up an alien encounter or other event, to extrapolate from Hopkins's position. Yet on this point Strieber and Hopkins now appear to be in theoretical agreement, since Strieber declared in *Transformation* his own dissatisfaction with his prior determination that the memories of the Whitman massacre were "screens" perhaps covering up a "visitor experience." It was because of the fact that the memories were too complex and painful, he said, that he began to investigate what really happened.

Second, though, Hopkins asserts that he believes that Strieber wasn't at the university at all. In essence, his position is that Strieber invented the story, as he believes Strieber is wont to do in many aspects of his life. Yet, in his interviews with me, Hopkins failed to provide a hypothesis or possible motive (other than his assertion that Strieber is "mentally unstable") to explain why Strieber would for years tell an invented story about having been at the Whitman shooting. Kunetka's statement, that Strieber was uncertain about whether he was at the site of the shooting even *before* writing *Communion*, indicates that, far from going around insisting that he was indeed present at the shooting, Strieber uninhibitedly expressed a certain degree of confusion about the subject. Such an attitude seems to be at variance with what one might expect from someone who would be trying to systematically invent a story about an experience he definitely knows didn't happen.

An incident of this sort can be easily used, therefore, by people to make whatever they will of it. I was impressed by the fact that Strieber was willing to tell me, as far back as April 1987, that he believed he had made a mistake in *Communion*, and that he was willing to attempt to correct the record. Given the lack of eyewitnesses to confirm his presence, it would have been far easier for Strieber to continue to maintain that he was not at the shooting than to assert that he was. Even Jim Bryce, whom in *Transformation* he said he remembered seeing in the student union building doorway, could not confirm his presence.

"When Whitley called me, he basically wanted to know if I could report that he was there," Bryce told me in an interview in January 1989. "And I said, to be as objective as possible, that I don't have any specific recollection of Whitley. I well could have seen him, but I don't know. But I can certainly report that I was at the student union, and was concerned about people walking through the doors."

Strieber did spend a year at St. John's University before returning to Texas to study English literature at the University of Texas. Jim Bryce said he knew Strieber fairly well during the time he was an undergraduate student, since both of them were in the same student organization. During our interview, he told me that one of the most outstanding impressions he had of Strieber at that time was of his overwhelming personal intensity. Byrce said he particularly remembers visiting Strieber at his Fountain Terrace apartment and having a casual conversation with him.

"He told me he hardly ever slept," Bryce said, "and that when he did sleep, it was only for short periods of time." Bryce told me that that single statement had made a big impression on him, implying he had at the time been inclined to believe it might be true. "I also remember that he was very much into Value Line investments," Bryce said. "I had the impression that he was involved in investing in shares of oil tankers and so forth. I knew that he had come from a family of some means, so that didn't surprise me."

Strieber considered a law degree, but found that option boring after a semester of law work at UT Austin. Instead, he packed off to London with hopes of becoming a filmmaker. Strieber described his time in London and his bizarre trip through Europe in both *Communion* and *Transformation*, which included an account of his strange "plane trip" to a land with adobe houses, a kind of "university," as he later described it. In *Communion*, Strieber describes fleeing from a strange young woman in Italy and landing up in Barcelona, where he "holed up in a back room of a hotel on the Ramblas." It was from that point on that the journey became extremely confused, with memories of the foul-smelling plane and being accompanied by someone who called himself a "coach."

Strieber wrote a poem after that experience, entitling it simply "Barcelona." Heretofore unpublished in its entirety, its first section reads:

> I lay in bed all afternoon
> there was no wind
> the sea was steel grey.
> I counted my breaths against the clock
> slept with my mouth open
> and woke up dry.
>
> Once upon a midnight we danced in circles
> beneath the waning moon,
> the blood-red moon of the Mediterranean,
> ate poppies
> and smeared ourselves with the fat of the bull.
> We flew when we danced—
> we danced a long time ago.
>
> A bull's death is not beautiful,
> the mouth opens and the tongue gags out
> the eyes roll back
> a bull dies for the minor frustrations of the poor,
> they shout to amuse the intellectuals to serve his birth
> and you wonder for the sake of progeny.
>
> Lightning in the south . . .
> A soft, evil smell rises from the street.
> We seem to see so many things
> the ships that never were
> the fairies at their ebat
> the descendants of bulls.

The last four lines of this section of the poem are particularly evocative of elements found in *Communion*, from the evanescent "ships" to the mention of "fairies," of which Strieber spoke as possibly being a category of being that has some relationship to his "visitors." The mention of the bull might be considered odd, too, in light of the ongoing and much-debated apparent connection between anomalous cattle mutilations and UFO phenomena.

According to Strieber, the confusion he experienced during that European trip was only one of several missing-time episodes in his youth. Despite those occasional periods of disorientation, though, he proceeded to move ahead with his career, eventually leaving London to pursue a series of small film-related jobs in New York.

His mother recalled that period in our interview.

"He came back from London and got a job in New York before he even came home," she said. "He wanted to live in New York. He didn't want to live in San Antonio. He worked with Barbra Streisand on a film.[7] But he didn't want to do that, he said, because unless you belonged to a union or were related to somebody high up in the movie business you didn't get anywhere. . . . Then he worked with Cunningham and Walsh advertising."

Strieber's career in advertising, he says, provided him with a stable base. He met and married his wife, Anne, and moved up in his business, all the while writing at night.

"He was a vice-president, but he said that didn't mean anything in advertising," his mother said. She confirms that he wrote eight novels before *The Wolfen* was published in 1978.

"Oh, yeah, and I had to read them, and he wanted me to criticize them, and, you know, that's a hard thing to do," she said. "When you love a person you don't want to put him down, but a lot of them weren't any good."

For what it is worth, Strieber's mother seems to take his story in *Communion* with a grain of salt.

"I had a funny experience," she said. "Mother lived to be, well, a week short of ninety-four, and she had her own house in Terrell Hills, and she got so she couldn't live alone. So she had Ina Wilson there, and Ina called me one day and said, 'Mary, I want to borrow that book that Whitley wrote, and if I like it, I'll buy it.' And I thought, 'That's pretty smart.' "

I haven't bothered to find out if Ina Wilson finally bought a copy of *Communion*. Certainly plenty of other people have done so. Yet despite the book's popular success, it appears that Strieber has become identified in the minds of a good portion of the reading public with

Communion alone. Perhaps one of the reasons for that phenomenon has been the fact that few journalists bothered to look seriously at his previously published works. After all, they were "fiction," so what could they have to tell us? Such an attitude, of course, flies in the face of the simple fact that a great deal of fiction is thinly disguised autobiography, and that the role of the imagination is often one of an amplifier of images that, in one way or another, may have a deep, personal connection to the mind and the life of the artist.

If one looks with an open eye, once can find numerous thematic resonances between Strieber's earlier fictional work and the visitor-related material in *Communion*. To some readers, of course, these parallels may in and of themselves constitute the outline of an elaborate literary hoax. I certainly wondered if such could be the case at the outset of my inquiry. Strieber remarked on his fictional work in *Transformation:*

> I reviewed my writings. Except for *Communion* and one recent short story there is nothing that relates directly to the UFO phenomenon. But the whole corpus of my work seems to reflect some sort of attempt to cope with an enormous, hidden, and frightful reality.
>
> My early poetry is full of references to being lost in time and dancing by night, to a very different view of life than fits convention: "God is wild; I am tame. . . . Night falls and an age ends. . . . We call and we answered through the thick foliage, by voices too strange to be called our own. . . ."
>
> The Wolfen were gray, hid in the cracks of life, and used their immense intelligence to hunt down human beings as their natural and proper prey.
>
> Then there was Miriam Blaylock, the vampire in *The Hunger*. She drank blood, and extracted from it the stuff of souls. They were the source of her immortality. And when her human consorts died, their souls remained forever trapped in their bodies, for all eternity. Like the Wolfen, a part of nature, Miriam describes herself as belonging to "the justice of the earth."
>
> *Black Magic* is a novel about secret psychic research and mind control.
>
> And *Night Church:* Again the issue was a force that could consume the soul.
>
> Was the force I had written about again and again my mind's

way of dealing with supressed horror of very real visitors? Only in *Cat Magic* had the force emerged in anything like a positive light, and in that book the "fairy" had been responsible for manipulating and controlling human society in such a way that the flowering of souls would be the outcome.[8]

There are even more specific areas of similarity between Strieber's fiction and the content of *Communion*. One particularly striking example may be found in his novel *Black Magic*, which deals with a Soviet plot to use psychotronic means to induce American Air Force officers to involuntarily launch intercontinental ballistic missiles, thereby provoking a war the Soviets were prepared to win. In one scene, an American woman is captured by Soviet agents in New York and subjected to the torture of having a golden needle, attached to an electric power source, plunged through a hole in her skull, into her brain.

In *Communion*, one of the first things Strieber describes having been done to him was the insertion of a metal needle into his brain.

There are other areas of resonance that emerge in specific images. Strieber wrote in *Communion* that he and Anne had an experience of hearing a voice emanate from their stereo. Perhaps a fictive analogue to that phenomenon might be found in the hypnotic television sets that turn on by themselves in *The Night Church*. Even the characters in that novel, members of a secret organization that has been conducting a genetic experiment through the centuries toward breeding a being who would become what pious Christians might call the antichrist, have this much in common with the visitors: They stealthily enter and leave people's houses unnoticed.

So too, for that matter, does Miriam Blaylock, the beautiful vampire in *The Hunger*. There is an extraordinary scene in that novel that elaborately describes Blaylock's secret nocturnal visit to the home of Dr. Sarah Roberts, a physician doing research into the prevention of the aging process, and her lover, Dr. Tom Haver. Not only is this scene highly erotic (as was Strieber's initially remembered experience with the visitors) but it also reveals an attempt on the part of the nocturnal visitor to directly influence Sarah Roberts's mind:

> Miriam went to the bed, sat down beside it, and contemplated her victim. She was a ripe little apple, this one. Very carefully, Miriam slipped back the bedclothes and revealed the

woman's neatly curved body. She longed to draw the life out of it but rather she hovered close, inhaling its sharp, humid aroma, listening to its little sounds. . . .

To begin the *touch* that would enter Sarah's dreams, she took her hand, which dangled off the edge of the bed, and ran her lips across the back of it, kissing lightly, brushing it with her tongue. Sarah inhaled a long breath. Miriam stopped awhile, then leaned close to Sarah and breathed her breath, smelling its sharp warmth, mingling it with her own. Sarah's head moved and she moaned. Her right breast was exposed and Miriam held it briefly in her hand, then slid her palm back and forth across the nipple until it became erect. She took the nipple between two of her long forefingers and squeezed until Sarah tossed her head. The girl's mouth hung slackly opened. Miriam covered it with her own, pressing her tongue against Sarah's with the utmost care. She remained like that for fully half a minute, feeling the faint movements of Sarah's tongue that indicated her unconscious excitement. She drew back and listened once more. Tom was still in stage three sleep. Sarah was nearly awake, making little noises as she dreamed. Miriam now felt powerfully drawn to her, could almost see her glowing dreams in her mind's eyes.[9]

This passage, from a book published in 1981, is a very curious prefiguring of Strieber's later representation of the visitors as practitioners of a most intimate "communion" with him.

There are numerous other resonances. Strieber makes references to an image of an "eye" in the sky in both *The Night Church* and *Communion*. Owls also figure as a factor, not only in *Communion* (where Strieber said he remembered seeing a barn owl at his bedroom window after his first recollected "visitor experience"), but in *Cat Magic* as well.

Strieber later interpreted the owl as a "screen memory" of his visitor experience, but added, in *Communion*, that his sister Patricia, also testified to having seen what she regarded as an owl. In a telephone interview from her home in Houston in April 1987, Patricia Strieber mentioned this experience and related it to me in her own words. As she put it:

"The only thing that happened to me that I can't explain was while, once again, I was up in the Texas Hill Country, at my grandmother's place. I was driving, I must have been coming back from Kerrville and going back there to Comfort, and a big white light came across the street, the road, and into some trees, and disappeared in there. My only question at the time was why it was so big and why didn't I hear it hit, if it was a meteor. And then I saw an owl flying in front of the car and it scared me half to death."

Patricia Strieber also told me she remembered one occasion when a large white owl, not normally seen in Texas, appeared atop a telephone pole in the backyard of the Strieber house. She added that when she was a girl, she would often see and hear a small "screech owl" outside her bedroom window. In a telephone conversation subsequent to our first telephone interview, moreover, she said that during the night immediately following our initial conversation, she heard and saw an owl outside the bedroom window of her house in Houston.

Clearly, Strieber deliberately evoked owl imagery in *Cat Magic*, in an encounter that occurs between two characters, one a young woman, the other a "fairy":

> Mandy instinctively lowered her eyes. It was more bearable this way, just looking at the woman's feet, no more than two inches long, naked in the snow. Then the feet rose out of her line of sight. She looked up, startled. The girl was floating in the air. Wings flapped and she was gone. A great gray owl hooted from the top of the rowan, its horns darkly silhouetted against the sky.[10]

In my April 1987 interview with him, Strieber offered some further observations on owls and the visitor experience.

"The owl image has emerged as one of the most predominant images of the whole experience, because not only am I involved with owl imagery, so are a lot of other people who have had the visitor experience," he said. "It's a very common image connected with it. The owl is also, as you know, the image of Athena, in her manifestation as the goddess of wisdom. It's also the symbol of hidden knowledge, and the owls and eagles are the symbols of light and dark knowledge among certain American Indians. The owl imagery is very interesting imagery, and indeed, during 1986, there was much more. Owl-stuff became involved not only with me in the country, but with some of my neighbors, one of whom remembered being taken out of his bedroom in the middle of the night by a giant owl, and that is before he knew anything about *Communion*.[11]

Even the idea of entities "eating souls," which Strieber said in *Transformation* was one of his fears of the visitors themselves, is to be found in *Cat Magic*. Strieber takes Amanda, his principal character, on a journey through an after-death state in which she encounters the psychic forces of her own mind as though they were real demons:

> It had the head of a human being. She thought, perhaps, the face was familiar. Was it Hitler? Stalin? She couldn't be sure. It bubbled words, "Help me, he-e-e-lp me . . ." Then it snarled, its body whipped out, and in an instant coils as hard as iron had swarmed about her.
>
> She saw flashes, she heard an old song, "Lili Marlene," a German song from World War II. And she felt hot wires digging into every part of her body, digging and exploring.
>
> She felt herself disappearing, becoming less than nothing.
>
> The wires were its teeth: it was eating her soul.[12]

Parallels and resonances with features of visitor experiences are relatively easy to find throughout his work. When I asked Strieber if he had ever thought about the similarity between the golden needle in *Black Magic* and the silver needle he described in *Communion*, he said, "You know, that was brought up to me this morning. I had not remembered it was in *Black Magic*."

Yet underlying the easily identifiable resonances, which to some readers might be sufficient information to conclude that Strieber had to be imagining the story in *Communion*, there remains one concept fundamental to understanding his work. To Whitley Strieber, predation is, in his words, "the justice of the universe."

This theme is glaringly obvious in his first published novel, *The Wolfen*, which described a race of ultraintelligent wolves with a sensorium and capability for stealth so advanced as to make humans easy prey. Like wolves themselves, the Wolfen only took the weak and sick—and those who suspected the truth of their secret existence.

The character of Miriam Blaylock, too, was a sublime predator, who deceived her victims but loved and cherished them with the gift of centuries of life.

In Strieber's young adult novel, *Wolf of Shadows*, he turned the tables on the conventional man-wolf relationship and dramatized a mother and daughter's adoption into a wolf pack as their only means to survive the winter brought on by a nuclear war.

It is extremely significant, then, that the first story Strieber wrote after his visitor experience was entitled "Pain."[13] Only one journalist, out of all the articles I have examined, has commented on this story, and then only to serve the purpose of supporting a satire of Strieber's work in *Communion*. I asked Strieber to discuss his interpretation of "Pain" in April of 1987.

"It's a remarkable and terrifying story by the way and I think it—I mean I call it remarkable because when I wrote it I was still totally unconscious of this material— but it had all risen to the surface within a few days of having written the story. Indeed, while I was writing the story, it all kind of emerged into the forefront of my mind. This was written after the *Communion* experience that happened in December of '85, and before I really had put the narrative together. I was actually writing the story the day that I remembered. My head began to hurt and I remembered the needle being put in my head. I was in the process—I hadn't finished writing it then.

"Let me tell you what the story involves. It involves a man coming into contact with a woman who is somewhat like Miriam Blaylock in *The Hunger*, not a vampire but a strange angelic demon whose purpose is to put people under so much pressure that they break through to a higher level of consciousness—and this, to me, is the whole essence of the visitor experience."

In more specific terms, "Pain" is the story of an author who goes "networking" into his city's community of prostitutes as research for his next novel. He finds what he is looking for—and much more—in the person of beautiful young Janet O'Reilly. As Strieber wrote:

> For my new book, to be called *Pain*, I wanted to know not only about prostitution but also about the various perversions that attach themselves to it. There are sexual desires so exploitative that people will not gratify them without being paid even in our exploitative society. These have to do for the most part with pain and death. For death is connected to sexuality— witness the spider. Who hasn't wondered what the male spider feels, submitting at the same time to the ecstasy of coitus and the agony of death?
>
> For almost all of human history it has been believed that

there is something to be gained by human sacrifice. There are lurid tales of it in ancient times, when it was practiced formally. In *The Golden Bough* Frazer comments that "worship of the feminine principle was everywhere and in all times associated with human sacrifice." This is, naturally, an outrageous misstatement of fact. All early religion was associated with sexuality and so with death; human sacrifice was an integral part of much ritual. There has forever been the notion that something higher than men had to be fed on human souls. Janet has taught me both the truth and the error in this concept. She has taught me with my own life's blood.[14]

Remarkably, too, this story contains the first recognizable instance of a direct mention of UFOs in Strieber's fictional work:

Ten years ago, in the course of another research effort, I met a man—since dead—who claimed that the National Security Agency had a document a hundred and thirty pages long which told the truth about UFOs, making an irrefutable case for civilization so far in advance of our own that we literally cannot see its manifestations except on rare occasions when they probe into our temporal space, much as the farmer enters the pigsty to check the health of his animals.

The underlying thesis of the paper is that this higher species is native to earth, and that—by their own lights—they use us as we use the pigs. I know that this is true because Janet has shown me that it is true. For reasons that will become clear, I was earmarked for special suffering. As my understanding has increased, I have come to love my tormentors, and share with them their own sorrow.[15]

"Pain" is much more, though, than the philosophical essay it appears to be in its opening pages. Though Strieber reveals his preoccupation with the fate of the earth, specifically through mentioning the potentially disastrous implications of the widening ozone hole in the atmosphere, the story moves into the drama of a man caught in the web of a spider woman who is far more intense than any ordinary sado-masochist. Eventually, the narrator, here named Alex, finds himself trapped in a steel locker box, to which Janet applies the flames of a blowtorch.

I have never known such suffering as I knew over the period of time she applied the torch to the outside of the steel box. She did not burn me but rather baked me slowly. I sweated, tickled, itched. The box became a humid hell. I screamed helplessly, totally given over to my pain. I cannot describe in words what I felt in those hours. But I can say that my spirit separated from my body, and its tragedy. It has done my real suffering in life. It must do the real dying. As the cup is not the wine, Alex is not me. Understanding this, I began to know myself a little.

To learn this lesson was the reason she had brought me here and submitted me to such suffering. The whole torment of a lifetime had been concentrated in a few hours. I was now at the threshold: she had taught me what is essentially needed to be well-prepared for death.

The heat had stopped.

"Can you speak?" I tried, but nothing came out. I wanted to speak, though, and she knew it. "Try harder, Alex."

Finally, my voice cracked to life. "Thank you."

"Well said. You've understood. Say it again."

"Thank you, thank you." [16]

This encounter between predator and prey did not simply result in carnage and feast. While Janet, as predator, is depicted as clearly enjoying the power she exercises, Alex, as prey, receives a strength that comes from a fierce appreciation of the fleetingness of life itself. He returns to his wife and home to savor every facet of his life: the smell of bacon and coffee at breakfast, the depth of his sensual love for his wife, all put into perspective by his awareness of death.

This picture of Janet O'Reilly might be all the more interesting in relation to the fact that Strieber believed the visitor who seems to have been in control of his first remembered "abduction" experience to be female. Was she, too, a "strange angelic demon whose purpose is to put people under so much pressure that they break through to a higher level of consciousness"?

"Pain" is a story that, in retrospect, aptly sums up Strieber's estimation of the "visitor experience" as an initiatory experience, deeply personal and different for each individual.

"I have hundreds of letters here," he said in April 1987. "Again and again people describe a terrifying approach or experience of some kind, followed by all kinds of parapsychological experiences, out-of-the-body experiences beginning to occur. There's a whole sea change, a change of nature almost. Very deep changes take place in these people.

"It seems to be, by the way, kind of like an initiatory experience, something like people involved in medicine rituals in Native American cultures would have gone through in the past—an immensely stressful experience that leads to greater enlightenment."

Clearly, *Communion* was representative of a "whole sea change" in Strieber, in which he purported to reveal himself as nakedly as he could, apparently letting light into the darkest corners of his personal experience. It was not an overtly political book, but it was radical in the sense that it was a sharp departure from the path that he had been previously following in his career. Its apocalyptic concerns about the ecological future of the earth (echoed and amplified in *Transformation*), however, resonate most with his work in *Nature's End* and *Warday*. The appearance of those two books reflected a growing politicization of Strieber's work as a writer. It is perhaps characteristic of Strieber, though, that he attributes the inspiration to write *Warday* to a night-time visitor.

Strieber surprised me with this account when I asked him why he switched from writing in the horror genre to that of documentary fiction with a strong scientific bent:

"I guess what happened was that in December of '83 I had in this office one of these experiences—although at the time I did not interpret it as a visitor experience—it was an apparitional experience, where I saw something quite apparitional. The first moment I looked at it I thought it could be somebody, but that was dispelled after a second because it was obviously some kind of hallucinatory thing, but it had—what it was, was a figure standing and looking down at me at about two-thirty in the morning. I had been sitting and toying with my work in a kind of dark state, feeling kind of at the bottom of things, when I turned around. I felt someone behind me, and I thought Anne had come into the room, even though it was very late at night, and there was this figure standing behind me—tall, staring down at me with a very sort of—wearing a cowl—with a very beautiful, intense sort of face underneath the cowl. I met eyes with it for a moment and it disappeared. I was a little startled, that's all. At that hour of the night, when you're tired, it's not unusual to have such an experience. It passed off instantly, it was never even a heartbeat. It was nothing important.

"However, I did notice there was a dramatic change in my work. I became passionate about writing it. I was on fire to write that book, but what was more important was the structure of it was in my mind then, the way I was going to go about it. I guess you could say I was inspired by a muse."

It may seem harder to find visitor-related themes in *Nature's End* and *Warday* than in Strieber's earlier fictional work. Yet both books deal with the human struggle to overcome very real fears about our capability to survive the problems we have created for ourselves. In *Nature's End*, in particular, there is a considerable amount of hope for the future for a dramatic increase in the intelligence of children, a change perhaps comparable to the shift that occurred when man arose out of his evolutionary predecessors. This hope is dramatized by Strieber and Kunetka's imaginings of a group of extraordinarily intelligent children living in a secret enclave on the California coast, who use their precocity to tap into the world's communications and computer network. Their goal? To create highly sophisticated models of world event trends—in the hope that they might intervene to gain time for the planet's nearly dead ecosystem to heal itself.

That strain of thinking is evident in the final chapter of *Communion*, in which Strieber speculates that perhaps the significance of the "visitor experience" is that mind itself is struggling to become more conscious. Strieber commented on his thoughts in this regard in our original interview:

"There has always been—well, not always, but especially in recent years, a kind of undertone of speculation that some sort of breakthrough of mind would take place," he said, "and what I'm driving at in that chapter is that it could be a very physical thing, it could be in effect that there were children born who were different, who were more powerful than those of us—the species—who bore them, bearing in mind that that must once have happened. That's where we came from, in one degree or another, and whether it happens suddenly or slowly, we don't know really the answer for sure yet.

"I guess what the chapter is really about is an expectation, or rather a hope for a change of consciousness, that mind would come more into harmony with itself, and less filled with desperate passions and intensities that blind us to what we are doing, because my feeling is

so strong that if it doesn't, that the world we have made is too dangerous to survive in."

This concern with the potential of a revolution of consciousness
in children is reflected in the one fictional work that Strieber has written since the publication of *Communion* and *Transformation:* a short
story entitled "The Pool." [17]

In the context of the scores of telephone conversations I have had
with Strieber over the past year and my own visits with him and his
family, I can say that "The Pool" fairly reflects many of the concerns
for the future of human life itself that I have frequently heard Strieber
voice. This story is all the more poignant in that it deals with an
interaction between a father and his young son, in this case analogous,
in one sense, to Strieber and his own son, Andrew.

When I told Strieber I had read the story, he said "Yes. I was
exploring some of my darker fears."

Its opening lines are highly evocative of some of the pages of
Transformation:

> That night, I woke up before I had stopped dreaming. I
> seemed to be running through a forest, dark and so wound
> with paths that it might as well have been pathless. At the same
> time I knew that I was lying flat on my bed. As I struggled to
> consciousness, it felt as if the entire top of my head were open
> and some sort of wind roaring through the exposed core of my
> brain. I heard a voice cry out, "I'm being caught inside a body,"
> and then I was fully awake. [18]

The story line is simple: A father goes outside early one morning
to find his son, naked, sitting at the bottom of the backyard swimming
pool. He rescues him, only to find his son furious with him for having
done so. From that interaction, though, father learns that son had
long ago begun to live with an adult sense of himself—and an attitude
of complete intellectual superiority.

He tells his father: "I'm not like you. I love you, but I'm not like
you. Your mind has an end. It's got a door, and the door is closed. I
was born without a door. When I turn my attention to my own thoughts,
it's different from the way it is with you. You go inside something to
think. I go outside. Your mind is a nice, neat room. Mine is like the
sky." [19]

Later, the father finds a small, homemade electronic device in his son's room. He flips its switch and something flashes in his mind. A moment later, he steps outside to discover that his son, indeed, had succeeded where first he failed.

Some readers may find Strieber's willingness to write about a father's despair at the suicide of his young son an indication of what they might label his own suicidal tendencies. I am not a psychologist or psychiatrist, and am unable to render any such judgment regarding Strieber. I do know, however, that such an interpretation fails to take into account a rather fundamental aspect of Strieber's practice of systematically confronting and exorcising his own fears by objectifying them, putting them out on paper and looking at them. It is a process that he described at some length in *Transformation*, and which seems to be understood by Strieber's wife, Anne, who has made a point of generally staying out of the glare of publicity her husband has received.

Anne Strieber gave me a lengthy interview in December 1988. I asked her if she could describe to me what it was like, nearly two years since the publication of *Communion*, to live with Strieber and his experiences.

"I'm really not someone who's had a lot of personal experiences [with the visitors]," she said. "The things that I've had were small, and in many ways were confirming to Whitley, but were the kind of thing that would have been ignored if Whitley had not had these memories.

"I do think that, as a person who has not had extensive experience, I can be objective. Even living with a person who has had some incredible experiences, I can be objective and help Whitley to be objective, and I have helped to make all of his books much more objective, and that's why they've been accepted by the general public. Most UFO books are terribly opinionated—the authors have decided what's going on. That's why they're only for buffs. They don't have anything to say to the average person who really wants to know but doesn't want to be preached to, doesn't want to be 'converted.' And I can also be objective with all of this material that I receive in the letters."

Aside from her role as "reality tester" for her husband, Anne Strieber has taken on the job of managing and responding to the extraordinary volume of correspondence they have received since the publication of *Communion*.

What is of concern to Anne Strieber, though, is the tendency for people to adopt specific belief systems in regard to UFO experience, thereby producing social settings in which people are given very dubious "answers" to their questions about the UFO phenomenon. She tries not to perpetuate this situation, feeling that otherwise, UFO experiences will "remain some kind of 'space myth.' "

Aside from being a wife to Whitley Strieber, Anne is also mother to a boy who, from his father's accounts, has had more than one experience with the "visitors." I asked her if she could describe how she and her husband have come to deal with Andrew's experiences in the context of their family life. Has it been their policy to try to isolate him from the experience? How has she felt about Andrew's having attended UFO conventions and other gatherings?

"I'm very glad he had a chance to go to those meetings," she said. "He sometimes will talk about his experiences spontaneously, and sometimes he just doesn't want to talk about it. We decided not to ask him a lot about it. I'm afraid he'd change his story in order to please us. I think he would be less likely to do this than many kids, but that's why I don't want him questioned by reporters and I don't want him questioned by us all the time.

"But he has talked about this quite a few times in great detail, telling us what was on the walls, what he ate, what he went out in, what they looked like. Something has happened to him, and some of the things he said happened to him are the things we read from all these people who have written to Whitley, so this can't be ignored."

Anne pointed out that she has therefore tried to simply listen to what her son has to say, which is part of the sensitivity she tries to practice in living and working in relatively close quarters with her family in their New York apartment. She also admits being glad that Andrew has gone to the MUFON conventions, so that he can judge for himself about this part of his life.

I first met Andrew Strieber in late November 1987, at the "Angels Aliens, and Archetypes" conference in San Francisco, at which his father was a speaker. Andrew sat with his father and mother throughout a number of lecture presentations by Jacques Vallee, Terence McKenna, Richard Hoagland, Michael Grosso, Richard Grossinger, and many other commentators on UFO and related phenomena. Andrew sat by me during a portion of the conference, and was particularly interested in Hoagland's slide show of photographs of anomalous facelike and pyramidlike shapes on the surface of Mars. He did not appear in any way disturbed by any of the presentations or any of the dialogue he heard.

Andrew and I spent a bit of time together exploring the rock garden of San Francisco's Miyako Hotel and its adjoining plazas in Japantown one morning before the conference. When we went up to the Striebers' suite to get Andrew's overcoat, he gave me an example of the spontaneous way in which he occasionally brings up the subject of the "visitors" and UFOs.

He pointed to the night table beside his bed and said he had awakened at about five-thirty that morning from the sound of one of his books hitting the floor after falling from the top of the table. He then said he looked outside his window and saw a "huge" ship floating in the air just outside the hotel.

I must admit I was rather surprised by Andrew's sudden candor. All throughout the conference, he had not said a word about UFOs to me nor had I heard him directly mention the subject to anyone else, even though we both had been accosted by a young man who spoke to us rather challengingly of the sightings he had been witnessing in Sonoma County, just north of San Francisco. Frankly, I found Andrew's nonchalance about the whole subject, especially in a place I considered to be a hotbed of "true believers," to be quite refreshing, and I had made a point of not bringing up the subject with him unless he chose to do so.

I have had a number of occasions to spend time with Andrew and his young friends playing video games and going to movies (in the company of his parents) and I can personally attest that he knows very well how to enjoy life, and has all of the interests of a normal ten-year-old boy, even including such extremely conventional enthusiasms as collecting coins and baseball cards. He is also, as I have learned, full of surprises.

He is growing up, of course, under most extraordinary circumstances, and he knows it. Yet I have seen that his relationships with his father and mother are very strong, and he gets a tremendous amount of support—intellectual, emotional, and spiritual—from both of them.

Spirituality in the life of Whitley Strieber, and therefore in the Strieber family, however, is not by any means a matter of participation in the activities of any spiritual organization or church. While both Whitley and Anne were involved in the activities of the Gurdjieff Foundation during earlier years of their marriage, they have both left that part of their lives behind them. Strieber told me that he left primarily because he felt that a change in the organization's leadership was having the general effect of shifting the group's focus from matters of substance to matters of form. Based on the teachings of G. I. Gurdjieff, a Georgian mystic who emerged out of Asia Minor between the two worlds wars to have a tremendous effect on the cultural elite of Western Europe and North America, the organization aims to help its members "wake up," said Strieber, and integrate the disassociated parts of their personalities. His personal views on human spirituality and personal growth were very influenced by his work in that group, Strieber will admit, but he makes it clear that he sees spirituality as being dependent on no particular system or teaching.

In this sense, Andrew Strieber is growing up in a household where he is encouraged to think about his own experiences for himself, yet his parents make it clear to him that he is free to talk about anything with them, anytime.

Since Strieber was raised Roman Catholic, however, and since Catholicism played such a big role in his own education, I concluded my first interview with him by asking him his views on spirituality and the Church, especially in the light of his visitor experiences. This was his response:

"Insofar as any human institution exists to foster, encourage, or reinforce guilt, if religion uses Christ and his teaching to bind spirits in guilt, then there's something wrong with that religion. That's why he was so friendly with Mary Magdalen. Christ is the symbol of freedom of the spirit. I think that organized Christianity is in a period of profoundly healthy evolution. In the Christian churches, the real Christian churches, there is a new determination to understand the words of Christ that has never really been there before, and it's very exciting to me. The Catholic Church, for this reason, is filled with ferment, because I think there is a tremendous bifurcation or splitting between the leadership and the laity, a splitting that is so profound that the nature of the experience of being Catholic will be completely different in fifty years. It won't be the same at all. The fundamentalists seem to me to be people who are frightened, terribly frightened, and what they are frightened of is their own loss of faith, and all of the yelling and screaming is a method of covering up for the fact that they don't believe anything at all, for the most part. As far as the new paganism is concerned, I'm very excited by it. I have participated in witch rituals, I have been very involved with people who are deeply involved with the new paganism and I do not find them to be in any way demonic or evil. On the contrary, what they wish to do is think of the planet as a single being to express through ritual worship their appreciation for what that being gives them. So their participation in that being—to me that seems a very valid and worthwhile thing to do.

Goodness knows the earth needs all the help it can get right now. I also don't see a real schism between them and genuine Christians. The two can certainly live together in harmony."

I asked him, then, to speak specifically to some of the political problems in the church regarding the status of women and the Church's policy on homosexuality.

"The ordination of women is inevitable," he said. "If it doesn't happen in the context of the established Church, then the Church will change to accommodate it. The Church is going to discover that grace is like a flowering tree, and not like a single flower.

"I believe there is room in the Church for every soul. The words 'the Church' to me encompass everything in terms of spiritual direction and growth, insofar as it flows out of the life of Christ. I think that there is room for homosexuality in the Church. I think that there is room for a more feminine Church. I think there is room for women in the priesthood. To me, the Church is an enormous open door—it is Saint Peter's of the spirit—and right now the papacy, instead of thinking of itself as Saint Peter's of the spirit, with those great open arms, it has closed itself off against the future, again, out of fear. The papacy is a fearful institution. Right now, it's terrified of its own crimes, because of the fact it's being steadily investigated by the Italian government and other governments and it's clear that the papacy is deeply involved, not the pope himself, but the institution, is deeply involved in criminal financial activities and apparently has been for a long time. It's afraid of the future, it's afraid of change. It's afraid of the enormous growth of the human population and the spread of ideas, and it has always been thus. One of the eleventh-century popes actually issued a statement condemning merchants and mercantilism and essentially saying that business was against religion. This was when money was becoming popular. It was against the spread of the merchant class, and it still is. It has always been a negative institution, and now we're coming to the point where we can't afford to have great institutions that are negative. So what will happen is the papacy will either change or die. It's a sink-or-swim proposition."

Strieber's critical stance toward his native religion, as radical as it might seem, is actually not all that different from the opinions increasingly being expressed in print by members of the North American Roman Catholic Church, particularly by women religious. It would be fair to say that although he does not participate in Church activities, Strieber's comments seem hopeful for some kind of major reform in the Church happening some time in the next century. Yet it is unlikely that he will choose to have a direct role in this movement.

It is no accident that Whitley Strieber's first successful novel was based on the idea of creating a race of highly evolved wolves. This man is nothing if not a lone wolf, skirting the edges of society, smelling and seeing things that ordinary people don't allow themselves to see, or have lost the ability to perceive. How curious it is that, in many cultures, the wolf and the coyote have long been identified with the mercurial archetype of the "Trickster."

The record of Strieber's life, as full of question marks as it may be about some specific incidents, makes one thing clear: If there is anything this man values, it is personal independence and spiritual freedom.

Throughout his life, from making rockets, "Frognik" balloons, and "antigravity" devices as a boy to his adult career writing novels and narratives that challenge our assumptions about the nature of human life itself, Strieber has stood outside the world of conventional wisdom and its institutions. In the process of doing so, he has no doubt gained his share of critics, but he also seems to have developed an incisive sense of humor that apparently delights even in the "scandals" of his pranksterish adolescence. Some people have told me that, despite having spent time with Strieber, they never have felt they've really gotten to know him. I can sympathize with their dilemma. It is not easy to enter into Whitley Strieber's subjective reality and understand the "high level of uncertainty" at which he has trained himself to live. I have confronted the difficulty of having to listen to many of his statements that, initially, seemed largely incomprehensible. Having learned that Strieber is accustomed to speaking occasionally in parables and stories, though, I have come to see what the moral imperative behind his own story appears to be.

As he would put it, that imperative is his commitment to live in such a way that we "enable ourselves to perceive something that is happening to us that is in reality completely inexplicable."

Does he know what that is or must be, apart from his own hypotheses and conjectures? He has consistently answered that question, in its strictest sense, in the negative.

"I don't now what it is," he has told me. "I think that UFO perceptions are a curtain, and I'd like to know what is behind that curtain very much."

Chapter 3

COMMUNION Goes Public

Response to *Communion* from the
Mass Media and Readers

When the time came for Whitley Strieber to tell his story of "abduction" to the world, the medium through which he spoke had a great deal to do with the reception of his message.

As Strieber put it to me: "The electronic media treated me much better than did the print journalists. At least on television you have some control over what goes out. You have no control over what they do to you in the newspapers and magazines."

Is that an accurate assessment of the way in which this story was handled by the media? At face value, Strieber's observation certainly expresses on overriding fact: *He* was as much under question as was his book. While the point may seem so obvious it needn't be mentioned, it must be observed that book reviewers and journalists interviewing authors for feature articles do not usually question the sanity of their subjects. For many of the journalists who approached Whitley Strieber, that question was *de rigueur*. Strieber's manner of taking the matter of his media treatment very personally, in light of that factor, is quite understandable.

Judging from the record of reviews and feature articles written on Strieber in 1987 and 1988 (as compiled by Lucius Farish and Rod B. Dyke of *UFO Newsclipping Service*), there were no banner headlines that read NOVELIST TALKS WITH MEN FROM MARS! Yet Strieber's story of *Communion* easily lent itself to a goodly amount of sensationalistic and sarcastic treatment by both print and electronic journalists looking for a good story. There were, nevertheless, notable exceptions where Strieber found a sympathetic and interested ear, in newspapers as well as on television. (Press coverage of *Transformation* was an entirely different matter, which I'll examine at the end of this chapter.) Like any other author, Strieber had to go through the standard public relations mill that processes people onto television and radio talk shows and arranges for telephone interviews with print journalists around the world. He made no secret that he found it all to be exhausting. (When I first telephoned Strieber for my own interview, I heard him ask Anne, in the background, how many more "phoners" he had to do that day. When she replied—I couldn't hear the number—he said, "They're a plague!")

In fairness to print journalists, there were many who took Strieber at face value and attempted to write feature articles that whetted the reader's interest toward learning more about the man and his reported experiences. Yet there were others who made a point of raking Strieber over the coals and satirizing his work, sometimes even without the benefit of an interview. It is somewhat indicative of Strieber's treatment by the print media that while newspapers paid close attention to *Communion*, no article that attempted to comprehensively discuss Strieber's abduction reports in *Communion* and *Transformation* has as of this writing appeared in any of the prestigious magazines of the East Coast Literary Establishment (*Harper's, The Atlantic*, etc.). Nor, for that matter, have those books been reviewed alongside other works on "alien abduction" in *The New York Review of Books* or other heralds of the literary industry. *Communion* was reviewed (surprisingly favorably) by *The New York Times*, but *Transformation* (as of this date of writing) has not yet been reviewed by that same publication. Despite the fact that these books have so far received little attention in mainstream intellectual venues, a goodly number of reviews and articles did appear in newspapers throughout the English-speaking world.

Gregory Benford, a physicist from the University of California at Irvine, was cautious in his March 15, 1987, treatment of *Communion* for *The New York Times*.

"For a scientist this is a difficult book," he wrote. "The U.F.O. digressions cloud the seemingly straightforward psychological aspects.

That many people have similar psychological recalled experiences may well be significant, though of what one cannot say. Perhaps this book will draw attention to a disquieting phenomenon."

What is remarkable about Benford's review is that he appears to have found the psychological aspects of *Communion* to be "straightforward," for some of Strieber's critics have felt that the psychological dimension of his narrative only detracted from his personal credibility.

What Benford notes with satisfaction, it seems, is Strieber's willingness to be somewhat skeptical regarding his experience:

> Whitley Strieber has recently written books on nuclear war and environmental collapse, and admits this may have biased his perceptions somewhat. Still, his detailed accounts of being carried off and subjected to weird, sometimes overtly symbolic acts are powerfully written and involving. "I had been captured like a wild animal on December 26, rendered helpless and dragged out of my den into the night," he writes. He renders both his strong reactions and his skeptical inner objections. When he undergoes hypnosis to recall previous encounters, he admits that "we just don't know enough about hypnosis to call it a completely trustworthy scientific tool in a case like this."
>
> He tries to subject his own memories to rigorous checks, though getting a handle on such events is slippery work. Witnesses saw only odd lights, heard inexplicable sounds. "It would be easy to say that the material revealed here is the work of a mind making opportunistic use of some nocturnal disturbances to gain contact with fears it needed to explore."

Benford's comment that *Communion* may draw more attention to "a disquieting phenomenon" is a noteworthy conclusion, inasmuch as it comes from a scientist. The scientific community's response to the whole subject of alien abduction is of great concern to people from the UFO community who maintain links to other publications. Jerome Clark (director of the J. Allen Hynek Center for UFO Studies), for example, reviewed both *Communion* and Bud Hopkins's *Intruders: The Incredible Visitations of Copley Woods* in the May 1987 issue of *Fate* magazine. In his introductory comments, he observed:

> Sociologist of science Ron Westrum calls UFO abductions "hidden events"—occurrences that, although they are in fact

widespread, remain unrecognized because they are unacceptable. A comparable hidden event, Dr. Westrum observes, was child abuse, a social problem whose existence even medical professionals, social workers and law enforcements officers failed to recognize until finally it was unavoidable.

Benford's response appears to have been the only review of *Communion* written by a member in good standing of the American physical science community, for the majority of responses to *Communion* in print were written by journalists, most of whom likely had little or no prior exposure to literature regarding abductions. Clark is an exception, however, in that while he functions as a contributing editor of *Fate* magazine, he has researched a number of UFO abduction cases himself. (His current opinions regarding the validity of Strieber's narrative are included in the following chapter.)

Clark did have some positive things to say about *Communion*, in that same review: "Still, no writer on the abduction experience—at least any who was writing from firsthand experience—has ever communicated so eloquently the trauma such events cause in the lives of those unfortunate enough to experience them."

Some reviewers focused simply on the question of the believability of the narrative in *Communion*. Wray Herbert, managing editor of *Psychology Today* magazine, reviewed *Communion* for *The Washington Post* (alongside *Intruders* and Gary Kinder's *Light Years: An Investigation into the Extraterrestrial Experiences of Eduard Meier*). Published April 15, 1987, his interpretation of Strieber's case was interesting, seeming to doubt the possibility that it is an elaborate hoax:

"Strieber, a gifted writer, is certainly capable of crafting a convincing narrative, and I have to confess that *Communion* gave me the chills. But Strieber has involved his family in this case, as well as personal friends and reputable psychiatrists whom he identifies by name. If it is a hoax, then a lot of people are party to it; the same is the case with the other two accounts."

Herbert's logic in analyzing the narratives presented in all three books is that they must fall into one of three categories: hoax, mental aberration, or actuality. In the ensuing paragraphs of his review, Herbert seems to be disinclined to accept the possibility that Strieber is crazy. While he says that the revelations that come out during hypnosis are unreliable, he goes on to give his opinion that "if there is a hallucination occurring . . . it is a massive hallucination involving friends and family and hundreds of others only alluded to here."

What is most remarkable about Herbert's conclusion, though, is his manner of rejecting out of hand as "unacceptable" the possibility that "these events took place." Having said that he doesn't think hoaxes or mental illness are involved, he admits that he is simply "not able to believe." Such a response was typical of many "incredulous" reviews, but ultimately skirts the larger issue raised by both *Communion* and *Intruders:* What are we to make of the proliferation of other "abduction" reports in society? One has to wonder whether what was being asked of the reader by Strieber, Hopkins, and Kinder was belief—or rather simply the ability to remain open to further questions.

One of the most negative reviews that *Communion* received in a newspaper, was that published on February 26, 1987, by Karen Liberatore, in the *San Francisco Chronicle.* Under the headline "Strieber's 'Communion': Gall and Lot of Blather," the reviewer (in a move uncharacteristic of other writers who largely ignored questions of the quality of Strieber's previous work) took a few swipes at his most recent fiction:

"Strieber is best known among the general (as opposed to cult) reading public as the co-author of the best-selling 'Warday,' and of 'Nature's End,' a real grabber that concluded there isn't much that we can do anyway to save the world, except to totally restructure civilization. 'Nature's End' was an anarchist's delight, as inspiring as Gilda Radner whining 'Never Mind.' ' "

Liberatore's main objection to the credibility of Strieber's story, it appears, stems from his statement in *Communion* that he regarded as a "screen memory" what he once thought was an actual memory of having been at the Charles Whitman massacre at the University of Texas at Austin in 1966. The reviewer cites a 1986 interview with Strieber in *Twilight Zone* magazine in which Strieber recounted the tale as though it were indeed a fact. His about-face, in *Communion,* for Liberatore, is damning evidence of a person who can easily lie:

"In 'Communion,' Strieber admits that the experience was a 'screen memory,' his euphemism, apparently, for a big white lie: Strieber wasn't anywhere near the tower. And he admits in 'Communion' that he has told other such fantasies, which brings us to his subtitle: 'A True Story.' Swallow 'Communion' whole and it could be your last sane supper."

Obviously, as noted already in Chapter 2, Strieber had some considerable problems with his own suspicion of the Whitman massacre memory as a screen memory, and later said he was convinced, through careful checking, that he was indeed present at the time of the massacre. It is worth noting that Liberatore chooses not to mention that the concept of screen memory originated in the psychological treatment of rape and trauma cases. It would be fair to say that, in the absence of such an explanation, a goodly number of the readers of her review would not understand the precise meaning of the term "screen memory."

But what of the admittedly "mystical" and "paranormal" elements in *Communion*? Diana Morgan's review of June 14, 1987, from the *Dallas Morning News* (also considering *Intruders* and *Light Years*) sounded a note characteristic of much press response.

Morgan quotes Strieber's description of *Communion* as a "chronicle not only of my discovery of the visitor's [*sic*] presence in the world but also of how I have learned to fear them less." She then goes on to say:

> Taking the place of his fear is his strange sense of mystical union with his abductors. During one encounter the aliens etch on his arm two small triangles, which he sees as universal symbols of bodily and spiritual wholeness. It could be, he says, that the aliens are using the triangles as a symbol of "shared aim, which is the continuation of life and the search for wisdom." This sounds a bit like paperback spiritualism. If Strieber was sane before his run-in with the extraterrestrials, his struggle to find in it an opportunity for greater spiritual growth and self-understanding seems to have sent him completely around the bend.

Morgan is entitled to her opinion, of course, but in fairness to Strieber it is difficult to see how the quotation she takes from *Communion* regarding Strieber's interpretation of the triangles is *ipso facto* evidence of insanity. Unfortunately, she doesn't provide us with a logical bridge demonstrating how prose that may be labeled "paperback spiritualism" is necessarily a sign of mental instability.

Morgan essentially throws up her hands, saying, "It is, in a sense, impossible to judge books like these." Her concluding observation, however, is a rather trenchant commentary on what may well have constituted a great deal of the public's interest in not only *Communion* but the other UFO-related books that appeared in 1987:

On one level, the accuracy of the accounts is beside the point. Both Hopkins and Strieber are spinning tales that will keep readers turning the pages as fixedly as any Stephen King thriller could. They are fascinating in the same way newspaper accounts of hijackings or shopping mall gunnings are. We don't really believe they could be true, but we nonetheless read on in horror. Of course, the truth is that deranged individuals do go on killing rages. And the aliens? That's for you to decide.

The Wall Street Journal, a publication that one might think would have chosen to ignore *Communion,* chose instead to review it with other books published in the summer of 1987. David Brooks did so on June 4, 1987, under a headline that read "Summertime Best Sellers: Irrationality Pays."
Brooks wrote:

Reason also flies out the window in "Communion: A True Story" . . . Whitley Strieber's account of how he was kidnapped by aliens from another planet. Mr. Strieber is a fantasy novelist who claims that aliens nabbed him from his cabin in upstate New York and gave him the once-over. . . . He makes his case fairly well, but his prose is so leaden that one finished the book not really caring if aliens exist.

David Finkle of the *New York Post* (May 22, 1988) was one of the few reviewers who compared *Communion* to *Intruders* and noticed a considerable chasm between Strieber's and Hopkins's points of view.

There are significant differences, however, between Hopkins's and Strieber's views. What Hopkins deduces from Kathie Davis's set-tos and others like hers is this: "It is unthinkable and unbelievable—yet the evidence points in that direction. An ongoing and systematic breeding experiment must be considered one of the central purposes of UFO abductions." Strieber never posits this theory. In addition, where Strieber notes that triangular scars show up on abductees, Hopkins mentions no triangles but insists that circular scars are the norm.

That difference in opinion was also noted by my colleague, Dan Goddard, an arts writer for the *San Antonio Express-News,* who surveyed the Strieber/Hopkins/Kinder books on May 24, 1987, and commented:

> Strieber used Hopkins as a consultant, but the two have reportedly had a falling out over the last third of *Communion*, which goes into bizarre philosophizing about the source of the 3-foot-tall characters with large eyes. Strieber thinks they may want to form a "triad" with humans, a major jump in our evolution.
>
> Strieber, though, is a successful writer who has demonstrated his ability to do massive research and then turn out best sellers like "Warday" and "Wolfen." He also has a long association with the Gurdjieff Foundation, based on the teachings of a Russian occult teacher who believed in a parallel, spiritual universe.
>
> Hopkins, on the other hand, approaches the subject from a firmly skeptical point of view. He thinks any utopian messages from the aliens promising peace on earth are probably just camouflage, a lot of "noise."

Finkle's and Goddard's observations are somewhat lacking in background and accuracy of detail. In retrospect, however, they have far more significance than might have been apparent to the casual observer in mid-1987. There are indeed significant differences between Strieber and Hopkins over the interpretation of "abductions," which have now developed into a public issue that affects dialogue in the UFO community. (This question will be discussed fully in the following chapter.)

It should be noted that Strieber was the focus of a number of major newspaper feature articles as a result of publicity for *Communion*, notably in the *San Francisco Examiner* (by Michael Heaton), *The Washington Post* (Curt Suplee), and, in the only article that looked into his family and early educational background, the *San Antonio Express-News* (which, as I mentioned in the Introduction, I wrote in May of 1987).

Some remarks by journalists made as much as possible of the monetary aspect of Strieber's contract with his publisher, as can be seen in Peter Turnbull's Scripps-Howard News Service story, headlined "Communion with Other Worlds," which went out on the wires on February 22, 1988. As Turnbull put it:

Whitley Strieber is angry. He believes that he has been abducted and subjected to terrifying, ongoing biological experiments by non-human "visitors" from another planet or dimension, and that the situation has been officially ignored and ridiculed.

Whitley Strieber is also getting rich.

Coverage of Strieber in England, when he took his book tour abroad, also seemed to have a slant on the commercial success that the book was enjoying.

In a review published May 21, 1987, in the *London Daily Mail*, Val Hennessey wrote:

> He [Strieber] was transported to a spacecraft, had probes inserted into various orifices by bug-like beings smelling of burnt cardboard, and was subsequently returned to his bed, traumatised, sore-nosed and filled with "an insane desire to come out with this in public."
>
> This desire was not as insane as you might suppose. The resulting book, *Communion—A True Story*, currently tops the U.S. *non*-fiction bestsellers having sold over three million copies, has earned its author a million dollars, and attracts 50 letters daily from hitherto closet alien-spotters."

Hennessey was clearly one journalist who ran away a bit with her story! *Communion* had been selling well, but the paperback version had not yet even been released in May of 1987, making the mass volume of sales she reported—three million copies—completely impossible.

The same theme of lucre was present to an extent in Yvonne Roberts's feature article (headlined "Take Me to Your Reader") in London's *Daily News*, published May 20, 1987. This journalist seems to have chosen to take a rather mordant, tongue-in-cheek approach to presenting Strieber, indicated by her use of capitalization for certain significant words:

> In the artificial light of a London hotel room, Mr Strieber, who also looks remarkably like John Denver after a particularly tough night, is low key to the point of passivity. If the "unknowns" have selected him to be one of the Chosen Few,

then they are obviously not opting for Earthlings Who Like a Good Time.

Sincerity is Mr Strieber's best asset—that and what he terms his Credibility. Unlike the sterotype of many who have seen an Unidentified Flying Object—never mind boarded one—Mr Strieber does not need the notoriety. In the States, he says, he was Already Famous.

In a feature by the *London Evening Standard's* John Preston (titled "The Night E.T. Came for Whitley Strieber," also published May 20, 1987) Strieber is seen dealing with a less than friendly reception.

"Oh God, he's a loony," muttered the photographer as Strieber strode across the lounge of his hotel. In the flesh, Strieber certainly looks as if he has just stepped off the bridge of Fireball XL5, but this surely is no discredit at all. What he is, though, is very earnest indeed. British journalists, he has found, have been giving him a rougher ride than he got in the States.

"In America I am a well-known author," he says a little huffily between sips of week [*sic*] chamomile tea. "No one imagines for a moment that I would come up with a fraud."

Over here he has already seen off one "witlessly sceptical" interviewer. "I told him to get lost," he says. "I couldn't think what else to do. After all, I am sceptical myself, not in a thoughtless way though, but in a thoughtful way."

Perhaps the most straightforward feature to appear in the British press was Ann Shearer's piece, "A Man Who Got Carried Away," which appeared May 20, 1987, in the London *Guardian*. Of all the articles that described his experience, it was one of the few that focused on Strieber's descriptions of his work with a group of scientists (including a psychologist who had been reportedly reading letters sent to Strieber by people claiming abduction) who agreed to consider with him the implications of his experience.

Already the thoroughly sceptical psychologist who has been sorting through the accounts sent to Strieber has noticed that those from men, in particular, seem somehow gentled, as if the barriers of aggression and fear may be lowering.

That psychologist is one of a group Strieber has gathered to inquire into the evidence. The group also includes a psychiatrist, and astrophysicist and scientists various, including one with a very secret job for the U.S. navy. . . .

What he wants now is for more scientists to shed their prejudices about UFOs and to start taking seriously the proliferating accounts of visitors in a new respect for people who have for so long been fearful of mentioning these experiences at all.

Shearer was one of the few reporters in either the United States or Britain, moreover, to discuss the political dimensions of Strieber's message.

And he [Strieber] is very keen that reports from his group make their way to government. "Either this is a mental health problem of some significance, or the visitors are real or it is an extraordinary mental state which can be used for growth. Whichever it is, the whole body politic has a right to know what's going on."

It should be noted that most of the features and reviews on Strieber that were printed in the British press were rather short (often less than half a tabloid page) in comparison with some of the treatments done by their American counterparts. Nor, for that matter, did Strieber find himself being compared to Hopkins and Kinder in Britain.

Attention to Strieber in American magazines was not the occasion of major, in-depth essays save for items that appeared in *Publishers Weekly* and *The Nation*. Both articles were quite critical of *Communion*, and essentially questioned Strieber's intentions in writing the book.

Thomas M. Disch's piece entitled "The Village Alien" (a reference to Strieber's residence in New York's Greenwich Village) in the March 14, 1987, issue of *The Nation* went so far as to openly suggest that readers would be justified in regarding *Communion* as a work of fiction: "Skeptical readers (and I freely confess I began as one) may feel that the million-dollar advance paid for the book is in itself reason to doubt the good faith of the author. For there certainly could be writers who might be tempted for such a price to invent such a tale out of whole cloth and swear to its truth."

Disch's piece was by far the most biting attack on Strieber and

Communion to appear in print, and all the more interesting in that it appeared in a publication that considers itself progressive. Disch opened his essay with an attack on what he evidently considered to be the grandiosity implicit in Strieber's story: "If Whitley Strieber isn't fibbing in his new book *Communion* (and the book's cover boldly affirms it is 'A True Story'), then it must be accounted the most important book of the year, of the decade, of the century, indeed of all time. For what Strieber recounts in *Communion* is nothing less than the first contact of the human race, in the person of Whitley Strieber, with an ancient alien civilization."

Disch tones down his hyperbole a bit in a second paragraph, though, admitting "there have been other, similar reports of U.F.O. sightings and contact with aliens." Still, he points to the book's potential stature as a best-seller and the fact that it represents the most extensive first-person UFO abduction narrative yet published as justifications for considering that it is "unique."

Disch's piece quoted extensively from *Communion*, featuring segments of text from the book pointing out Strieber's self-described skepticism, the influence he said he felt from reading Jenny Randles and Peter Warrington's *Science and the UFOs*, his speculation that UFO phenomena seem to be unfolding according to a design, comments on the problem of screen memories, an account of the rectal probe experience he said occurred while he was among the "vistors" and the resulting period of stress he experienced with his wife, his description of having a visionary experience (a rush of symbols), his one-on-one encounter with the female visitor, and his questions as to the nature of the mind itself. It is quite a list, indeed.

Disch also goes somewhat deeper than most other journalists in examining Strieber's short story, "Pain," mentioned in *Communion* as the first piece of new fiction he began to write after his abduction experience (but prior to fully remembering it). After two quotes from the story that illustrate the sadomasochistic themes in "Pain" (in which we meet the character of Janet O'Reilly, a blond dominatrix), Disch observes: "The textual parallels between 'Pain' and 'Communion' are even more extensive and systematic than this précis can indicate, but it would be hard to deny the virtual identity between the fictive Janet O'Reilly and the nameless alien who abducts Strieber and, in one rather breathless paragraph of hypnotic transcript, has something like sex with him."

Disch concludes that there are only two ways to deal with these parallels: Either (1) Strieber made up both stories, having "made the imaginative equation between the 'archetypal abduction experience' and the ritual protocols of bondage and domination," or (2) the story represents "the first surfacing of materials repressed by the aliens, who had, only days before the story's writing, taken Strieber aboard their saucer and given him a hazing." Of course Disch observes, Strieber would no doubt defend the second possibility as being what in fact occurred.

As it turned out, Disch and Strieber did finally have a conversation (albeit on the telephone), which followed close upon the heels of a telephone message Strieber apparently left for Disch. Reproduced in full in the text of the essay, the message is a plea for Disch not to do a "vicious hatchet job" on *Communion*. In their subsequent conversation, Disch said he protested to Strieber that "not having read what I'd finished writing, he was arguing with straw men." Strieber replied, Disch said, by saying that "he could tell where I was heading just from my condescending tone of voice, and the questions I'd been asking about 'Pain.' " (Disch had checked with Dennis Etchison, who edited the anthology in which "Pain" was published.)

The tongue-in-cheek manner in which Disch decided to conclude his essay is fairly indicative of what must have been a fair amount of heat between him and Strieber:

> What Whitley could not have imagined at that moment (and what I was certainly not going to tell him after so many minutes of vituperation) was that I was no longer a skeptic about U.F.O.s, that in fact, in the course of writing this essay I have been in contact with alien beings, and though my aliens—the Winipi (pronounced Weenie-pie; singular, Winipus)—are not of the same race as those in touch with Strieber (who are known, and feared, throughout the galaxy as the Xlom), the Winipi are well-informed of the purposes of the Xlom and the grave danger they represent.

In the concluding paragraphs of the essay, Disch produced a "transcript" of a conversation between himself and a "Winipus" regarding Strieber's sad fate as a "human minion" of the Xlom, "who will do anything for money." It is a clever—and extremely biting—piece of satire.

Six months later to the day, Strieber and his book faced a challenge from another critic, this time from within the publishing industry itself. In an article from its August 14, 1987, edition titled "When Is a True Story True?" *Publishers Weekly* gave the floor to Edward Beecher Claflin (identified as "an author and the publisher of Brookside Press"). The timing of its publication was significant, in that *Communion* had at that time (as Claflin himself points out in the opening of his article) enjoyed twenty-three weeks on *The New York Times* best-seller list. Perhaps some people in the publishing industry were wondering why.

At the top of his article, Claflin quotes James Landis, then publisher of Beech Tree Books; Sherry Arden, then president and publisher of Morrow; and Rena Wolner, then president and publisher of Avon, as having had no problem with determining to publish *Communion* as nonfiction.

> "There was no discussion about whether to publish this book as fiction," James Landis, publisher of Beech Tree Books, told *PW*. "It came in as *Communion—A True Story*, and that's the way we published it. I see it as a memoir. Whitley Strieber is saying, 'This happened to me.' I don't see any more reason to doubt this memoir than I would doubt the autobiography of a Hollywood actor or actress."

Arden and Wolner are quoted by Claflin making remarks that are essentially expressions of their enthusiasms for *Communion* and Strieber. If either of them chose to directly address Claflin's concerns as to the propriety of publishing *Communion* as nonfiction, they are not so quoted. Claflin goes on to provide for his readers a capsule version of Strieber's story in *Communion*, a précis of Strieber's performance as a witness to his experiences on television, and a biographical note on the author. Nor does Claflin ignore a number of acerbic quotes from people (including Gregory Benford, who reviewed the book for *The New York Times*, quoted as saying he subsequently considers *Communion* to be part of a "deplorable trend in book-publishing"; Thomas Disch of the *The Nation*; and Philip J. Klass, leader of the UFO "debunkers"), all highly critical of Strieber's book.

The segment of Disch's article dealing with Strieber's telegenic qualities is particularly interesting, in that it represents one of the few

places where a print journalist made reference to the reception afforded *Communion* on television.

"My next guest," announced Johnny Carson on May 6,
1987, "claims he's been visited by nonhuman beings. It's a
very strange, bizarre tale, and we'll hear his story tonight."

"It was a little figure three-and-a-half feet tall with a rectangular shield," said Strieber, speaking directly into the camera.
"I was carried out of the room. It felt real. The creatures inserted needles and began operating on my brain. I realized my
eyes were open. I began to scream. Then I said, "Let me
smell you."

"It was a wonderful spot on *The Tonight Show*," recalled
Rena Wolner. "But the promotion has been a great strain on
Whitley. He had to discipline himself to be able to respond to
all this publicity."

"Whitley is such a wonderful guest [on shows]," Sherry Arden said. "He doesn't look like a kook-head or a nut. He's
terribly well-spoken."

Carson said he first saw Strieber on CNN and was so impressed with his presentation that he decided to invite him to
The Tonight Show.

"There have been some very good hoaxes," Johnny pointed
out to his guest. "Maybe some people out there are saying,
'How do we know he didn't just sit down and write it?' What
do you say to them?"

"I know that many people are suffering," Strieber replied.
"Those people have a right to relief from their suffering."

It appears that Claflin is attempting to make the point that television shows do not, by their very nature, get to the substance of any
issue, especially something as complex as Strieber's story. Seen in the
cold black and white of print, Strieber's reply to Carson's question
clearly does not directly answer it. Was it evasion, or was it an attempt
on Strieber's part to make a point to Carson that he felt was more
important than defending, for one more time, his personal credibility?
Claflin appears to prefer to make his points by implication, letting the
reader make the inferences to which he would lead him.

In the final segment of his essay, subtitled "Where Is the Truth,"
Claflin makes the point that Strieber's message appears neither au-

thoritative nor specific: "Strieber, however, does not claim to be an authority on the subject of UFOs. In *Communion* and in his publicity appearances, he makes a point of emphasizing that he does not know who the aliens are, where they come from or what they want."

After providing his readers with a restatement of a hypothetical "dilemma" similar to that experienced by Morrow (man provides manuscript of alien encounter, will takes tests, book will surely become best-seller if well published, author wants you to call it a "true story," etc.), Claflin then poses his final challenge, rhetorical as it may well be: "*QUESTION:* Will you publish this book?"

The objective of Claflin's article, it appears, is to prick the conscience of the publishing industry into considering the consequences of publishing implausible tales as nonfiction books, and to look beyond the potential bonanzas that can be reaped from best-sellers of the "bizarre." Determining whether Claflin succeeded in doing so, or whether he even made his case in an adequate manner, is beyond the scope of this report, but it is important to note that Strieber requested of *Publisher's Weekly* the right to reply to Claflin's article.

In a piece entitled "What Communion Really Said," published on October 2, 1987, Strieber replied to Claflin with an opening paragraph that read:

> When William Morrow & Co. offered a million-dollar advance for *Communion*, I worried that they had overpaid for the book. Little did I know what would happen: that the book would be warmly adopted by a public eager to question the nature of alien abduction, but that it would also unleash a thunderstorm of media hysteria.

This piece is interesting for the record, in that it is an accurate statement of Strieber's assessment of his treatment by the media. As he put it:

> One segment of the media operated on the assumption that *Communion* should be dismissed because its claims were a danger to the public's intellectual health. A few publications and one television show elected to pander to the notion that the public wants to believe in aliens. Both of these positions assume that the public is gullible and stupid. They bear no

relationship to the thoughtful response that *Communion* actually received.

Strieber produced a list of some of the negative responses his book had received in the print media (including mention of the remarks by Benford quoted by Claflin), making the implied point that these reviews had attributed to him claims regarding the visitors that Strieber never actually made. "I was astonished," he said, "as the whole sense of my book was not to make claims but to ask questions."

He had better things to say of television and radio: "I got a more rational reception in the live electronic media. As often as I possibly could I delivered my message: 'We do not know yet what is happening to people. It seems very real, but there isn't any proof that it is aliens.' "

The sum of Strieber's protest against Claflin's piece comes toward the end of the essay:

> This magazine ran a lengthy article . . . addressing the question of whether or not *Communion* should even have been published. The suggestion was that the nonfiction publication of a book making such outrageous claims was questionable.
>
> But where are the outrageous claims in *Communion*? They aren't there, unless extracted by out-of-context quotation.
>
> *Communion* was written to bring into question the idea of alien abduction. It was intended to enrich speculation about this experience by placing it in historical perspective and—at the same time—acknowledging its power and the startling sense of physical reality that accompanies it.

Strieber's public statement that his book was intended to *question* the idea of alien abduction did not sit well with some members of the UFO, particularly Budd Hopkins, who strenuously objected to any public statement that seemed to diminish the reality of the phenomenon. (See Chapter 4 for discussion of the Hopkins-Strieber conflict.) No doubt there were some readers who felt that Strieber was being melodramatically apocalyptic in his final paragraph, yet few statements express so succinctly Strieber's underlying concerns:

> I again ask the question that I asked in *Communion*: Why are people seeing spaceships in the skies and encountering aliens

in their midnights? Is the inner mind—or perhaps the universe—warning us that we cannot remain sane unless we correct the vast political, social and environmental problems that threaten us as much psychologically as physically? We must address this issue responsibly, correctly—and soon.

Television treatment of *Communion*, of course, was quite different, owing to the nature of the medium, with each appearance by Strieber in promotion of his books occurring in the context of a talk show.

While Strieber characterizes the treatment his stories have received at the hands of the electronic media as having been better than that displayed by their colleagues in the world of print, there is at least one notable exception. Strieber points to his experience on *The Phil Donahue Show* (broadcast February 23, 1987) as having been the most difficult of his experiences on television.

In an interview with Strieber on that subject, I said, "I noticed on your New Dimensions interview, for example, that you said you had to deal with a jeering squad on *The Phil Donahue Show*."

Strieber replied: "More than a jeering squad. He whipped the audience into a frenzy of jeering. When I was first starting to tell my story, when I said I heard a sound that woke me up in the house, he grabbed the microphone and said, 'A toilet flushing,' into the microphone, and brought the house down. His purpose was to wreck me with that thing. It's what he set out to do. I mean he's a hateful man, and he hates me and everything that I stand for. He despises anything new, and anything that implies his ego isn't the largest thing in the world. He's also a very simple and rather pitiful little man. He's not a particularly bright man, and not a particularly kind man, and he's aware of his shortcomings, very aware of them, and that makes him suffer a lot."

I asked Strieber about the other people on the show.

"With me was Brian O'Leary, and there were a couple of New Age people," he said. "A channeler, another New Age person was involved, which had nothing to do with me. There were sort of two shows welded together to make, I think, to damn us both, in that if I didn't make the channelers look ridiculous, then they would make me look ridiculous. That was the idea."

The interchange that followed then was particularly interesting:

CONROY: When you were originally negotiating to get on the show, did they reveal to you that you would be on with these people?

STRIEBER: No. We didn't find out until we actually arrived there.

CONROY: So they were deceptive?

STRIEBER: Absolutely. Very deceptive.

CONROY: Uh-huh. Was this the first time you were on with Brian O'Leary, or had you been on with him before?

STRIEBER: No. That was the first time.

CONROY: Was he there as a photographic expert?

STRIEBER: No. Just as a scientist who was open-minded about these things. I got Brian involved in the show myself, and he proved to be an excellent addition to it and managed to turn the audience in our favor a couple of times by causing them to laugh with us.

CONROY: I guess you would categorize that experience as having been the worst, perhaps, of your whole treatment on the tour.

STRIEBER: Mm-hmm. But it didn't hurt me. The book jumped from eleven to seven on the best-seller list.

Is there any justification for that remark in view of the way Phil Donahue, the show's host, dealt with Strieber?

It is rather telling, perhaps, that Donahue made reference to a toilet only a few seconds after Strieber began to speak on his show. As the dialogue went:

DONAHUE: You believe you've been visited by extraterrestrials, it says here, Whitley.

STRIEBER: I know. It sounds incredible, but my thing happened in a totally physical world.

DONAHUE: You were in your bedroom.

STRIEBER: I was in my bed.

DONAHUE: You heard a whooshing sound in the living room—not unlike a toilet? [Laughter][1]

Strieber, appearing to be somewhat annoyed, explained that the sound was more akin to that of "someone waving a flag."

Donahue then asked his guest for details of the "figure" whom Strieber had said he'd seen entering his bedroom during his first remembered abduction, and Strieber responded by going through his by-then already rather standard description. In the midst of his description, though, he interrupted himself to say to Donahue, in a pleasantly remonstrating manner, "You can laugh." Donahue immediately responded, "I'm not laughing, I'm not laughing, I am not. Believe this, it would be hypocritical for me to put someone on the program . . . ," to which Strieber rejoined, jokingly, "You know what, maybe they'll get interested in you, now that I've been on the program!" (The "they" to whom he was referring, in that context, was clearly meant to be the visitors.)

After going on with his narrative a little further, Strieber found that his tale was eliciting nervous laughter from a fair number of audience members, whereupon he had another exchange with Donahue on the subject of laughing.

> STRIEBER: It's easy to laugh at something like this.
> DONAHUE: You're upset if we laugh . . ."
> STRIEBER: No, I'm not upset.
> DONAHUE: It's a nervous thing, it's the only thing we've got.
> STRIEBER: You've got to understand that what happened seemed so real that, after it was over, I thought I was losing my mind. I thought I had had a psychotic episode.[2]

The visual images that accompanied this series of exchanges were indicative of some of the audiences' reactions, in that, after Strieber said he was taken out of his room and into the woods, the screen shows two matronly ladies turning to one another with looks of disbelief turning to amusement. Donahue, after expressing his hope that Strieber wasn't upset, could be seen to have a certain amount of frustration on his face. For his part, Strieber's eyebrows were beginning to knit and an expression of earnestness bordering on defensiveness began to overtake him during these exchanges. At one point he emphatically insisted that he was telling the truth, and had taken medical and lie detector tests to discover even if he was lying to himself.

Strieber's reception on the show was additionally influenced by the fact that he appeared as one member of a panel that included a number of other people involved with affairs Donahue described as "paranormal," including a gentleman who "channeled" an entity during the broadcast. Given that his appearance did not occur in the context of a specific focus on his own story and the subject of "UFO abductions" in particular, it would have to be said that this show is not representative of other electronic venues where Strieber had the show to himself.

Such a case occurred, for example, when Strieber appeared on *The Larry King Show*, broadcast March 25, 1987. There was some laughter involved in this instance, too, but without a live audience's reaction it appears Strieber and King succeeded in actually hitting it off rather well.

> STRIEBER [describing his abduction]: . . . They took me forcibly out of the house.
> KING: Whitley. [Laughing nervously]
> STRIEBER: I know it.
> KING: You gotta realize—you're a very successful author. Were you a believer in this kind of thing, pre-this, the kind of guy who would say "they're coming"?
> STRIEBER: The last time I was interested in this was the age of twelve when there were *This Island Earth*, and so forth— the horror–science fiction films of the fifties.

As Phil Donahue did on *The Phil Donahue Show*, King began to laugh when Strieber described one of his visitors as wearing a large, broad-brimmed helmet, yet he said to Strieber, "I'm not laughing at you, I'm laughing with you." It would be fair to say, moreover, that while Strieber visibly showed that he was upset with the way his appearance on *The Donahue Show* was proceeding, he apparently felt much more at ease with Larry King. King seemed to good-naturedly revel in the spirit of Strieber's story, even at one point indirectly suggesting that the visitors would be welcome guests on his show, as the following segment of dialogue shows:

> STRIEBER: There are two ways of looking at it. One is that there is no physical proof of their existence, at all. Therefore, our strongest social institutions, like the scientific community, can't really look at this.

KING: I don't follow. What if they went to Johns Hopkins University?

STRIEBER: But they won't because it gives them total control over the situation. They are out there doing exactly what they want to do, the official scientific community is just ignoring it, those scientists who try to study it spend half their time trying to protect their careers at the same time.

KING: Why don't they visit the political community?

STRIEBER: Because if they . . . But maybe they do. Maybe this has happened to people in political life. What if, Ed Meese, it had happened to him? He could never say it, he could never say a word about it.

KING: Because he'd be laughed at.

STRIEBER: He'd be destroyed.

KING: One would think, "Why don't they come here, on a live television show?" What are we going to do then, man?

STRIEBER: If they want total control of the situation, they're going to stay away from our social institutions and they're not going to let us prove their existence.

KING: What are they doing, studying us?

STRIEBER: I don't know.[3]

This segment is of some interest, too, because it shows to a certain extent the manner in which Strieber could direct his interviews and interject points rarely expressed in the print media. Strieber's observations about the visitors' interest in maintaining their hypothetical control over humanity are similar to comments he made on a number of other television shows, not only in promotion of *Communion*, but of *Transformation*, as well. Those observations are indicative, moreover, of the manner in which television interviews on occasion went well beyond simply allowing Strieber to recount the narrative of his abduction.

One other feature of Strieber's electronic record is the fact that he was able to make the point that after writing *Communion*, he had not yet arrived at the conclusion that the visitors are, indeed, intelligent extraterrestrials. An allied point that he often made, too, was the need for treating people who claim to be witnesses to these kinds of experiences with dignity.

One example of this kind of dialogue occurred on the CBS show, *Nightwatch*, which aired on April 1, 1987, hosted by Charlie Rose.

> ROSE: What was the evidence that took you over into believing that what had happened to you was a realistic experience involving extraterrestrial beings?
>
> STRIEBER: Well, you're taking it even farther than I am, even now.
>
> ROSE: Okay.
>
> STRIEBER: Where I am now is I am very convinced that something extremely strange is happening to me and to a lot of other people, and there are two things that concern me about it. First of all, the people are not being treated with the kind of dignity that they should be treated with. They are traumatized and they suffer. There is no reason that society has to laugh at them. [4]

Strieber didn't get around to making the second point, whatever it was, in a direct way. However, a little later in the same show he was asked a question that was not often dealt with in the print media, regarding alleged UFO secrecy on the part of the United States government.

> ROSE: You did a lot of research on this afterwards. What did you find out? Wrap it up for us, and whether this government, that we all care about, is being forthwith and aggressive in trying to find out what these experiences are about.
>
> STRIEBER: No, I don't think it is at all.
>
> ROSE: Okay.
>
> STRIEBER: I think that the assumption has been that this is nonsense, on the part of the government, and on another level, they have hidden anything that seems anomalous, especially when it comes around military bases, because they obviously don't want it to come out in public that they can't control our own airspace which if these visitors are real, it would be the case, that we can't, in fact, control our own airspace.
>
> ROSE: Do you think the government has done everything it can, at least to assimilate the information, even though maybe not sharing it with the public?

STRIEBER: I don't know how to answer that question. I'm not privy to what the government does internally.[5]

Another point that Strieber had an opportunity to make via the electronic media that was often ignored by print journalists was his estimation of the spiritual dimensions of the visitor experience. Strieber's appearance on *Nightwatch* was one such instance.

ROSE: Your investigation led you to what understanding about all this?

STRIEBER: Well, primarily, my investigation didn't lead me very far. What led me a long way, though, was after *Communion* came out, I began to get letters. I've gotten over seven hundred letters from people this has happened to; long, complex letters from articulate, intelligent people, often in the professions, often very highly educated, and it led me to two conclusions, really. One is that something extraordinary is definitely going on, and two is that it is frightening initially, but it leads people to a very great opening of the mind, even to a spiritual reawakening in some cases, and therefore I don't perceive it as necessarily being a bad thing or a negative thing at all.

ROSE: Even if it's just within the mind.

STRIEBER: Even if it's within the mind.

ROSE: It causes people to open up their minds . . .

STRIEBER: Yeah. It's essentially a productive experience, whatever it is, even though it starts out being terrifying.

ROSE: Is there a common denominator between your experience and these other people who wrote you or contacted you since you have gotten so much attention?

STRIEBER: The experiences have been quite varied. They tend to follow a pattern of experience, period of terror and fear, followed by opening of the mind.[6]

Other shows on which Strieber appeared on the *Communion* tour included *People Are Talking*, a production of San Francisco television station KPIX, on February 17, 1987 (hosted by Ann Fraser and Ross McGowan); *The Tonight Show* (already referred to); and radio talk shows too numerous to mention. Strieber's reception by Fraser and Mc-

Gowan was generally friendly, as was the treatment he received from Carson, who essentially let him speak without much cross talk.

The promotional tour for *Transformation*, in comparison with that of *Communion*, was quite different in a number of respects. For one thing, there was considerably less press coverage of *Transformation* in the print media (both feature articles and reviews) in part because Strieber had deliberately delayed the mailing of review copies of the book to newspapers until after the North American electronic media tour was over. Strieber explained that action to me by saying that he had come to trust people in the electronic media more than their counterparts in print journalism. He added that he trusted people in general to respond genuinely to his story.

It could be said, moreover, that Strieber and his story had naturally lost some of their novelty value for the press, which had fallen all over itself to cover the release of *Communion*. Nevertheless, there was quite a wide array of response generated from *Transformation*, even if it was somewhat more diffused than that *Communion* had received.

Karen Liberatore of the *San Francisco Chronicle*, in a review published September 22, 1988, raked *Transformation* over the coals much as she had done with *Communion*. Remarkably, she again introduced Strieber to her readers via his novel, *Nature's End*, which she described as "perhaps the most depressing end-of-the-world book ever written." According to Liberatore, Strieber's writing in *Transformation* "flails away at 20th century skepticism regarding phenomena not easy to understand or explain."

Liberatore's generally tongue-in-cheek approach to presenting Strieber's accounts of his further visitor experience focuses on her perceptions of what she implies is a messianic strain in Strieber's understanding of the visitors:

> He tells us, too, why they're here: to save us, if only we'd accept the challenge "to see" as he himself finally has.
>
> And he explains why he, of all contactees, is privy to the truth of the visitors' mission—because of the ozone crisis, the cataclysm Strieber believes the visitors can help avert, and a crisis, more importantly, that just happens to be his specialty.

Dennis Stacy, editor of the *MUFON UFO Journal*, also took a rather dim view of *Transformation*, though his September 25, 1988, review for the *Houston Post* focused on a different perceived problem.

Now comes *Transformation*, which has the cash-register ring of a continuing series of sequels written all over it. (The issue of what Strieber believes really happened to him is no more resolved here than it was at the end of *Communion*.) . . .

On the one hand he argues for the physical reality of the phenomenon by citing stories in the UFO literature of crashed saucers and government-retrieved bodies; on the other he argues that the visitors are the same ethereal entities as the angels, fairies and perhaps even goblins of yore that have both plagued and inspired mankind since time immemorial.

What Stacy concludes is that Strieber is unable to "maintain some sense of proportion about events, however weird and personally perplexing they might be." As he puts it:

Confusion may be the only possible reaction to such startling events. But even so, it should not be allowed to reach out and color everything it touches, as it does in *Transformation*, hauling in visions of golden cities, dreams, out-of-body experiences, childhood fears and every unexplained light in the night skies, not to mention psychic presentiments of personal and global extinction. Someone needs to make more, not less sense, out of all this phantasmagoric New Age stew, but if not Strieber himself, then who?

Perhaps I was one of the few reviewers in the country who gave *Transformation* a relatively friendly reception, given the fact that I had been examining Strieber's case in some detail for quite some time. In my comments, published on the book page of the September 25, 1988, *San Antonio Express-News*, I pointed out something central to Strieber's narrative ignored by Stacy and Liberatore: *Transformation* is primarily an account of Strieber's confrontation with his *fears* of the visitor experience. I directed the reader's attention to parts of his narrative with a local connection:

San Antonio readers may be particularly intrigued by Strieber's account in "Transformation" of his recurring "dark neighborhood" dream, a sequence in which he as a boy "flies" on his bicycle down Elizabeth Road, across Broadway and deep into the night in Olmos Basin for a rendezvous with—something.

There is clearly a poetic quality to Strieber's writing here that instantly evokes a sense of exhilaration and mystery. It is not the sort of style, however, which would convince persons desiring more documentation and facts to fully accept his claims. . . .

"Transformation" is not a book intended to convince the skeptics, but rather a work which purports to offer some guidance to people trying to understand the morass of public information (and perhaps "disinformation") about UFOs and their "occupants."

Does it succeed in doing so? It does, in the sense that Strieber's personal account of contacts with "visitors" appears to be striking a resonating chord among people who say they have had the same experiences, but long felt too afraid to discuss them in public.

Yet for the general reader who has never had a "visitor experience," the book offers an intelligent introduction to the panoply of psychological and physical phenomena, historical anecdotes and speculation associated with UFOs.

As of this writing, *Transformation* has still not been reviewed by *The New York Times*, nor have there been any major feature articles on the book in the United States press that have come to my attention through the *UFO Newsclipping Service* or other sources. After a few weeks on the *New York Times* best-seller list (reaching its highest point at the number 7 position), *Transformation* seemed to reach a falling-off point in terms of North American media attention. In conversation with Strieber regarding the reception of *Transformation*, he remarked on the avalanche of letters he has been receiving since early September 1988, when *Transformation* was first published, which he said have been arriving in much greater numbers than in the case of *Communion*.

Strieber's promotion of *Transformation* also took him to Australia and New Zealand, occasioning some coverage in the press "down under." On October 15, 1988, *The Age*, a Melbourne newspaper, published a feature based on an interview with Elysabeth Wynhausen conducted at Strieber's New York apartment.

Apparently, she and Strieber didn't exactly have a love feast. Wynhausen wrote:

> For a start, he spent the first 10 minutes of the interview acting as if I had come armed with a pair of pliers just to get at his molars. He kept his mouth clamped shut, after answering questions with a word or two, and he could not have looked more pained if I had got the pliers out.

Nor did things get much better.

> Not sure what to make of him, I asked *the* question, framing the inevitable insult as politely as possible. "Are reporters most inclined to think that you're a raving lunatic, that it's all a fraud, or that there is some psychological explanation?" One to Wynhausen. "The dumber ones think it's a fraud," he said. Two to Strieber, even if he had thrown back his head and shut his eyes again.

The picture Wynhausen painted of Strieber seemed to focus largely on his fears, which it seems Strieber had little problem expressing to her. Indeed, it might seem Wynhausen concluded by suggesting Strieber is a wee bit paranoid.

> With almost everyone in a state of unpreparedness, the extraterrestrials could take over at any moment. Last year [quoting Strieber], ". . . I discovered how open the skies are to visitors. Some friends saw an object over the city at night. . . . As an experiment I called the relevant police precinct to report it. When he heard "UFO" the duty officer said, "Let 'em come," and hung up the phone.
> See?

Wynhausen was clearly unimpressed with Strieber, and perhaps the feeling may have been mutual, but Strieber's response may also have been indicative of a feeling of frustration he expressed openly in at least one television interview for *Transformation*.

On *Good Morning America*, Strieber was asked by hostess Joan Lunden to give the audience an "update on his adventures with aliens."

LUNDEN: Are there new meetings with the aliens?

STRIEBER: Well, I wouldn't say it works quite like that. I'd say it's more an attempt on my part to respond to this, rather than turn away from it. When I realized that they probably were real, I began going out into the woods in the dark, the woods that they seem to have taken me to, and so forth.

LUNDEN: Because you say that you really wanted to try to forge a relationship with them.

STRIEBER: To try. Yeah, why not? If they are real, it seems like that's the thing that I should try to do.

LUNDEN: There was one point, I think, December twenty-third, 1986, you talk about, a year after the incident . . .

STRIEBER: Right. They came back.

LUNDEN: They came into the bedroom.

STRIEBER: They woke me up and the first thing I did was I went for a camera that I had there, because I have tried many different ways of getting some kind of proof of them, because I'm a little sick of going out with this story with no proof. But anyway, at that meeting they asked me, "What can we do to help you?" and I said, "The truth. You could help me fear you less." And once I began to get past the fear I began to understand a little bit more about this.

LUNDEN: Well, wouldn't another thing that they could do to help you is to give you some kind of—

STRIEBER: Proof?

LUNDEN: —evidence, so that you could show people that they really do exist?

STRIEBER: It would have been very helpful, but since they had prevented me from using the camera, there was really no point in asking for that, I didn't think.[7]

The remarkable thing about this interview, looking at it in retrospect across the months of his previous experience with the *Communion* tour, is that here an interviewer is addressing Strieber with an a priori attitude that, for all practical purposes as regards the interview, the visitors are to be discussed as though they were real. What is different about Strieber, too, is that he speaks of his visitors now as entities whom he has in fact come to accept as real. While it is obvious from the early part of the interview that he refuses to be backed into a corner speaking about "meetings with aliens," gone are the frequent comments to the effect that perhaps the visitors are reflective of a new, unknown mental state.

Strieber's media tour for *Transformation* occasionally included eyewitness testimony of encounters with the visitors by people claiming such experiences (or what seemed to them to have possibly been such experiences). Such was the case with *Live with Regis and Kathie Lee*, as well as with what was probably the all-time high point of Strieber's media exposure, a one-hour special edition of *The Late Show*, entirely dedicated to exploring UFO phenomena, with Strieber leading off the show.

Broadcast September 16, 1988, on Fox network affiliates, this particular show featured not only Strieber, but also appearances by William Moore, coauthor (with Charles Berlitz) of *The Roswell Incident*; Brian O'Leary, a space scientist and former astronaut; and John Gliedman, a research psychologist from New York who has acquainted himself with many of the people involved in the "alien abduction" scene and their literature. In addition, the show featured first-person testimonies by four people who claimed to have had unusual experiences that might be interpreted as having occurred with nonhuman entities: Deanna Dubé, Raven Dana, Lorie Barnes, and myself. A group of more than sixty people from the Los Angeles area claiming to have had alien contacts was also present in the audience.

Strieber received something of a hero's welcome when he walked out onto the stage on this show, with resounding cheers greeting him from the audience. Unlike some hosts who appeared to spontaneously generate their questions, Shaeffer read his questions from cards, reflecting the considerable amount of planning that had gone into the way the show would be handled. Shaeffer also treated Strieber with a visibly greater amount of deference than did some other talk show hosts.

Interestingly, the discussion on this show went immediately to the subjects of "proof" and "control" in relation to extraterrestrial entities.

SHAEFFER: Let's just say I'm totally skeptical of the whole deal. I'm going to ask you why is it there is no physical proof of unidentified flying objects.

STRIEBER: Well, there's a very interesting possible reason, and that's this: As long as there's no physical proof, our government, our scientists, military, medical professionals don't get involved, meaning that there's nobody telling the ordinary person what to think about this. Everybody can make their own decision. Everybody can—they can turn away from it, be skeptical as they want, turn toward it, deny it, accept it, whatever they want to do. It means we're completely free, on the one hand, and on the other hand, because our official authorities aren't involved, the visitors are in complete control of the situation.

SHAEFFER: Hm.

STRIEBER: And I think that that may be changing. I think that we're just on the edge quite possibly of getting physical evidence, that, incredibly, contact of some kind may very well be under way.[8]

This show was unusual, also, in that Strieber used it as a venue for showing a transparency of his brain taken from the MRI test of March 18, 1988, and explained that he thought there was a good possibility it was a step toward a kind of physical proof regarding the probes that he says he experienced being put into his head.

Yet this show was a significant shift from any other in which Strieber had spoken of the visitors, in that it placed him and his experiences in a much larger context that reflected, to a certain extent, the state of current dialogue about certain issues in UFO research. In particular, the presence of William Moore enabled this show to confront the questions that still remain unanswered regarding whether or not there is a secret government organization named MJ-12 that is involved in managing alien affairs. Additionally, Moore presented the audience with information on the alleged crash of a flying disc on July 7, 1947, and the subsequent retrieval of disc fragments and four alien bodies from the Coronado ranch near Roswell, New Mexico. Strieber attested on the show to the fact that he had visited the Roswell area with Moore and was convinced that it was very likely a crash had occurred, officially making himself a player in the game of an alleged United States government UFO coverup.

The presence of Brian O'Leary on the show served as a vehicle for comment on the remarkable (and by now relatively famous) series of photographs and videotapes from Gulf Breeze, Florida, which display what appears to be a very unusual aerial craft in unusual maneuvers. O'Leary testified that the work of a number of scientists had not been able to find any evidence of a hoax reflected in the tapes and photographs.

John Gliedman, the research psychologist, made the point, however, that if visitor abduction experiences seemed to have a mystical component, it was entirely possible that they were analogous to encounters with angels recorded in centuries past. If modern-day people have encounters with space beings from UFOs, he reasoned, perhaps this is the result of the science-fiction-oriented culture in which we live, in which television shows like *Star Trek* have had a tremendous influence on the popular mind. He also did not dismiss the possibility of temporal lobe epilepsy transient events having caused these experiences in the minds of people who were otherwise perfectly healthy.

The first-person narratives from people in the audience served the purpose of giving the general audience some feeling for the manner in which abduction and other types of UFO encounter experiences seem to manifest in people's lives.

This overall discussion, as cursory as it had to be for the purposes of television, nevertheless put Strieber and the issue of abductions into a context that had previously never existed: the question of the existence of real alien beings. From the manner in which the show was structured (and Strieber had a great deal to do with its final form) this special edition of *The Late Show* made the overall statement that, for Whitley Strieber and a lot of other people of credible backgrounds, the visitors are now a de facto reality.

Perhaps the most unusual outcome of press coverage to derive from *Transformation*, however, did not relate directly to Whitley Strieber but rather to his wife, Anne, and their son, Andrew. It appeared in the form of an interview with Anne conducted by freelance journalist Barbara Clayman, published in the October 1988 issue of *Ladies' Home Journal*. The interview followed an excerpt from *Transformation* that related the story of what Whitley described as his son's abduction. This was the first time that Anne had been interviewed for publication.

As might be expected, Clayman's questions to Anne dealt primarily with the manner in which the visitor experience has affected her marriage with Whitley and the development of her son.

LHJ: How has the visitor experience affected your son emotionally?

ANNE: I think my son is very special and very lucky because he didn't have to feel that we were laughing at him and not believing him. He is growing up in a unique situation, yet he is like the rest of the individuals who had experiences. He puts them out of his daily life. He doesn't go around and talk about them with many people. In his own way he is still an ordinary kid who likes to read *Mad* magazine.

LHJ: Have the visitations affected your marriage in any way?

ANNE: When Whitley was so troubled by his memories before he found out what was causing them, we were having terrific fights and great unhappiness. Neither my son nor I could figure out what was wrong with Whitley and why he had such sadness. Everyone expected that when he finally came to me and said, "Well, I've been hypnotized and this is what I remember . . ." I would have been terrified. Actually, I was quite relieved and grateful that our problems didn't originate with me or our son.

This interview also broke some ground in providing Anne an opportunity to speak about the many letters she and Whitley have received since the publication of *Communion*. Anne has assumed the rather gargantuan task of reading those letters, seeing that they are replied to, and making sure that they are classified in an intelligible order, all of which, I can personally testify from seeing her work, she has certainly done with diligence. Yet prior to these few published comments, there had been little known about Anne's work in establishing a network of communication for people involved with the visitor experience.

LHJ: Certainly there are people who don't believe your husband's story. How does that make you feel?

ANNE: I understand these people, because I used to laugh about UFOs; I used to think it was ridiculous. I understand why someone would say, "How could this be true?" . . . [But] I've corresponded with so many people to whom it's happening. I have read letters from and met so many nice, sober, ordinary people who have had these experiences that I have no choice but to believe what they are saying.

In relation to her own marriage, Anne mentioned the fears that occur in relationships where a visitor experience has transpired:

ANNE: We get hundreds of letters from men and women who tell us that they have kept their experiences a secret. I understand their concerns and their sadness all too well. What causes a husband or wife to reject the reality of their spouse's experience is fear: They are terrified that the world might be different from the way they see it. We all try to get our lives in order and under control, and when this idea of visitors comes into your life, everything is turned upside down.

Clayman left what is perhaps her most personal question for last.

LHJ: Do you have any desire to be taken by the visitors yourself?

ANNE: At this point, I am interested in getting to know the visitors in a more direct way, in having an experience. At first I wouldn't have said that because it was enough for me to cope with Whitley's and Andrew's experiences and those of thousands of others. Currently, I'm learning about what I might need to do inside myself to be more open to the idea of visitors. I have to find out in what ways I am afraid, in what ways overcontrolled, perhaps, and too wedded to everyday life. I think that if I take this journey inside myself, I may be able to help other people to take it, too.

I interviewed Anne Strieber myself in December of 1988, and asked her to specifically describe her project of dealing with all the response Strieber's media exposure has generated. It is a job that has come to form a major part of the Strieber family's life.

CONROY: Anne, you have been in a very remarkable position, reading these letters.

How soon after *Communion* came out did you begin to get mail?

ANNE: I could say days, but really very soon. We were already set up, but I had to hire a full-time secretary. We have to open them all, to make sure the return address is on the letter, because people will send manuscripts, books, tons of things with no return address in it.

CONROY: Just a tremendous amount of hand labor there. I presume that you read all the letters as they came in.

ANNE: I certainly did. I categorized them. I had a more elaborate system, but now I've decided that I only want certain ones. You can't keep them all, so I only keep a couple of categories.

CONROY: So about how many letters, more or less, do you have on file now?

ANNE: Oh, about twenty-five hundred. They're definitely culled letters, the ones that have real information. There might be only a little information, but it's real information.

CONROY: Have you put some of these letters into the computer now?

ANNE: Oh yes, we have a program and we're putting them in. We have between an eighth and a fourth of them, although we don't type the whole letter. We only type the important part. We leave out the parts like "I'm married with two kids," and things like that, and also opinions, unless they're very interesting with new ideas. We just put them with certain types of material, and we give everybody a number, so that we can set them out and give them to people to research them. If that researcher wanted to get in touch with certain people, then we could look it up in the computer and find out who that number belonged to.

CONROY: I see. So right now, I take it, all this work is preparatory to some larger research project taking place.

ANNE: Yes. We're hoping to get the Communion Foundation going, a nonprofit. What we are doing is to get professionals—we have some on-line already—to do some research projects with this. We want them to not only do research projects, but publish the results in either mainstream or scientific publications, not the UFO publications. The UFO community has been talking to itself long enough.

We are more interested in people who have a publication history—a couple of psychologists are interested. I would also like to get a physicist, somebody who knows something about particle physics, and we'd like to get a couple of biologists, an anthropologist, a linguist. These types of specialists I would love to have.

We have a program called ZyIndex, which is the most sophisticated that we could find, where you can call up phrases and words—like if you're interested in the color of the light, you could get all the letters that mention that. . . . This actually makes it so that you're able to develop some statistics from these letters. While it's not a huge sample, it's the biggest sample, by far, that has ever been gathered. . . .

I think the average person doesn't realize this, but UFO researchers work with very poor samples—maybe they have ten cases. That's why scientists don't take them seriously. . . . And this data—while it's undoubtedly influenced to some extent by Whitley's books—I feel it's a much purer sample than has ever been seen before.

Most samples are gotten as the results of questionnaires, and questionnaires always limit the material. Or UFO researchers tend to run into these cases by knowing somebody who knows somebody. I would like to see this stuff in as scientifically objective a way as any other data, and have it analyzed, because the UFO community has ruined its objective data by doing this kind of research, so scientists will naturally reject it because it's not being researched in the right way. That's why they ignore it, and that's why people refuse to accept it, because to the scientific community—and we can all be very annoyed at them, sure—but to them it does not exist because it has not been collected correctly and it has not been analyzed correctly.

CONROY: I understand you had some correspondence with the psychologist, Kenneth Ring, who has pioneered near-death-experience research.

ANNE: He was interested in UFOs. He's not in that community, but he has talked with people in it, and I think he's beginning to notice these similarities. And in relation to the book, I think one of the biggest surprises was that the experience changes people so much—it's like it came to people as a spiritual journey, it changes people in a spiritual way. . . . Also, many people report out-of-body experiences and other types of classic spiritual experiences after having had a UFO experience. It kind of awakens them in some way.

CONROY: I'm sure you're aware, of course, that some people, Budd Hopkins in particular, have a very different take on this. Talking to people out in the UFO community, it appears that a lot of people who consider themselves professional UFO investigators are very hot on the idea of an extraterrestrial-hybrid genetic experiment taking place.

ANNE: Yeah, well I hope that hasn't spread too much beyond Budd Hopkins.

CONROY: Well, I was wondering if you had seen any reports of this genetic business in the letters.

ANNE: I must say, of the UFO investigators who have written, most of them have no UFO experiences. And the ones who have had experiences have had mild experiences, like seeing a shooting star, or seeing a strange glow in a field. I never got one letter from a UFO investigator who had a major experience. That doesn't mean there aren't any, but I think it's very telling that of all the ones who have written, there's not even one worth saving, worth putting on disc.

Now, the genetic stuff. As Whitley told you, I also noticed that we have literally no letters that mention the Budd Hopkins's taking-the-fetus scenario. None of them, except for the ones that have been either heavily influenced by his book, *Intruders*, or—most cases—hypnotized by him. There are only a few [of these] letters, but it just struck me that the ones who have been hypnotized by him—and it's only a few [of the] people who wrote—followed the scenario exactly. It's like they're religious converts. It's really rather sad. . . . There were no others.

But the genetic idea—the evidence we do have of it is from letters from many people. Now, this is not something I think statistically very healthy—you get a lot of letters where they say "They felt like family," or "I've always felt I didn't belong on this Earth, when I was little I would look up in the sky and I would tell my mother I came on a spaceship."

It is easy to scoff at the stories in the letters Anne Strieber has read, but in a way they represent the best indicators of the effect that all of the publicity about Strieber was having, and the surest documentation of the length and breadth and depth of the penetration of Strieber's presence into the public mind. In telling his message so publicly, Strieber in effect made it possible for other people to reveal, for the first time, stories once thought too strange to tell, much less publish.

Chapter 4

Earth Man: Unless You Change Your Ways, Your Planet Will Be Reduced to a Burning Cinder

---

Communion in Relation to the
American UFO Community

The North American UFO community may not be very large, but it is certainly complex. It is so factionalized, however, that it is hard to describe it as a "community" in the sense of having a common sense of purpose and direction. UFO organizations now in existence range from research groups that attempt to maintain serious links with the academic community to semireligious "contactee" organizations led by persons unabashedly claiming to be spokespeople for an angelic hierarchy. New on the horizon are the "extraterrestrial abductee support groups" that have arisen in recent years, owing largely to the work of UFO researcher Budd Hopkins, who worked with Strieber at the beginning of his inquiry into the "visitor experience."[1] While some groups work toward establishing UFOs as a serious field of study, others claim to teach people how to spiritually interpret purported personal experiences of encounters with extraterrestrials. In between those extremes lie thousands of people who might ordinarily have no contact with such groups but are interested in obtaining substantive information about UFO phenomena, motivated perhaps by strange personal experiences that seem to defy conventional explanation.

How is the outside observer to regard these UFO groups? Is there any one of them that can be regarded as a reliable source of honest, accurate information—or do they simply foster the latest fashions in irrational fantasies about spacemen, their content drawn from contemporary science fiction culture?

Worse, do some of them display the same characteristics as "cults," which discourage rational thinking and a healthy social life among their members?

Given the enormous success that *Communion* enjoyed, what relationships does Whitley Strieber now have to the people whom, in large part, he did not need to convince of the reality of his experience?

Has Strieber taken the road to becoming a UFO cult leader, thereby discrediting the UFO community, or is he doing something else— perhaps even challenging some of the concepts in the UFO community's prevailing consensus reality?

Given the predominant intellectual and political attitudes of our times, all UFO-related organizations (save for government-sponsored research teams) have long been represented in the mainstream press as existing on the fringes of society. Some, at one time or another, have indeed been characterized by critics as being cults or havens for cultists determined to impose an alien-oriented creed upon unsuspecting individuals. The question of cultism is legitimate, as it is becoming difficult to ignore the manner in which highly sophisticated mind-control techniques are being increasingly employed in a variety of sectors of society. The bloody legacy of the suicide-massacre of nine hundred People's Temple members in Jonestown, Guyana, on November 18, 1978, stands as a reminder of what can happen when mind-control techniques are misused by a completely unscrupulous individual.

Given the extremes to which some destructive cults have already gone in denying liberty to their members, it may well be said that the charge of cultism is, in our day and age, a serious one. After all, how is the public to know if organizations that on the surface appear to be legitimate might not actually be run by dangerous and unstable individuals? The Reverend Jim Jones, leader of the People's Temple, was treated during the mid-1970s as a respectable member of the San Francisco political scene, and met regularly with elected officials and community leaders. While his behavior was even then regarded in some circles with suspicion, Jones's position as someone apparently tackling the problems of poverty in San Francisco's black ghetto provided him with sufficient leverage to cultivate a positive public image—until members of his group were seen to shoot U.S. Congressman Leo Ryan on national television, after which Jones and his followers killed themselves.

Questions of UFO cultism have not been extensively addressed in recent years by some of the organizations that regard themselves as representing the mainstream of the UFO community. The question is a sensitive one, and understandably so, for people within the UFO community who regard themselves as rational thinkers have all too often had to encounter more than their fair share of ridicule. Organizations such as MUFON (the Mutual UFO Network, based in Seguin, Texas), CUFOS (the J. Allen Hynek Center for UFO Studies of Chicago, Illinois), and others regard themselves as centers for serious research. Moreover, they publish journals that attempt to maintain high standards for intellectual content, displaying a vigorous and healthy debate on issues in contemporary UFO studies, known by them as "ufology."

Although ufology is so new that it has yet to become regarded as a respectable intellectual discipline in the world of North American academia, this field of inquiry has generated an extraordinarily rich literature representing contributions derived not only from people with a background in physical science but increasingly from people with backgrounds in folklore, anthropology, sociology, and, of course, literature and the arts. It would be hard to characterize these organizations, which openly encourage a free hearing for divergent opinions, as being cult groups.

One independent researcher, however, has explored the ramifications of UFO cultism in some depth in a book entitled *Messengers of Deception*. Jacques Vallee, Ph.D., a computer scientist originally trained in mathematics who became a research assistant to J. Allen Hynek, Ph.D., an astronomer and former Air Force UFO consultant who became the grandfather of contemporary North American ufology, surveyed a fair variety of groups active in North America and Europe during the 1970s. Vallee's book was unique at the time in that he accepted the possibility that the UFO phenomenon was something more than could be explained by standard means, yet seriously challenged the assumptions of the contactee movement and much of the work of UFO researchers that UFOs and their "occupants" necessarily came from "outer space." Instead, Vallee argued, it behooves us to look at the radically new belief systems being advanced by contactee groups and inquire whether these movements represent the results of highly sophisticated attempts at mind control.

Vallee went so far as to propose that we regard UFOs as real physical objects whose function is to manipulate human beliefs. Moreover, he proposed, there is no reason for us to suppose that the "manipulators" behind such craft are necessarily extraterrestrials or necessarily humans. After illustrating the wide spectrum of beliefs being advanced by people claiming contact with extraterrestrials, Vallee concluded his book with the observation that as faith in religion has been breaking down for centuries under the onslaught of science, so too is confidence in science now breaking down under the weight of a new mythology heavily connected to the UFO phenomenon. New beliefs that negate the importance of both science and religion are the result, leading Vallee to wonder what kind of "brave new world" we may indeed be entering.[2]

In addition to traditional contactee groups that have developed their own lore about extraterrestrials, other members of the UFO community, such as the Unarius Educational Foundation (based in El Cajon, California) and the Aetherius Society (of Hollywood, California), center heavily upon activities associated with "channeling," once known in the late nineteenth century as "trance mediumship." While some people within the ranks of the research-oriented UFO groups may not wholly discount channeling as a source of possibly useful information, it nevertheless remains an observable fact that a wide gulf separates the activities of groups such as MUFON and CUFOS from those of channeling-related organizations.

Members of anticult groups such as CAN (the Cult Awareness Network) have alleged that groups practicing channeling justify the suspicion of practicing mind control upon their members.[3] However, little published research has emerged from members of anticult groups on the social and psychological dynamics of chanelling-oriented UFO groups. The main accusation leveled against such groups is that the phenomenon of channeling induces a mild hypnotic trance in the channeler's audience members, thereby rendering them susceptible to influences from the channeler delivered in the course of the "reading."[4]

There seems to be an unwritten agreement between these two poles of the UFO community not to engage in much open criticism of one another. Members of research organizations may largely dismiss the claims of contactee groups as constituting an essentially social response to the stress of UFO sightings, or simply as the desire to be "taken away," but they do not do so very vociferously. The channelers, for their part, seem to be largely oblivious to the researchers and their controversies regarding issues of "alien abduction" and alleged United States government UFO secrecy.[5] Because most UFO-channeling organizations have played a negligible role in relation to some of the questions raised by Strieber's *Communion* and *Transformation*, I will refer primarily to that part of the community that has made a serious attempt, hard as it might be, to relate its research to the tangible world we agree that we know. All UFO and alien abduction research, of course, is hampered in terms of public credibility by one, simple overriding fact.

No one has yet produced a single, indisputable "alien" artifact or body.

This problem, curiously enough, appears to have been compounded by a lack of willingness on the part of some members of the North American UFO community to even consider the implications of reported UFO abductions. The problem to which I refer might be called that of the "missing aliens," and it has much to do with the historical development of UFO research. From the period of 1947 through 1960, UFO research focused on investigation of reports of unidentified *flying* objects. A number of writers who have explored the subject of an alleged United States government UFO cover-up contend, moreover, that a great deal of effort was expended even by many UFO investigators during the 1950s and 1960s to make sure that cases that involved reported landings of UFOs and reports of UFO occupants did not see the light of day. Chief among the UFO organizations alleged to be active in ignoring abduction reports is the now defunct NICAP (the National Investigations Committee on Aerial Phenomena), which was purportedly interested in achieving respectability for the organization's appeal for a congressional investigation of UFOs. According to contemporary researchers, NICAP-related ufologists censored abduction-related material from UFO reports they used in their public presentations.[6] This attempt on the part of some factions of the early UFO community to put a nuts-and-bolts spin onto UFO stories eventually led other researchers to explore the areas of reports that were being ignored because of their strangeness and apparent absurdity. Consequently, there gradually developed what might be called the hard and soft poles of the UFO research.

At the "hard" end of the research are situated writers and research-ers concerned with the study of cases characterized by what is con-sidered to be hard physical evidence, as well as those investigators who have been laboring over the documents associated with the problem of the alleged government UFO cover-up. Researchers of the hard persuasion have tended, in the past, to come from the ranks of the military, scientific, and technical communities, and have generally been influenced by their training in the physical sciences.

At the "soft" end of the spectrum one finds researchers who are primarily concerned, not with the physical reality of UFO phenom-ena, but rather with their general significance and meaning. At one end of this soft pole we find investigators (e.g., Jacques Vallee, Hilary Evans, Jenny Randles, and others, often of English and European backgrounds) who may use social science-derived methodologies and theories to analyze the possible meaning of UFOs as a social phenom-enon, as well as to make observations on the pyschological dynamics of people reporting contacts with "entities" of varying descriptions. At the other extreme of the soft pole, one encounters people who claim that the only way to understand UFOs and "visitors" is by the inges-tion of psychedelic drugs as part of a shamanic vision quest (e.g., Terence K. McKenna).[7] Somewhere between these two extremes are located the investigators who would have us look very closely at the phenomenon of "UFO abductions" as related to us through texts de-rived from hypnotic regressions (e.g., Budd Hopkins, Jerome Clark, David Jacobs, and others). Such investigators in general deplore the use of psychoactive drugs in relation to UFO research, are interested in varying degrees in the psychological processes characteristic of "ab-ductees" and are generally sensitive to the question of the manipula-tion of abductee information through leading questions during hypnosis. Soft-pole investigators are characterized by diverse educational and professional backgrounds, but it is reflective of a change in the sensi-bility of UFO research itself that Budd Hopkins, one of the most prominent UFO investigators who uses hypnosis in his research, is a noted visual and plastic artist.

Whitley Strieber's own introspective approach to self-investigation, as revealed in *Communion*, falls in the latter category, of course, though it is radically different from Hopkins's approach in a number of ways. It would be fair to say, moreover, that his account is probably the most detailed first-person narrative of purported human-"visitor" inter-actions yet published, and all the more interesting for Strieber's abili-ties as a professional writer.

Yet the very fact that Strieber is, by his own account, a "highly imaginative" writer has, from the inception of *Communion* as a manuscript, been something of a problem for some prominent mem-bers of the UFO community. In retrospect, it seems that the very process by which Strieber wrote *Communion*, in which he submitted early versions of the manuscript to Hopkins, David Jacobs, and Jerome Clark, led to the opening of a deep rift between Hopkins and Strieber, who had previously been close associates during early 1986, when Strieber was first attempting to deal with his "visitor experi-ences."

Hopkins gave me his thoughts on the early *Communion* in our first interview: "When I finally saw the manuscript, I was quite horri-fied and I thought it was totally unpublishable. . . . I was very upset, and it had a lot to do with making suggestions on how to handle things, what to leave out, and general sort of strategic decisions. See, one has to realize one very basic thing. He [Strieber] has little experi-ence as a nonfiction writer. I have a great deal of experience as a nonfiction writer. His sort of anything-goes attitude, that's a product of being a horror story writer and very different. It is interesting, too, that many, many interviewers would ask me, 'Can he be trusted?' because of the quality of his writing, which has this sort of—as they point out—'It was a dark and stormy night' quality, a sort of setup for the horror thing."

In essence, Hopkins said, he was concerned about the believability of Strieber's initial text, which he felt simply would not be accepted by readers. As Hopkins put it:

"He said he was led off his airplane by his penis, by these little—naked—things; it was the kind of thing where I said 'Whitley!' He had no sense as to what would go down with the reader and what wouldn't. I mean, writing fiction is one thing, but there are other rules. He got a practically line-by-line criticism from David Jacobs, and Jerry Clark made a lot of suggestions, and I certainly made a lot of suggestions, and there were many, many hundreds of changes that the editors made to the book. So it was finally whipped into shape, thanks to a lot of other minds, but at the time it was bizarre beyond belief. A lot of it was very, very good, but a lot of it was extremely bizarre."

Strieber admits to having ultimately left out some of his experiences from the content in *Communion*, but he insists that he was faithful to what he describes as the "high level of strangeness" of his experiences. Hopkins's insistence upon having a major impact on the style of his book (not to mention his insistence that Strieber did not know how to write nonfiction) did not sit well with Strieber, as can be seen in the criticism he now makes of Hopkins's work.

"He and Jacobs are censoring the experiences of people with visitor experiences in order to fit them into a theory they have about extraterrestrials," Strieber told me in a December 1988 interview. "If some of the experiences in people's lives don't fit with their theories, they just exclude them. In my books, I have maintained an account of the experiences which is very close to how strange and bizarre they really are. That is why my books have gotten such a tremendous response, while *Intruders* was a failure."

Hopkins, of course, asserts that *Intruders* was not a failure (it made its way onto *The New York Times* best-seller list, though it did not by any means stay there for the length of time that *Communion* did). As events turned out, relations between Hopkins and Strieber (as well as between Clark and Strieber, and Jacobs and Strieber) began to deteriorate after Hopkins submitted his criticisms of the manuscript. Perhaps relations might have been more cordial at that time had it not been that Hopkins was himself preparing to launch his own new book, *Intruders*, upon the market. According to Hopkins, he was originally hopeful that a joint appearance of *Intruders* and *Communion* in the bookstores would be a watershed for publishing on the subject of UFOs and aliens. He recalled having proposed to Strieber that Morrow and Random House (Hopkins's publisher) "could make publishing history by advertising our two books in one ad."

However, no plans were ever made for such a joint advertising program. Hopkins said he was surprised and infuriated, moreover, to suddenly hear from his publisher that Strieber had written a letter suggesting that it would be much better for the reception of *Intruders* if its release were delayed by several months. Hopkins refers to that letter as a "betrayal" by Strieber of a trust that he had carefully developed. He referred to the day when he was informed of his publisher's receipt of that letter as his own "Pearl Harbor Day."

Strieber has explained that his motive in attempting to convince Random House not to publish *Intruders* as planned was to save it from being overwhelmed by what he saw was the imminent best-seller status of *Communion*. Strieber even wrote a letter to Random House offering a quotation that could be used on the dust jacket. Hopkins refused the offer of the quote from Strieber, and terminated his relationship with Strieber, essentially saying that he could not trust him. Since that time, Hopkins has not spoken to Strieber, nor corresponded with him.

In the course of three lengthy interviews and a number of subsequent telephone conversations, Budd Hopkins made quite an effort to inform me of the particulars of his problems with Strieber and of the nature of his own work with abductees, for which I am quite grateful. He did send me copies of all of his correspondence with Strieber, and invited me to speak with a number of his associates and some of the abductees with whom he has worked. Among the papers that Hopkins gave me was a document detailing his observations about Strieber that he had been sending around to people in the UFO community, essentially as a warning about working with him. The upshot of all of this communication for me as an investigator was really not very fruitful. I was told a number of stories about Strieber that, in essence, amount to rumors, because I was provided with no means of verifying them with uninvolved third parties.

I also spoke at length with David Jacobs, Ph.D., off the record, and he also gave me a good deal of information that I could not check. As a reporter, I cannot give credence to information that remains at the status of a rumor. I can say, though, that it was very clear to me that the message I was getting from Hopkins and a number of people associated with him was that, in their opinion, Strieber is both mentally and emotionally unstable and therefore not to be trusted.

At more than one point, Hopkins said to me, "I wish that Whitley Strieber would just go away" and, "I would just like to have him out of my life." Considering his difficult experiences, I can certainly understand his feelings. However, I must say that Hopkins exhibited a fair amount of emotion, especially in relating to me the record of his experiences with Strieber.

I could write a book about the controversy that has raged between Budd Hopkins and Whitley Strieber, but I am afraid it would make rather dreary reading. As an outside observer, I cannot help but note that what transpired between the two men had a great deal to do with questions of control. Hopkins made it clear from the outset that his professional problems began with Strieber's mention of elements of his story that he considered just too bizarre to be believed. Apart from the question whether Strieber exhibited what Hopkins took to be emotional instability during the time of their association, the question remains whether Hopkins's attempt to edit Strieber's narrative was appropriate.

However, it should be said that, despite all of the rancor that developed between these two men, Budd Hopkins has insisted all along that he believes Strieber did indeed have an alien abduction experience. In a way, that insistence has perhaps been his own way of sticking by Strieber, perhaps whether Strieber liked it or not.

One example of the manner in which he maintained that position was by writing a letter to the editors of *The Nation* in response to the article "The Village Alien" by Thomas Disch, previously discussed in Chapter 3. Hopkins told me that he retracted it after his colleagues had received "threats" from Strieber regarding its publication, but asked me to reproduce it in this book as a summary of his position on Strieber. I agreed to do so, and it follows:

Dear Editor:

Thomas Disch's suspicions about the veracity of Whitley Strieber's book *Communion* are cleverly stated, though poorly investigated. Disch's readers, unfortunately, were not told that the book contains the results of a polygraph test that Strieber took and passed, nor were they informed about the various psychological tests and evaluations that were carried out by qualified professionals. Though I am mentioned in the book a number of times as the investigator who worked with Strieber—for months there were nearly daily phone conversations, psychiatric interviews and many visits—Disch never felt curious enough to question me about the case. Literary criticism alone seems to satisfy him, and the similarities he found between a Strieber short story and the nearly contemporaneous *Communion* evidently constituted proof of something nefarious. By contrast, after a many levelled [sic] inquiry I concluded months ago that Strieber had indeed undergone complex and disturbing UFO experiences, an opinion I still hold.

I agree with Disch that *Communion* raises difficult questions. Strieber—an inexperienced writer of non-fiction—is a skillful science fiction and horror novelist, and his literary habits show. In the past few weeks I have had to defend the author's truthfulness to a number of writers put off by the book's style and some of its shakier assertions. I suppose every horror story aspect is a little like Frank Morgan in the *Wizard of Oz*, busy behind a curtain, spinning dials, causing machinery to belch smoke. There is too much of this in Strieber's book, but it constitutes a literary weakness, not a deliberate fabrication. Strieber wrote *Communion* in the first six months after he first discovered the reasons for various periods of "missing time" in his life. I know, having investigated over one hundred similar cases during the past twelve years, that no one should undertake the publication of such disorienting recollections, feelings and speculations in such a short period of time. Perspective is essential, and Strieber was so advised. But the book was written anyway, and I believe that some of its strengths as well as many of its weaknesses are attributable to the speed of its composition. Despite the smoke, the stylistic infelicities and the dubious hypothesizing the book is still an honest attempt by a very shaken man to deal with unimaginable events.

Budd Hopkins

Strieber, of course, would no doubt take exception to Hopkins's evaluation of his text in *Communion*. What Hopkins might regard as "smoke" is to Strieber the very bizarreness of the visitor experience itself. He is now quite adamant on the necessity of maintaining faithfulness to the "high strangeness content" of his "visitor experiences," and would recommend that faithfulness to others who would write of theirs. At a certain point in our conversations on this subject, he told me he had recently received a letter from a man who told him that he remembered a visitor experience in which *he* was led off the flying craft *by his penis.* He said he was profoundly affected by reading a letter that confirmed such an apparently bizarre and incredible detail of his own experience.

In the latter part of 1988, Strieber became increasingly vocal in his criticism of Hopkins's work, writing a number of articles questioning many of the assumptions about hypnosis and group dynamics that he says Hopkins holds. Moroever, he has extended that criticism to the UFO community in general, which he says has tended to poohpooh the value of his work.

One organization of which Strieber has been especially critical is MUFON, which he initially recognized as having played a key role in helping him over the crisis of adapting to his visitor experiences.

Dennis Stacy, editor of the *MUFON UFO Journal*, was in touch with Strieber by telephone during the time he was writing *Communion* and seeking contacts in the UFO community. As I mentioned in the Introduction, Stacy had a copy of the manuscript of *Communion*, which, I learned in a later interview, Strieber had personally sent to him. I asked him what were some of his initial impressions of the book.

"From my perspective," Stacy said, "it was interesting but it was also not really anything new to the UFO community. What did strike me was that it seemed to be ongoing, which is, of course, always interesting, and then that seemed to hold out the possibility of being able to verify the experience, either by a third party or objectively, possibly photographs, whatever. In other words—a crude idea—that you would spring a trap on it and get a picture."

Stacy also pointed out that he found many other long-standing members of the UFO community felt similarly, and that he could understand the resentments of researchers who had been freely sharing their information with one another for years, only to find that someone with no experience in the field was making large sums of money off his personal story.

Strieber's relation to MUFON, however, was not always from a critical stance. Shortly after the publication of *Communion*, he wrote a letter to the MUFON general membership for publication in the *MUFON UFO Journal* expressing his gratitude for the support and understanding he had received through MUFON. Over a year later he would write a letter to that same publication protesting what he believed was the unfair manner in which MUFON's leadership had been making public statements belittling the importance of *Communion* as a tool for understanding the UFO phenomenon.

Walt Andrus, president of MUFON, expressed his reservations in regard to *Communion* in a telephone interview I conducted with him in April of 1987. As he put it at the time: "*Communion* does not make any significantly new contribution to the UFO literature."

It was then Andrus's opinion that none of what was represented in the story of *Communion* actually took the UFO community any closer toward establishing the physical reality of the UFO phenomenon, a goal that has long served as a criterion for researchers of the "hard" pole of the spectrum. Moroever, Andrus was not interested in discussing the psychological aspects of the book.

A year later, though, when I interviewed Andrus about his current assessment of Strieber, he was much more generous with Strieber.

"I know Whitley Striber as a personal friend," Andrus said, "although the last time I saw him up at American University in Washington, D.C., he had such a big crowd of people around him there was no chance for private conversation going on whatsoever. However, he has been a member of MUFON and subscribes to our monthly magazine. Back when he was putting together *Communion*, he allowed Dennis Stacy and myself to read the original manuscript, which included penciled marks, revisions, and so forth. . . . It was quite a pack and I read and read, waiting for him to tell us something I didn't know. Well, he never did, because in reality, his abduction was a very mild case compared to most—a lot that we've investigated.

"But I have to give Whitley credit, because he certainly put his reputation on the line as a best-selling author in writing his book—publishing his personal experiences. Because after having a record of best-sellers, he could have destroyed his whole reputation with publishers, and also the public, by publishing *Communion*. They would have said, "He's a nut!"

I asked Andrus why he thought the public responded so well to the book.

"Well remember, he is a very, very fine writer," he said, "and one of the difficulties in reading the book is how much is Whitley's experience and how much is speculation, theories. All those things creeped in, and he's such a good writer that this appealed to people. I think 251t's the answer, not that it came from his own experience. Because books like *Intruders* are much deeper material and much more meaningful material which is not in Whitley's book.

"I felt that Whitley really wrote his book prematurely, because he only had a few hypnosis sessions with the doctor before he was already writing, before he had really completed any in-depth study at all. That's why we find the problem that he hasn't told us anything we don't know, because he never got that far."

Jerome Clark, who is an editor for the CUFOS journal and *Fate* magazine, makes the point that Strieber was initially very welcome in the UFO community: "A lot of people welcomed Strieber with open arms and thought that, since he was a major writer coming out with this story, perhaps there might at last be a favorable hearing given to this kind of story. I myself wrote an article in *IUR* [*International UFO Reporter*] saying that I thought this was a great thing, and put my reputation on the line."

According to Clark, though, he and many of his colleagues now feel "very disillusioned" with Strieber, owing to what Clark considers to be Strieber's erratic behavior in relationship to them. Of particular concern to Clark were reports that Strieber was telling people claiming abduction-type experience not to work with ufologists, as well as other comments critical of the research that Clark and others conduct on an ongoing basis. Money was also a factor, it appears, in that Clark claims Strieber promised CUFOS donations of as much as $5,000 to further their research, and then allegedly reneged on his promise.

When questioned on the point of the proffer of financial support, Strieber said: "Jerome Clark is 'disenchanted' because I give the Fund for UFO Research money but not his organization, CUFOS. I don't give them money because I don't think they are very good. Their handling of the Gulf Breeze matter[8]—sending it out on a national mailing declaring it a hoax—is a case in point. They sent out this mailing on the basis of testimony from a neighborhood teenager and their own assessment that the UFO didn't 'look right.' In my opinion they did this because they were jealous of the fact that MUFON got hold of the case first."

Clark had a number of complaints about Strieber that did not affect his immediate group. For example, he mentioned to me that Strieber had only given about $100 to the Fund for UFO Research, a nonprofit organization in the Washington, D.C., area that has financed a number of UFO-related studies.

I asked Strieber about that allegation in November of 1988, and he replied by saying he had given $2,500 to the Fund for UFO Research, and was planning to give a $5,000 matching grant. He also provided me with copies of two of his canceled checks deposited by the Fund for UFO Research totaling $2,500.

One other allegation Clark made against Strieber was that he had persecuted Jenny Randles, a noted British UFO investigator (and coauthor of *Science and the UFOs*, which Strieber said he read on the night before he remembered having had a visitor experience), with unnecessary legal action.

Strieber filled me in on his view of what occurred between himself and Jenny Randles in a letter dated December 7, 1988. He wrote: "I attach a copy of the poem I mentioned as well as some material about the Randles affair—the part that Jerome Clark knows but conveniently "forgot" to mention.

"Randles libeled me on the radio and was forced to broadcast an apology. I could have sued her for damages and costs, but elected not to do so because she has no money."

Strieber also provided me with a tape of the original broadcast in which Randles made the comment he found offensive, as well as a copy of a tape in which an announcer for Piccadilly Radio reads an apology for the statements made in the original broadcast.

I reproduce here my transcript of the tape from the March 3, 1988, broadcast. Randles's comments were as follows:

> I wrote a book called *Science and the UFOs* and a horror novelist called Whitley Strieber decided to get it bought for him for Christmas. And the very night that he got the book he had a very strange experience in which he claimed he was kidnapped by this UFO and examined by these strange entities who were very interested in his nether regions. . . . And he made an awful lot of money out of this and it was, in fact, based on that book that the Dynasty[9] program built their own UFO story. But unfortunately his book is a virtual direct reproduction—which is a very appropriate word, considering what the aliens did to him—of my book. I am not making claims that he actually invented his story based upon my book. I leave you to draw your own conclusions.

Strieber's material about Randles included a copy of a letter from her dated May 14, 1988. It read (style and punctuation reproduced exactly as in the original):

Dear Mr. Strieber:

On March 3rd 1988 I appeared on Piccadilly radio in Manchester, England to discuss the issue of UFO "abductions." On that program I made statements that created the impression that your book "Communion" was a plagiarism of a book I co-authored with Peter Warrington: *Science and the UFOs.*

I wish to apologize for these and any other statements which have created false impressions about "Communion". I realise that the book is entirely your own work, and that it emerged from what you sincerely believe to have been actual experiences and was not concocted as a fraud to make money, or for any other reason.

I further acknowledge that the cover of my book "The UFO Conspiracy" contained, without your knowledge, an extract from the book "Communion", for which the publishers did not have your permission or authority to use, in a manner which you consider to imply endorsement of my book. You were not, in fact, asked whether you did, or did not, endorse the book. The use of this extract, in a way with which you honestly disapprove, was not done with my knowledge or consent.

You are free to publicise this letter in its entirety or in part as you wish. I will not publish or make further derogatory statements about you or your book, or any statements intended to imply that it is anything other than a sincere and honest effort to get at the truth.

Sincerely yours

Jenny Randles

I telephoned Randles at her home in London, thanks to some help from Walt Andrus, and she readily agreed to tell me her account of what had transpired between herself and Strieber.

Apparently this affair began when Randles's book *The UFO Conspiracy* (released in 1987 by Cassell Publishing Company) appeared with a quote from *Communion* on the dust jacket. The quote was Strieber's mention of having read *Science and the UFOs*. It appeared without Strieber's permission. According to Randles, *The UFO Conspiracy* was published while Strieber was in England promoting *Communion*, and this apparently provoked Strieber to make some comments regarding Randles to a British journalist.

"He was amazed that Strieber just laid into me with all kinds of very strange comments about how I was in business to make money and I was using and abusing people—words to that effect—I in fact heard a tape recording of the conversation which the journalist made of that interview, so I know that he wasn't misrepresenting it," Randles told me. "Strieber was clearly very angry. He also was going on about how I had placed this quote on the cover of the book and it wasn't true."

Randles did admit she thought the quote was a "little bit naughty, the way they'd done it."

"Later in America, when I arrived at the MUFON conference in Washington several people said I should keep clear of Strieber," she said. "So I decided there and then that I should clear this up, so I literally walked up to Strieber—he was surrounded by a group of people—and I introduced myself and proposed that we should chat and sort this out. He first off said 'I don't want to speak to you' and was sort of gruff and angry. I said, 'Look, you don't understand what's happened, I'd just like to explain to you what's occurred.' So he agreed and we went into a corner and we discussed it for some time. I explained my position as to exactly what happened, that it wasn't in any way my fault, that I was sorry for any upset that he seemed to feel about it. And he completely changed in the space of a few minutes to now saying that well, he understood, et cetera, and we should stick together, we should be friends, we shouldn't antagonize one another, and I entirely agreed. He said he'd read *UFO Conspiracy* and his exact words were, in fact, 'I found it a very nice book.' He said, 'I probably would have been happy to endorse it, if I had been asked.' It seemed fair comment to me. He actually offered, then and there, to write a foreword to my next book.

"Nevertheless, when I went back to Britain, I told the publisher that it might be expedient for future editions of the book—and especially the paperback edition—that they not include the same quote. That was an entirely voluntary act on my part. . . .

"I was therefore extremely surprised, to say the least, in February of 1988, about eight months after that conversation, that I was advised by Cassell that they'd received these legal letters stating they were going to take action for the use of that cover quote. Fortunately, as I say, I insisted that they delete the quote from future editions. So they were making all kinds of claims from the original letters—it just seemed very odd that after the amicable discussion we had in Washington, this suddenly happened."

Piccadilly Radio broadcast a formal apology for Randles's comments made on March 3, 1988, and there, for now, the matter seems to have ended. Randles did confirm to me that she wrote the letter to Strieber included in this book, but she declined to discuss it in detail, offering me information on her interpretations of UFO abductions instead.

All such disputes aside, I asked Jerome Clark what was his professional estimation of Strieber's narrative in *Communion*, especially in comparison with other UFO abductee accounts.

"I think that when you are dealing with people who've had any kind of extraordinary experience, a UFO experience, a bizarre, anomalous adventure, what you want is someone who is articulate, who can communicate what happened to him in a way that people can understand, but who is also kind of pragmatic and matter-of-fact— someone who you can be reasonably sure is telling you what happened without a lot of embellishment and subjective reading into the experience. So the ideal percipient of anomalous experience is a reasonably intelligent individual who is not in the throes of certain kinds of spiritual longings which he will read into his experience. And I think that Whitley, by acknowledgment, is someone who has deep spiritual leanings. I think that his interpretation of the personality and the motives of these entities is very, very different from that of the typical percipient."

I asked Clark what the "typical percipient" got from an "abduction" experience.

"They come away with no sense of spiritual wisdom," he said. "To the extent that they feel any kind of association, any kind of spiritual or emotional bond, with these entities it's really elemental and somewhat mysterious because it belies the details of their experience—in which they report being treated like laboratory animals, in a cold, clinical manner by entities who are uncommunicative and uncaring."

Clark generalized about abductions in his remarks, too, saying, "Basically, if you've seen one abduction, you've seen them all."

This idea of there being a common pattern to UFO abductions was one that I encountered in a number of individuals. One of the most notable proponents of this concept is Thomas E. Bullard, Ph.D., currently a librarian at the University of Indiana, Bloomington, whose doctoral thesis on UFOs as contemporary American folklore brought him into a study of abduction literature financed by the Fund for UFO Research. His two-volume study, *UFO Abductions: The Measure of a Mystery*, is by far the most monumental survey yet done of accounts of the abduction phenomenon.

I spoke with Bullard and asked him how Strieber's abduction compared to those of others he had studied.

"One thing I should say at the outset is that we never before had an abductee tell his own story," he said, "especially someone as articulate as he is, who can describe all his inner feelings, his struggles, and fears. So in that sense he is quite unique. As far as it compares, a lot of it compares very well. There are some peculiarities. He has the standard bedroom intrusion. He is taken out in the woods and they perform some operation on him outside the ship. Now that's very unusual. It's not unheard of, but it's unusual. Then when they take him inside the ship, there's often a kind of antechamber or holding room, it may not be as clinically clean as the rest of the ship, but it's very unusual for them to take a person there. If there's any kind of dirty or poorly constructed part of the ship, it's usually a large area that they take a car into. But to take a person into what he so well described as a place with dirty clothes around, that's unheard of, especially to carry out an operation in anything but a clean environment.

"And the fact that he described the air as being very dry is unusual. It's always heavy and moist, so that's different."

When I asked Bullard about Strieber's subjective reaction to the abduction in *Communion*, I noted that he screams. I asked him if this was normal for an abduction.

"Most people have been so well controlled that they don't make any outburst," Bullard said. "I suppose you could take Betty Hill's case though—when they put a needle through her navel, she cried out and said 'This is painful,' and they were very surprised about that, so I guess it isn't all that uncommon.

"One of the things that struck me was that the beings wouldn't let him look at them very clearly. He could look around the ship, and learn. That's something a lot of people report, but his describing the exact way it took place, that's interesting."

Bullard recounted a number of other remarkable observations on Strieber's case, and made it clear that while it was unusual, it did seem to have a sufficient amount of "classic" elements for him not to discount its reality.

Still, there remain many aspects of his story that are quite bizarre.

It seems that the general consensus among some of Strieber's more vocal early critics was that the inclusion of elements in the narrative that seemed excessively bizarre would not only militate against the public's acceptance of the story, but also bring Strieber's sanity into question. The fact that he had a facility for verbally relating the products of his own imagination, moreover, was regarded by some ufologists as more a liability than an asset.

One well-respected and highly recognized researcher, however, holds a different view regarding the matter of the psychological (and paranormal) elements in *Communion*. Raymond Fowler, author of *The Andreasson Affair* and *The Andreasson Affair, Phase Two* among other books, is one of the most veteran UFO investigators in the United States, having begun his research activities in 1966. His work with Betty Andreasson, a middle-aged American woman, is specifically concerned with a case of apparent alien abduction.

"Whitley's books are really sort of a journey through Whitley's mind, they're not your typical documentary," he said in a telephone interview from his home in Massachusetts. "They get readers to feel and experience what he was going through. It's hard reading sometimes, but you end up really empathizing with someone who's really trying to find the answers."

Some readers of *Communion*, however, exhibited a tendency to dissect his experience in terms of the details cited in the book, with an eye toward evaluating the degree of substantiation provided by Strieber for the information that he puts forth as being factual.

Michael Swords, Ph.D., was one of the first to do so within the UFO community in an article published in the May 1987, *MUFON UFO Journal*. Billed as a "reader's guide" to *Communion*, the article in its very first paragraph creates an interesting dichotomy in regard to Strieber's narrative: "An experience, or set of experiences, can be essentially internally or externally activated. Given the extreme richness of the experiences, and the extreme poverty of external impact, this set of experiences seem best judged as internally activated."

From his own analysis of the witness testimony in *Communion*, Swords appears to have come to the conclusion that none of it is of sufficient weight to lend any credence to a rational discussion of Strieber's experience in terms of ordinary events in space-time as we know it. He appends a list of footnotes to his article that point out specific instances of inadequacy in the testimonies provided in the book. He makes the point, for example, that Anne Strieber, Whitley's wife, does not figure as a corroborative factor through words quoted from her by Whitley. Moreover, he discounts the testimony of physical scars on Whitley's body, inasmuch as it cannot be determined who inflicted them or even whether they occurred at all.

Despite the fact that Swords makes severe criticisms of the witness testimony in *Communion,* he nevertheless enthusiastically endorses a program of reflection that would focus on exploring four alternative hypotheses for explaining Strieber's experiences, given that they were likely "internally activated."

Swords's first offering is the "clinical hypothesis," which he says would be the skeptic's choice; Strieber is seen as essentially mentally unstable, reacting to mental stress with creativity.

Second on the list is the "spiritual hypothesis," involving "a true encounter with the deepest reaches of the person himself." Swords posits this as an encounter with an "inner self helper" that would put the personality through a spiritual death and transformation.

Third is the "scientific hypothesis," which would explain Strieber's experience as pointing to "another ontological segment of universal reality not previously known but potentially explorable." Real "other beings" set off experiences in space-time, in this version, introducing possibilities of multidimensional and/or time travel.

Lastly, Swords proposes consideration of the "ultimate hypothesis," which posits that perhaps "other intelligences from whatever aspect of reality are interacting with us at our place in Space-Time not for academic research, or pragmatic needs, but for a more Cosmic purpose in line with the Design of the whole created universe."

Swords ends with a list of questions about whether Strieber's experiences are somehow verifiable and repeatable, saying that he believes all of his proposed hypotheses should receive serious attention.

Strieber replied to Swords's article in a letter dated April 24, 1987, published in the same issue of the *MUFON UFO Journal.* He objected strenuously to Swords's immediate dismissal of any external point of reference for his experiences:

> Overall the care you took to try to diminish the validity of the witness content of the book strikes me as suggestive that you began your undertaking with a less than objective set of preconceptions about the nature of my experience—no doubt because what has happened to me is too strange to fit the desired model of an experience with more-or-less comprehensible visitors.
>
> The tendency among UFO investigators to unconsciously seek after a hoped-for-outcome interests me. I wonder if you

do not secretly hope that some sort of comprehensible "nuts and bolts" ETs will eventually emerge into common life, and we will be able to gain sensible and understandable knowledge from them. Certainly the lectures you have given and the material you have written in the MUFON journal *[sic]* would suggest you hold this outcome very dear to your heart.

Later in that letter, Strieber stated what has come to be something of a summation of his problems with certain UFO researchers.

The truth is that there is an eerie combination of internal and external material here, made more difficult to sort out by the fact that the stress and extreme strangeness of the experience disrupts the ability of even the most well-intentioned witness to provide an accurate report of his or her encounter.

The absurdity of UFO investigators dismissing this sort of testimony based on the fact that it is often contradictory and full of confusion again suggests the subordination of good thinking to emotion, in the sense that the investigators are overly eager to dismiss that which does not fulfill their wishes.

I was warned by other abductees before writing *Communion* that it would be dismissed by the scientists and engineers in the UFO community because it dealt primarily with the spiritual and metaphysical aspects of the experience. . . . The abduction experience is *primarily* a mystical experience, in the sense that the stresses generated are similar to those created by initiation into mystery cults of the old animist religions. And the postlude experienced by abductees—one very different from that reported in accounts carefully edited and "massaged" by UFO investigators—is usually replete with spiritual and paranormal life events.

The abduction experience as it really happens is far more strange than UFO literature would suggest—far richer, far more important, far more filled with implications about the nature and future of man.

I suspect that all or most of the abduction experience as reported by UFO investigators may suffer from a sort of unintentional fictionalization. They have been subtly altered to suggest that a quite comprehensible force is behind them. [Italics Strieber's]

In the rest of that letter, Strieber stated that his primary concern was not discovering the identity of the "visitors," but rather "how to make this difficult and stressful experience useful, at least endurable, to those who have it."

After the publication of *Transformation*, Strieber began to put that statement into practice by attempting to communicate more directly with people who wrote him through planning a newsletter that will eventually serve as a means for linking the various groups that have arisen around the country in response to *Communion*. Through establishing the Communion Foundation, moreover, Strieber has begun to finance some research into the more debatable areas of ufology, specifically the question whether a secret government agency known as Majestic 12 (also known as MJ-12) has been managing "alien" affairs in the United States since 1947.[10]

I telephoned physicist and UFO researcher Stanton Friedman, Ph.D., who has been pursuing the MJ-12 story for years, to ask him about his estimation of Strieber's contribution to UFO research.

"Oh boy," he said. "That's a difficult question—to UFO research. We go in several different directions.

"Whitley's experience obviously isn't unique in the sense that obviously he's not the first abductee down the pike. It is unique in the sense I know of no other professional writer who has put words to the experience, in public, so that, for many people—and I've been in this field for a long time, since 1958 and very active since '67—in recent years, at least, Whitley has made a contribution to research on a couple of different levels. One is he got an awful lot of people talking about the subject. It's a subject that he has helped bring out of the closet, if you will, and that's good because, if you think about it for a minute, the more respectable the individual, the less likely he is to come out of the closet unless he becomes certain that he isn't the first guy to go down the pike. And so Whitley, I think, regardless of whether people buy everything that he says, he is obviously an intelligent person—this is not a dink, this is not a George Adamski—and so his coming out of the closet has been a very good thing in terms of reawakening concern and interest in publishers and all that sort of stuff. That's on the one hand.

"On the other, he has forced discussion among the UFO community, as well as among many others, about things like the relevance of hypnosis, the legitimacy of control systems—these esoteric sorts of questions. But he has pushed the discussion. He is also making a matching contribution on a research project on MJ-12. You know, I've got a long history in this field, and one of the greatest frustrations for me has been that I'm not rich. You know *The Roswell Incident* got started with me, the first three stories, and then I shared them with Bill [Moore] and then we went full speed ahead and I was supposed to get a big acknowledgment in the book and I didn't. I thought I was paying my dues for a book by Bill and me, but thanks to dear Mr. [Charles] Berlitz, that fell away. I didn't get my acknowledgment, and I was very unhappy with the book.

"But my phone bill was running eight hundred to a thousand dollars a month, and the frustration has been when you know things to do. Now I've spent time at fourteen archives and it's been so frustrating to want to devote full time in a scholarly, straightforward, sensible way when you can't afford it. The Fund [for UFO Research] has been good, because they've paid expenses on a couple of trips. . . .

"But this time around, with Whitley's grant assuring I will get the support that the Fund has requested, it's going to make a hell of a difference, to get paid for my time. That grant will be extremely important."

Friedman sees it as absolutely essential to provide journalists and other public communicators with accurate information about UFOs—hence the importance of research.

"What I found consistently across the country—and this has an impact on people's reaction to Whitley, as well—is that I talked to a lot of journalists, a lot of people who are going to make television programs, and documentaries and what have you—you know, most of which never come to fruition," he said. "What I find is that, almost invariably, they have vastly underestimated the amount of data that's out there. They haven't done their homework—they think they can round it all up in a week, read a few tabloids, and that's all there is to it. So I very quickly disabuse them of this because there's an enormous amount of information out there.

"The problem is that most media people think that all viewpoints have equal value. And I find this, as a scientist, a totally objectionable viewpoint.

"I think that this research opportunity could provide a real incentive—from the Fund's viewpoint. There were some people who were hesitant—'Can we raise money, actually, in large chunks? and secondly is there research to be done?'—so his providing the last package of dough and presuming I do a decent job, no matter what the results are, I think that may provide a real incentive for the Fund and other groups to say there are other people involved in supporting decent pieces of research."

There are some areas of research dealing with abductions in the UFO community, however, that are less popular than the classic question of government cover-up. One is the area of UFOs and cattle mutilations. This topic has seen a great deal of attention from Tom Adams, of Paris, Texas, who along with his wife, Christa Tilton, edits the *Stigmata* and *Crux* newsletters, as well as from Linda Howe, a television journalist and producer currently living in the Denver area. Her award-winning 1978 video documentary, *A Strange Harvest*, was the first (and only) serious, in-depth journalistic examination of the cattle mutilation phenomenon ever aired.

Howe is one UFO investigator who does not see the UFO abduction phenomenon as essentially a mystical experience. In fact, she sees a parallel between the human abduction experience and that of the mutilation of cattle, as hard to believe as it might sound. Moreover, she tends to hypothesize that the aliens are involved with us in a big, cosmic con game.

I interviewed her by telephone from her Denver-area home.

CONROY: At least one person who has been abducted has reported seeing something akin to a cattle mutilation while aboard a vessel of some sort, a UFO. So this has led you, I understand, to remark that you see a parallel between the human abduction and the cattle mutilation phenomena.

HOWE: Correct.

CONROY: Could you expand on that?

HOWE: The case you're referring to is the Judy Doherty case, from the documentary film that I did, *A Strange Harvest*. During the making of the film I had begun exploring what was happening to the animals, with the idea that maybe it was an environmental contamination problem. During September, October, November, and December of 1979, I heard one off-the-record UFO story after another from deputy sheriffs, ranchers, fellow journalists, in association with the mutilation phenomenon.

In December or January, I was sent an audio cassette of a

hypnosis session in a doctor's office in Texas. It had been sent
. . . because the doctor realized that it involved some kind of
craft, some kind of beam, and an animal. . . . The researchers knew I was working on animal mutilations. . . . When I
heard [the tape] and the description of the pale beam of yellow
light with an animal squirming in the light, I knew that I had
to at least talk to the woman. And I did, over about two or
three months, trying to persuade her that, because of the incident in 1973, she might shed light on a film I was doing. . . .
And I contacted Leo Sprinkle[11] to do the hypnosis work.

When in March of 1980 the crew and Dr. Sprinkle and I
finally met with the woman, the four hours that he worked
with her was the very first time since 1973 that she saw, in the
hypnosis session, a brown-and-white calf as the animal that
was being taken up in this pale beam of yellow light. And in
the hypnosis she could see two small—she calls them "little
men"—with gray skin and eyes that had vertical pupils in pale
yellow irises—not the large, black-eyed creatures with the slits
for a nose and slits for a mouth and slits on the sides for the
ears, and no other definable features—with long arms that had
four appendages only—no opposable thumb, and at the end of
those appendages, long dark, clawlike nails. She watched them
excise parts from this calf, lower the calf back down into the
pasture in this pale yellow beam of light, and she knew that
the calf was dead when it landed on the ground.

That was the first encounter I had with what might be an
eyewitness account of an animal mutilation by beings that were
not human. The problem was it was a hypnosis session, and
they are not accepted as being highly credible. Leo Sprinkle
did a series of normal psychological evaluation tests on the
woman, and found her to be completely normal. The woman
herself went to the doctor in the first place, in the original
hypnosis session, because she had suffered migraine headaches
since 1973, when she and four of her family members had
watched this very bright light pace their car for about forty
minutes outside of Houston.

So there was a multiple eyewitness of five people to the original object in the sky. All five people to this day remember the
strange object. All five people remember Judy pulling the car

over to the side of the road, getting out, trying to see whatever it was more clearly. They all remember that she walked to the back of the car and everybody said that they thought she'd gotten back into the car, feeling nauseous and thirsty, complained to the other family members, and then driven home. Whatever this light in the sky was, it paced the car all the way to the house where they were going, and proceeded to do all kinds of strange antics in the sky, that all of the family members still remember today. The part that was only revealed under hypnosis is this strange duality of Judy feeling like she was standing by the side of a car, by the road, and yet some other part of her was inside of the craft watching these beings excise parts from the calf.

Now that description of people feeling like they're in two places at once has come up repeatedly in the human abduction literature. So has missing time. The family members realized when they got home that they had lost, I believe, about an hour and fifteen minutes that night. So here is a mutilation-related case that ties in every detail to the human abduction cases—missing time, the fact that Judy also saw her daughter examined on the craft by the beings—and she had also watched them excise parts from the calf. If that is true, it would be the one and only story that I know in which both the mutilation of an animal and a human abduction were juxtaposed in time.

After describing two cases in detail, Howe told me that many of the excisions seen in cattle mutilations dealt with the removal of the cows' and bulls' sexual organs. In light of this information, I opened the question whether Howe saw a parallel between such activity and the "genetic experimentation" spoken of by Hopkins, in which he reports people having lost sperm and ova during abductions. I also broached the question whether Howe saw the human abduction experience as having a mystical component, or rather as primarily a genetic operation.

> CONROY: Now, is there anything that you have seen in the pattern of the human abductions that—to get more specific now, talking about the removal of sperm and ova—anything in the patterns of the manner in which this is done that parallels

things that might be seen in the removal of sexual organs and so forth from mutilated cows and other animals?

HOWE: Well, I think that the comparisons are there, very much so. Sperm and ova in the humans, vaginal examinations in the cows and other animals, the removals of entire vaginal tracts and uteruses and the removal of penises and scrotum completely from the male animals. The skin—circular pieces of skin removed from the cattle, only hide deep, just like taking only a little hide-deep piece of flesh in the leg or some other part—

CONROY: And that would be parallel to the so-called gouging of flesh reported in human abductions?

HOWE: Exactly. And then there seem to me to be experiments by these intelligences about pain and fear. In humans, several abductees have spoken about how they have been subjected to excruciating pain. The woman in the Cimarron case had a vaginal exam—she's screaming and screaming, and she said she wanted to die. And then suddenly, something is done to her head and she begins to feel better. In other cases, people have felt like whoever the creatures are, that they're actually looking for thresholds of pain tolerance. Some abductees have suggested that they have that impression . . . .

Howe: That comes back to your question, which is so difficult to answer in a direct way: spiritual versus genetic experiment. There are so many complex patterns in all of this that what does provoke me the most is the idea that this intelligence could also be manipulating us spiritually.

CONROY: In other words, providing us with, so to speak, surrogate mystical experiences, while at the same time removing something from us either physically or psychically?

HOWE: Yes. . . . One of the things that keeps occurring to me is that perhaps the large black-eyed gray things are like somebody else's worker bees. That beyond them, controlling them, is perhaps an intelligence we have yet to encounter, and that it is this intelligence that is involved with this planet, and perhaps a lot of other planets, doing a variety of experiments because it is advanced beyond our comprehension in its ability to manipulate the physical universe. And that this intelligence might not necessarily exist full-time in the particular dimen-

The Strieber family, 1972. From left to right: Bruce Simpson,
Patricia Strieber Simpson, Daniel Simpson, Richard, Mary, Anne,
Whitley, and Karl.

Whitley at the Strieber family home in 1952

Whitley Strieber, after two and a half years of visitor experiences

The Strieber cabin in upstate New York

The bedroom where the abductions took place

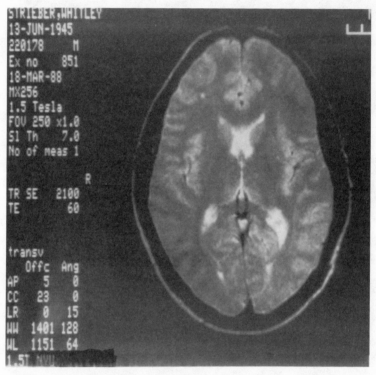

STRIEBER,WHITLEY
13-JUN-1945
220178   M
Ex no   851
18-MAR-88
MX256
1.5 Tesla
FOV 250 x1.0
Sl Th   7.0
No of meas 1

R

TR SE   2100
TE   60

transv
    Offc Ang
AP   5   0
CC   23   0
LR   0   15
WW 1401 128
WL 1151 64
1.5T

ABOVE AND OPPOSITE: Results of Whitley Strieber's Magnetic Resonance Imaging Test, March 18, 1988

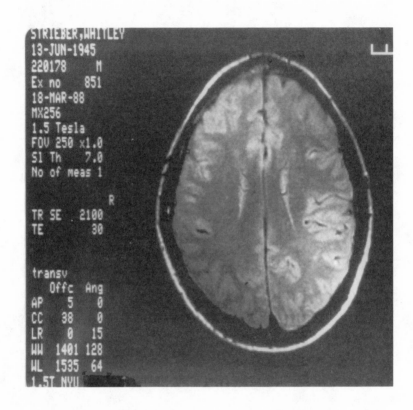
STRIEBER,WHITLEY
13-JUN-1945
220178   M
Ex no   851
18-MAR-88
MX256
1.5 Tesla
FOV 250 x1.0
Sl Th   7.0
No of meas 1

                    R
TR SE   2100
TE   30

transv
    Offc Ang
AP   5   0
CC   38   0
LR   0   15
WW 1401 128
WL 1535 64
1.5T NYU

Aerial photograph of San Antonio, Texas, with the Olmos Basin area

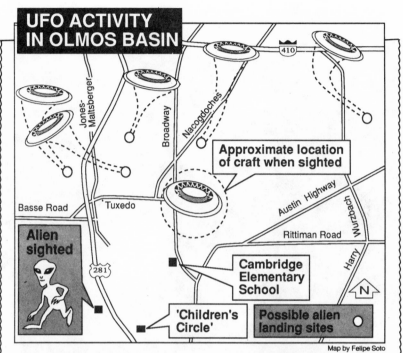

UFO ACTIVITY IN OLMOS BASIN

410

Jones-Maltsberger

Broadway

Nacogdoches

Approximate location of craft when sighted

Basse Road

Tuxedo

Austin Highway

Wurzbach

Rittiman Road

Harry

Alien sighted

281

Cambridge Elementary School

N

'Children's Circle'

Possible alien landing sites

Map by Felipe Soto

IF YOU'RE LOOKING to make contact with an outer-space visitor, Olmos Basin seems to be the hot spot. According to Whitley Strieber's books and sightings by San Antonian Ron McAtee, the area may have attracted a lot of UFO activity. McAtee, for instance, believes he saw a spaceship near the basin while he was standing in the Cambridge Elementary School playground. He also has sighted what he believes may be an alien near where U.S. 281 cuts through the basin. Strieber writes about an alleged "children's circle" in the woods behind Incarnate Word College, where he believes the aliens took him as a child. The additional circles on the map mark spots McAtee believes spaceships could land.

Map that appeared in the *San Antonio Express-News Sunday Magazine*, October 30, 1988

Philippe Mora and Whitley Strieber, on the "Gray Room" set, during the making of the film *Communion*

sion we live in. One of the intriguing ideas for me is the possibility that we could actually be at the end of a microscope that actually has its eyepiece in another dimension and that the grays themselves, as peculiar and strange as they are, may have been constructed precisely to interface in this dimension. That they are worker bees, creatures that carry out the bidding, almost on a high-minded robotic level, with no feeling, no sense of compassion. They are simply tools.

That also might explain why people seem to have a genuine encounter with something else that is not the black-eyed grays, whether it's the blond humanoid types or something else, in which they actually seem to have a level of communication that leaves them affected in a compassionate way. . . . I would challenge anyone to find a transcript dealing with the grays in which they felt compassion. . . .

There may be something akin to a chess game being played out here on a very complex level having to do with those unseen energies as well as the grays and the others. So when Whitley Strieber and Budd Hopkins come onto the stage with their experiences, I think that they are in some ways consistent in this regard: If the planet is an experiment, then individual humans may be experimented upon, also. This appears to me to be the masses of abductees who are taken for only physical reasons, nothing else. I agree with Budd Hopkins on that point one hundred percent. The majority of the abduction cases seem to be primarily for one thing and one thing only: to collect physical, biological tissue. Not any interest in communicating, not any interest in anything that humans would relate to as human communication or emotion.

In Whitley Strieber's case, his story began in great fear. His first title for his book was *Body Terror*. It became *Communion*, he says, at the insistence of the gray extraterrestrials he was dealing with. The ones that he has described, to my knowledge, are the large-black-eyed, small gray skinned ones, the ones that I'm beginning to suspect may be akin to somebody else's worker bees—robots.

Whitley Strieber has tried to describe his relationship with the grays as having the potential for some kind of spiritual transformation. I'm suspicious of spiritual transformation in the name of any creature that has no compassion. . . . Compassion, as I define it, is to feel a love and a connection with life and our fellow creatures. To me, it is one of the most important ingredients of human life as I understand it.

While Strieber has provoked his share of criticism from the UFO community, he has certainly also made some friends who share much of his point of view. One person with whom Strieber immediately struck up a cordial relationship was Jacques Vallee, Ph.D., the previously mentioned computer scientist whose books on the UFO phenomenon have long held respected spaces on many a researcher's bookshelf. Formerly associated with the late J. Allen Hynek, Vallee now lives in San Francisco.

The January 1989 interview that Vallee gave me, in my opinion, covers many areas of concern raised by this chapter: cultism, proper use of hypnosis in investigation, different ways of thinking about UFO research itself. It is also a representation of the voice of one of the UFO world's most independent thinkers. Even though he is far more a computer scientist that a ufologist, I include his comments here, for they are directed toward the UFO community. While Vallee works on the periphery of UFOdom, I think it appropriate that he have the last word in this chapter.

CONROY: How did you and Whitley Strieber meet?

VALLEE: We met at a conference in San Francisco called "Angels, Aliens, and Archetypes," [12] and we had a bit of lunch together with some other people. I introduced myself, and we started to talk about *Magnolia*, [13] and we became friends immediately.

CONROY: What were some of the things that he said that struck you?

VALLEE: What I find refreshing with Whitley, is that he knows literature, and he knows history. Most of the people who tend to gravitate to UFO research—or to the paranormal in general—have grown up in the traditional American culture which does not emphasize history. They think of an old book as a book that was written in the 1930s. Whitley shows a kind of interest in history—in the history of ideas, the history of science—that you find in Europe, in a lot of the more traditional

European education. So, that created a bond between us of common interests.

CONROY: Had you read *Communion* at the time you met Whitley?

VALLEE: Yes, I had read *Communion* and I was puzzled by it, like many people have been. I think meeting Whitley made a big difference in my assessment of the book.

CONROY: What was it you found puzzling about it, and what was it that changed after you met Whitley?

VALLEE: Well, when somebody gives you a personal story, a personal statement of an experience, it makes a big difference in your assessment of the person. . . . So, after meeting him, and realizing how he thought, and what else he did, and what else he was interested in, then I could go back to the book and read the book again.

CONROY: Well, on your second reading of the book, did you find more there than before?

VALLEE: Yes.

CONROY: One often reads of so-called "classic" UFO abduction experiences, or one reads of "classic" animal mutilation cases. There seems to be a tendency to try to hypostatize the experience or define that there's some kind of template—a procrustean bed, perhaps—into which one can fit these sorts of experiences. What did you find on that second reading?

VALLEE: One thing I found was that Whitley's experience was *not* the typical UFO experience. It was not "I believe in UFOs because I saw one and furthermore little people came out of it and took me inside it and did this and that to me." He says, "I don't know what this is, but I woke up and I saw this, and I had this impression, and I was terrified by this and that. By the way, a few days later, there was this strange disc in the sky." And the reader can make what he wants of it. On my first reading, that approach to it was obviously striking, but it was a little too slick—combined with his very professional style. [And] the fact that he had written some very good science fiction before, sort of made me cautious. At the same time, on the second reading, having met Whitley and being able to visualize him in that situation, he was then able to take me step by step through his experience. I wasn't reading a story anymore; I was living through the experience with him, and that made all the difference.

In fact, what he describes is much more what I hear from witnesses. What I hear is not the classic UFO abduction story. What I hear is, I find, a witness who is confused, who is terrified, traumatized by an experience—who very often doesn't know where to stop. Who is deluged with images and impressions. Usually what happens is some UFO investigator comes along, hypnotizes the poor guy, and out of it comes a classic experience. That's what I've objected to for a long time, and Whitley, because he's gifted with a command of the language and has experience with introspection, was able to deliver the experience in a much clearer way. That's why his book was so successful.

CONROY: Let's talk about this in relation to your previous research. For the purposes of background, how did you develop the strain of thought that led to your book *Passport to Magonia?*

VALLEE: I first approached the problem from an astronomical perspective, looking at the statistics of the sightings, trying to relate them to things in the sky, then looking for patterns on the ground, in geography and time, that could be correlated. I failed, but in the process of failing, I generated a lot of data and kept looking for patterns in that data. And that led me to the realization that as that body of data expanded, so to speak, both in time—across cultures—and in space, it led me to the question of exactly "When did all this start?" I was still pursuing the idea that if the phenomenon was real, it must be—the best explanation was that it was from outer space. Today, as you know, I still think it is one of the hypotheses. We'll never be able to prove that it isn't, but I don't think that's the best possible hypothesis at all.

In the process of looking at exactly when this began, the link with the body of literature, especially from medieval times, about similar entities soon became obvious. I was led to that by the large mass of information from the French data about landings. I was looking through some notes recently and I found a statement by one of the American groups, NICAP, which was one of the best groups in the sixties, I think after the time of

Socorro,[14] saying that in the past there have been only a few examples of landing reports, which were generally unreliable. And, it's just amazing that people would have said that in the mid-sixties. By the mid-fifties we had hundreds of documented landings, with small creatures and such associated with them.

It was going over that material that convinced me to start looking for the link in terms of behavior, of the behavior of these creatures—the link to Magonia.

CONROY: To backtrack for a second to the NICAP era, if I'm not mistaken, there is a statement in *Dimensions* to the effect that NICAP had political reasons for not paying attention to landing and entity-related phenomena, in that they were interested in getting Congress to investigate UFOs.

VALLEE: Of course. We are in danger of falling into the same pitfall right now, in that there is a movement now to demand new congressional hearings about MJ-12 and everything else. In order to do that, of course, one has to ignore a great part of the absurd material which is part and parcel of the UFO problem. That was a situation where NICAP, in those days—at least part of the explanation was that they were just embarrassed by the landings. And the other part of the thing was that most of the landing reports came from Europe, and they didn't trust anything that came from Europe. They had blinders. They were really looking exclusively with American data. It was also part of the Air Force effort—a cultural bias. Whitley, of course, is remarkable, in that he is free of that bias.

Now, in saying all this—if I had been with him in his cabin in New York, I am not saying that I would have seen the same thing. I don't know what I would have seen, and that's a question I ask myself all the time. Would the phenomenon have been there? Would I have been able to perceive it? Are there phenomena that one perceives when the person next to him would not perceive it? That is the most difficult, most troubling aspect of this whole thing.

CONROY: So, you reached a point where you became receptive to *Magonia* material.

VALLEE: Of course. Once you do that—you just don't stop. One source will lead you to another, and another, and another. This was not a small amount of literature. [Even though] people like Budd Hopkins have implied that this was just a vague folklore. This has been a major source of concern for scholars for several centuries.

CONROY: This eventually led to your hypothesis that there is some kind of metalogic, a spiritual or psychic control system going on.

VALLEE: One of the things that led me to the fact that the phenomenon did not begin in 1947 or even 1900, was that that behavior seemed to be similar, if not constant, through history. The other thing that led me to that was just looking at the trends in the shape and structure of current waves,[15] recent waves, and noticing that the phenomenon behaves like a schedule of reinforcement, in other words like a training system. So there was both a historic component and a modern component.

CONROY: This leads me to some questions about *Messengers of Deception*. I was wondering how you evaluate your work in that book, now ten years later, in the light of the transition from what was previously a, so to speak, "contactee" UFO subculture, to what has now become, apparently, an "abductee" subculture.

VALLEE: That's a tough question. I think the jury is still out regarding *Messengers of Deception*. . . . [It] was written after the frustration I had with the cults. We tend to forget that there was a time when there were a lot of people joining cults. I saw a lot of UFO witnesses who had no place to turn. The only people who would listen to them were the cults. The cults, of course, had the answers—wonderful, wonderful answers—and I was just very frustrated with them. I felt that somebody had to have the guts to say, "Look, this is a complex phenomenon, we don't understand it. It is real, and the solution is not to worship it, or to blindly follow anybody who pretends to have an answer. Let's step back and look at what it's doing to us."

In the process, I had to dredge up a lot of things that I had in my files that the UFO experts had been keeping away from, that they just did not want to deal with. . . . Again, the book just scratched the surface. The problem with the structure was that—and in this I will take full responsibility for it—as it was written, the book was not a logical development of a theory or idea. So, if you did not read it carefully, you could be left with the impression that I was saying that the phenomenon was a human manipulation, which is absolutely *not* what I was saying. But I left that impression. I can understand why people were discouraged.

CONROY: I had a problem with it myself.

VALLEE: Well, what is encouraging to me now, is that, in light of the current movements with MJ-12 and all of that, I'm very glad that I wrote *Messengers* the way I did, because I think all of that is coming back now, coming back with a vengeance. For example, the "Cover-Up" documentary[16] was a perfect illustration of that. You just watch that documentary and go back and read *Messengers*, and you'll agree that maybe the book was a little ahead of its time.

CONROY: Yes, there are some very curious politics in the development of that television special, I found.

VALLEE: The more you dig into it the more wonderful it becomes. It's very strange.

CONROY: Anticult people have expressed their concerns of Whitley himself becoming the leader of some new cultural phenomenon that could become cultlike. Do you think that this is a misapprehension?

VALLEE: I think Whitley could be a catalyst for new ideas in the field, including some ideas that border on the mystical or the religious. . . . [But] Whitley has no interest in being a cult leader, he doesn't say that he has the answer. I think he stresses that he does *not* have the answer. You know, a cult has a high demand of dogma that you follow and so on. A cult has very well-characterized social values. Any sociologist can recognize those features, and they are not present in anything I've seen Whitley do until now. I don't think that's his personality or his interest. He is becoming a focus, clearly, for a lot of reports from people who share his experiences, but I don't think those people are looking for a single answer. . . .

CONROY: There seems to be a growing dichotomy among people who are concerned about abductions, in that Budd Hopkins, Jerry Clark, and David Jacobs and others of their colleagues have formed an association which seems to be trying to typologize the abduction experience and to typologize "abductees." Moreover, they seem to have a rather predetermined manner of dealing with abductees in their support groups. Whitley, on the other hand, is more anarchic in his approach to dealing with people—he corresponds with them and meets with them on occasion—and insists that, in essence, the experience is mystical. Whitley has alleged to me that Hopkins is trying to create a model of abduction which will be acceptable to people in the social and behavioral sciences. Do you see any indication of that kind of effort on the part of people who consider themselves serious ufologists?

VALLEE: Well, you've raised a whole number of things. I think that there is nothing wrong with trying to come up with a typology or taxonomy of abductions and abductees and classifications and so on. That's one of the things that science does well, and why not use it? Certainly Budd Hopkins and Jerry Clark and David Jacobs are the right people to do it. They have a lot of data and they've had firsthand experience with it. . . . I think Tom Bullard has done some of that and that's good work, so let's see how far it goes. Good luck on convincing the social scientists on anything! I think if you've read the books by Hilary Evans, who is certainly one of the good minds in this business, you'll see that he handles the same material in a completely different way.

[But] my concern is not with that kind of activity. I think hypnosis is often mistaken for a scientific tool that gives you correct answers—complete answers—all the time, which is a huge misunderstanding of hypnosis. I am obviously outside my field, and Budd Hopkins and David Jacobs will immediately jump on me, and they are right. It's outside their field, too.

In the few cases where I have advised use of hypnosis with some witnesses, I've gone to professional psychiatrists who were M.D.'s and used hypnosis in a clinical practice. And what they told me convinced me of the great, great care that should be taken when applying hypnosis to this kind of problem. So, I think that, when hypnosis is done by a researcher who already knows about the UFO problem and has a strong personal belief, I think that's scientifically worthless.

CONROY: Do you think it's therapeutically worthless, also?

VALLEE: (Pause) I think it raises some very complex ethical

considerations. I know that some of these researchers say, "Look, nobody will talk to these people; at least I'm doing some good, I'm giving them an explanation." I think there is an interesting ethical debate there. . . . Very often, UFO witnesses will tell you, or imply, "You're a scientist. Please tell me this was a helicopter! Please tell me there was some good explanation of this," or "Please tell my wife this was some new prototype from Vandenberg Air Force Base." You have to tell them, "No, it wasn't a helicopter, it wasn't a prototype." The next question is: "Well, what are those things?" And you have to say, "We don't know." I think that's the honest reply. Budd [Hopkins] is infuriated when I say that. He says, "Look, these people need an answer, let's give them an answer, and the best answer we have is that they were abducted by extraterrestrials."

Well, you know, I don't believe that. My approach to that is to tell people, "Look, science doesn't deal with certainty. Science is not what's in the science books. Science is addressing the mysteries of the world. There are many mysteries. . . . And that's what science is all about."

Sure they have been disturbed, but the very fact of being able to talk to somebody who doesn't deny their experience is therapeutic. I have seen people to whom I've [suggested], "Let's sit down calmly and go over this." If you have some amount of charisma, or at least trust—if you can establish a basis of trust and people know that you're not going to sell them a theory, that you're going to listen to them—you give them permission and they will tell you things. You see the same thing happen with people who have been molested when they were children. There are things that people have never told anybody. When they find someone they can trust, whom they can rely on confidentially, and who shows some regard for them as a person, then a simple conversation in some coffee shop somewhere can be extremely therapeutic. You just need permission to look into their own souls, so to speak, or their own experience. It's a very emotional experience for both people, and there is an ego trip that takes over. . . . There is a power trip associated with that.

That's the other thing that worries me. I don't believe anymore that some of the researchers into abductions are doing it for the good of the people or out of concern for the human race, I think it's become a huge power trip. That bothers me. There is nothing wrong with having an ego, nothing wrong with selling books, but you shouldn't be mistaken about your own motivations.

CONROY: What you are implying, then, is perhaps the power of Whitley's narrative derives from the fact that it seems to have given permission to many, many people, throughout the country or throughout the world, who've read his book, to suddenly admit to themselves things that happened to themselves and tell this to other people.

VALLEE: Yes. Let me complete what I just said. . . . Philip Klass would say that hypnosis is done unscientifically and it just dredges up things that didn't really happen and convinces people that they've been abducted. I don't believe that. I believe that the hypnosis, if done unscientifically, clobbers an experience which is indeed a latent experience and should be retrieved. I think something happened to these people, I think there is a UFO phenomenon, and to that extent I agree with Budd Hopkins, I agree with David Jacobs, I agree with Jerry Clark, that rushing into hypnotizing these people is not the way to do it. In fact, it's detrimental, because of the fact it overlays preconceived ideas on top of a very, very complex matrix of images and emotions and everything else. What Whitley has done is to go farther than anybody else in describing that matrix.

CONROY: I imagine that you are aware that Hopkins and Clark are extremely critical of Whitley and regard him as mentally unstable.

VALLEE: Yes.

CONROY: What do you think might be their motivations for doing this? Whitley claims that it is because they cannot deal with what he calls the "high strangeness factor" in his experience, and he accuses them of editing that out of the accounts of abductions that they deal with. . . .

VALLEE: My reading of that is that indeed there is a need to rationalize a problem at all costs, and that need is satisfied—and it is a normal drive—if you get rational answers. The problem is that, of course, there are creatures described in connection with UFOs that behave in an absurd way. So, now we recapture the rational approach by saying, "Aha! What they are doing is a very complex scientific survey of our planet that involves genetic manipulation and so on." Again we have succeeded in rerationalizing the experience.

The problem is that, when you look at the theory, of course, it doesn't explain the facts, because if you were doing genetic manipulation or scientific surveys of the earth or all that, you obviously wouldn't do it that way. So, you really have not explained anything, but you *look* like you've explained something. The more the facts continue to contradict your explanation, the more frustrating that becomes, and then you have to lash out at anybody who doesn't quite agree with you. I have been the target of those attacks, [though] not as much as Whitley. . . . There's nothing you can do about it. It's a normal thing. But I think that as the evidence continues to accumulate, that this particular theory is not the answer.

CONROY: I get the feeling that you keep a certain distance from the UFO community.

VALLEE: I see the UFO problem as a subset of a larger problem that I'm interested in, which is the paranormal in general. Most of the UFO community is only interested in UFOs—they've never heard of some of the other things that I'm interested in. . . .

There are many people who are true scientists, true researchers. I don't think the answers are going to come from an organized group or any one particular theory. We are a long way from that, and so I'm not ready to join anything. I certainly talk to everybody.

I asked Vallee, now that he'd known Strieber for over a year, what he thought of *Transformation*. He replied to the effect that the question of Strieber's mental stability seemed, after his reading of the book, unnecessary. "This may be a phenomenon that you maybe need to be a different personality to appreciate. Maybe it centers, at least in some cases, around people who have a different way of dealing with reality."

Chapter 5

Invasion of the Body Snatchers: The Sequel

American Mass Culture Lies in Wait for *Communion*

J. Allen Hynek, during a break in the 1984 MUFON convention in San Antonio, gave me a brief interview. I asked him what he thought was the American public's general attitude toward the subject of UFOs, particularly because at that time there had not been any major UFO sighting "flap" in years.

Without hesitation, he said, "After America went to see Steven Spielberg's *Close Encounters of the Third Kind*, UFOs have become 'real.' The only thing is, now that they're real, people's next response is, 'So what?' "

I found Hynek's observation to be trenchant, for it implied that we Americans no longer attach much importance to distinguishing between fabricated and real events. It also seemed to indicate a certain sensitivity on the part of the American entertainment industry toward specific hopes and fears at a mass level in the general population. After all, one of the myths of contactee groups during the 1950s and 1960s was the concept that there would someday come a time when UFOs would descend upon the earth in a "mass landing," or that at least one truly certifiable, undeniable sighting would occur and be recognized by officialdom, thereby vindicating their vigil and changing the course of history. No such events occurred, of course, so it was up to

Hollywood to provide us with a surrogate experience. Instead of thousands of UFOs landing in the parks and plazas of American cities and towns, we were given the nightly spectacle of one, huge mother ship landing on the silver screens of thousands of movie theaters across the country. For many "believers," it was the next best thing to real "alien" contact, given the fact that the producers had employed Hynek and other ufologists as consultants in an effort to make the film as true to life as possible. For the rest of us, it was entertainment.

In the years that followed *Close Encounters of the Third Kind*,[1] the filmgoing public has seen a proliferation of science fiction films in which the alien has assumed the status of a protean cultural icon, a catch-all for images ranging from bizarre monsters and galactic policemen to gnostic savants and cute, cosmic teddy bears. We've even seen the return of the "pod people" in the last decade, with the remake of the classic *Invasion of the Body Snatchers*,[2] that now legendary fable of middle-American xenophobia. The future has arrived, and with it the aliens as tools used as much by filmmakers to titillate our fears and fantasies as to (somewhat less frequently) boldly question our assumptions about prevailing social norms.

Given the now pervasive presence of aliens on the silver screen, could any new film about alien intervention in human life be anything other than simply entertainment? Is there some kind of neutralizing factor in the American public's inordinate ability to consume (and swallow) just about any kind of product, even a story of "alien abduction"? What makes Strieber's "visitors" any different from previously seen aliens, anyhow?

These questions and others confront the makers of the film version of *Communion*, a project over which Strieber has insisted that he maintain artistic control. Slated for release in autumn of 1989, *Communion* the film poses some considerable artistic challenges. To quote Strieber: "It can't be filmed as an actual documentary. What I was trying to do when writing the script was to capture the emotional impact of the experience as it affected me and my whole family. It is a drama about a family under tremendous pressure from an unknown source."

Philippe Mora (whose most recent films include *Death of a Soldier* and *The Howling III: The Marsupials*), takes the helm as director in this project, written and filmed during a time when most of Hollywood was in creative limbo because of the ongoing writers' strike. Yet there was no consequent lack of talent for the film. In fact, the principal actors are rather stellar: Christopher Walken and Lindsay Crouse take the roles of Whitley and Anne Strieber, respectively. Strieber wrote the screenplay himself. When the film finally makes it into the movie houses, it will be the first feature-length film for theatrical release dealing with the subject of aliens to be based, not on a work of fiction, but upon the real-life experiences of a contemporary American family.[3]

Strieber was not entirely new to the film business, having already formed a partnership with Mora to create a company they called Pheasantry Films. (Mora and Strieber had originally worked toward making a film based on Strieber and Kunetka's *Warday*.) In October of 1987, I asked Strieber to explain some of the circumstances around the genesis of *Communion*, the film:

"In *Variety* it was reported that we were making the film with Allied Vision International in London, which is true," he said. "They are one of the financing entities, along with Bancannie. We tried to get one of the big distributors, like MGM or Columbia or Orion to take the picture on the basis of me and Philippe retaining total creative control, but they would not do it. They would not allow us to have total creative control. So we decided to finance the film independently, which is the route we took."

Richard Strieber, Whitley's brother, handled a great deal of the negotiations for the film version of *Communion* and was present at that same interview in my office. "It's important to point out that one of the problems with giving up a certain amount of creative control is that it will hamper the establishment of a viable, functioning production company, and our goal, of course, is to establish just such a company," he said.

Yet while Whitley Strieber single-handedly wrote the *Communion* screenplay, the actual job of putting it onto celluloid fell into the hands of a man who has known him for twenty years. Philippe Mora, though born in Paris, is an Australian citizen who has been residing in the United States for the past twelve years. While he has eleven films to his credit, Mora was in fact a painter in his early career, working and exhibiting in London from 1967 through 1972. It was there in 1968 that he met Whitley Strieber, then a student at the London School of Film Technique.

In an interview in December 1988, I asked Mora what it was he remembers of Strieber at that time.

"Well, Whitley had a tremendous sense of humor," he said. "He still does, and we got on in that regard. We got on intellectually, I guess. We were interested in similar things, we had the same taste in motion pictures, and the arts, and really that's what we were talking about, as I recall, most of the time. It was books, and movies, movies, movies."

Curiously, though, Mora said he never saw any of Strieber's early films, so he was unable to render an opinion on his friend's capabilities as a film student.

As fortune would have it, Strieber left London to return to the United States, while Mora became a London-based filmmaker.

"In London I made documentaries," he said. "I made *Brother Can You Spare a Dime*, which was a history of America in the thirties, and another feature called *Swastika*, which became quite famous because we found Eva Braun's home movies in the Pentagon in Washington. It was amazing footage, it was extraordinary footage, showing Hitler and the intimate circle at Berchtesgaden in color. That was in 1973. I did a musical film in 1969 called *Trouble in Molopolis*, which starred Germaine Greer, as an interesting little footnote. She was an actress then, just before she wrote her book, *The Female Eunuch*."

Later Mora went to Australia to make a film with Dennis Hopper called *Mad Dog Morgan*, and has had a career moving from genre to genre ever since. I asked him if he considered versatility to be one of his strengths as a director.

"Certainly it's something I set out to do," he said. "I've always admired the Hollywood directors of the Michael Curtiz school, who were able to jump from various genres. He directed *Casablanca*, and everything else."

I used this theme of changing genres in opening my interview with Mora.

CONROY: Would you consider *Communion* to be a jump into a new genre for you?

MORA: Well, *Communion* really is a genre unto itself. It's not really a genre picture. It has some obvious similarities to some serious science fiction films, but I've always called it science faction, because it's based on a true story. So it's not a fantasy, and in that sense it's a unique kind of project, because it's made from a true story.

CONROY: How were you brought into the project?

MORA: Well, Whitley and I were working on *Warday* to-gether, before Whitley wrote *Communion*. I think it was like early '86 when I met Whitley in New York, and I hadn't seen him for a while. And that's when he told me he'd been having these experiences. It was in '85 that he started having them, isn't that right?

CONROY: Yes.

MORA: So it was early '86 when I had lunch with him in New York. He obviously was very bothered about something, and after I promised I wouldn't laugh at him, he told me that he believed he'd been abducted by these beings. That was when he was just beginning to write it all down. It was something I was very interested in, being an old friend of his. It was such a fascinating story, and obviously he was terribly sincere about it. There was absolutely no doubt in my mind that something was up, because of his intensity at that lunch. I think I was one of the first people to be privileged to read the first version of *Communion*.

CONROY: What was your feeling, what were some of your thoughts, reading the manuscript?

MORA: I found it incredibly convincing. You know, from about that point on, we discussed making a film at some point.

CONROY: The purpose of that lunch in New York was to discuss the possibility of a production of *Warday?*

MORA: No, I had just finished a film called *Death of a Sol-dier*, which was a true story about American troops in Australia in 1942. I was screening it in New York, and I was calling up old friends to have a look at it, and I called Whitley up. He came over and saw it, and really liked the film and we just renewed our friendship. That was all there was to it. After that period we started developing *Warday*.

CONROY: How far did it get?

MORA: Well, it got pretty close. This is how Christopher Walken got involved in the *Communion* movie: We were going to use Christopher Walken in *Warday*, and we got quite close to doing it, and then it became quite obvious that *Communion* was fascinating to so many people and that it was crazy not to do that first. So we switched to *Communion*.

CONROY: What was it about [Walken] that you wanted?

MORA: A couple of things. Firstly, it's very hard to get any so-called stars to convincingly portray a writer, an intellectual, because it's a difficult thing for an audience to grasp what a writer does. [With] other characters—a builder, or any sort of physical activity—it's easy to understand what the person does. But to actually portray intellectual activity on the screen is very difficult. I thought Christopher Walken could do it. The other thing is, the whole crux of this movie is that it's about a man who thinks he's going crazy—or he's not going crazy, he's been abducted by these beings, which is even more extraordinary. Either way he's facing these incredible things in the unknown, or he's going crazy. Now that sort of *a priori* demands a great actor. And in my opinion, Christopher is one of the best actors around, and has the depth to pull this off.

CONROY: What was his response when you approached him with the idea of playing Whitley?

MORA: Well, it was very favorable. He said he'd like to do it, so we went down and met with Whitley at Whitley's apartment in SoHo. . . .

Then Lindsay Crouse, she plays his wife. You know, I'm tremendously pleased with her performance. I think she's done a fantastic job. The interesting thing about casting her is she's married to a famous writer.

CONROY: Yes, David Mamet, if I'm not mistaken.

MORA: Yeah, so she has a whole other perspective on this, from the intimate point of view—all the creative angst that could go on in the process of creating a book. And I felt that was really valuable to this, because Anne wasn't a character, really, in the movie and, in reality, she hadn't had these experiences at that point. What bothered her was a fear of her marriage falling apart. Again, there's sort of a complex personal drama going on, which is why we needed an actress who could do it. Lindsay, in my view, is perfect for that.

In the movie, obviously there are a few levels to all this. Obviously, there is the level of *Communion* itself, which is the issue of what happened to Whitley, and the extraterrestrials, or rather, terrestrials that we haven't seen before—people or beings from another dimension or whatever these things are. And then there is the point of view, of what this did to the family, and how the family kept together against this threat. . . . This is shown in the film pretty clearly.

Then, the other level of it was sort of examining the creative process of a writer coming up with a work. In this case it was based on something that affected him deeply, but there was still a lot of creative angst going on. That's where the supportive wife came in. You put all those things together and you've got a fascinating story.

CONROY: Who is the actor who plays the boy, Andrew?

MORA: His name is Joel Carlson, and he was chosen by— they call it "reading actors." I read a lot of these kids here, and I got it down to three. . . . So I then had Lindsay and Christopher come in and meet the three finalists. We all mutually decided that Joel was the one that they were most sympathetic to.

CONROY: What were some of the qualities about him that you found winning?

MORA: I thought that he was totally unaffected and unpretentious. This is something that comes across on screen, he's just a pure little actor, fantastic.

He met the real Andrew. When they were filming, Andrew came out, and they became friends. Obviously, Joel was a couple of years younger than Andrew, because by then it was a couple of years later. But they got along very well.

CONROY: That must have been quite a fascinating experience for Andrew—to meet his cinematic counterpart.

MORA: Yes, absolutely. I think it was quite a dramatic experience for Whitley and Anne, too, to suddenly see these things being portrayed.

CONROY: Yes, I'm sure. . . . Well, I really don't know anything about the film business, but from my point of view as a journalist I've read that there seems to be a custom of directors not liking to have writers on the set. I don't know if that's true or not, but how was it, having Whitley and Anne on the set?

MORA: Well, when we were actually filming there was no one present; that is really for the actors. . . . It's very tough acting for film, because you wait in a trailer for eight hours, and then someone snaps their fingers and you're expected to put in a good performance, you know, on call. So any distractions are very complicated, but Whitley's involvement was total with me throughout the picture. I would say that ours was a much closer relationship than the normal director-writer relationship. Ours was a total collaboration from day one, so really he was sensitive to my needs and I was sensitive to his, and these issues never really came up.

CONROY: I'm wondering about the technical challenges this film represented, of making believable alien figures.

MORA: Well, the special effects are complicated, because there are four different kinds of aliens. There're the little blue guys; there's a little robotic, toylike figure that came in like a scout into the bedroom before the blue guys burst in. Then there was the, for want of a better description, the *Communion* figure—the one with the big dark eyes, taller, feminine, kind of figure. Then there's a fourth figure that we reveal in the film. It's a figure that Whitley saw once—a version of the *Communion* figure that actually showed that the face was a kind of mask, and there was something underneath.

From the technical point of view, it is complicated. We used every conceivable form. We used puppets, we used little people inside suits, we used remote control robots, sculptures, masks, the whole smorgasbord, if you like, to make it work. . . . The whole story is cinematic, with layers of reality. Is he imagining it, or is he not imagining it? The film really takes the position of "What do you think?" . . . It makes for a fascinating movie.

CONROY: There are some people out in the skeptical community, such as Philip J. Klass—I imagine you've heard his name once or twice—who are making comments already about the film, in advance of having seen it. Klass in particular is raising a red flag, saying this film will only incite unnecessary public anxiety about "abductions."

MORA: (Laughs) That's terribly funny. How could he know if he hasn't seen the film?

CONROY: Speaking about humor, Whitley, as you mentioned, is something of a prankster in his personality. Does this aspect of his personality come through in the film?

MORA: It does, yeah. Not in the sense of pranks, but his sense of humor. . . .

CONROY: With the exception of the more or less benevolent

and saintly aliens who come forth from the mother ship in
Close Encounters of the Third Kind, and the cuddly little fellow
in *E.T.: The Extra-Terrestrial,* most aliens have been either
sort of cosmic policemen like Michael Rennie in *The Day the
Earth Stood Still* or monsters, essentially. I don't know of too
many other types.

MORA: No. Well, I think Whitley subscribes—I'm not going
to put words in his mouth—to the point of view, and I certainly do, that Jacques Vallee has expressed in his latest book,
Dimensions, that these things are much stranger than just being
able to be explained by these clichéd ideas of extraterrestrials.

But getting back to a serious response to Philip Klass: Just
for the record, there's no way that this thing could cause anxiety, because this is a very serious attempt at trying to get a
grasp on what this experience is. I think you'll see, when you
have a look at the picture, that if anything—inasmuch as it
examines it from every angle—it's much more of a calming
conclusion than an anxiety-causing movie.

CONROY: Is that because in the end there's a personal resolution of conflict in the film?

MORA: On a human basis, everything stays together. And I
must say, I was very aware of the danger of making a picture
that would scare the shit out of everybody, because film is such
a powerful medium. It was something, too, that Whitley was
very concerned about—to spread some kind of paranoia or
something like that. So, in fact, the film is exactly the opposite
of what Philip Klass is saying. It's not *Alien.* It couldn't be
further removed. If anything, I would compare it to *2001: A
Space Odyssey.*

CONROY: In the sense that there's a transcendent element
there?

MORA: And it examines the issues seriously. *2001* was the
first movie that seriously examined these issues in nontabloid
fashion. I'm making the comparison strictly in terms of content, not in terms of being a "space movie," because *Communion* is not a "space movie" at all. It's more internal space, or
psychological space.

CONROY: There are no rocket ships, no flying discs in the
picture?

MORA: The only flying saucer in *Communion* is a wooden one in Andrew's schoolyard.

CONROY: But there were some strange flying lights that I saw one day, watching the dailies with you in New York. There was some strange ball of light that seemed to come out of the right-hand edge of the screen.[4]

MORA: We never found out what that was. We wondered if it could be a taillight on the helicopter. The pilot said it was impossible for it to come out like that and sweep back again. The camera was in a fixed position.

CONROY: Are you going to include that in the film?

MORA: No.

CONROY: There was also something that appeared to be anomalous, a light in the sky that I saw in a scene that was shot from the top of one of the multistory buildings in SoHo looking down onto the roof garden. Do you remember that—there was some sort of streak in the sky?

MORA: Yeah.

CONROY: Is that in the film?

MORA: I think that is in there, with no editorial comment about it.

CONROY: Now that you've finished editing the film, is there anything you could have done differently?

MORA: I make every film knowing that I'm putting every ounce of energy into it, so I'll have no regrets that I could have done more. And that's how I feel about this. I'm tremendously pleased with this picture. It's easily the best picture that I've done. I'm very pleased with the performances, and I think Whitley's story is an incredible one. I have no complaints, no misgivings. That's in all sincerity.

CONROY: I understand. Would you estimate that it was the most fascinating subject matter that you've ever worked on?

MORA: Yes.

CONROY: Speaking of fascination, Whitley took the liberty of mentioning that once, when you were staying at his cabin, that he believes something possibly occurred to you one night. Do you feel like talking about that?

MORA: Yeah. Well, . . . Whitley and I went out for a walk before we went to bed, about ten-thirty at night, with Anne, and we saw what must have been three or four meteors, in the space of about twenty minutes, crashing through the sky, plus quite a bit of space junk flying around.

CONROY: What do you mean by "space junk"?

MORA: It looked like satellites, high up. The meteors were lower down. The satellites were moving up there, but moving not at an unusual speed. In other words, it looked as if it were a satellite, but I'm calling it space junk. I don't know what it was.

Then we all went to bed, and I still believe—I had one of these nightmares, quite vivid dreams. Now, you've got to bear in mind that I had been working with Whitley on the script, and I was psyched up, although I can't say [that] when I went to bed I was. I was relaxing. I had the experience of lights blasting through the bedroom window, lights blasting under the crack under the door of the bedroom—I tried to turn the light on in my room, and I couldn't turn it on and I was pushed back into the bed. All the while I was consciously saying to myself, "This is a hell of a nightmare."

Then I remember being outside the guest room door, in the kitchen area, and the whole cabin lit up—every opening, every exterior opening, the whole thing was lit up with moving lights. And I looked through to Andrew's bedroom. The door was open, and he was asleep, lit up. I remember Anne rushing up to me and saying, "Whatever you do, don't wake Andrew." And then I woke up the next morning, . . . very scared.

CONROY: Because of the complete bizarreness of the experience?

MORA: Yeah. And, you know, some of that feeling I definitely put in the movie. Even visually, with the lights. It was identical to what Whitley had described. Now again, we're on the high wire of: What was it? I believe it was a dream.

CONROY: Nothing comparable to that has happened in your life since then?

MORA: No. Not that I'm aware.

Strieber has on occasion said to me that he seems to have something of a "Typhoid Mary" effect on others, passing on the "visitor experience" as though it were some kind of contagion. Mora wouldn't go any further in speculating about his experience, but it is a rather curious one in the context of the experiences of other people who have visited his cabin. I have spoken to two women who remember sleeping on cots in the living room of Strieber's house only to be awakened, they said, by brilliant light streaming into the house from all the windows.[5]

If Mora is unwilling to voice any complaints about *Communion*, the movie, the opposite is certainly true of Strieber. When I asked Strieber in December of 1988 to bring me up to date on the structure of the company and the business of making the film, we had the following dialogue:

> STRIEBER: Philippe and I own the production company, fifty-fifty, and my brother has a small nonvoting share of it. There are two investors: one in London, and one in Sydney. There is one distributor at the moment: Vestron Pictures, for international distribution, and there is at the moment no U.S. distributor. This is a very contentious, constantly squabbling bunch of people, this group of investors and distributors. They are extremely difficult to deal with. Again, the creative end of it has been excellent, but the business end of it has been miserable. It's taken up far more time than it should, and I've so far spent about one hundred thousand dollars on the movie, just in terms of expenses, and not received a penny. And I'm beginning to suspect the likelihood of my receiving anything on this is very small. So I will have made a movie from a number one best-seller, lavished my time and effort on it, and had it be a very frustrating and not very rewarding experience. Certainly my relationships with the people involved have been pretty stormy and miserable. . . .
>
> I'm not comfortable with the attitudes the investors take. One of them seems to be at the point of litigation all the time, and the other seems curiously indifferent to things like tendering funds on schedule, and so on and so forth.
>
> The Vestron distributors' script notes lacked a great deal, I thought, in terms of depth and I was glad that they didn't have any power to enforce their ideas on us. For example, there's a very powerful scene in the movie where little Andrew tells Whitley for the first time he has encountered the visitors. The

Vestron people wanted that taken out because they didn't think it was enough like their idea of a seven-year-old and the way a seven-year-old would act and talk. Of course, the scene is taken from life, and I asked these people if they had kids. None of them did. So I left the scene in. They've been extremely unpleasant about the music for the picture. It's been an awful experience.

CONROY: Is the issue of a U.S. distributor also a matter of contention, at this point? (December 1988)

STRIEBER: There's been a lot of interest from one particular distributor that I think is absolutely second-rate, and I don't want anything to do with them, and so far the film hasn't been shown to anybody. We will show the film when it's finished.

CONROY: This is interesting, perhaps, as an indication of the trials and travails of an independent film these days. You're not dealing with a big studio, you're working outside the system, so to speak. Do you think this is characteristic of the problems of other people who are trying to do the same sort of thing?

STRIEBER: Oh yeah. It's characteristic.

While Strieber described his relationship with the people making the film as being "fairly stormy and miserable," he apparently expended some considerable effort toward improving his relationship with Philippe Mora. As this book was going to press, I discussed the matter with him. Strieber summed things up by saying, "We had a very difficult period when it was time for him to take over creative control and direct the picture. But the relationship survived—just."

It appears that perhaps Whitley Strieber did not end up having the absolute degree of artistic control over his film that he initially desired, but it would be fair to say that he did have a much greater degree of control over the film than would have been the case had he gone through a major studio. The appearance of films dealing with an "alien" theme in 1988 (*Alien Nation*, which featured James Caan, Mandy Patinkin, and Terence Stamp; and *My Stepmother Is an Alien*, with Dan Aykroyd and Kim Basinger, being two of the most notable examples) shows that Hollywood filmmakers and others continue to be just as fascinated with the popular appeal of this theme, if not more so, as it was in the 1950s, and are playing around quite a bit with the "alien" as a character.

What is significantly different about *Communion*, though, is that it represents a departure from the use of the alien as merely a fictional device or metaphor. Moreover, according to Mora, the film moves far away from using the figure of the alien purely for shock and horror value alone. Anyone familiar with *Communion* will be aware that the book was subtitled "A True Story," making the "visitors" who appear in certain scenes in the film into potentially much more than simply figments of Strieber's imagination. Certainly Strieber now regards them as real, independent entities. Moreover, the fact that a great deal of the drama of the film is based upon the conflict that occurred between Whitley and his wife, Anne, during his initial period of adjustment to what was happening to him gives an objective frame of reference to the film that is greater than the author's imagination.

Perhaps the fact that *Communion*'s visitors are not being presented as fictional devices may cause a certain amount of the filmgoing public to scoff at the film. It will be interesting to observe, too, whether some of the film's strongest critics may arise from the science fiction community. On more than one occasion, Strieber has commented to me that he finds some people in the science fiction world to have expressed generally hostile reactions to his book. One such comment was precipitated by a visit we made to a science-fiction and fantasy bookstore in New York City, in which the paperback edition of *Communion*, then the number 1 book on *The New York Times* best-seller list, was displayed at the very bottom of a bookshelf of other best-sellers, only a few inches from the floor.

Is there any substantiation for such an opinion? Perhaps so. The hostility of professional stage magicians toward the apparently paranormal feats of metal-bending displayed by Uri Geller may serve as an analogy of the attitudes of some science fiction fans before reports of UFOs and psychic phenomena.[6] In an article published in the May 1977 issue of the *Journal of Occult Studies*,[7] author David Swanson reported the results of a questionnaire administered to 184 people in four groups, three of whom were university students in courses on parapsychology, flying saucers, and the occult, respectively. The fourth was a sample from a group of people who had attended a science fiction convention in Boston. The questionnaires were designed to test for relationships between reading of science fiction and interest in paranormal subjects, as well as for the respondents' experiences with psychic phenomena and UFOs, in addition to their beliefs regarding such matters.

The results of the study are summarized in the abstract: "People who read extensively in Science Fiction do not tend to have psychic experiences and people who have strong psychic beliefs do not tend to read Science Fiction. The study discovers the existence of two mutually exclusive groups whose activities and interests do not appear to overlap even in unrelated areas such as UFOs."[8]

While the sample is small, and the study may be flawed in methodology, the observations pointed to in its conclusions are nevertheless interesting points of departure for thinking about what impact a film such as *Communion* may have upon what some authors have described as an already well-defined popular folklore regarding UFOs.

That such a folklore exists is an easily enough documentable fact. Photojournalist Douglas Curran's extraordinary book, *In Advance of the Landing: Folk Concepts of Outer Space*,[9] is perhaps the most comprehensive compilation ever published of contemporary North American UFO lore. Inasmuch as Curran personally drove over much of the continent to meet with and photograph prominent and not-so-prominent advocates of the idea of extraterrestrial contact, the images in this book, enhanced by a series of exceptionally well-written and informative essays, demonstrate the manifold ways in which UFOs and aliens have become firmly entrenched in popular thinking about life beyond the earth.

One of Curran's photographs, taken in the home of noted "abductee" Betty Andreasson, shows some remarkable images that are all the more interesting for their relation to Strieber's text in *Communion*. In a shot of a living area in which some of Andreasson's models of alien creatures are on display (one of them not entirely dissimilar to the image on the cover of *Communion*), we can also see three framed prints depicting three different species of owls (one of them a barn owl) on two of the walls of that room.[10] Skeptics might say, of course, that Strieber had perhaps included owls in his "abduction" narrative because he had found out that other abductees have a fascination with owls. Yet the coincidence, for what it is worth, remains.

While this anecdote may seem spurious, its relevance lies in its demonstration of the fact that some aspects of UFO folklore seem to share a common structure in images that may, or may not, have some relationship to actual events of a paranormal nature.

Yet the folklore of any people is a very curious thing. Its principal characters shift and change continually. While in the last forty years our aliens have been linked in the cinema with our fears of extinction and desires for adventure in space, the advent of a film such as *Communion* seems to be squarely placing the visitors—"real" as they are considered to be by Strieber—in the central character's inner, psychological space, as well. They are made to *commune* with them. This lack of a flashy "space age," high-tech motif in *Communion*, while a departure from Hollywood tradition, seems to be finding parallels in other recent films dealing with the concept of aliens.

Alien Nation, which was written for the screen by Rockne S. O'Bannon (and novelized by Alan Dean Foster) is a particularly noteworthy addition to the alien genre. In keeping with the political landscape of the late 1980s, this is a film dealing with the alien as cosmic refugee. While many reports of extraterrestrials associated with alien abductions describe such beings as highly secretive, the aliens in this film are quite public, announcing their presence by landing their flying-saucer-shaped craft under the full glare of television lights in the southern California desert. Upon telling the authorities that they are slaves who mutinied and commandeered their spaceship, they are welcomed into American society and officially dubbed "newcomers." Popularly, though, they are called "slags," and find themselves subject to a fair amount of racial discimination and bigotry. Given that the setting for the film is a grimy Los Angeles of the not too distant future (a place where immigrants from many countries form a prominent part of the local community), the characterization of the alien in this film is a social commentary of the most obvious sort.

Another relatively recent release, *Man Facing Southeast*,[11] an Argentinian production, likewise takes the alien theme and gives it an unusual twist. Because the text of this film is in Spanish, it has had only limited popular exposure. Nevertheless, its setting—an impoverished Latin American insane asylum—and its hero—a young man who exquisitely plays Bach organ fugues, calls himself Rantes and says he hails from another planet—provide the elements required for a thoroughgoing examination of what we normally consider "sanity" and the purposes of psychiatry itself. The film's development of the character of Rantes into something of a gentle messiah-figure who attracts a loyal following among the other inmates of the asylum is challenging, as are the implications of the destiny he faces at the hands of the asylum's authorities.

Back in the United States, though, perhaps the first film to deal

with the "illegal immigrant" metaphor, race, and the psychic component of UFO phenomena was John Sayles's 1984 feature, *The Brother
from Another Planet*. In this very contemporary comedy, Joe Morton
plays an alien whose spaceship crashes into the waters adjacent to New
York's Ellis Island, where generations of immigrants once passed. We
find he resembles a normal young black human in all respects save
two: He is mute, and his oversized feet are graced by huge, knobby
toes. As he passes through the old building that once housed the Ellis
Island immigration center, the alien clairvoyantly sees and hears the
figures and voices of people dressed in the peasant clothing of nine-
teenth-century Eastern Europe, reinforcing the metaphor implicit in
his own odyssey. Once in the city, he finds he way to a bar in Harlem
where, accepted as a "brother," he eventually gets his own social worker
and makes a living psychically repairing video games. Complete with
an apparition of the legendary "Men in Black" often described by UFO
witnesses, *The Brother from Another Planet* stretches the alien metaphor to its limits as a vehicle for social reflection about ourselves.

Strieber's "visitors," in contrast, at least as he describes them in
both *Communion* and *Transformation*, seem to function as mirrors of
his state of mind as an individual. Their relationship with him is personal and specific. That relationship stands in very marked contrast to
cinematic alien figures who came to earth to speak to humanity as a
whole, as did Michael Rennie, the cosmic cop in *The Day the Earth
Stood Still*. The relationship that Strieber describes is somewhat comparable, though, to what Karen Allen and Jeff Bridges portray developing between a young earth woman and an alien who assumes the
form of her recently deceased husband in John Carpenter's *Starman*.
Abducted by the alien and forced to drive him across country to a
rendezvous with his kinsmen, Allen's character tries to escape, only to
end up falling in love with her captor and being gifted by him with a
son. Still, *Starman* remains a simple love story, and detractors who
might note a parallel with human abductee accounts could describe
the response of Allen's character to the starman as an example of the
"Patty Hearst syndrome," in which the captive falls in love with her
captor.

Yet while a film like *Starman* romanticizes and perhaps oversim-
plifies an experience of being abducted by an alien, it nevertheless
does convey something of the emotional intensity that some abductees
describe in connection with their own experiences. Perhaps because it

is presented as a contemporary, cinematic fairy tale, we are able to more easily accept its transformation of the Karen Allen character's initial fear of relationship with an unknown force into a magical intimacy full of wonder and awe.

Will *Communion*, the film, based as it is on real events in the life of the Strieber family, adequately convey the human drama and emotional current that Whitley Strieber describes in regard to his own "visitor experiences"? Will audiences, too, experience a transformation of their own fears of the unknown through seeing this film? Or will it simply promote public delusion and unnecessary anxiety? Or, could it perhaps even be that this film will facilitate a more conscious relationship between humanity and the visitors—whoever or whatever they are?

That judgment remains to be made. For Whitley Strieber, though, there is no doubt that his estimation of what *Communion*, the film, took from him through being adapted from *Communion*, the book.

"An absolutely brilliant film is coming out of it," he said, "but part of it, at least, is spattered with my blood."

Chapter 6

The *Facts*, Please

Responses from a Noted UFO Skeptic,
Scientists, and a Therapist

A grain of salt is a useful, indeed necessary tool, when evaluating UFO "abduction" stories.

We owe it to ourselves to remain capable of critically evaluating information from Strieber and other "abductees" that purports to describe or characterize the "visitors" or "aliens" in any way. These kinds of stories present a variety of special problems. For one thing, we have no widely recognized yardstick with which to measure them.

If someone came to us and told us a tale of having escaped from Nazi Germany by crossing the Alps on foot, it might be possible, simply from a detailed interrogation, to determine whether he was telling the truth. We could inquire into the particulars of his route, ask for the names of the villages by which he passed, the length of time it took him to make the trip, and so forth. Depending on his answers, and our knowledge of the terrain, we could become reasonably certain that he was not pulling a hoax. Further inquiry could determine, through documentation, the date of his entry into Switzerland and the details of the proceedings of his request for asylum. Certainty, in such a case, is possible.

In evaluating a story of "alien abduction," however, this same kind of certainty is simply impossible, since we do not know the territory that has been traversed by the abductee. All UFO investigators admit this fact, yet nevertheless point to patterns of evidence and testimony that, when viewed as a totality, show the recurrence of similar if not identical features in story after story.

The overriding factor that renders pointless nearly all popular discussions of UFO-related phenomena is the fact that *we have no socially accepted and tested body of knowledge about UFOs and their "occupants,"* certainly not in the manner in which we have knowledge about animals and plants, or ourselves, for that matter. In other words, save in the company of small groups of UFO investigators who have endeavored to maintain a high degree of rationality in their investigations, we still have no common vocabulary, no common scheme of knowledge on which to base our discussions of UFOs. This is not to say that progress has not been made toward achieving such a degree of development, but the simple fact remains that there is no field that so amply provides people with room for the projection of their own fantasies or for the manifestation of their intellectual biases (often motivated by understandable but often self-damaging political concerns about being accepted as "legitimate") as does UFO research.

As simple a fact as this is, it is often lost upon members of the UFO community, some of whom claim to have intimate, personal knowledge of aliens, their behavior, and intentions. They very well may have such knowledge, but it is not the kind of knowledge that can become socially accepted, for it is not testable. What is significant in the public dialogue about such matters, of course, is that people with such testimonies are no longer being automatically regarded as crazy. Yet a change in public attitudes does not necessarily create the circumstances for the development of a rationally based consensus about what UFOs are, if indeed it may be once and for all socially and scientifically established that some of them represent more than mere illusions that we construct from naturally occurring or technologically produced (man-made) phenomena.

Because of the lack of a high degree of intellectual rigor that has characterized so much of what has been published on the subject of UFOs, we have come to see the development and increasingly public emergence of a group of professional skeptics who take apparent delight in "debunking" the writings of any and all writers who attempt to consider UFO phenomena seriously, as a subject that may require more than an ordinary explanation. Among the most visible of these authors is Philip J. Klass, formerly a senior editor of *Aviation Week and Space Technology*, whose books[1] have generally been characterized by a tone of concerned alarm at what he takes to be the public's general credulity. While there is plenty of cause for sharing his concern about our own gullibility, Klass also gives his readers reason to question just what kind of skepticism he and some of his colleagues practice. Owing to occasional lapses of discipline among some journalists' and media talk-show hosts' use of the English language, the term *skepticism* itself has received an exaggerated aura of automatic respectability in certain mass-media circles, especially in relation to UFO stories. The term has become a label that automatically denotes the philosophical orientation of a person who, through the use of reason and common sense, explodes the irrationalities and contradictions that are often simply assumed to be discoverable in *all* cases where extraordinary (or "paranormal") experiences are reported or unusual claims are made.

Described as such, "skeptics" may make a claim to being socially useful folk who prevent us from falling for intellectual fraud, thereby helping keep society sane. Problems arise, however, when journalists who interview the professional skeptics are incapable of distinguishing between arguments that show balanced, rational skepticism and polemical attacks masquerading as skepticism, designed for the sake of grinding an ax.

Traditionally, though, within the historical development of Western philosophy, *skepticism* was, as put by *Webster's Third New International Dictionary*, "the doctrine that any true knowledge is impossible, or that all knowledge is uncertain: a position that no fact or truth can be established on philosophical grounds."

By corollary, *skepticism* was also "the position that universally reliable knowledge is unattainable in particular areas of investigation."

Of course, *skepticism* as we tend to think of it in terms of "debunking" activity is closer to that same dictionary's related definition of it as "the method of suspended judgment, systematic doubt or destructive criticism characteristic of skeptics," combined with "an attitude of doubt or disposition toward incredulity in general or in regard to something in particular."[2]

Unfortunately, given some of the arguments advanced by prominent professional UFO skeptics, one has to wonder if what is being practiced is in fact a program of "suspended judgment" or rather the exercise of a rhetorical campaign intended to steer questioning minds away from inquiry into UFOs and "abductions," founded on the skeptics' a priori philosophical position that no certain knowledge about truly anomalous UFO phenomena is possible. I call this brand of doubt *irrational skepticism* to distinguish it from legitimate critical thinking.

There can be no doubt that the work of the professional skeptics is not entirely in vain. To the extent that they hold up a bulwark against a completely credulous acceptance of any kind of UFO-related story as gospel truth, they do a service for rationality. It is sometimes the case, though, that some skeptics seem to arrive at a conclusion as to the impossibility of a certain anomalous phenomenon, and then go about trying to prove their point. Such reasoning is evident, for example, in Robert Sheaffer's book, *The UFO Verdict,* in which he contends that famous abductees Betty and Barney Hill must have mistaken Jupiter for a UFO that followed their car. He arrives at his conclusion by analyzing the number of objects they reported seeing in the sky on the night of their reported abduction (September 19, 1961). The Hills said they saw two starlike objects, one of which was the UFO that presumably abducted them. Sheaffer insists that "if a genuine UFO had been present, there would have been three objects near the moon that night: Jupiter, Saturn and the UFO." Because the Hills produced an apparently "faulty" report of the sky, Sheaffer infers that "the conclusion is inescapable: no unusual object was present."[3]

One might argue for hours, ad nauseum, whether the Hills' presumably "faulty" report of the number of starlike objects in the sky is sufficient evidence for invalidating their entire story. What is interesting in Sheaffer's approach to analyzing this case is his apparent eagerness to throw out the entire testimony of Betty and Barney Hill through demonstrating that they could not have seen a UFO. In the light of the many abduction reports of subsequent years, though, the question of the reliability of their report of the presumed physical presence of the UFO becomes, in retrospect, largely irrelevant. There are other considerations that are clearly much more important than that of the UFO's alleged presence, not the least of which by any means is the welfare of the people who report UFO abductions as having occurred in their own lives. Are they to be treated as reliable witnesses, or are they to become automatically suspect as "mentally unstable"? What are we to make, too, of the increasing number of reports of abductions that reveal similar features, both psychological and physical? Are they all symptoms of a mass delusion, or should they be studied as the legitimate experiences of sane people? At the moment, we have virtually no public debate on questions such as these, which still linger at the fringes of respectable intellectual inquiry and discussion.

As a result of this sad state of affairs, we have to ask another difficult question: Is it possible to have any kind of objective knowledge about this phenomenon that can be shared in a social way, in the way we talk about "ordinary" subjects such as cars and kidnappings, for example? The intellectually honest answer to that question must take into account whether there remains a portion of UFO and visitor-related phenomena that defies explanation by ordinary means. Clearly, if one takes the position that all UFO phenomena are reducible to explainable causes, then we may in good conscience talk about the phenomena as we do other ordinary things. Such a position, however, runs the risk of ignoring a considerable amount of evidence (e.g., cattle mutilations that could not have been caused by predators; burns, rashes, and scars on UFO witnesses; and "landing" marks on the ground) that do not easily lend themselves to an ordinary explanation. If, for the sake of argument, one accepts that there may well be certain such phenomena that do indeed prove themselves to be truly anomalous, are they then subject to systematic investigation? The history of contemporary UFO research is one long, sustained answer of *yes* to that inquiry, but the question of reported human-"visitor" interaction, having only recently become a subject of study, has produced many a methodological problem for investigators who value rationality, both within and without the UFO community.

Yet, in the course of my investigation, I have come to see that there exists quite a continuum of "skeptical thinking" about the subject of UFO abductions, and I would be doing a disservice to rationality itself if I were to characterize all legitimate UFO skepticism as the thinking or writing of any one person or group. Such a continuum is composed, at one end, of people who deny the reality of paranormal phenomena in relation to UFOs and spend their time attempting to convince the rest of the world that such matters are a waste of time; and at the other end, of people who have inquired into certain paranormal phenomena and found instances of true anomalies their best professional tests cannot explain. This latter group has, without coming to any final conclusions, dedicated themselves to trying to help people who are perplexed by the anomalies they have encountered in their lives.

In between these two poles—both of which are populated by people who confess no belief whatsoever in the paranormal—one might find persons of scientific training who attempt to work as mediators between the two extremes. Such persons, while maintaining a highly rigorous approach to thinking about such paranormal phenomena as alien abduction, nevertheless maintain personal contact with people in both the orthodox scientific communities and people who are deliberately challenging those orthodoxies.

It was of particular importance to me in this research to obtain the viewpoints of people who were willing to knowledgeably comment on the alien abduction phenomenon from a rigorously skeptical point of view. Naturally, I requested an interview with Philip J. Klass, and he readily agreed. (To his credit, he even tracked me down through my mother after, when leaving my telephone number on his answering machine, I made an error in one of the numbers.) However, I also attempted to obtain interviews from people in highly recognizable and distinguished positions in the world of physical science and psychology. Many inquiries in the world of academia and even the aerospace community revealed one fact to me: Top-flight people were reluctant to be drawn into this area of discussion.

This experience caused me to look for scientists and professional people who were peripherally involved with the alien abduction phenomenon in the United States. The closer I looked at these people, the more I found that their credentials and backgrounds were not only sound, but revealed a degree of curiosity in their personalities that had drawn them into becoming knowledgeable in the area in the first place.

I speak specifically of three individuals: John Gliedman, Ph.D.; Rima Laibow, M.D.; and Brian O'Leary, Ph.D. Dr. Gliedman was educated as a research psychologist at the Massachusetts Institute of Technology, and is now writing a book relating advances in quantum physics to problems in cognitive psychology. Dr. O'Leary holds his doctorate in astronomy from the University of California at Berkeley, is a former astronaut chosen for the aborted Mars project of the 1960s, and is currently working on a project to stimulate a Soviet-American manned Mars expedition. Dr. Laibow, a graduate of the Albert Einstein College of Medicine in New York City, is a psychiatrist in Dobbs

Ferry, New York, and her work is relevant because she has offered her professional services to eleven persons claiming abduction experiences, discussing her experiences with colleagues, and has been writing up the results of her clinical experience for submission to professional journals.

Dr. Gliedman and Dr. O'Leary I knew from their association with Whitley Strieber. Both of them have known Strieber for some time and had been in close contact (often daily telephone conversations) with him during the period when he was first dealing with his visitors. Yet while both men lent a sympathetic ear to Strieber's experiences, neither specifically endorsed any one hypothesis to explain what was occurring with Strieber. In essence, both of them acted as counselors, yet from a strictly scientific point of view. I decided to interview them both at length as a means of testing their impressions of Strieber's understanding of himself, and in an attempt to get a handle on how they regarded the intellectual problems posed by alien abduction stories.

I contacted Dr. Laibow through Budd Hopkins, who informed me that she had begun working with people from his support group in New York. As I proceeded in my research, it became increasingly apparent to me that it was imperative that I address the treatment of persons with abduction experiences within the existing frameworks of medical psychiatry and psychology. As I cast about the country for information, it was clear that very few psychotherapists have become publicly recognizable for their work in this area. Dr. Laibow, although her involvement in this area is rather recent, impressed me with having made an attempt to become quite knowledgeable in the area. She is all the more remarkable for remaining skeptical about the phenomenon but stating that she no longer considers all reports of alien abductions necessarily to be the result of, in her words, a "psychotic fantasy."

I believe that this chapter may serve, therefore, to illustrate the variety of ways in which the phenomenon of alien abduction may be viewed from a skeptical point of view, with responses ranging from outright denial and debunking to therapy performed without a diagnosis of psychosis.

Since Philip J. Klass has achieved the highest public profile as a skeptic in this area, I began my inquiry by interviewing him, by telephone, from his home in Washington, D.C. I asked him to begin by giving me his overall appraisal of Whitley Strieber and his "visitor experiences."

Since he was well prepared for our interview, I include his comments verbatim as follows:

> KLASS: I think that there are, considering his story, there are three possible explanations. One is that the incident or incidents (plural) occurred essentially as he describes. I could sooner believe that he was abducted by Santa Claus, the reason being that I have spent more than twenty-two years of my life as a hobby investigating famous UFO cases. As an editor of *Aviation Week* magazine I can think of no more exciting story that they could publish, no more exciting story that I could write than to say, "I've investigated a UFO case, I cannot find an earthly or prosaic explanation for it, therefore I suspect that we may have visitors from other worlds." I can think, really, of no more exciting story. In twenty-two years I have yet to find such a story. I'm sometimes asked, "Well, haven't you found a case that you could not explain?" To give a short, meaningful response to that, in one of my books and in many of my lectures, I have offered that if, at any time that I'm alive, an honest-to-goodness extraterrestrial craft should land anywhere in the world, or crash, or a physical artifact should be found and examined by the National Academy of Sciences and they were to say this thing could not be made on this earth—anything that would irrevocably, unquestionably prove beyond all doubt that we've had at least one extraterrestrial visitor—then I would say to those who've bought my book, "Mail your book back to me, and I will refund not the ten percent or twelve percent royalty that I was paid for the book, I will refund the full purchase price of the book, as long as my lifetime savings hold out." I always add, "Get it in the mail fast, because I'm going to be bankrupt!" And, considering that I just turned sixty-nine, it would be a little late in life to start over again, and I'm sorry to take so long, but I think it demonstrates that I am utterly convinced, after twenty-two years, that there is no evidence that we are being visited by extraterrestrial craft.
>
> So, if one then says that is not a possible explanation for Whitley Strieber, then there are two other explanations. One

is that he is intentionally lying, the other is that he is a very mentally disturbed person. One can consider the first of those alternatives—that he is intentionally lying. I don't think anyone would question that Whitley Strieber is fundamentally a very smart, very intelligent, a very well-read guy. If Strieber were intentionally lying or concocting this story, I feel he would do it far better, that there would be far less flaws or discrepancies in his story, or stories, than one finds. For example, referring to his most recent book—and here I refer to a chapter that I've just written—Strieber makes the statement in his new book that he has intentionally tried to keep his son—Let me see if I can find the exact words, stand by just a moment, yes. On page twenty-seven, I'm referring to *Transformation*, he says that he and his wife have a firm policy of keeping their son, Andrew, "strictly isolated from talk about the visitors." Seven pages earlier, Strieber wrote that Andrew had been told "little" about the visitors. Well, isolated and "little" are somewhat at odds. On page two hundred eleven he reports that when Andrew awakened one morning, he reports that Andrew was "full of questions about the visitors. . . . We never discuss them with him unless he brings them up." But in fact, in late June of '87 when MUFON had its several-day UFO conference here in Washington—there were two panels on UFO abductions, one of which Whitley appeared on. Following that, it was close to midnight—he and I spoke about his accusation against me— and he introduced me to his young son. Now how can you claim that you keep your young son isolated from talk about UFO abductions and bring him to a several-hour symposium on UFO abductions in which eight different people described their accounts? So what I'm saying, Ed, is that if he were, in my opinion, intentionally falsifying, he is smart enough and clever enough to recognize these inconsistencies. With his intelligence, if he was trying to spin a tale, he would be much more clever and consistent.

Klass went on in the interview to discuss a confrontation that occurred between himself and Strieber at the Mutual UFO Network conference held in Washington, D.C., during the latter part of June 1987. Apparently, both of the men raised their voices at one another during the course of a reading by Strieber of the results of one of his lie detector tests. According to Klass, Strieber angrily shouted to the audience that Klass had accused him of being a liar. Klass said that he, loudly, asserted that he had not. There followed a conversation between the two men that, Klass said, resulted in an agreement for Strieber to send Klass a videotape of a New York television talk show in which he supposedly made the assertion that Strieber had denounced. According to Klass, after an exchange of letters in which Strieber sent him copies of the transcript of the show in question he was left with the impression that Strieber could not keep track of his own activities.

KLASS: This one exchange with him, to me, was added confirmation of my suspicions that he is suffering from temporal lobe epilepsy, as his own psychiatrist suggested, or some other transient mental illness. And temporal lobe epilepsy, from what I know of it, the characteristics match very closely those of Whitley Strieber. Now, in the book, the hardcover that you have, I point out the discrepancy between what Whitley Strieber wrote in *Communion* and what I subsequently learned. In *Communion* he wrote that, after Dr. Donald Klein had written to him in July of '86, suggesting that he might be suffering from temporal lobe epilepsy, Strieber writes, he underwent tests by two neurologists and they found no evidence of it. Yet, in a letter of May third or ninth, he wrote to me saying that the tests were still continuing. Now in *Transformation,* he provides another version, which is at odds with the other, and here I'll quote from my new chapter in my book. "In *Transformation,* he says he was tested for temporal lobe epilepsy on December sixth, 1986, and no abnormalities were found. Now, also, according to *Transformation,* his book *Communion* was out in the bookstores in late January of '87. I don't know what kind of a publishing or printing schedule his publisher has, but if a book is out in the bookstores in late January, surely it must be on the printing presses by early December. Yet according to *Communion,* he had undergone tests by two neurologists for temporal lobe epilepsy and they found no abnormality. In *Transformation,* he speaks of *one* test on December sixth, 1986, which found no abnormality." And as I mentioned, in his letter to me, which I already mentioned, he said that one of the neurologists had not yet completed his investigation. Now, in *Transformation*, Strieber offers another account, which claims he took the one test for TLE on December sixth, 1986 and another beginning March fourteenth, 1988, more than a year after *Communion* was published. And that test, he reports, using CAT scans, computerized axial tomography and MRI, magnetic resonance imaging, and if he had gotten a completely clean bill of health earlier, one wonders why he would continue to have such tests run. So, in my opinion, based on what Strieber has said, and what I have learned in my limited correspondence with Dr. Donald Klein, I am inclined to believe that he is a victim of temporal lobe epilepsy.

I refer the reader to the text of my written interview with Dr. Klein and my analysis of the medical tests in Chapter 1. The documentary record of Strieber's tests and the testimony of Dr. Klein does not reveal any contradiction between their content and Strieber's accounts of them in *Communion* and *Transformation*. The fact that Strieber referred to one EEG in *Transformation* simply omits mention of the second one he had administered because of his own urge to do so, and he accounted for that test in *Communion*. Because the second test did not have nasopharyngeal leads and sleep, Strieber himself did not regard it as having the same import as the original EEG with leads and sleep.

However, as I mentioned in Chapter 1 in my questions to Dr. Klein, Klass asserts that Dr. Klein was not the real author of Appendix I in *Communion*. Klass brought this up on his own in my interview with him.

KLASS: The rumor circulated in the movement and it came to me secondhand, allegedly from Budd Hopkins, I guess you certainly know the bad blood between Hopkins and Strieber.

CONROY: Yes.

KLASS: Hopkins refuses to talk or correspond with me so I could not check out the rumor, I could not check out that he is the source of it and that is why I did not identify him as the source of it, but I wrote to Dr. Klein pointing out that I was doing this book and that I had heard the rumor that Strieber, not Klein, had written Klein's statement which was published in *Communion* and I was writing to ask was that true. And in my book I paraphrase Klein's letter because I did not have his permission to quote verbatim—I didn't ask for it.

The following quotation is drawn from *UFO-Abductions: A Dangerous Game,* and represents the gist of his assertions about Appendix I in *Communion:*

> In correspondence with Dr. Klein, I learned that when Strieber called him to request a statement on his "clinical condition" for use in the book, the psychiatrist sought guidance from Strieber as to how much he should reveal and what Strieber might consider to be confidential. It was agreed that Strieber first would draft a statement indicating the range of information he was willing to reveal. Then Dr. Klein would revise the statement so it "accurately portrayed my view of the situation within the limits of his authorization." Clearly, Strieber did not invite Dr. Klein to offer a candidly complete statement.[4]

I do not know whether Strieber invited Dr. Klein to offer a "candid and complete statement" for the appendix of *Communion.* However, I know that he did invite Dr. Klein to do so for the purposes of his interview with me, as Dr. Klein points out in the text of his letter to me.

Klass said that since his book came out, he has not discussed this matter with him.

"I did not quote verbatim," he said. "After the book came out apparently Strieber complained to Klein about what he had told me. Klein's office called me and his secretary left a message on my machine, you know that he wanted to talk to me, but it was clearly concerning my book. I tried to return the call—he was out of town. I then sent him a copy of what I had written, and I have heard no further from him. I returned his call, to the best of my knowledge I sent him a copy of what I had written, and I have heard no complaints from him."

The more I spoke with Klass, the more it became evident to me that he had come to have the opinion that Strieber was not a normal, healthy person, and that this was the basis of his rejection of Strieber's

stories and the whole alien abduction phenomenon. I then followed
that line directly in my questioning.

CONROY: So, since you have reached the conclusion, it seems,
that Strieber is suffering from a mental disturbance—
KLASS: Yes.
CONROY: Has this led you to—well, I don't want to tempt
you to overgeneralize—but do you feel that many abduction
accounts that people are volunteering represent, essentially,
mental disturbances?
KLASS: Ed, if you were to ask me why do people commit
crime, there would be no single answer. A drug addict may
mug to get money for his habit; some of the Wall Street mil-
lionaires have different motivations. So there is no single motivation for it. As I point out in a new chapter in my book,
based on talks given by [Budd] Hopkins and his principal pro-
tégé, Dave Jacobs, at the MUFON conference in June, this
past June, in Lincoln, Jacobs acknowledges that many of what
he calls the "unaware" abductees are psychologically disturbed
people. They have panic states, they're afraid to be in the base-
ment, afraid to be in the backyard, afraid to be in an elevator,
some of them have out-of-body experiences, et cetera, et cetera. It is their thesis that these are the results of abduction
experiences. I would put the cause and effect in the other direction.
CONROY: You would reverse them.
KLASS: And so I would say that at least some of the abduction claimants are psychologically or mentally disturbed people. I would not call them crazy—I would underscore that,
that in fact, I quote Budd Hopkins in my original edition as
saying that Strieber was the first abductee that he had worked
with that he had urged to see a good psychiatrist. So I would
consider Whitley Strieber to be at one extreme. Another motivation that I would consider is the opportunity to become a
celebrity, a local celebrity, appear on national talk shows or at
least local ones.

I asked if one of his reasons for practicing the art of skeptical inquiry was a personal belief that irrational behavior in individuals seems

to lead to social conditions in which a fascist political takeover is possible.

KLASS: This is a position held by Paul Kurz. I don't think Paul would object to my saying that I don't share his fears as strongly and I think that some other members of the executive council of CSICOP, of which I am a member, feel that maybe his fears on this are a bit more extreme than our views on it. But since you raised that issue, let me digress. If you and I had been talking two years ago and you said to me, "Phil, what harm does it do to believe that a light in the sky that you saw last night might be a spaceship with strange-looking advanced creatures?" my response two years ago would have been, "Ed, it's a fairly harmless myth." I can cite you a Minnesota middle-aged couple that parked their car in northern Minnesota in the wintertime, going without food, and the woman died while waiting for a spaceship to come and pick them up, an elderly Florida couple that fell under the sway of a chap from Oregon who told them that flying saucers landed on his ranch, they sold all their property and moved north to buy property, but these are isolated cases. But two years ago I would have said to you—and I think the recent election maybe demonstrated this—that there is a great danger in gullibility or credulity, especially in a republic or democracy, in the sense that a majority of the people become too credulous and someone comes along—and here I'm divorcing myself from the recent campaign—but if a candidate comes along and says, "I can increase social security, I can increase defense spending,' and says, 'I can reduce the deficit, I can do these miracles'—if the public is too credulous and gullible, such a politician, and again, I'm not referring to either Bush or Dukakis, could become the president of this country.

Additionally, I use a very simplified analogy. My wife and I live in a small town house in downtown Washington. We have a little patio and we feed the squirrels regularly. For eight years we've fed them, we've never harmed them, and so on. And they will come moderately close, but not up to eat out of our hands. Why? Because nature has taught them—it's instinctive, I should say—that they must be wary and cautious. And if squirrels were much more bolder and trusting, they probably would disappear as a species. So, skepticism, if you will, is nature's way of protecting the species. This would be my assessment, my personal view. I have no ambition that I can stamp out belief in UFOs. I've often said that I only wish that I could live as long as the myth of extraterrestrial visitors. I don't think anyone in CSICOP has any hope or ambition of stamping out belief in astrology or parapsychology, et cetera.

Now, that was the scenario I spelled out two years ago. Today, I believe that this abduction cult—I call it a cult intentionally—does have very dangerous implications, because—and I touched on this in the original edition—I strike even harder at it in some of the new chapters after hearing Hopkins and Jacobs suggest that maybe we need to throw out all the basic principles of psychotherapy, and as a result of UFO abductions. They suggest that all or many or most psychologically troubled people—that their problems are not due to their childhood or prosaic causes—but are due to the fact that they were all abducted as children. And so here are these amateur psychotherapists serving as psychotherapists for people, at least some of whom are mentally troubled, and should be going to experienced, trained psychotherapists, instead of amateurs. In fact, it is to me almost analogous to discovering that you have a brain tumor and going to your local butcher shop and asking him to do the surgery.

CONROY: I see.

KLASS: So that is my concern. And the widespread publicity—best-seller list—that *Communion* achieved, and the new movie coming out, I think is sending and will send hundreds of people to the amateur UFO abduction therapist who should really be going to trained, skilled psychotherapists. Budd Hopkins, and I quote him in a new chapter from an interview in *UFO* magazine, cites a father—a man he's talked to—and Hopkins said apparently as a result of reading Hopkins's book, and *Communion*—led him to suicide. Hopkins also mentions two young children he's talked to, who have contemplated suicide, seemingly because of concern that they have been or will be abducted. I don't remember if I included in my book an

English grandmother who killed her two young granddaugh-
ters, I think seven, eight or nine—stabbed them in cold blood—
to keep them from being abducted by extraterrestrials. Again,
are those isolated cases? Yes.

CONROY: I think Hilary Evans told me about that.

KLASS: Yes.

I explained to Klass that I had recently edited and reworked many
of the chapters of a book entitled *Combatting Cult Mind Control*,
which had rekindled my concerns about the activities of destructive
cults that irresponsibly use mind-control techniques on people. I asked
him, "Do you feel that the UFO abduction cult that you are describing is characterized by a kind of credo or cult belief system?"

KLASS: Yes, and I'm delighted that you've worked in the area
you've described. I had an experience a few years ago where a
parent called because a young teenage daughter had run off
with a UFO cult that was going to be taken away from this
earth—I forget the name of the couple that was promoting it.
Now the interesting thing, and you'll find it in my book as I
trace the history of this, Betty and Barney Hill, never, to my
knowledge, claimed that their children were abducted or that
they were abducted a second time. And in fact, in the early
years of the abduction tales, it was a one-time experience. Budd
Hopkins and Strieber have added what I consider is a very dangerous element of suggesting that this is an extraterrestrial genetic experiment, that you or I or whoever have been selected,
you see, and that they will come back, typically, to abduct a
person a second or third or fourth time. But, worse than that,
for me, is the fact that if you have been selected for the experiment that your children will undoubtedly be involved—they
will be abducted, your teenage daughter will be impregnated,
your grandchildren, your great-grandchildren, ad infinitum.

CONROY: To paraphrase the Bible, it seems that you're suggesting they're saying that the sins of the "aliens" shall be visited upon the sons, yea, unto the third and fourth generations.

KLASS: Very apt. This, to me, is the dangerous thing, and
imagine that you or I—I'll use you as a guinea pig here—are
psychologically disturbed, you know, maybe your father was

alcoholic or your mother was alcoholic, or whatever, and you had an unhappy childhood, and this had a more or less permanent effect on your outlook on life. You come to talk to a conventional psychotherapist, presumably they would try to convince you that, all right, that's in the past, you can't undo that, but you've got a life ahead of you, so focus on the future, not on the past.

CONROY: There's a positive future possible for you.

KLASS: Exactly. There's a possibility, if you will work at it, to escape the past. If you go to Budd Hopkins under the same conditions, undergo hypnosis, and under hypnosis you're in a very suggestible mood, he then convinces you, perhaps unwittingly, that you've been a victim of a UFO abduction, then that is something from which there is no escape for you. Whitley Strieber's elaborate burglar alarm system doesn't protect him. My goodness, I can think of no more horrible thing, it's almost as if one believes in witchcraft and somebody casts a spell on you. Even there—and I don't know that much about witchcraft—but even there, the spell is only on you or me, not on our subsequent generations and humanity. So there is this brainwashing, and the tragic thing is that Hopkins, Jacobs and others use hypnosis, it is a key element in the cult. Now Hopkins proudly announces that "Well, in ten percent of my subjects I didn't need hypnosis," but the majority undergo hypnosis, and under hypnosis the subject is in a very suggestible mode. As a matter of fact, Dr. Simon, Betty and Barney Hill's psychiatrist, when I first interviewed him back in 1966, he said it's almost a master-slave relationship where the hypnotist is the master and the subject is the slave. Well that may be overstated, but . . .

CONROY: I understand the point, that you're under a great deal of influence.

KLASS: The Reverend Jim Jones, maybe his preaching was sort of a form of mass hypnosis, but he did not use individual hypnosis. You can imagine how much more effective he could have been in implanting his wild ideas if every subject underwent personal hypnosis. My added concern about this cult is that hypnosis is the cornerstone of its modus operandi.

CONROY: I see your point. It's very clearly expressed. . . . I have to thank you, Phil, for laying some of the groundwork here. Inquiring into this world is not an easy matter because people get very emotional.

My interview with Klass covered a number of other areas of concern, ranging from his estimation of recent television shows regarding UFOs and alleged government secrecy (he thought they were bunk) to considerations of defending ourselves against the aliens (he was theoretically in favor of using Star Wars-type technology against them, were they ever proved to be real). Yet upon concluding my interview with Klass it became clear to me that his stated concern is for the psychological health of society as a whole. In this regard, his critique of UFO researchers Budd Hopkins's and David Jacobs's work as "amateur psychotherapy" is interesting. Klass seems to be making a defense of traditional psychiatry, but he is not terribly specific about it, either. For example, while he urges people who think they've been abducted to get professional help, he doesn't say what kind of therapy he thinks will be of greatest help to them.

Is Klass's attack on Hopkins and Jacobs justified? I asked Budd Hopkins about Klass's assertion that he was urging the abandonment of the basic principles of psychotherapy by suggesting that all psychological problems stemmed from alien abduction scenarios. Hopkins found that assertion to be "outrageous" and "a complete distortion of everything we've been trying to do." Hopkins pointed out that he has been very carefully building bridges to members of the psychiatric community who were willing to learn about the special problems of people who have experienced abduction-type events in their lives.

As I mentioned, Hopkins put me in touch with Dr. Rima Laibow, who quickly consented to being interviewed at length about her work with people referred to her by Hopkins. I was interested in seeing how a psychiatrist with no previous experience or interest in this area would respond to the challenge represented by these sorts of cases, and expressed that interest at the outset of our conversation. The text of our interview follows:

> DR. LAIBOW: As a psychiatrist, my issue is not to determine the event-level reality of any of this, because I'm not trained to do that, . . . I am a person who deals in distress and the relief of distress, and there's no question in my mind that this

phenomenon is associated, in many people's experience, with distress.

I am neither a buff nor a believer. As a matter of fact, I basically ignored the entire topic, figuring that it represented a variety of some kind of psychotic fantasy in a life event. When I was younger I'd heard about the Betty and Barney Hill case that was bantered about by the media, and I thought, "Well, that's just a way of being psychotic." . . . As a psychiatrist, I later encountered patients whose delusional systems included being abducted by aliens. I encountered other patients whose delusional systems involved aliens, but they had to do with control of their thoughts by men from Mars by means of radio waves and fairly standard twentieth-century kinds of delusional thinking. Without any kind of evidence, I made the association that one kind of alien was like another, that one kind of thought about aliens was like another, that it was all basically the same crazy stew.

Then a patient I had been working with for a long time and knew well, whose fantasy material had been available for us to work on in quite an intensive way for quite a long time, came to me in February [1988]. She had seen the cover of Strieber's first book on the subject, and was deeply shaken, feeling that some of this material pertained to her. I was completely at a loss to know how to deal with it, because this was a demonstrably nonpsychotic patient saying things that I had previously assumed were psychotic. I was committing an error of circularity—I felt the only kinds of people who said these kinds of things were crazy, and the way I could tell that was that only crazy people said this kind of thing—circular reasoning. But as I considered the clinical realities of a nonpsychotic person who was not in an acute decompensation, who should not, by the previous standards I had used, have been having these experiences, I realized that I had to find out more about the experiences. I did a great deal of reading on my own. I read *Communion*, I read Budd Hopkins's books, I began looking for someone who could provide me with some expertise. I contacted Budd.

He was very generous with his time and expertise and experience, and we spent a lot of time talking, and he made his library available to me, and I read quite extensively on the subject and discovered that many of my previous assumptions were demonstrably wrong. . . . I then began seeing patients at Budd's request, who are in this category [abductees] of being disturbed, and I looked for clinical disturbances very hard.

This began in February of 1988, but this required a significant outlay of energy and investigation on my part . . .

CONROY: Before you felt you were ready to see patients . . .

DR. LAIBOW: Yes, and before I felt that I could speak knowledgeably about the phenomenon. I was willing to see patients before that, but I didn't really understand in a way that led me to be comfortable, that I was at some point in my own thinking that had a conceptual framework in which to work. So I began seeing patients.

I'm trained in the use of medical hypnosis and I was doing clinical work, therapeutic work without the use of hypnosis. I was using hypnosis to investigate the source of the difficulty. And I found several very interesting things. I found some very powerful clinical discrepancies between what I expected and what one, in general, would expect, given the kind of common wisdom position about this whole topic, and what I was actually seeing with these patients. The discrepancy between the expected psychosis and the actual lack of psychosis was important. I did see people who were anxious, I did see people who were extremely uncomfortable in a variety of ways, but given the underlying subjective reality of their experience, it made perfectly good sense to be worried and frightened. One man carried three flashlights, so that whatever happened, he would never, ever be caught in the dark without a light source, because his fear was so great, so enormous. But, if you have been terribly traumatized, and darkness has been part of that trauma, it makes some kind of sense. Without trauma, of course, it's a very bizarre thing.

So, that was the first clinical discrepancy—the lack of the magnitude of pathology that I expected to see. The second was the quality of the associative realities of these people. If, for example, a woman has been raped, she has only a limited number of symbolic and dynamically meaningful associations to the make and model of the rapist's car. She can have some feeling about it, but that's not the issue for her. The issue is her helplessness and vulnerability, the violation of her own integrity, her guilt, her this, her that—whatever. The associative chains to those triggers, if you will, are endless, given world enough and time, there's no limit to the associative complexity that can be followed from that in a therapeutic setting. . . .

So if, on the other hand, a sane patient was someone who fantasizes deeply, indeed, from the associative complexity and symbolic meaning of the make and model of the rapist's car, and the shirt that he was wearing had the same richness as any other aspect, because they are her observation, and they were chosen out of the entire wealth and diversity of possibilities, like any element in a dream can provide the springboard for associative investigation, that really is just as diverse and rich as the human mind. Now in a trauma victim, I look for some of that information, and I am seeing in these people differential associative patterns. They act as if they did not create a fantasy and then respond to it in terms of those associative chains. I find that utterly fascinating. If it's a trauma of external event level, then it makes perfectly good sense. If it's a trauma based on an internally generated or perceptual state, then this is utterly fascinating.

CONROY: And new, so to speak.

DR. LAIBOW: And new. It's something I'm not familiar with, that's for sure. So I was really kind of struck by that. The third clinical discrepancy that I'm finding is that everybody tells the same story.

CONROY: In other words, there's a structure to the abduction experience?

DR. LAIBOW: It's not just that it's sort of similar, that there's a structure. There is a very precise structure, very precise structure and it's world-wide. It doesn't matter whether you live in Australia or the homelands of South Africa, or whether you live in Portugal, or whether you live in the favelas outside of Rio or whether you live in the corporate canyons of New York. It's basically the same story. . . . . Now, if it's a dream, if it's a fantasy—if you or I are both concerned about, let's say, helplessness, we will construct a dream, a fantasy, an internal scenario that reflects your past history and life and your personal symbology, I would be the same, and the dreams would, the surface, look very different. They might both be dreams about falling, or dreams about flying, or screaming and not being able to make a sound, or whatever, but they would be very different stories. They would be able to be story-typed, in the folkloric sense, only at the superficial level. That's not the case here. And if these are internally generated fantasies, they ought to be widely divergent. The ones that are widely divergent are either the products of poor investigation or the investigator didn't know what was going on and the individual was allowed to confabulate and create supplementary material or was encouraged to do so, which is very interesting. So that when a meticulous investigation is carried out in which the investigator is very careful about the kind of suggestibility that is present and avoiding stimulating it, then you get the stories spilling out spontaneously, in a way that is true to type. Now that's really very challenging. Another clinical discrepancy has to do with recovery and the process by which that's accomplished. People talk about hypnosis and suggestibility. Now when I do, first of all, between twenty and twenty-five percent of these stories do not involve hypnosis, and they should be different from stories created by the hypnotist creating what he or she needs.

CONROY: Very crucial point.

DR. LAIBOW: Absolutely. There's no difference. The hypnotically recalled stories—they're less fragmentary, they flow one part into another, but they still are the same stories. And in those cases where the entire episode is recorded without hypnotic recall, you have the whole story and it's the same. And in those cases where you have a fragment, it's a fragment that belongs in a recognizable portion of the ABCDEFG sequence. Now that's very, very interesting. . . .

Now, as a hypnotist I use suggestibility and leading-question technique all the time when dealing with abduction phenomenology, whatever it is. I attempt to mislead and interject my material or what the patient will perceive as my expected material, constantly, as a check. When I can change the story of a highly suggestible client in the state of a hypnotic trance, I know that I'm dealing with confabulation. When I'm dealing with an abduction scenario, however, I have never been able to do that.

CONROY: That's extraordinary.

DR. LAIBOW: People will argue with me. That's definitely new to me, to have a hypnotic subject in a trance argue and say, "No, goddammit, no!" That's fascinating. Where's the suggestibility? I'm having trouble finding it. I look hard for it.

CONROY: How many people have come to you?

DR. LAIBOW: I have worked directly with eleven people. I attend the support group that Budd runs in New York as an interested psychiatrist, and I attend the support group in Philadelphia that Dave Jacobs runs. Therefore I've come into contact with maybe sixty, sixty-five people total, whom I've not worked directly with but whom I've spoken at great, great length with, both in group sessions and in one-to-one interactions. So this hypnotic suggestibility just doesn't seem to be part of the situation. Now there's one final discrepancy that I'm seeing, which is that these folks, by and large, are experiencing stress in the form of PTSD, the posttraumatic stress disorder. That's a fairly complex and important disorder, and it accounts for the flashbacks, it accounts for the somatic responses, it accounts for the sleep disturbance, and so forth. Now, PTSD is, as far as we know, only produced by event-level trauma. If this is not event-level trauma, then this is a new variety of PTSD and we have to redefine our understanding of the disorder and look for a better model. Because we have the disorder, what we do not have is a proper understanding of the etiology of the disorder. On the other hand, it raises the possibility that our understanding of the etiology is perfectly sound, that PTSD *is* the consequence of event-level trauma, and that therefore these people are suffering event-level trauma.

CONROY: It certainly raises the level of intriguing questions.

DR. LAIBOW: Yes. And for me, one of the really powerful points that keeps me from coming squarely down on the side of any one answer is because, there it is, and, as I said, it is not known that PTSD will occur in the absence of external trauma. And that raises some very interesting considerations. If this is not event-level trauma, why then (a) is it being produced as a worldwide phenomenon and (b) why is it so astonishingly consistent even among people who are totally outside the flow of the modern world, including very young children?

CONROY: Uninfluenced by science fiction culture and so forth.

DR. LAIBOW: Right, and illiterate folks whom we tend to think have not read *New York Times* best-sellers, and why is it so astonishingly consistent?

It's a very significant part of what I think about, and compared to the number of people that I see for other diagnostic categories, it's a small part of my practice, but it's an enormously important problem, because potentially we're dealing with a phenomenon that is huge, really, incomprehensibly huge numbers of people.

CONROY: Being a member of the psychiatric profession, have you had an opportunity to begin to discuss this with some of your colleagues, and do you see any interest in the profession?

DR. LAIBOW: Well, I am in touch with maybe eight colleagues—I consider psychologists as much my colleagues as psychiatrists—therapists around the country who are being confronted with this material in much the same way that I was. And we've been talking about setting up an informal network, and I think that that's tremendously important. On the other hand, I have written a paper about the discrepancies we have been talking about, and I shared it with a number of colleagues and the reactions have been mixed. Some people simply tossed the thing into the circular file, because it deals with a forbidden topic, which is a fascinating subject sociologically. This information is sequestered and is forbidden, and subjected to ridicule that keeps it from being seriously considered. So for many otherwise quite thoughtful, sagacious folks, this is a forbidden topic: "We know it's true, but we know we don't have to deal with it."

However, a number of other people, including some people who previously have been publicly identified as skeptics on the whole topic, have looked at what I have had to say with a much more open eye, and that's rather gratifying.

Dr. Laibow's testimony, although it comes from someone who is relatively new to this kind of psychiatric practice, offers an interesting challenge to some of the assertions of Philip Klass. Her assertion that she finds no real tendency to change narrative in the people with whom she works is intriguing. In addition, the other discrepancies she mentions seem to indicate that the level of trauma being experienced by the "abductees" is very possibly related to a real event. It will be fascinating to see how her work progresses, and what kind of dialogue she may be able to generate within her professional circles.

The "report by Elizabeth Slater" that Dr. Laibow mentions is something of a landmark effort to conduct psychological tests on UFO abductees, sponsored by the Fund for UFO Research. Released in January 1985, the report was authored by Ted Bloecher, Aphrodite Clamar, and Budd Hopkins. In brief, the report states that "a battery of standard tests failed to detect any psychopathology that could be reasonably expected to be a cause for UFO abduction reports." This report would be an especially interesting point from which professional psychotherapists might begin an inquiry into the problems of UFO "abduction."

Clearly, some psychologists would argue that a clinical situation is not the best condition under which to try to do research into the phenomenon of alien abduction. While Dr. Laibow will be the first to point out that she is not engaged in research, she cannot help but come up with information that may be useful. I turned to someone trained as a research psychologist, with a rigorous background in the neurological structure of the brain, for greater insight into how to approach the problems of thinking about abduction experiences. Dr. John Gliedman is particularly interesting, moreover, for while he maintains a firmly skeptical stance, he has been Strieber's friend for over six years. "We'd been good friends for quite a while before he started talking about his experiences," he said.

I asked Gliedman to describe how he first learned of Strieber's "visitor experiences."

DR. GLIEDMAN: Well, he came by and we had lunch, I think it was February of whatever year after his first visitor experience in *Communion*. Maybe it was late January of '86, and I had seen him—well he had some earlier experiences in October—during the fall, and he seemed perplexed. We all have our ups and downs, and I thought he was just in a period where he was working something through. At lunch he sort of unloaded and told me what had been happening to him, and I just listened. It was the beginning of a very intense period where we would talk virtually daily for long stretches of time, and we would compare together possible interpretations of what was happening. I just felt as a friend it seemed appropriate to talk to him about this. He was deeply troubled. Also, being a science fiction nut from way back and being most interested in the way the mind works, and other related questions, it was something that I found intrinsically interesting beyond my perception that it was very important for him to have a friend. And very soon—I don't remember exactly when he started to see Don Klein—he told me pretty quickly that he was seeing a therapist, and I thought that was excellent, and he really wanted to talk to a couple of people about it. I think I became a major connection for him while he was seeing Klein. I must say it was quite an intense and interesting experience."

CONROY: How did Whitley characterize what was happening to him? Could you describe the kind of language he used?

DR. GLIEDMAN: Well, he was careful to— I may be wrong about this, but I'm pretty sure he couched this as, "Well, you know I think I could be going mad, but I don't know," he said. "Some very disturbing things have been happening to me and here they are." The point was that he questioned the reality of the experience at the same time that he put the experience on the table for me. That was the essential thing. And that indeed became the dominant thread of our conversations. There were many, many interpretations of what was going on, including some of the interesting ones that have been advanced by Michael Persinger. But what he did do was tell me about some of the places that he thought he had been taken to, although it was quite a while back and I did not keep a diary or chronology so I am quite as unreliable a witness here as anybody else. That is my recollection. There was a lot of material that eventually found its way into *Communion* that I heard over lunch. He definitely told me that he had been taken somewhere by strange aliens, that he remembered seeing somebody on a table, eating something but it didn't look much like food and they didn't look all that much like humans.

CONROY: It seems Whitley was willing to consider arguments drawn from research into experimental psychology, and other such arguments.

DR. GLIEDMAN: The position that I immediately adopted and that he found useful in organizing his own thinking was that obviously something incredibly intense had happened to Whitley. I never have doubted the veracity of the intensity of it. The fundamental question that is presented by any intense, first-person experience is to what extent does supplementary evidence accompany the experience and allow someone who does not have the experience to understand what went on and to accept one or another interpretation of what went on. If Whitley had shown me a communicator that said "USS Enterprise" on it and when I pushed the button I saw a holographic image of Starbase Central, seventy-five light-years away, then I would have raised instantly one widely popularized interpretation of what was going on. As is the case with almost all of these kinds of experiences, they combine the quality of intense meaningfulness within the first person and a frustrating lack of external corroboration. So I felt from the start that when something like this happens to you, you have a personal responsibility to make sense of it in terms of your own life, but it is a very separate issue whether this experience can be integrated into what you might call—to use jargon—the consensual reality of society. That is, if you don't have a bolt from the spaceship or you don't have a Hollywood monster's bat wing to show me, we can be talking about a religious experience, we can be talking about a symptom of temporal lobe epilepsy, we can be talking about a possible allergic response to common or not-so-common chemicals, or even a response to electromagnetic phenomena, one way or another. We can be talking about somebody who's been abducted by real flesh-and-blood aliens. We don't know, but my problem, as a third-person observer, who believes in the scientific method, is how to interpret it. You can't just deny it.

CONROY: Did you-all ever discuss the possibility that perhaps, indeed, he might have been abducted by normal human beings and somehow subjected to mind-altering drugs and behavioral conditioning of some sort?

DR. GLIEDMAN: We discussed more possibilities than I've ever seen discussed in print. I mean we discussed that, and we discussed the possibility that that was just a paranoid fantasy, we discussed many families of temporal lobe interpretations, and particularly, I am very interested in the suggestions that Persinger has made over the years, that there may be a connection between geophysical earthquakes or whatever—or shifts in the earth's crust—which release very substantial amounts of energy. There was an article in *Nature* a couple of years ago which reported it had been demonstrated that this can actually produce things that look like flying saucers—lights. This was done in a laboratory setting. So I'm very intrigued by the possibility that there may be a tie-in between geomagnetic activity and let's call them "transcendental experiences" in people, and not just abduction experiences but straight religious experiences. Now this is just one of many possibilities that I would like to see systematically explored.

Since Michael Persinger seems to have figured so prominently in Gliedman's thinking, and moreover has written extensively on the relationship between the temporal lobe and mystical or UFO-related phenomena, I turned to Dennis Stacy, editor of the *MUFON UFO Journal* and a San Antonio-based free-lance writer, for information he had gleaned from a recent period of in-depth research into Persinger's work. Under contract with *Omni* magazine, Stacy produced an article on Persinger's research that appeared in the December 1988 issue of the *MUFON Journal*. He also conducted an extensive in-person interview with Persinger (previously unpublished, parts of which he has permitted me to reproduce here, from a paper Stacy has entitled "Temporal Lobe Effects and Mystical States of Consciousness"):

Dr. Michael A. Persinger is a clinical neuropsychologist and professor of neuroscience and psychology at Laurentian University in Sudbury, Ontario, where he directs the Neuroscience Research Group. He is the author of more than 100 technical papers in a variety of fields that impinge on the impact of electromagnetic fields with biological organisms and human behavior, a discipline in which he is considered a world authority. He is also the author or co-author of six books, including *Space-Time Transients and Unusual Events* (1977, with Gyslaine Lafreniere), *Weather Matrix and Human Behavior* (1980), and *ELF and VLF Electromagnetic Field Effects* (1974).

His most recent book, *Neuropsychological Bases of God Beliefs*, was published by Praeger last year.

Persinger is one of the foremost proponents of the theory that the majority of luminous phenomena, so-called UFOs, are in fact the product of geomagnetic forces unleashed within the earth's crust by tectonic strain. Aside from their electrical and magnetic components, these forces may also have previously unknown components capable of influencing human perception and consciousness.

QUESTION: Why did you associate mystical states of consciousness with the temporal lobe of the brain?

PERSINGER: The hypothesis that temporal lobe excitability is tied to these kinds of experiences goes back to the clinical literature, in which we know that there are certain personality and subjective experience features that are associated with electrical foci in the temporal lobe, specifically epileptic foci. The argument has been that this is unique to the epileptic population. What we did, basically starting back in 1982–83, was to devise a questionnaire, a kind of psychological inventory, that contained a lot of the temporal lobe signs, such as feelings of vibration before you go to sleep at night, or the feeling that you get a sign or signal that is meaningful to you only, these kinds of things.

Once we set up the questionnaire and standardized it, we found that the normal population shows these symptoms, too, and that they appear to lie along a continuum. We then decided to see if there was any electroencephalographic (EEG) validity to these items people were responding to. And indeed, we found that people who scored very highly on this temporal lobe sensitivity scale also showed a very significant correlation with alpha activity from the temporal lobe.

This got us very excited because the temporal lobe has been implicated in mystical experience on the one hand, and creativity on the other, specifically language and the ability to put words together in new ways. The next step was to select people who were very high on this temporal lobe sensitivity scale and see if they had any special properties. Because we assumed that the temporal lobe was labile, or prone to excitability, we argued that weak EM fields that are pulling in the same frequency as the temporal lobe should specifically affect this process.

At the same time we'd learned that suggestibility was tied to temporal lobe signs. We realized that we were on to something, because people who were high on temporal lobe sensitivity scores also showed increased suggestibility, that is, hypnotizability, using the technique developed by Spiegel and Spiegel, who wrote *Trance and Treatment*. The first thing we did was to determine if we could influence people's temporal lobe signs by exposing them to magnetic fields. We did this by exposing them to flashing light at various frequencies that flashed at the same frequency as magnetic fields pulsed to the head, particularly on the temporal lobe plane. The results were published in "Perceptual Motor Skills."

What we were trying to do in that scenario was stimulate a close encounter experience, relying heavily on subjective accounts of UFO literature, in which people often report a flashing light that had a sleepy effect on them. We attempted to determine if the light flashing frequency in conjunction with, that is, synergistically, a magnetic field being applied to the brain would enhance suggestibility and imagery. What we found was that there was indeed a change in imagery, and that the imagery was specific to those kinds of properties that are unique to temporal lobe activity; feelings of floating, movement, certain complex visual sensations. It's not unusual for people to feel they're floating, moving, spinning through time, or whatever, when the temporal lobe is stimulated. The excitement was the realization that we might have a way of stimulating such temporal lobe components so that they actually appeared in subjective imagery.

QUESTION: Were you successful?

PERSINGER: Eventually, yes. But first we needed to get more specific, because the equipment we were using was pretty crude. So we devised a computer-controlled helmet that allows us to control the shape of the field applied across the temporal lobe plane, and its temporal characteristic, whether it's spinning like a vortex or whatever.

We then brought in people who were extremely sensitive as

defined by our temporal lobe scale. The first question we asked was could they detect it? We found that they could not detect it in terms of being voluntarily able to say, yes, it's on or off. But they could use it as a cue.

QUESTION: As a cue? Could you explain, please?

PERSINGER: Well, I can tell you what happened with one particularly sensitive subject. Every fifteen seconds we presented a card, followed by fifteen seconds blank period, during which time the subject would try to anticipate what was coming next. With certain symbols [on the cards] we turned the field on during the blank or dark period, and she had to guess which of the five symbols would appear. We always had the field associated with one particular symbol. We saw that even though she could not identify subjectively when the field was present, her ability to guess correctly that symbol which followed the field presentation got better and better with trial. This suggests that people may use these fields as subtle cues, even though they may not be aware of their presence.

This became very relevant in terms of trying to understand that the brain can discriminate and respond to different kinds of very subtle, external magnetic fields, without the individual necessarily being aware of it, except through their imagery. If you begin to look at their imagery, then, their dreams, or what they're imagining, you may begin to discern the fact that these fields are present.

QUESTION: This ties in with your earlier work on the correlation of geomagnetic activity, usually associated with tectonic strain, and certain spontaneous psi phenomena, does it not?

PERSINGER: Exactly. During this same course of experiments, which ran approximately six to eight weeks, we found that the card-guessing accuracy was negatively correlated with geomagnetic activity in the area. On days of high geomagnetic imagery she had very low, almost below chance, scoring. Our next study was to take these fields and see if we could interfere with the psi process, and indeed we could. We now think this has something to do with the prepared state of the brain, and the temporal lobe particularly. The geomagnetic field simply adds to, or is conducive to, that state of the brain many people associate with psi phenomena. . . .

QUESTION: Theoretically, I suppose you could induce temporal lobe epilepsy . . . since such seizures are usually characterized by electrical spiking. But Whitley Strieber, the very popular American writer who recently claimed to have been abducted by extraordinary, non-human beings, says he was examined for TLE and no such spikes were found.

PERSINGER: About twenty per cent of people with clinical epilepsy don't show any EEG change at all, and that's even during the time of display. Between seizures it is very typical for no obvious pathology to show up on the EEG. I think Strieber misinterpreted our work, to be honest. What we're saying is that the TL signs we see in mystical and many related altered states of experience, including close encounter experiences, have a lot in common with the symptomology of TLE. That does not mean to imply that people who show these things are always temporal lobe epileptic. Our data indicate that there is a continuum of TLS along which we are all distributed. At the very extreme end are the TL epileptics who also suffer other adverse side-effects because their seizures are usually uncontrolled. But the normal person is also susceptible to these things, particularly during times of personal stress or crisis, like identity crises, mid-life crises, loss of loved one and so on.

And some individuals are simply prone to this all the time, and they are the individuals we find are the creative ones. That's the positive side of TL sensitivity. The critical feature is this continuum we seem to find, and that includes about 500 people now in our inventory. . . .

What seems to be evident from this work is that in many of the mystical experiences the temporal lobe properties—movement, odd visual experiences, the profoundness, the fact that it's true reality, the intense meaningfulness, the cosmic significance of it all, the desire to proselytize, to spread the word, the sense of the personal, as if one is particularly chosen—these are all classic temporal lobe signs. They aren't paid much attention to in the clinical population, because you're usually dealing with people that are also cognitively impaired. But when there is no cognitive impairment, such as the normal individual, then these types of behavior can very often show some unusual and I think exciting combinations of words. You can see this in the writing of Whitley Strieber and other people whose work is allegedly acquired through these sort of extra-self sources of information.

QUESTION: Would you also include out-of-the-body and near-death experiences in this category?

PERSINGER: I would say the whole context of feeling that there's another self giving you information, whether it's identified as the Great Spirit, an extraterrestrial, or just another personality, that whole operation is extraordinarily similar to temporal lobe phenomena, as well as the kinds of symptoms shown.

In a second interview with Dr. Gliedman, I asked him to outline what, in the light of his interest in Persinger's work and his own background as a research psychologist, he would consider to be a rational and skeptical approach to dealing with the "visitor experiences" reported by Strieber. I asked him if he had formulated a model for that type of experience.

DR. GLIEDMAN: Well the problem is that there are too many models for it. We have to find a way to distinguish experimentally between different interpretations. Until we do that, we're all in the armchair, speculating, unless the experience has happened to us. Speculation, alone, is not enough, because we have to live with whatever has happened, and that's an entirely different set of questions.

Speaking as a skeptic, a sympathetic skeptic, I'm afraid that there is a great misunderstanding about science, which is common among nonscientists, at least in my experience, which is that scientists are always scratching their heads, struggling against all odds to come up with models that are logically consistent with the phenomena, and that when they come up with a model, a hypothesis, the work is really done because it's so hard to come up with a model. In many cases, the reverse is true. Coming up with a model which is logically consistent with the data is almost child's play. The problem, in fact, is that you can come up with so many models that are compatible with the information that is available. The real trick is dreaming up some sets of experiments in which all of the different, logically consistent models make different enough predictions that you begin to weed them out.

The poet Paul Valéry said, once, that one part of his mind was constantly producing new poetic lines, new ideas for poems and whatever, and another part was selecting the good stuff. Well, in science there is a similar division of labor. On the one hand, everyone is coming up with beautiful models all the time—or in many areas of science this is true—but experimental design serves a critical function. It isn't just a question of sitting down and looking at somebody's model and being critical about it. Often that's very useful because you discern logical inconsistencies or things that are unconvincing, but again the real nitty-gritty comes when, instead of being sort of a literary critic, as it were, you're able to go over to the laboratory and run experiments and actually pin your rival's model down and your own model down, and your rival's model predicts "A," and yours predicts "not-A."

The trouble with the phenomena which Whitley's experienced is that it is particularly susceptible to logically consistent interpretations of the most diverse sort. In order to sort things out, it requires experimental effort. One of the reasons why I'm so intrigued by Persinger's work is he is one of the few experimental psychologists who take an interest in finding non-obvious physical explanations for mystic experience. And it is possible that Whitley's experience is a mystical experience, but beyond that there is your classic Christian mystical experience, the vision of God—name any religion. He's put his finger on some very funny physical phenomena, which I think psychologists would do well to study much more closely. There is the possibility, among other things, that some people have brains which are prone to interesting states as a result of electromagnetic energy, which may be shifts in the earth's crust or simply man-made transmitters.

Gliedman pointed out, however, that a program of designing an extensive series of experiments to explore the physical dimensions of mystical and other anomalous experiences is highly unlikely, given the major cutbacks that have been occurring for nearly a decade in the national science budget. Basic research, he noted, has suffered the most. However, he did state that he believes such research would be very profitable.

Gliedman is interesting, also, because he is one skeptic who recognizes that there is some validity to the approaches now being developed to help abductees cope with their experiences.

"I think support groups are immensely useful," he said. "Very often people who suffer from a particular problem are as competent as anyone else in inventing strategies for coping with the problem."

There are other perspectives on the visitor experience, of course, not the least of which is the question whether the "visitors" might not, indeed, relate somehow to the world of outer space or other dimensions. One perspective that Strieber sought in that regard he found in the person of Dr. Brian O'Leary, whose background in astronomy, planetary science, and his training as a astronaut (though his program was canceled) was no doubt of great interest.

O'Leary and Strieber came into contact in 1986 during a time when there was a flurry of interest in exploring the significance of certain anomalous features found on the surface of Mars that appeared to have the form of a gigantic face and a series of pyramids, among others. Both O'Leary and Strieber were involved in these activities, and Strieber had actually contributed funds toward the continuance of that research.

O'Leary's relationship with Strieber was very similar to that shared by Strieber and Gliedman.

"Basically he was confiding in me," O'Leary said, "and I was listening to his description of his phenomena, and there was a part of me that said, 'Why not?' because I've had a number of experiences myself which one would categorize as 'weird,' so I listened. But another part of me said, 'Now Brian.' You see, I go around the world and give lectures, and a lot of people ask me about UFOs, and up until around the time I met Whitley, I kind of pretty much pooh-poohed it. I didn't say they didn't exist—I don't have that kind of arrogance. Nor did I say, 'Yes, they exist.' I would actually say, 'That's a fascinating question and we can't really go into it and I don't really have a position on it; I haven't had the experience myself.' Having met Whitley, I said, 'I'd better look at this a little more.' It was then that I started to get to know other people, actually Vicki Cooper [editor of UFO magazine], in fact I knew her even before she started the magazine, I was one of the people who encouraged her to start it. I wrote an editorial for her first issue that gave them encouragement to do a good job.

"So, it was coming at me from all directions, and I began to take a closer look at these things. So rather than considering Whitley as an anomaly, I consider him more as an articulate spokesman for what appears to be a very pervasive phenomenon, and the probability that this is a hoax put on by Whitley and it could be thousands, perhaps millions of people, the probability of that being one big gigantic hoax is about as close to zero as anything I know of, just from my range of experience with humans. So, although I don't have any experimental proof for UFOs, there certainly is a great deal of evidence out there that deserves much closer attention."

O'Leary said that he began to speak with other people who claimed to have had abduction-type experiences, and came into closer contact with UFO researchers when he moved to Phoenix in the spring of 1987. He mentioned that he had become close friends with the people who run the Center for UFO Research in Phoenix, an organization formerly associated with the late J. Allen Hynek.

"Of course, I have great respect for Hynek," O'Leary said. "I used to share podiums with him to give talks occasionally. I'm working closely with Brian Myers and Tina Choate, who are the people who have taken over here. I fairly quickly became their science adviser and have been working fairly actively at looking at various cases, primarily from the point of view of photographic analysis and basically just being a good listener. I've been like a sponge, taking a lot of this in. I've not come out with any strong public positions yet. I guess one of the things I've been advised is that the whole UFO community is like a can of worms. It's better for me not to get my neck out there too much. I think people will acknowledge that the whole community is very, very difficult to work in.

"Where I see an opportunity for scientists here is that people who are highly trained as scientists, with a great degree of scientific credibility in the scientific community can address some of these questions, like the 'Mr. Ed' pictures, which some of us have spent some time processing. We've also worked with Bruce Maccabee, who's also been very cooperative. So, I've been networking in a loose way, looking at evidence as it comes in. People call me often and I tend to piece it together and gestalt it. So it's not only Whitley who's my source of information, it's a consensus that, yes, the phenomenon is real, and yes, it has a spiritual dimension, which I'm fairly familiar with, more so than Whitley, because Whitley hasn't had the spiritual background."

I found it interesting that O'Leary, given his scientific background and bent toward examining the UFO phenomenon from a technical point of view, would countenance such a viewpoint. In response, I pointed out to him that many people in the UFO community have been asserting for some time that the UFO "abduction" experience is not by any means necessarily mystical, but rather seems to have evidence pointing to some kind of genetic manipulation being practiced upon us. I asked if he believed we had sufficient information and evaluated research reports to be able to responsibly advance such a hypothesis.

"I don't really know," he said, "I can't say that with authority. I can venture a guess, and it's pure speculation, and I've been listening and soaking up data, and like you, as a reporter, sometimes it's difficult to get a consistent thread, but it sounds like there is an element of that. But I'm also guessing that, if these are other-dimensional beings, and by other-dimensional I mean able to conquer the time-space problem—they can become physical, they pop in and pop out—my guess is that there is a hierarchy of beings and what Whitley confronts and what Budd Hopkins has documented, we're talking about just one small section of the whole hierarchy."

I asked O'Leary if he felt that such a hierarchy was comparable to differences to be found in humanity among people of varying levels of awareness.

"The best analogue I can think of is imagine we are a bunch of aborigines and we're doing our thing and a giant 747 flies overhead," he said. "And you can say it's a big, silver bird and start to characterize it. Somebody parachutes down and a couple of people confront the person that was in that silver bird and come back with all sorts of stories, even mythologies, of what their experience was. Maybe somebody else in the tribe sees another airplane which has different characteristics. One might be military in intention and another one might be some sort of rescue or anthropology group. And it's a rather poor analogy, probably, because the sheer grandeur of the experience is so great. If one confines one's investigation just to Whitley, then we're kind of missing a lot of data. He's like a data point for what is obviously a very complex phenomenon."

O'Leary's immersion into the world of UFO phenomena may hardly strike persons who identify "skepticism" with hostility, and they may question my decision to have included his comments in this chapter. It is true that O'Leary is one of the most open-minded people I have encountered in my investigation, and it is that willingness to look at all the evidence that is thrown at him that demonstrates a truly scientific mind. More than that, his willingness to act upon and make contributions to UFO research seems to provide a model for a critical, active skepticism.

Having surveyed the attitudes and thinking of a fair number of "UFO agnostics," I hope that I have provided a foundation for thinking critically and flexibly about the subject of skepticism itself. I cannot help but observe that, at the base of Philip Klass's skepticism, there lies a profound suspicion of the general population, a vision of people as being easily made into suckers and victims. While such a view is certainly justified from the sad history of fascist political movements and other tragedies in this and past centuries, it also negates the strong signs to the effect that people are much smarter than many authors might tend to believe. In the face of a phenomenon that continues to manifest at many levels of society, might it not be more scientific to look at it as closely as possible—and expand one's own educational background, question one's own intellectual prejudices—than to deny its existence?

Is it fair, moreover, to attempt to debunk an abduction story by asserting that its author is "mentally unstable," a term that will be popularly interpreted, for better or worse, as "crazy"?

Perhaps the viewpoints elucidated by Drs. Laibow, Gliedman, and O'Leary may provide us with a more constructive path toward rationally—and constructively—examining the problems posed to both individuals and society by reports of UFO abduction.

Chapter 7

Little Green Men:
From Ireland—or the Pleiades?

A Survey of Speculation About the
Identity of the "Visitors"

The Proud Angel fomented a rebellion among the angels of heaven, where he had been a leading light. He declared that he would go out and found a kingdom for himself. When going out at the door of heaven the Proud Angel brought prickly lightning and biting lightning out of the doorstep with his heels. Many angels followed him—so many that at last the Son cried out, "Father! Father! the city is being emptied!" whereupon the Father ordered that the gates of heaven and the gates of hell should be closed. This was instantly done. And those who were in were in, and those who were out were out; while the hosts who had left hell flew into the holes of the earth, like stormy petrels. These are the Fairy Folk—ever since doomed to live under the ground, and only allowed to emerge where and when the King permits . . . On certain nights, when their *bruthain* [bowers] are open and their lamps are lit, and the song and the dance are moving merrily, the fairies may be heard singing lightheartedly:—

> Not out of the seed of Adam are we,
> Nor is Abraham our father;
> But the seed of the Proud Angel,
> Driven forth from heaven.

—Story told by Roderick Macneill, then ninety-two years of age, to Alexander Carmichael, of the University of Edinburgh, and J. F. Campbell, his colleague, in October 1871, on the island of Miunghlaidh, Barra, Scotland.[1]

In recent decades, the phrase "little green men" has become almost universally adopted by cartoonists, humorists, and other purveyors of contemporary folklore as a synonym for "extraterrestrials." In the world of nightclub comedy and on the pages of sophisticated magazines, short, pudgy-bodied entities with pairs of antennae in place of ears have long enjoyed a stylized, stereotypical status. They are said to be the sort of folks whom hapless drunks encounter while staggering home in the early morning, or the inevitable products of an LSD hallucination. As creatures who have supplied Hollywood with more than one morsel for popular consumption, they have been relegated to a limbo of the imagination inhabited as well by the elusive Bigfoot and the somewhat sinister Loch Ness monster. In the consensus mentality of our culture, we have come to regard little green men as figments of a pathological imagination, excessive mention of which in conversation might still be regarded by some people as sufficient provocation for putting witnesses in straitjackets.

Ironically, though, the phrase "little green men" carries a dual meaning in our culture. Only a hundred years ago, its use in casual English-language conversation would have been automatically understood to refer to "fairies," "leprechauns," the "wee people" in general, of whom folklore and tradition have given us innumerable stories and legends. By some transmutation of the popular imagination, though, belief in fairies has been far outstripped by belief in the existence of extraterrestrial beings. In short, fairies and leprechauns are out, and "aliens" are in.

It would not be an exaggeration to say that few creatures in our culture's fabulous bestiary have exerted more influence over our collective mind than the alien, as can be seen from even a casual perusal of science fiction literature and cinema. While outer-space villains were a staple of pulp science fiction in the 1930s and '40s, in the 1980s we have seen the term alien become inextricably linked in the public mind to the horrific image of the extraterrestrial monster around which revolved the movie *Alien*. Nor was Hollywood slow to provide us with the necessary corrective to such a nightmarish specter. Just so our children might sleep at night, Steven Spielberg supplied us with a warm, friendly extraterrestrial (endowed with magical powers and big, cute eyes) who arrived on earth hygienically devoid of all negative alien connotations and, in good American style, was known by an acronym-style nickname: E.T.

As a result of the enormous commercial success of Whitley Strieber's *Communion*, the general public now has yet another image of what is considered alien or extraterrestrial, although Strieber has gone to great pains to avoid saying his "visitors" are natives of another planet somewhere in the universe. The image reproduced on the dust jacket and paperback cover of *Communion*, magnetically attractive with its huge, slanted eyes, prominent forehead and vestigial mouth and nose is now well on its way to becoming something of an icon in American popular culture, as much for its own power as for the fact that it somewhat resembles other images of aliens previously distributed by UFO publications and other authors, not to mention the little men who emerged from the mother ship in the movie *Close Encounters of the Third Kind*.

Yet while Whitley Strieber describes some of his visitors as being short, he by no means says that they were green. If anything, Strieber's accounts of his visitors break just about every possible cultural stereotype that has been created regarding aliens. That break is amply indicated by Strieber's insistence on calling the entities that intervene in his life "visitors" instead of "extraterrestrials," "aliens," or "intruders." Yet that refusal to use a certain label does not signify that his visitors are dramatically different from what other persons who claim to have been "abducted" have called aliens. Remarkably, some of them seem from his accounts to bear at least a superficial physical resemblance to some of the short, bald-headed, big-eyed creatures whom Budd Hopkins called "extraterrestrials" in *Intruders: The Incredible Visitations at Copley Woods*. The publication of *Communion* and *Intruders* at approximately the same time in early 1987 certainly had a corroborating effect for the general reader unaccustomed to thinking of aliens as "real." Here were two books by apparently sane, distinguished men who took these entities seriously, as having some existence apart from the imagination! Yet both books left unanswered the one compelling question that must inevitably flow from granting the possibility that the visitors may be real:

Who (or what) are they?

"Visitors," "Deros," and the Public's Credulity

Strieber's use of the term "visitors" to describe the anomalous beings with whom he says he has had contact in a variety of states of consciousness is indicative of their principal characteristic: They are elusive. They do not stick around long enough for us to get to know them on our terms. They are secretive, communing with us one moment, then gone the next. Owing to their evanescent nature, the visitors are perfect suspects for being regarded as nothing more than the figment of the imagination of a highly creative writer. Indeed, Strieber has on more than one occasion remarked on the irony that, from his point of view (regarding them as a de facto reality in his life), the visitors couldn't have chosen a more unlikely and ostensibly less credible advocate for the actuality of their existence. Yet, he also remarks that such an irony is indicative of what he has come to expect of the visitors—that they deliberately shroud their actions in the appearance of absurdity.

What is most remarkable about Strieber's public relations work in promoting *Communion*, though, is that he has effectively communicated his message despite the apparent absurdity of his position as a writer of Gothic horror and science fiction. As a result, he has persuaded his readers and many people affected by his public statements to consider the possibility that the visitors are unlike anything they've ever thought about before—especially the standard-issue aliens provided to us by the machinery of popular culture. By giving his entities such a neutral name, Strieber has taken a tack very different from previous writers and publishers who demonstrably and deliberately practiced the art of such a literary hoax originated with a science fiction writer named Robert Shaver, creator of the "Deros."

Shaver came to the attention of Ray Palmer, publisher of the pulp magazine *Amazing Stories*, in the early 1940s, according to John A. Keel in an article published in the Fall 1986 issue of *The Whole Earth Review*.[2] Keel (who later became a respected writer on UFOs) maintains that Shaver initially wrote a letter to Palmer that described his knowledge of a subterranean race of "freaks" called "Deros," who presumably controlled life on earth's surface through their fiendish use of machines that emanated powerful energy rays. While Keel says he read Shaver's letter and threw it in the wastebasket, Palmer saved it, published it in *Amazing Stories* (with no noticeable concern for checking Shaver's veracity or sanity) and found that, in Keel's word, "a flood of mail poured in from readers who insisted every word was true because *they'd* been plagued by Deros for years" [emphasis Keel's]. Palmer found Shaver had written reams of material on the "Deros," bought it, contracted for more, and made the "Deros" a big, continuing hit for years in the pages of *Amazing Stories*.

Shaver's source of information about the "Deros," by the way, was a voice that he heard while welding. Shaver also wrote a novelette entitled *Earth Slaves to Space*, which Keel says "dealt with spaceships that regularly visited the Earth to kidnap humans and haul them away to some other planet."[3]

Are Strieber's "visitors" simply another recapitulation of Shaver's fiendish but laughable "Deros" in modern, more sophisticated form? Can it be said that Strieber, long noted for novels that explored some of our most fundamental fears, finally hit upon the formula for the ultimate sensation—and the ultimate ego trip? Or has he, in fact, succeeded in articulating his own true-to-experience impressions of entities who, he conjectures, may have played a role in the development of human consciousness? Whatever may be one's personal response to such questions, it is undeniable that Strieber has at last broken through the barrier of social stigma that has long prevented us from even talking about what appear to be visitor-related phenomena in rational terms.

Whitley Strieber brought the visitors into America's homes with every copy of *Communion* left open on a coffee table or bedside nightstand. No doubt more than one reader had to pause while reading the book, wondering whether he or she would meet a visitor while sleeping, or perhaps suddenly remembering some dream frighteningly similar to the experiences Strieber described.

The "Visitors" as Part of the "Entity Enigma"

Toward the end of *Communion*, Strieber offered his own list of speculations about who the visitors might be. He conjectured that they could indeed be from one or more other planets; that they could be from earth but so completely unrecognizable to us that we have not previously regarded them as real; that they might be from another dimension; that they might be time-travelers from the earth's future; that they might surge up from within us as creations of our own imaginations; or that they might be hallucinations caused by some natural phenomenon such as magnetism or extremely low-frequency electrical currents. Strieber even speculated that the visitors might be humans in a highly evolved state who have passed through the gates of death and returned to work with us.

Each one of Strieber's speculations about the identity of the visitors is tantalizing in itself, offering a fascinating (but not necessarily fruitful) intellectual journey to anyone who would explore them in their length and breadth. One of the few hypotheses that Strieber didn't mention was the possibility that the visitors might be inhabitants of a "hollow earth," an idea that actually has a certain amount of acceptance in certain UFO circles.

In actuality, Strieber's line of thinking is reflective of the vast array of experiences connected with and explanations offered for what some investigators have come to call the "entity enigma." At first glance, it would seem that the content of Strieber's story is no different from hundreds of cases on record of people reporting terrifying experiences with "bedroom visitors," ghosts, poltergeists, apparitions, religious visions, and what have been regarded as demons. The entire array of such phenomena is beginning to be studied by serious ufologists with training in the psychological and social sciences, most notably by Hilary Evans, whose *Visions, Apparitions, Alien Visitors: A Comparative Study of the Entity Enigma* makes an attempt to thoroughly survey the colorful panoply of anomalous phenomena concerning strange, nonhuman beings.

Books such as Evans's are particularly useful in gaining a degree of insight into the problems associated with evaluating "abduction" stories, which have characteristics quite different from traditional accounts of house hauntings and poltergeist activity. They also contain enough information for any imaginative writer, it would seem, to use in concocting his or her own abduction experience story, and no doubt many a reader of *Communion* who was aware of the availability of works such as Evans's wondered to what extent Strieber was influenced, if at all, by such information. Questions about Strieber's intentions naturally pose considerable difficulties to anyone who hasn't had anything resembling the experiences that he describes in *Communion*, or those described by other investigators of "UFO abductions." Even if some people might believe they have had experiences such as Strieber's, they might have just as much reason to question their own sanity as to seriously regard the experience as having some kind of objective reality apart from their own imagination. As a consequence, we are left with a *social* problem in evaluating testimonies such as those delivered to us by Strieber and other presumed UFO "abductees." Is there any way in which we can rationally evaluate the ostensibly incredible stories that we are being told by persons who speak to us in all apparent sincerity? Can one possibly approach an understanding of who Strieber's visitors are by obtaining an in-depth understanding of his story, or are we all being led down another primrose path, overcome by curiosity about 1980s-style "Deros"?

No one can rationally read a book like *Communion* without confronting those concerns, a factor that has no doubt played a predominant role in the success that *Communion* has enjoyed. We are fascinated, I would say, by the questions the book raises as much as by the strangeness of its narrative. As a result, sales of *Communion* have no doubt benefited from both the controversy and the adulation that have followed its meteoric course through the marketplace. Then, too, Strieber's descriptions of his experiences are so richly textured that they have most likely led many a reader into a "willing suspensing of disbelief" for sufficient periods of time to make the thought of the visitors' reality not inconceivable. Since large segments of the American population have been documented in more than one poll as already believing in the likelihood that UFOs are indeed physical spaceships carrying real aliens, millions of potential readers are receptive to reading a book that purports to explore what an apparent human-alien contact might be like. It doesn't matter that Strieber refuses to cast his experience in language that refers to interplanetary travel via "spaceships" or "aliens." The public clearly wants to learn more about what it believes it already knows, and is tantalized by the prospect of actually getting a firsthand account of aliens.

Yet Strieber himself has maintained that he does not precisely know who his visitors are, thereby upsetting the applecarts of many of his readers. In an interview he gave me in April 1987, Strieber said, "Bear in mind that I think of the visitors primarily as a mode of perception. I don't necessarily assume, by any stretch of the imagination, that they are visitors from another planet." In actuality, the thrust of his entire public record points toward his willingness to seriously consider the possibility that the world of the visitors abuts ours, though in another "plane" or "dimension." When asked if he could be more specific about the nature of the "visitor experience," Strieber said, "I don't know what it is. I think UFO experiences are very much a curtain, and I'd like to know what's behind that curtain very much."

Then, of course, there is the factor of *fear*. Whitley Strieber frankly admits in *Communion* that his initial response to the visitors was complete abject terror, a fear so great that, as he put it in *Communion*, " 'Whitley' ceased to exist." Nor was the process of adjustment to his experiences, when he was gradually remembering them while under hypnotherapy, an easy one. He acknowledges that there were moments when he had feelings of what he took to be paranoid delusion, and consequently questioned his own sanity. Strieber's own account of his gradual perception of the visitors as entities who had a real, independent existence and who directly affected his life is characterized by his emphasis on the fact that, in order to know the visitors, he had to overcome many of his deepest fears.

In other words, as Strieber once put it to me in conversation, "you have to *earn* whatever knowledge you have of them."

Fairy Tales, Jung, Archetypes

Strieber's philosophical stance in regard to his visitors is significant, in that it is considerably at variance with the traditional, popularly held conception of the entities reported in association with UFO sightings as being, of necessity, extraterrestrial in origin and/or necessarily benevolent in intent. In fact, some of his comments in *Communion* indicate he believes that visitor behavior may be fruitfully compared with that attributed to the legendary entities known as "fairies." As he put it: "Maybe the fairy was a real species, for example. Perhaps they now floated around in unidentified flying objects and wielded insight producing wands because they have enjoyed their own technological revolution."[4]

While Strieber's speculation that the fairy may travel through the air in UFOs is certainly no more than an educated guess, it is interesting to observe that more than one Irish source has recorded the belief that the fairy were, indeed, of nonterrestrial, in fact heavenly, origin. As folklorist D. R. McAnally, Jr., relates in his *Irish Wonders:*

> According to the most reliable of the rural "fairy men," the fairies were once angels, so numerous as to have formed a large part of the population of heaven. When Satan sinned and drew throngs of the heavenly host with him into open rebellion, a large number of the less warlike spirits stood aloof from the

contest that followed, fearing the consequences, and not caring
to take sides until the issue of the conflict was determined.
Upon the defeat and expulsion of the rebellious angels, those
who had remained neutral were punished by banishment from
heaven, but their offence being only one of omission, they
were not consigned to the pit with Satan and his followers, but
were sent to Earth where they still remain, not without hope
that on the last day they may be pardoned and readmitted to
Paradise. They are thus on their good behavior, but having
power to do infinite harm, they are much feared, and spoken
of, either in a whisper or aloud, as the "good people."[5]

While Strieber does not *reduce* the "visitors" to of necessity having
to be "fairies" (or anything at all, for that matter), he nevertheless
stringently avoids making any mention of them as "extraterrestrial aliens."
Such an approach may hardly seem scientific either to people in the
UFO community or to the professional skeptics, for reasons distinct to
each community. While the mainstream scientific community continues to pooh-pooh the entire UFO phenomenon and insist that only
deep-space listening programs will put us in touch with aliens, the
UFO community in general has been so committed to believing that
UFOs transport extraterrestrials that it is reluctant to consider any other
possibility. Nevertheless, Strieber has advanced his position in all seriousness. Indeed, the strength and persistence of his own public communications about the visitors, delivered from such an unconventional
point of view, have intensified the debate in the UFO community
over whether the "extraterrestrial hypothesis" (the belief that UFOs
and their "crews" *must* be from outer space) is a serviceable concept.
To reduce the debate to basic terms: Are the visitors something akin
to leprechauns, or are they "space brothers" from, say, the Pleiades?
  That question, of course, is unanswerable when simply posed as a
rhetorical device, and even more unanswerable in terms of any kind
of objectifiable evidence. Perhaps some concerns, however, are not
best addressed head-on, but do better when approached indirectly. Since
we have previously dealt with the larger question of whether Strieber's
account reflects insanity or dishonesty, we may presume that the visitors certainly do have an objective reality *at least* "in his own mind,"
a psychic reality, if you will. We are culturally conditioned to regard
the psyche as a scientifically insignificant nonentity, but such attitudes

only ignore the entire development of contemporary psychology. If we grant that the visitors are indeed psychic realities for Whitley Strieber and other abductees, then they may be susceptible to an analysis on their own terms, much as the characters of a dream (or perhaps the personages encountered in a fairy tale) may be analyzed by someone skilled in interpretation. Owing to their high level of strangeness, the visitors have recently been compared by some ufologists to what psychologists call the "Other," which leads into the possibility of regarding them (along the lines of the psychology of Carl Jung) as *archetypal* realities, having a legitimate psychic existence in the unconscious mind of Whitley Strieber. Such an approach to understanding the visitors does not by any means rule out the possibility that they may also have a very solid, corporeal aspect, too. In the absence of being able to refer to a solid visitor body, though, we have no choice but to examine the question of how the visitors behave or (to use a verb that does not presuppose that they necessarily have a biological nature), "manifest" themselves at the level of the psyche.

Carl Jung introduced the term "archetype" into modern psychology as a result of his extensive analysis of the symbolism he found revealed in his patients' dreams. Jung came to regard the archetypes as autonomous forces at work at the deepest levels of the mind, crystallizations of a very real psychic energy that manifests in dream imagery in a variety of forms. Archetypes such as the Father, the Mother, anima and animus (ostensibly "female" and "male" aspects of the psyche), and the Child are examples of ways in which these forces display themselves in images (and sometimes even as "presences") that have a symbolic meaning to the person in quest of maturity. To Jungian psychoanalysis, a mature individual is characterized by a quality that has come to be called "wholeness," or the ability to effectively integrate in one's personal life thinking, feeling, intuition, and sensation—what Jung held to be the four primary faculties of human consciousness. One function normally predominates to the exclusion of others, in this system, but an integrated person has learned how to accord equal weight to information he receives from each faculty.

While it would be a mistake to try to fit Whitley Strieber's visitor experiences into a Jungian box, Strieber himself makes so many references to the manner in which the visitors affected his unconscious mind (using terms he himself borrowed from Jung) that one is forced to ask if a Jungian approach is useful in regard to understanding Strieber's story.

What did Jung mean when he used the term "unconscious"? In *Archetypes of the Collective Unconscious,* Jung wrote:

A more or less superficial layer of the unconscious is undoubtedly personal. I call it the *personal unconscious.* But this personal unconscious rests upon a deeper layer, which does not derive from personal experience and is not a personal acquisition but is inborn. This deeper layer I call the *collective unconscious.* I have chosen the term "collective" because this part of the unconscious is not individual but universal; unlike the personal psyche, it has contents and modes of behavior that are more or less the same everywhere in all individuals. It is, in other words, identical in all men and thus constitutes a common psychic substrate of a supra-personal nature which is present in every one of us.[6] [Italics Jung's]

If we are willing to forgo the insoluble problem of establishing some kind of genus-and-species classification for the visitors, we may explore the possibilities of considering the visitors as functions of the "collective unconscious," as "archetypes" through an interpretive approach outlined by the noted Jungian psychologist Marie Louise von Franz in her book *Interpretation of Fairy Tales.* As she puts it:

In terms of Jung's concept, every archetype is in its essence an *unknown* psychic factor and therefore there is no possibility of translating its content into intellectual terms. The best we can do is circumscribe it on the basis of our own psychological experience and from comparative studies, bringing into light, as it were, the whole net of associations in which the archetypal images are enmeshed. The fairy tale itself is its own best explanation; that is, its meaning is contained in the totality of its motifs connected by the thread of the story. The unconscious is, metaphorically speaking, in the same position as one who has had an original vision or experience and wishes to share it. Since it is an event that has never been conceptually formulated he is at a loss for means of expression. When a person is in that position he makes several attempts to convey the thing and tries to evoke, by intuitive appeal and analogy to familiar material, some response in his listeners, and never tires of expounding his vision until he feels that they have some sense of the content. [Italics in original]⁷

If we might for a moment regard Strieber as "one who has had an original vision and wishes to share it," his compulsion to write *Communion* and communicate his experience is certainly reminiscent of the kind of condition of which Von Franz is speaking. Yet it is important to remember that what she is referring to is *the compulsion of the unconscious mind itself* to communicate its truth, behaving as though it were a person who has seen something extraordinary. In other words, the unconscious has a way of erupting into our awareness, forcing us to meet the archetypes as though they were, in fact, somehow real. That process of eruption and encounter, she would have us know, is what is communicated in fairy tales. Yet Von Franz goes on to make an interesting generalization about fairy tales. She writes, "In the same way we can put forward the hypothesis that every fairy tale is a relatively closed system compounding one essential psychological meaning which is expressed in a series of symbolical pictures and events and is discoverable in these."⁸

What is the "one essential psychological meaning" that Von Franz believes is contained in every fairy tale? As she expresses it: "This unknown fact is what Jung called the Self, which is the psychic totality of the individual and also, paradoxically, the regulating center of the collective unconscious."⁹

Looked at closely, it could be said that *Communion* bears a remarkable resemblance to Von Franz's definition of a fairy tale. Surely Strieber was in a position of trying to convey "an original vision or experience" through a "series of symbolical pictures and events," because his "visitors" were, from the very beginning, a very real "*unknown* psychic factor."

Am I proposing that we try to analyze Strieber's experiences as though they were a dream or a fairy tale? I am. Yet in doing so, I by no means intend to give the definitive interpretation of Whitley Strieber's visitor experiences. In fact, we are in no position to even begin to analyze Strieber's experiences before attempting to understand "the whole net of associations" in which his archetypal images (i.e., the visitors) are enmeshed. Before moving into such an analysis, though, we might try to "circumscribe" what we know of the visitors through what Whitley Strieber tells us, drawing on our own psychological experience as a gauge of his story's merit, and to illuminate his story through making careful comparisons with other, similar stories. It appears we have no choice but to follow that difficult path, in which we can only proceed from one question to the next, hopefully refining our inquiry at each successive step. If we are to be fair to Strieber, too, we will have to follow his lead into some rather difficult intellectual terrain, where the possibility of misunderstanding and misinterpretation is very high. The dangers of misinterpreting Strieber's narrative are especially great at this time, moreover, since such a great deal of commentary on *Communion* has been published, some of it deliberately intended to impugn Strieber's credibility and sanity.

The "Visitors" as a "Mode of Perception"

What does Strieber mean by saying he thinks of the visitors as "a mode of perception"? Does he mean that one must be in an altered state of consciousness in order to even "see" them? Has Strieber seen his visitors while under the influence of drugs? Readers of *Communion* will remember Strieber's statement (later successfully tested, for what it is worth, by a polygrapher) that he does not now and has not in the past used consciousness-altering drugs. However, simply because he has eschewed the use of psychoactive drugs does not mean that Strieber does not see consciousness itself as a variable. In a talk he gave to the "Angels, Aliens, and Archetypes" conference on November 20, 1987, in San Francisco, Strieber pointed out to the audience that he had trained his capacity to direct his conscious attention through exercises that he learned in his work with the Gurdjieff Foundation in New York (an organization founded to foster the practice of the system of psychological self-transformation propounded by the mystical author and artist G. I. Gurdjieff).

As he put it: "I believe that the techniques I learned in that training—particularly a form of double-tone chanting—have enabled me to remain conscious in some experiences with the visitors where I otherwise would have been unconscious."

Clearly, Strieber has made the task of satisfying our simple curiosity about the identity of his visitors a difficult one. By stating that he sees a link between human perception itself and the nature of the visitors, Strieber has introduced into the UFO dialogue the idea that one's own state of consciousness has a part to play in understanding the visitor experience. While Strieber does not deny that there is an objectively real component to the experience, he nevertheless presents an element of what might be called "radical subjectivity" into his interpretation of it—radical in the sense of plunging to the roots of the mind itself.

How, then, given the intellectual problems it poses, might it be possible to even begin to get a sense of the identity of Strieber's visitors, assuming for the sake of argument that they are indeed something more than a figment of his imagination or a hallucination? Perhaps it might be best not to confront the problem directly, but rather, yielding to its difficulty, use something akin to intellectual judo in beginning to try to answer it.

As a point of origin, it may be useful to survey notable speculation about the identity of "aliens" or "visitors," drawn from an examination of some of the more highly visible and influential contributions to UFO literature written in the past forty years. Though it might seem an extremely unlikely area in which to look for parallels, it may also be profitable to delve into the world of Western ceremonial magic, where can be found a formidable tradition of reported communication and/or interaction with nonhuman entities of many descriptions. This tradition is different in several ways from the traditions of the spiritualist movement, and is not to be confused with its contemporary manifestation, now known as "channeling." What distinguishes it from other traditions is its formal, ritualistic aspect and the fact that some contemporary occultists, particularly those working within the Ordo Templi Orientis, a magical order founded by the controversial Aleister Crowley, have claimed that there is a relation between the entities with which they are in contact and some UFO phenomena. This claim has gained attention in recent years through the writings of Kenneth Grant, Crowley's successor as head of the OTO, as well as through the popular writings of Robert Anton Wilson, in his *Cosmic Trigger* and other books.

Is there any relationship between the "nonhuman" entities associated with UFO sightings and visitor experiences and those supposedly summoned into magical circles by magicians such as Aleister Crowley? The question is apropos of Strieber's approach, I believe, because both Strieber and the magicians see nonhuman entities as related to our modes of perception, to the dynamics of our consciousness itself.

After making that survey, we may have the foundation necessary to turn, in the following chapter, to a closer examination of Strieber's own text in *Communion*, casting an analytical eye on his descriptions of the visitors themselves and their various forms of behavior, as he remembers them. Moreover, we will follow up his own suggestion that the visitor experience may be understood through an inquiry into the traditions of human-fairy interaction as recorded in a certain old Irish fairy tale. While fairy lore might seem like the last place to look for an understanding of what happened to Strieber at the hands of the visitors, it behooves us to follow up the clues that he has planted in *Communion*, and see where such a path might lead us. As descriptive as he is, there are many things that Strieber left unsaid in *Communion*. Still, he did not leave us bereft of the means for more fully understanding what, it seems, he would have us know.

The ETs: Venusians, Pleiadians, and other "Space Brothers"

In the world of UFOs and aliens, there has never been any lack of people who are ready to tell the world "the truth" about UFOs. In the period immediately following Kenneth Arnold's famous 1947 sighting of nine "flying saucers" above Mount Rainier (a date often mistakenly taken as the beginning of contemporary UFO sightings), the world was entertained by the declarations of George Adamski, whose sensational testimony in *Flying Saucers Have Landed* (coauthored by British writer Desmond Leslie) reported his alleged November 20, 1952, encounter near Desert Center, California, with a "Venusian" who wore a one-piece body suit and long blond hair. The Venusians communicated to Adamski their concern about recent atomic bomb tests, a message that was subsequently to become increasingly common in alien-human contacts. In subsequent works, Adamski reported what he took to be the presence of English-speaking Venusians on earth, walking the streets of Los Angeles in ordinary business suits, indistinguishable from ordinary earthmen. He even claimed to have been taken by them to the moon, where he said he saw that its dark side was inhabited by men who could boast of clean cities and beautiful homes. Other early writers, such as George Hunt Williamson in *Other Tongues—Other Flesh*, produced equally incredible claims about UFO-related alien intervention in human affairs, laced with a good deal of religious fervor and dubious anthropological speculation. (Williamson was a colleague of Adamski's who reportedly accompanied him on his trip to Desert Center, and later signed an affidavit attesting to having seen a being matching Adamski's description of the Venusian.) Williamson also advanced the idea that there was some kind of cosmic good-versus-evil struggle going on between "beneficent" Pleiadians and "maleficent" natives of Orion—an interesting theme, in that Pleiadians would later figure so prominently in subsequent UFO stories.

In the years that followed, the books of Erich von Däniken trumpeted to the world his dubiously documented "ancient astronaut hypothesis" (though the term "hypothesis" is quite misleading) through his commercially successful *Chariots of the Gods?* and other books. The author did not bother to specifically identify his "ancient astronauts," preferring instead to assert that the advanced pre-Columbian civilizations of South America could not have arisen without the direct intercession of visitors from space. Needless to say, such a viewpoint has not been appreciated by Latin American intellectuals, and has hardly been introduced into the legitimate anthropology being done in the region. As popular as they were only a decade ago, Von Däniken's speculations have largely dropped out of current UFO debates for their manifest failure to make any contribution toward an understanding of UFO abduction phenomena as they are currently being reported.

As it turned out, the advocates of the position that UFOs and their occupants *must* be from other planets (what is known in UFO circles as the "extraterrestrial hypothesis," or ETH) initially advanced their arguments with so little regard for civilized rules of intelligent discourse (making claims completely unwarranted by the evidence they put forth to support them) that the public debate on the subject of UFOs remained largely paralyzed during the late 1960s and 1970s. While members of UFO organizations continued to advocate the ETH, members of the scientific and intellectual establishment found it easy to destroy their arguments on the basis of their fallacious reasoning, inadequate or falsified evidence and/or intellectual naïveté. Within the UFO community a greater degree of sophistication in researching and discussing anomalous phenomena certainly developed, but no major books or publicity campaigns that affected the mass audience emerged as a result.

And so the debate about the origin of UFOs and the nature of their "occupants" languished until the spring of 1987, when the publication of yet another book supporting the "extraterrestrial hypothesis" surfaced, in concert with *Communion* and *Intruders*. Gary Kinder's *Light Years: An Investigation into the Extraterrestrial Experiences of Eduard Meier*, brought to the American public the story of a Swiss caretaker who had already achieved a fair amount of fame in Europe for his remarkable color photographs of what he described as "beam ships," as well as for his stories of visitations by humanlike entities who, he said, claimed to be from the Pleiades, a cluster of seven stars in the constellation Taurus.

Although Kinder's book is written in a highly popular style and is completely devoid of the kind of documentation or bibliography that might help an independent researcher verify his claims, it is nevertheless a rather compelling story. Though Meier is reportedly a relatively uneducated, simple man, he has favorably impressed some of the world's most ardent pursuers of UFO-related information by both the force of his arguments and his remarkable photographs. He has also provoked vociferous accusations from other UFO researchers that he is perpetrating an enormous hoax. According to Kinder, the photographs attributed to Meier are quite extraordinary in both their quantity (Meier says he has literally hundreds) and in their quality, not to mention their mode of execution. (Kinder states that Meier claims he just takes his old 35-millimeter SLR camera out to the site when "called" and snaps the shutter without regard to adjusting the f-stop or the focus.)

One of the more curious aspects of Kinder's book is his account of Meier's relationship with his Pleiadian visitors. According to Kinder, Meier responds to all of the mentally received summonses from his visitors. His principal contact with the Pleiadians, according to Kinder, is an entity in the form of a beautiful, blond-haired woman named "Semjase." Moreover, Meier's own thinking has been profoundly influenced by Semjase, Kinder says, in that he has come to believe that all of our earth-based religions are encumbered by antiquated myths. As a result, according to Kinder, Meier is given to making strong statements highly critical of organized religion here on earth. The people from the Pleiades are here to help us evolve spiritually, he is reported to say, insisting that organized religions are preventing us from evolving as we should.

In this respect, the content of some of Meier's testimony, even though apparently made more credible by his high-quality photographs, fits to a certain extent within the pattern of some flying-saucer "cults" that had a brief period of efflorescence in countercultural California during the 1970s. Most notable of all was the One World Family Commune of Berkeley, which operated a restaurant on Telegraph Avenue. Jacques Vallee included an essay on the One World Family (whose leader, Allen-Michael Noonan, claimed to be the spirit of the archangel Michael) in *Messengers of Deception*, and it has also been mentioned in a less objective and informative manner in *UFOs: What on Earth Is Happening*, a fundamentalist Christian attack on UFO messianism by John Weldon and Zola Levitt. Part of the One World Family's philosophical justification for existence was its assertion that all world institutions were hopelessly corrupt, and that it was necessary to form a new alliance with the "space brothers" in the interest of saving humanity. Nor were they loath to express that idea by very striking visual means. On an outside wall of the restaurant, for example, was displayed a colorfully painted mural depicting a priest in Roman collar, a farmer in blue-jean bib overalls, and a U.S. Army soldier in helmet and olive drab fatigues standing beneath a hovering flying saucer emitting a beam of light that encompassed them all. The mural's legend read: FARMERS, SOLDIERS, CLERGY: UNITE!

While such imaginative and almost cartoonish graphics no doubt added to the group's countercultural charm (especially to alienated young students and/or dropouts), the thread that runs through both Meier's commentaries on religion and the One World Family's appeal to form an alliance with "space brothers" is nothing more than common *despair*. Humanity, embroiled in problems too complex to solve by itself, must seek the aid of higher, more evolved beings in solving its problems. While Meier's testimony may well deserve serious consideration in its own right, it is rather significant that his "message" received a fair amount of public attention during early 1987, at the same time *Communion* and *Intruders* appeared in the bookstores. Once again an old theme in the saucer literature repeated itself: salvation through benevolent intercession from above. It is very important to emphasize here what a world of difference exists between the approaches taken by Strieber, Hopkins, and Kinder in writing their books. It would be a severe mistake for armchair observers of the UFO scene to take what appears to be the political or religious radicalism they see in pronouncements such as Meier's and generalize from them that all writers in the UFO community share the same viewpoint. Neither Strieber nor Hopkins engaged in explicit ideological or religious rhetoric in their respective books, nor did Hopkins do so in his earlier work, *Missing Time*. Both Strieber and Hopkins, moreover, were dealing with abduction phenomena of an emotionally charged and terrifying nature, experiences far different from the rather pleasant ones that Meier reported having enjoyed aboard the so-called "Pleiadian" "beam ships."

Interestingly, the Pleiadian mysteries as expounded to Meier by Semjase have been recently resurrected in another book, entitled *The Fellowship*, by Brad Steiger, the author of numerous popular works on UFOs and entities whom he unabashedly refers to as the "space brothers."

While many of the UFO-related stories that Steiger reports may have been faithfully recorded, his most recent book is reflective of much of the rhetoric that seems to accompany the impulses within part of the UFO community to form a new religion. Indeed, Steiger comes right out and says at the beginning of his book that "the UFO contactees may be evolving prototypes of a future evangelism. They may be heralds of a New Age religion, a blending of technology and traditional religious concepts."[10]

Steiger's use of vague terms in a nonspecific context (e.g., "technology" and "evolving prototypes") and his penchant for using emotionally charged and uninformative rhetorical devices (such as "traditional religious concepts" or "future evangelism") make it occasionally very difficult to wrest any shred of precise meaning from his pages. Indeed, Steiger himself seems oblivious to the problem of trying to provide people with some basis of information that can be rationally discussed and evaluated. Rather, it appears he sees himself as a cosmic evangelist, interpreting UFOs, and the "space brothers" as emissaries of "higher consciousness." While such writings may be inspirational for many people, they do little to elevate the general level of public discussion regarding the full spectrum of phenomena—physical, mental, emotional, "psychic," and social—accompanying reported UFO abductions, nor do they deal seriously with the problem of trauma often experienced by many people who report what they consider to have been abductions.

Indeed, the growing attack on the "extraterrestrial hypothesis" that can be found increasingly represented in the pages of American UFO publications (e.g., the *MUFON UFO Journal* and *UFO*) is reflective of an increasing dissatisfaction within the UFO community itself with the manner in which advocates of an extraterrestrial origin for aliens appear to be using their speculations as the foundation of a new UFO-centered religion. The arguments that advocates such as Steiger make ultimately turn into appeals for belief in a certain set of propositions, not reasoned requests for more well-qualified researchers who might take on the rather thankless task of trying to understand abduction reports in their entirety, especially in their fearsome aspect. "Explanations" of UFO-related events that hinge upon one or another particular "metaphysical" teaching seem to suffer from a tendency to distort reports of visitor-human interaction to suit the author's purposes, as is certainly the case with Steiger in the overgeneralizations he makes about such contacts in his film *The Truth About UFO's and E.T.'s.*

Speaking as the film's host and narrator, Steiger describes his own childhood experience of encountering a short, big-eyed alien as having been "tranquil" prior to the moment when he lost consciousness. On the basis of that experience, Steiger goes on to say, a feeling of "tranquility" characterizes the moment of close "contact" immediately prior to loss of consciousness in most reported visitor-human interactions. Steiger notes that abductees are often frightened and agitated by seeing a UFO land prior to their close encounter, and return to that state of fright after awakening from their moment of tranquil loss of consciousness. What is remarkable about Steiger's description of such a "classic" abduction experience is that it is simply false to fact in the light of Hopkins's research and Strieber's narrative, not to mention the thousands of letters that Strieber has received from people who have reported abductions that do not reveal the pattern Steiger would have us accept. In the same film, Steiger also conveniently avoids dealing with the thorny problem of what happens after people lose consciousness in the visitor experience.

The possibility may indeed exist that by means yet to be developed, some UFO phenomena may one day be "proved" to be of a truly extraterrestrial origin (whatever that designation might really mean in terms of the physics of interstellar travel), but for the moment it appears that the advocates of the "extraterrestrial hypothesis" are moving more toward the creation of a New Age religious movement founded upon tenets of *irrational belief* than toward improvements of their hypothesis that would make it more testable.

Inside the Mind, Inside the Magic Triangle

While such observations concerning the problems of making a religion out of UFO contact may seem obvious to the seasoned reader of UFO literature, they tend to get missed so frequently in public discussion of abduction phenomena that I believe my emphasis is not misplaced. Would it be unreasonable to observe that in the face of the mysteries posed by UFO sightings and apparent visitor experiences, the human imagination rushes in to fill the gaps created by our own ignorance, aided by plenty of emotional longing for some kind of relief from life's tedium?

The questions opened by considering the relation between visitor abduction phenomena and the human mind are formidable. Could there be some kind of link between the visitors and the human imagination itself, that faculty of visualization so intimately connected with dreaming and the world of unconscious and subconscious imagery? Do visitor experiences have some kind of reality grounded in the apparent structure of the unconscious mind (as we understand it through the psychological system of C. G. Jung)? Are they reducible to being "archetypal experiences," or do they have a nature that is both inner (subjective) and outer (objective) simultaneously? Is it legitimately possible to speculate that the visitors, as Strieber intimates in *Communion*, are deliberately engaged in a process of entering the unconscious mind, of "communing" with us in a way that changes our own perceptions of what we have come to consider reality?

As "far-out" as they may seem, questions such as those are beginning to be asked with greater frequency within the world of the UFO community, but an interesting perspective on such inquiries comes from entirely outside the ranks of UFO investigators. Contemporary occultism (a highly diverse movement composed of people interested in exploring the reach of the mind and the nature of reality by meditational, ritual, and other means, often incorrectly branded as "Satanism" by yellow journalists and unscrupulous fundamentalist religious leaders) has begun to address the significance of the UFO and visitor phenomenon, and in so doing has forced some researchers to view the apparently outlandish and irrational claims of traditional occultism in another light.

One of the most prominent contemporary figures in this context was Aleister Crowley, whose life as an advocate of a system of magical self-transformation continues to elicit both praise and condemnation forty-one years after his death. In recent years, his self-appointed appellation of the Great Beast seems to have resulted in a corresponding popular cultural fascination with the cabalistic significance of "666," that title's supposed numerological analogue, especially among adolescents who follow the music of heavy-metal rock and roll groups and other culturally dissident members of society. His magical society, the Ordo Templi Orientis, continues to operate in a low-key manner in Britain and the United States.

As the son of parents who fiercely adhered to the extremely strict precepts of an ultra-Protestant sect known as the Darbyites, or Exclusive Brethren, Crowley developed a visceral hatred for the fundamentalist Christianity of his childhood and a corresponding fascination with ritual magic that led him to seek initiation into the then-flourishing Order of the Golden Dawn. With such distinguished members of the English empire's cultural elite as William Butler Yeats, Arthur Machen, and Florence Farr (a noted actress of the day, once lover to George Bernard Shaw and herself a prominent Fabian), the order promised its initiates the possibility of an evolution to a transhuman state through following a graded system of ritual and memory work that presumably opened the neophyte's consciousness to ever more subtle realms of perception. Such an evolution of consciousness was attributed to contact (through the practice of magical evocation) with such nonhuman entities as one's own "guardian angel" and other "angels" pertaining to different "spheres" of the cosmos.

According to Francis King in his somewhat sensationalist but highly informative biography entitled *The Magical World of Aleister Crowley*, Crowley was one of the few members of the Order of the Golden Dawn who actually attempted communication with angels. He did so through conducting a ceremony for communicating with his "holy guardian angel" as described in an early-Renaissance cabalistic text known as *The Sacred Magic of Abra-Melin the Mage*. Crowley also attempted to contact nonhuman entities through the practice of an obscure system known as the Enochian Calls, developed by John Dee, one of the most brilliant mathematicians of Elizabethan England, who is reputed to have taught the art of navigation to Sir Francis Drake.

While Crowley's Abra-Melin ceremonies (which he conducted on the shore of Loch Ness) were aborted and there remains little record of his experimentation with the Enochian Calls, he did claim to have received a number of psychic "transmissions" of information that he regarded as being of extraterrestrial origin. It has remained the task of Kenneth Grant, Crowley's spiritual heir, to elucidate some of the OTO's material in this regard, a project that took the form of a book entitled *Outside the Circles of Time.* The author makes clear throughout the book his opinion that contemporary manifestations of lights in the sky and human-alien or human-visitor contact are related to the world historical crisis, with humanity on the precipice of global catastrophe. Moreover, he contends, we cannot understand these phenomena without understanding some of the deeper, and indeed darker, aspects of the mind in both its unconscious and subconscious aspects.

In the introduction to *Outside the Circles of Time,* Grant observes that only recently has it been possible to reevaluate Crowley's work in a manner that "lifts it out of the exclusively 'occult' framework." It is the task of his book to introduce certain ideas left undeveloped by Crowley, he says, adding:

> That these ideas have remained undeveloped until now is not surprising when it is realized that Crowley's death in 1947 coincided with the occurrence of an unprecedented wave of inexplicable phenomena relating to space, and the mysterious objects that sometimes appear in it. Since that time a totally new scene has emerged and the more sensitive members of the human race have consequently become acutely aware of the possibility of consciously directed and self-intelligent life existing outside or beyond humanity.[11]

Grant returns to this theme later in the book, in the chapter "Nu-Isis," in which he expresses the theme of despair at man's apparent inability to save himself from destruction without some "external intervention," without a "veritable miracle." As he puts it:

> Some believe that the UFO phenomena are part of the "miracle," and a mounting mass of evidence seems to suggest that mysterious entities have been located within the earth's ambience for countless centuries and that more and more people are being born with innate ability to see, or in some way sense their presence.

Prayer for deific intervention in ancient times has now become a *cri de coeur* to extra-terrestrial or interdimensional entities, according to whether the manifestations are viewed as
occurring within man's consciousness, or outside himself in
apparently objective but often invisible entities. New Isis Lodge
has in its archives the sigils of some of these entities. The sigils
come from a *grimoire* of unknown origin which forms part of
the dark quabalahs of Besqul, located by magicians in the Tunnel of Qulielfi. The *grimoire* describes Four Gates of extraterrestrial entry into, and emergence from, the known Universe.[12]

In the last paragraph, Grant makes a deliberate connection between what he believes are the entities connected with UFO sightings
and what he claims to know as entities that (or who) have been contacted and identified by himself and his colleagues, through the traditional means of ceremonial magic. The "sigils" that Grant refers to
are line drawings of a very distinctive nature, diagrams that serve as
the signatures, if you will, of entities presumably accessible to the call
of the trained magician. A *grimoire*, of course, is a directory of such
sigils, as well as a manual for their employment, for the purpose of
obtaining information of benefit to the magician or the transaction of
business in the form of services rendered by the entity to the magician.

As to the manner of ceremonial evocation, that procedure traditionally involved the inscription of a floor with two diagrams: a magic
triangle, into which the entity would be summoned, and a magic circle, within which was to be drawn a pentagram inscribed with appropriate sigils and cabalistic lettering. According to Francis King, Crowley
himself used this method in conjunction with the Enochian Calls of
John Dee in his ritual evocation of Choronzon, an entity that Dee
and Edward Kelly reported they evoked in Elizabethan times. Grant
refers to Choronzon as "the Guardian of the Abyss," and notes that
Kelly describes him as "that mighty devil," while Crowley regarded
him "as the first and deadliest of all the powers of evil."

According to Francis King, Crowley's interest in evoking Choronzon was motivated by his desire to become one of the "Secret Chiefs"
of his order, a spiritual ambition that had been with him for years. In
a subsequent angelic evocation (or "Aire"), Crowley reported he was
told by an angel that he might well become a master of the inner

planes, but he would have to "cross the Abyss," or, in other words, undergo a complete ego-death, to do so. The "abyss" in Western occultism has become a code word for that "dark night of the soul" that traditionally precedes experiences of divine illumination, yet it is also understood that one must deal with a challenge from the "gatekeeper" of that abyss. It was this "Dweller on the Threshold" or "Guardian of the Abyss" whom Crowley wished to confront and conquer in his evocation of Choronzon.

As King relates the story of that evocation, which Crowley performed with the aid of his associate Victor Neuberg:

> In the eleventh Aire Crowley received the intimation that although he had unconsciously crossed the Abyss—the psychological barrier between ordinary men and the Secret Chiefs— he must now, in the tenth Aire, cross it consciously. To this end he and Neuberg prepared for a ceremonial evocation to Choronzon, the "mighty devil" of the Abyss. This was done on 6 December at Bou Saada, where they walked from the town to an isolated valley floored with fine sand. A large circle of rocks was constructed, around it were drawn protective Names of Power, and outside was drawn a large triangle. This last was designed to be the place in which Choronzon, "first and deadliest of all the powers of evil," was to manifest himself, and around it further protective "names of power" were traced in the sand. At the points of the triangle Crowley sacrificed three pigeons so that the elemental force derived from their blood would provide a material basis for Choronzon to manifest himself.[13]

In a most unusual and dangerous move, Crowley even went so far as to place himself *inside the magic triangle* where Choronzon was to appear. As King puts it:

> In other words, Crowley was to be the first magician in occult history to keep his body in the mystic triangle and offer it for an evil spirit to manifest itself through. During this process Crowley was to be in full trance, his everyday consciousness in "a secret place" and unaware of the doings of Choronzon.[14]

King continues:

> After Crowley had called the Aire Neuberg heard a voice
> cry out "Zazas [sic], Zasas, Nasatanda Zasas." This voice, which
> according to Neuberg simulated Crowley's own voice, went on
> to utter various blasphemies. Then Neuberg began to see things.
> He beheld in the triangle a woman's body resembling that of a
> prostitute he had known in Paris. She tried to seduce him, but
> he, deciding that it was Choronzon who had adopted this form
> in the hope of getting within the protective circle, resisted. The
> woman—or the demon—then changed its shape, apologized
> and made an appeal to Neuberg's pride by offering to lay her
> head beneath his foot in token of submission. Neuberg resisted
> this blandishment also. Choronzon turned into an old man,
> then into a snake, then into the form of Crowley, who begged
> for water, a request which Neuberg refused.[15]

After a verbal duel with the demon, Neuberg invoked a spirit named
Aiwass, the presumed entity whom Crowley "channeled" in writing
The Book of the Law, and ordered Choronzon to "make a clear statement of his nature." Choronzon identified himself as "Dispersion,"
and returned to blaspheming. While Neuberg was feverishly attempting to transcribe everything, the "demon" reportedly was able to throw
sand onto the border of the magic circle.

As King narrates the story:

> This being done Choronzon, taking the form of a naked
> man, jumped into the circle and threw Neuberg to the ground.
> They fought in the sand, the demon making frantic efforts to
> tear out Neuberg's throat with his teeth, until the latter was
> able to drive him back into the triangle and repair the circle
> with his magic dagger.
>
> For some time Neuberg and the devil went on arguing, the
> latter threatening all the tortures of hell, the former denounc-
> ing Choronzon as a liar. Then the demon vanished, leaving
> Crowley alone in the triangle to trace the word BABALON in
> the sand as an indication that the rite was ended. Together the
> two magicians lit a purificatory fire and obliterated the circle
> and the triangle.[16]

Of course, it may well be said that the demon with whom Neuberg fought was no one else but Crowley himself, the bestial part of his personality unleashed by the powerful atmosphere of the ritual. What was the outcome for Crowley, though, in psychological terms? According to King, "both magicians were satisfied with their achievement; they were convinced that Crowley had conquered Choronzon, and was now a full Master of the Temp.e." As Israel Regardie, Crowley's amanuensis and frequently cited biographer put it, the remaining "Aires" in Crowley's use of the Enochian Calls were "lyrical paeans of joy and gladness," in recognition of Crowley's victory achieved by "crossing the Abyss and subduing its sole inhabitant, the Demon Choronzon."

The invocation of Choronzon is of some interest here in considering the argument, advanced by some occultists but little discussed by ufologists in print, that UFO occupants are understandable as angels, perhaps "fallen angels." (We are not culturally accustomed to thinking of fairies as having any relation to the angels, but, as we have seen already, the concept of the fairies as fallen angels was an Irish folk belief at least a century ago.) The evocation of Choronzon (in the sense that it was prelude to a deliberate ego-death) is also of some interest in the light of Strieber's philosophical comments in the conclusion of *Communion*, where he speaks of the process of human-visitor interaction as analogous to a process of spiritual transformation. Yet while identification of the visitors as angels (or fairies) has not found its way into the mainstream of most researchers' concerns, the assertion that the angelic hierarchy is indeed involved in UFO phenomena has increasingly found its way into print. One early example of such a contention may be found in a book entitled *An Introduction to the Keys of Enoch*, authored by a former instructor at the California Institute of the Arts' School of Critical Studies named James J. Hurtak. The book was published in 1975 by Hurtak's now defunct Academy of Future Science in Los Gatos, California. Hurtak mixed a Hebrew cabalistic view of the universe as being administered by angels with an interpretation of the Apocalypse as a mass landing of UFOs to take away 144,000 "elect," a kind of early New Age version of the fundamentalists' "Rapture."

Crowley's fascination with contacting nonhuman entities was intimately connected with his own estimation of himself as the prophet of a "new aeon" (the term "New Age" hadn't yet come into currency back in the 1920s and 1930s), and his penchant for contacting spirits which he described as "evil" certainly added to his reputation as the Great Beast. Of interest to our inquiry, though, is the fact that Crowley, according to Grant, claimed to have contacted an extraterrestrial entity named Lam in 1919, who Grant asserts is intimately connected with the star systems of Sirius and Andromeda. The star Sirius's connection with extraterrestrials, of course, is legendary. Robert G. K. Temple, in particular, has explored a possible connection between visitors from the star Sirius and the Dogon tribesmen of Africa in his fascinating book *The Sirius Mystery*.

Grant goes on to assert that other OTO members have subsequently contacted Lam, making use of his image as painted prior to 1945 by Crowley. If there can be any legitimacy granted to coincidences of the imagination, it is quite interesting that Crowley's painting "Lam" depicts an eggheaded face characterized by a vestigial nose and mouth and two eyes in narrow, elongated slits. Its resemblance to the image on the cover of *Communion* is remarkable, save for the dimensions and qualities of the eyes.

Comparisons between the entities associated with practitioners of ritual magical means and "UFO occupants" are becoming a noticeable part of other new works in UFO literature, as is evidenced in George C. Andrews's *Extra-Terrestrials Among Us*. Quoting at length from *A True and Faithful Relation of What Passed for Many Years Between Dr. John Dee and Some Spirits*, a book edited by Meric Causabon and published in London in 1659,[17] Andrews directs our attention to an incident that Dee recorded in his diary on April 30, 1586, as having occurred while he and his associate, Edward Kelly, were residing in Prague.

Dee recounts how Edward Kelly had been approached by a "little man" whom he took to be a gardener, who, after apparently pruning some trees, spoke to him saying, "*Quaso dicas Domino Doctori quod veniat ad me*" (a request that Dee come to see him). The little man then went over by some cherry trees, whereupon "he seemed to mount up in a great pillar of fire." When Dee came to the garden, he claims that he suddenly saw the miraculous reappearance of several of his books that had been recently burned (in unexplained circumstances). Interestingly, one of these was the Book of Enoch, an apocryphal book of the Bible (Enoch being the man who was reportedly taken whole into heaven and transformed into an angel) as well as some of Dee's writings on how to call angels. Remarkably, the little man appeared again and bade Kelly follow him to the mouth of a furnace where the books had been burned on April 10 of that year. As Dee related the incident in his diary:

> And coming hither, there the spiritual creature did seem to set one of his feet on the post on the right hand without the Furnace mouth, and with the other to step on the Furnace mouth, and to reach into the Furnace . . . and as he reached into the Furnace there appeared a great light, as if there had been a window to the back of the Furnace, and also to E.K. the hole which was not greater than the thickness of a brick unstopped, did seeme [sic] now more than three or four brick thickness wide, and so over his shoulder backward he did reach E.K. all the rest of the standing books, excepting the book out of which the last Action was cut, and Fr. Pucci his Recantation, also to E.K. appeared in the Furnace all the rest of the papers which were not as then delivered out.
>
> That being done, he bade E.K. go, and said he should have the rest afterward. He went before in a fiery little cloud, and E.K. followed with the Books under his arm all along the Gallery, and came down the stairs by Fr. Pucci his Chamber door, and then his guide left E.K. and he brought me the books unto my place under the Almond-tree.[18]

How does Andrews interpret this and other passages from Dee? As he puts it:

> The characteristics of the "little man" whose feet "seemed not to touch the ground by a foot height," who moved "in a little fiery cloud," and who suddenly went up into the sky "in a great pillar of fire" turn up consistently in modern encounter-with-occupant UFO reports.[19]

Perhaps Andrews is stretching his point, but the fact remains that the years of collaboration between Dee and Kelly (a somewhat disreputable fellow who nevertheless seemed to have enough clairvoyant abilities to have kept himself in Dee's employ) constitute one of the most remarkable documented instances of a deliberate attempt to establish communication with nonhuman beings. In this case, Dee understood his entities to be angels, and was continuing a tradition of angelic evocation that may be traced back into the religious practices of ancient Israel.

Another curious reference to entities summoned by means of ceremonial magic may also be found in Jacques Vallee's recently released *Dimensions: A Casebook of Alien Contact*, in which Vallee cites an interesting passage from an early-Renaissance book entitled *De Subtilitate*. The book's author, Jerome Cardan, was a noted mathematician, physician, and occultist in the early sixteenth century. He was the son of Facius Cardan, who, according to Vallee, "recorded his observation of seven strange visitors directly related to the creatures of the elements." Interestingly, Vallee downplays the reference to a ritual magical invocation to which Jerome Cardan alludes at the beginning of his account of his father's experience. Son described the incident as he had heard father relate it:

August 13, 1491: When I had completed the customary rites, at about the twentieth hour of the day, seven men duly appeared to me clothed in silken garments, resembling Greek togas, and wearing, as it were, shining shoes. The undergarments beneath their glistening and ruddy breastplates seemed to be wrought of crimson and were of extraordinary glory and beauty.

Nevertheless all were not dressed in this fashion, but only two who seemed to be of nobler rank than the others. The taller of them who was of ruddy complexion was attended by two companions, and the second, who was fairer and shorter of stature, by three. Thus in all there were seven. He left no record as to whether their heads were covered. They were about forty years of age, but they did not appear to be above thirty. When asked who they were, they said that they were men composed, as it were, of air, and subject to birth and death. It was true that their lives were much longer than ours, and might even reach to three hundred years' duration. Questioned on the immortality of the soul, they affirmed that nothing survives which is peculiar to the individual. . . . When my father asked them why they did not reveal treasures to men if they knew where they were, they answered that *it was forbidden by a pe-*

*culiar law under the heaviest penalties for anyone to commu-
nicate this knowledge to men.* They remained with my father
for over three hours. But when he questioned them as to the
cause of the universe they were not agreed. The tallest of them
denied that God had made the world from eternity. On the
contrary, the other added that God created it from moment to
moment, so that should He desist for an instant the world would
perish. . . . Be this fact or fable, so it stands. [Italics Vallee's] [20]

Vallee's use of italics in the reference to secret treasures is prompted
by his interest in showing a similarity in this account with other references he cites in the same book to the reputed relation between
"fairies" and hidden wealth. It is Vallee's contention that an analysis
of behavior attributed to legendary nonhuman beings as reported in
centuries past may provide us with a better understanding of the UFO
abduction phenomenon and reported visitor behavior. His reference
to ceremonial magic, moreover, may be seen as a reflection of his
larger interest in the psychic component of UFO and visitor experiences. It is interesting, too, that in his paraphrasing of the conclusions
of the Reverend Robert Kirk of Alberfoyle, Scotland, as to the characteristics of the fairies, Vallee writes: "They can be made to appear
before us by magic." [21]

Kirk was the author of an eighteenth-century book entitled *The
Secret Commonwealth of Elves, Fauns and Fairies*, which to this day
is considered by students of fairy lore as one of the most detailed accounts of fairy life yet written. Evans-Wentz said of Kirk: "It was the
belief of the Rev Robert Kirk, as expressed by him in his *Secret Commonwealth etc.* that the fairy tribes are a distinct order of created beings
possessing human-like intelligence and supernormal powers, who live
and move about in this world invisible to all save men and women of
the second sight." [22]

Vallee's book's lack of an overview of Western occultism, however,
leaves the reader not familiar with the subject in something of a quan-
dary, as entities are variously (and apparently indiscriminately) called
"fairies," "gnomes," "elves," and "sylphs" with little description of their
distinguishing characteristics (a factor that would be of importance if
one were to take such entities seriously as having some real existence).
A theme that Vallee does not develop, moreover, is the presumed

"elemental" quality of the visitors whom Facius Cardan presumably invoked. The concept of the "elemental" as a creature of air (sylph), water (undine or nymph), fire (salamander), or earth (gnome) is a fundamental feature of the hermetic philosophy of the Middle Ages and Renaissance, with no doubt an even older origin in the Middle East. Nevertheless, Vallee has provided an extraordinary amount of documentation to support the notion that many aspects of what may generically be called fairy behavior may also be found comparable to that displayed by what Strieber calls "visitors" and others call "aliens."

Visual descriptions of presumed extraterrestrial beings, similarities in the names of entities supposedly invoked by magicians living centuries apart, and dazzling accounts of Renaissance man's encounters with "shining" men do not, at first glance, provide one with anything other than a basis for marveling at (or deploring, depending on one's point of view) the persistence of such ideas, practices and stories in our culture. Yet the literature of occultism and its sister field, folklore, may still prove useful in interpreting information that comes to us from the accounts of modern-day "abductees." Indeed, it is one of the few points of reference we have in our literary culture for trying to make some comparative sense out of first-person testimonies of abductions such as those in *Communion*.

Of course, we will always have to deal with the nagging question of the reality of the "entities" invoked in the course of ceremonial magic, whom some ufologists would have us see as related to contemporary "UFO-nauts." In that regard, the comments that Hilary Evans makes at the conclusion of his *Visions, Apparitions, Alien Visitors* might at least be reflective of how one investigator attempted to deal with what seems to be the problematical reality of such entities:

> The entity experience has a material basis that can be reasonably conceived of as a physical communication, fabricated by an autonomously operating part of the percipient's mind, either on its own or in liaison with an external agent; expressed in the same encoded-signal form as any other mental communication; presented to the conscious mind as a substitute for the sensory input from the real world; and occasionally being given a temporary external expression utilizing some kind of quasi-material psi-substance.[23]

While some scientifically inclined readers may throw up their hands at a phrase such as "some kind of quasi-material psi-substance" (whatever that term might refer to), the salient aspect of Evans's attempt to grapple with the question of the entity enigma's material reality is his emphasis on it having a *communicative* feature. The entities of which we have some documentary description all reportedly show a distinct tendency to communicate with us—*they have something to say*. If such a generalization might hold water, we may be on the track of finding out who the visitors are by paying attention to their apparently nonsensical messages.

After all, to what can we compare modern reports of beings who seem to break the laws of physics if not to the accounts of supposedly nonhuman entities with whom "magicians" of past eras (in some cases among the most distinguished scientists of their time) claimed they conversed?

Contemporary UFO "Abductions" in Retrospect

The extraordinary manner in which Whitley Strieber described his own visitors, however, becomes most apparent if we compare his account, not with reports from the distant past, but with some of the more prominent cases reported in the UFO abduction literature of the past few years, and attempt to obtain some useful points of reference for comparing identifying elements in those stories, as they relate to the nature of the visitors or extraterrestrials themselves.

There seems to be something of a shift taking place in both the perception and understanding of the abduction experience in these stories, moving from an emphasis on trying to establish the actuality of the abduction experience and the UFOs themselves toward an appreciation of symbolic imagery and psychic phenomena as also being part of the abduction experience. I emphasize commercially published American accounts here because of the simple historical fact that, in terms of widely published UFO abduction narratives, those stories produced by North American abductees and UFO researchers have been the most spectacular and highly disseminated instances of their kind. Owing to their rejection by official investigators, moreover, elements of many abduction stories have begun to be integrated into mass popular culture through the mass media, a phenomenon that takes place with particular alacrity in the United States (certainly to a much greater degree than in many third world countries) because of the pervasive influence of the mass media.

Stories of UFO abductions had certainly found a place in contemporary American folklore and popular literature before the publication of Whitley Strieber's *Communion*. Most of these stories, though, have been recorded by people who did not themselves have the abduction experience. Very few first-person narratives by abductees have been published, leaving the majority of the stories to be accounts of other people's experiences by professional writers or UFO investigators. In examining these publications (both first-person and third-person accounts) it is important to separate the publications into two distinct groups, since the first-person accounts require a different kind of evaluation than those written by investigators or professional writers. Questions of personal honesty and sanity become paramount in first-person accounts, along with whether the book was ghost-written. In third-person accounts, concerns about faithfulness to detail in quotation, professionalism in handling evidence, thoroughness in research methods, and the intellectual sophistication of the interpretations offered by the author come into play.

Pre-*Communion* First-Person UFO Abduction Stories

One of the earliest published firsthand accounts of a UFO abduction (aside from the Adamski-related materials) was entitled *Flying Saucers and the Three Men*, written by Albert K. Bender. Bender was a relatively young man (employed as a factory clerk in Connecticut) when he wrote the book, and had been a prominent UFO enthusiast for some time. He organized and led a successful popular organization known as the International Flying Saucer Bureau in the late 1950s, at a time when public interest in UFOs was just beginning to coalesce. The book is introduced by Bender's friend Gray Barker, a journalist who explains he edited the book in a few places for the sake of style, but maintains he left Bender's own words largely intact. Barker's statement is a credible one, in that Bender's fantastic accounts of meetings with sinister "Men in Black," visits to underground cities beneath the

South Pole, and mysterious appearances of strange blue lights and sulfurous smells are laced with rather uninteresting biographical anecdotes throughout the balance of the book's pages—revealing a rather unsophisticated writing style.

Bender's book is significant in the history of UFO literature for the fact that he claims it was the intervention of three "Men in Black" who forced him (through threat of death) to cease his UFO-related activities until such time that he had a sign that he could tell the story of his abductions to the world. Among the various entities most often reported in connection with UFO phenomena, the notorious "Men in Black" have achieved a certain legendary status. They are usually described as being swarthy-complexioned, almond-eyed fellows, somewhat gruff and threatening in manner. Moreover, they have a penchant for dressing in black, double-breasted suits and driving black limousines. (Bender even described his "Men in Black" as sporting homburgs!) They are the mafiosi of contemporary UFO folklore.

Bender definitely feared his visitors, who told him they were here on earth to extract precious minerals from our water supply, and would leave the earth when their mission was accomplished. One of his experiences included the now famous "operating room" motif, where Bender described a group of female aliens rubbing some kind of lotion onto his completely naked body, an experience he admitted having definitely enjoyed. As one of the first published testaments of a UFO abduction to receive wide circulation, *Flying Saucers and the Three Men* offers the careful reader a narrative with many features subject to possibly fruitful comparison with other, subsequent abduction stories. (For example, the blue lights and sulfurous smells that preceded the appearances of Bender's "Men in Black," the time of his first abduction having been 4:00 A.M., and other features of his story can be found in other UFO abduction narratives, including *Communion*, both in published form and as unpublished letters.)

Another first-person account of a UFO abduction was published in 1978 as *The Walton Experience*, with authorship attributed to Travis Walton, a forestry worker. According to the reportedly eyewitness testimony of his fellow workers on a tree-cutting crew, Walton was zapped by a blue beam emanating from a flying saucer-type vehicle on November 5, 1975. Under hypnosis, Walton was reported to have said he was taken aboard a UFO where, after an initially frightening encounter with round-headed, large-eyed humanoids, he had a series of experiences that also seemed to involve an operation on his body. Aside from the humanoids, Walton said he met a large, muscular blond-headed man wearing a helmet, who responded to none of his questions but took him to an operating room, where he lost consciousness. Walton had no further information to relate from his experience, nor did he venture to speculate as to the reason for his aliens' having conducted his abduction. Indeed, his account of his experience is remarkably poor in detail in comparison with that found in Bender's book, and there is no comparison with the degree of detail found in *Communion*.

Walton's story received a great deal of publicity, and attracted serious attention from L. J. Lorenzen, an experienced and respected UFO investigator, who was at that time director of APRO, the Aerial Phenomena Research Organization. In addition, Walton was hypnotized by a Dr. James Harder (type of doctorate unspecified in the book), who collaborated with APRO in investigating cases such as Walton's. While controversy certainly surrounded the question of the quality of the investigators' work, there is another unsettling aspect of *The Walton Experience*. In its style of exposition, it bears the marks of a professional ghostwriter.

My suspicion about the absolute authenticity of Walton's account is in accord with an objection first voiced by noted skeptic Robert Sheaffer, who rejected the Walton text as "obviously ghostwritten" in his previously mentioned book, *The UFO Verdict: Examining the Evidence*. While there remain unanswered questions about Walton's experiences, it is notable that *The Walton Experience* could be seen as one of the first abduction stories to have been accompanied by a public relations campaign. Walton appeared with Lorenzen on a pilot for the television program *The Unexplained*, hosted by Leonard Nimoy ("Mr. Spock" of *Star Trek* fame), and his story was accompanied by a series of highly colorful illustrations by an otherwise unidentified artist named Michael Rogers, copies of which were advertised on the book's final page as being for sale.

The question whether Walton wrote his own story may be immaterial to UFO enthusiasts who believe that Walton was telling the truth as he saw it. (It is interesting to note, too, that Walton failed a lie detector test administered to him at the request of the *National Enquirer* by Jack McCarthy of the Arizona Polygraph Institute.) Whatever may be the final verdict on Walton, he continues to maintain that he was telling the truth. He may yet emerge onto the national UFO scene as a spokesman on the abduction experience, since plans are afoot to make a major motion picture based on his book, according to the Spring 1988 issue of *UFO* magazine.

The Travis Walton case may also be seen as one example of the unfortunate mismanagement of an abductee's contact with the mass communications media. While much has been said in UFO literature about the manner in which a hypnotist's leading questions can create a narrative that the abductee comes to accept as an explanation for his or her experiences, little investigation has been done into the manner in which abductee narratives may be affected by testimony before a series of inquisitive and not necessarily well-informed reporters and even hostile or careless media people. In Travis Walton's case, his experiences with the press were so difficult for him that he kept an unlisted telephone number for nine years following his reported abduction.

Third-Person Accounts of UFO Abductions

As early as 1965, the case of Betty and Barney Hill, who claimed to have been abducted by a UFO in New Hampshire in late September 1961, became widely known through the publication of John G. Fuller's *The Interrupted Journey: Two Lost Hours Aboard a Flying Saucer*. A former columnist for *Saturday Review*, Fuller also wrote *Incident at Exeter: Unidentified Flying Objects over America Now*, which recounted his investigation of another UFO-related event. Serialized as well in *Look* magazine, the story had a tremendous popular impact, though there was little official or academic inquiry into the Hill case as a result of the publicity they received.

Fuller's book is competently written and speaks well for his patient investigation. Inasmuch as the Hills were examined and underwent hypnotherapy by a psychiatrist named Benjamin Simon, the book contains extensive passages that purport to be verbatim transcripts of hypnotic regressions undergone by both Betty and Barney (a stylistic feature shared, of course, by *Communion*). What is revealed in those transcripts is a moving account of the Hills' fear and terror in the face of their experience, characterized by what they described as their meeting with large-eyed humanoid creatures. Betty Hill reported experiencing temporarily intense pain when a needle was inserted into her abdomen. She also produced a diagram that she claimed had been shown her by her abductors, which she interpreted as indicating the aliens point of origin as the star system Zeta Reticuli. Her insistence upon this point has provoked strong criticism from many sides, notably from Jacques Vallee, who points out the absurdity of Betty's map as a diagram of the Zeta Reticuli area, questioning why her abductors would use star maps drawn to depict the appearance of Zeta Reticuli from earth.

Despite the controversy that surrounded it, the story of Betty and Barney Hill became a landmark UFO abduction case, and was the first such report to become widely known in the English-speaking world, not only through Fuller's book, but through the film *The UFO Incident*, shown on NBC-affiliate television stations in the fall of 1975 and repeated a year later. No major American narrative that competed for media play with the Hills' story was to emerge for over a decade.

In 1979, shortly after the publication of *The Walton Experience*, author Raymond E. Fowler interested Prentice-Hall in publishing *The Andreasson Affair*, the result of his extensive personal investigation of the experiences of an American middle-aged woman named Betty Andreasson, who recounted a series of what could be described as transcendentally transformative experiences with apparently nonhuman entities that she said occurred in 1967. Also making extensive use of hypnotic regression techniques, Fowler's investigation revealed something apparently new in abduction literature: elements of imagery in the abductee's experience laden with a great deal of symbolic, even perhaps religious significance. The late Dr. J. Allen Hynek, former professor emeritus of astronomy at Northwestern University and then director of the Center for UFO Studies at Evanston, Illinois, added his approbation to the book by writing its introduction. Hynek noted in his introduction that although Fowler had previously been an advocate of the "extraterrestrial hypothesis" in his previous book *(UFOs: Interplanetary Visitors)*, he was of the opinion that *The Andreasson Affair* would lend weight to a reevaluation of that hypothesis, particularly in the light of the paranormal phenomena increasingly noted in UFO cases.

(Hynek's comments are all the more interesting because he originally became a UFO investigator through a contract to work for the

U.S. Air Force in 1949. Although initially hired to participate in the Air Force's general "debunking" activities, he later broke with his employers over what he felt was the suppression of "undesirable" evidence in the Air Force's Project Blue Book reports and became one of the field's most respected independent researchers.)

One of the most dramatic elements of Betty Andreasson's story is her account of a visionary experience in which she perceived a great bird immersed in flames, as though illuminated from behind, which gradually died down to nothing but ashes, from which emerged a "claylike" worm that slithered away from the scene. That this visionary image is remarkably parallel to the classical phoenix that rises from the ashes is all too obvious, as has been extensively remarked since the publication of the book.

Of particular significance is that, for Betty Andreasson, the vision was tantamount to a religious experience. In the same regressive hypnosis session in which she remembered the vision of the great bird, Fowler reported, Betty said she heard someone speaking in a loud voice. As Fowler recounts the incident:

> Now she hesitated and repeated what she heard: " 'You have seen, and you have heard. Do you understand?'
>
> "They called my name and repeated it in a louder voice. 'No, I don't understand what this is all about, even why I'm here.' And they—whatever it was—said that 'I have chosen you.' "

After Betty questioned the voice about whether it was God, the voice replied, "I shall show you as time goes by." Such a reply, according to Fowler, did not satisfy Betty, a woman of deep Christian feeling and belief. When she expressed exasperation at the voice's refusal to tell her specifically why she had been chosen, Betty became defensive. As Fowler described it:

> Betty defensively proclaimed her Christian faith. . . . "There is nothing that can make me fear. I have faith in Jesus Christ!"
>
> " 'We know, child,' the voice answered. 'We know, child, that you do. That is why you have been chosen. I am sending you back now. Fear not. . . . It is your own fear that you draw to your body, that causes you to feel these things. I can

release you, but you must release yourself of that fear *through my son.'* "

The words "through my son" suddenly became the catalyst for the most moving religious experience that I have ever witnessed. Betty's face literally shone with unrestrained joy as tears streamed down her beaming face:

"Oh, praise God, praise God, praise God. (Crying) Thank you, Lord (Crying, sobbing) I know, I know I am not worthy. Thank you for your Son. (Uncontrollable sobbing) Thank you for your Son." [Italics Fowler's][24]

Despite the depths of her own experience, Betty Andreasson has not emerged as a major spokesperson for UFO abductees, though her work has had a considerable impact on opening the minds of many readers to the interior dimensions of the abduction experience. Even Strieber has been moved to comment on the book, and is quoted on the cover of the new paperback edition of the book as saying, "Something extraordinary happened to Betty Andreasson. Maybe she encountered non-human visitors or maybe something even more strange. Whatever the origin of her experience, her immensely powerful story awed me. Its rich and provocative imagery will remain with me forever."[25]

Budd Hopkins: The Emergence of a UFO Abductions Specialist

No overview of published third-person abduction stories would be complete without mentioning the work of Budd Hopkins, whose two books (*Intruders* and *Missing Time*, both previously mentioned) have proved to be two of the most recognizable works of their kind in print. With a record of having investigated anomalous UFO-related phenomena since 1964, Hopkins is widely respected in certain parts of the UFO community. In a recent article in *UFO* magazine, author Michael Grosso quotes UFO historian David Jacobs as having addressed the 1987 Mutual UFO Network (MUFON) Symposium with the assertion that Hopkins's book *Intruders* is "monumentally important." Though Grosso appears to be of another opinion, he goes on to say that Jacobs would have us believe that *Intruders* signifies the dawn of a new day for UFO research, "a breakthrough of unimaginable and incalculable importance." Grosso interprets the gist of Jacobs's statements about Hopkins's work as follows:

"The breakthrough comes in knowing 'unequivocably' *why* the extraterrestrial intruders are here. Alien abductions enable us to consider the 'motivations of the intelligence behind the phenomenon' " [italics Grosso's][26]

The way in which Jacobs phrases his praise, characterized by what could easily be regarded as rhetorical hyperbole, gives Grosso ample ammunition for questioning whether or not Hopkins has, indeed, given us "unequivocal" knowledge of the "motivations" of the "extraterrestrial intruders." Yet the praise that Jacobs heaps on Hopkins is only one example of the general adulation he has received in much of the UFO community (most notably his receipt of MUFON's highest award at a testimonial banquet in 1985). Consequently, Budd Hopkins has emerged as one of the most prominent investigators of UFO abductions, with a research methodology that relies heavily on hypnosis, some of which he conducts himself. In the course of his investigations, Hopkins says, he has encountered many descriptions of beings whom he refers to as "aliens," many of whom seem to be described (at least physically) in a manner in accord with some of the descriptions offered by Strieber in *Communion*. Both of Hopkins's books contain illustrations by various abductees of small, lanky, hairless humanoid figures characterized by bald, bulbous heads with large, slanted black eyes.

The graphic similarity of the figures produced by Hopkins's numerous different hypnotic subjects is very striking, and would seem to lend credence to Hopkins's position as an advocate for the idea that the aliens are indeed very physical extraterrestrials who come here from another planet to conduct a variety of very physical operations on human beings. Hopkins will grant that it remains to be finally determined toward what ends such operations are being conducted, but he insists on their reality as objective events occurring in the physical world we inhabit.

The "operations" that form a significant feature of the narratives revealed in Hopkins's research include the implantation of small objects in abductees' physical bodies, the creation of incisions or gouges in flesh that leave noticeable and inexplicable scars, unspecified procedures that result in burns and even the extraction of sperm and ova to be used in the creation of human-alien crossbreeds. In *Intruders*, Hopkins documents a case of a reported "missing pregnancy," in which a young woman, given the pseudonym "Kathie Davis," reported having lost the fetus she was carrying by completely inexplicable means, only to have an abduction experience during which, she said, she was shown what she interpreted to be her child—half human, half nonhuman. An illustration of this child by "Kathie Davis" is included in *Intruders*.

Hopkins's attitude toward such matters is nothing less than alarm. He expresses outrage at what appears to be a matter of physical rape of the abductees by a group of aliens apparently interested, he postulates, in replenishing their own failing genetic stock and learning nurturing skills from human mothers. Though Hopkins paints his aliens as having the same physical description as those reported by Whitley Strieber, he essentially characterizes them as a gang of highly sophisticated rapists and burglars—as, indeed, intruders.

Given Hopkins's tendency to see his "extraterrestrial intruders" as violators of our basic human rights, it is possible to see how areas of considerable disagreement might arise between him and Strieber. While Strieber does not deny that there are certain aspects of visitor behavior that are often terrifying to their subjects, he nevertheless sees them as part of a larger cathartic process that is aimed at the spiritual and psychic evolution of the person having the experience. In Strieber's view Hopkins is not interested in evidence that might lead the researcher to seriously consider such an interpretation.

In a conversation with Whitley Strieber and his wife, Anne, held in their New York apartment in February 1988, he maintained that Hopkins's view of the visitors as emotionless intruders was reinforced by his refusal to listen to testimonies of postabduction psychic experiences reported by the abductees themselves. Strieber explained that the "abductee support group" he mentioned in *Communion* met on several occasions at the Striebers' New York apartment for the reason that Hopkins's wife was becoming increasingly uncomfortable with the event being held at her apartment. During the course of the meetings at the Striebers' home, Whitley said, "some people began volunteering stories about having left their bodies or other psychic experiences after their abductions. Budd wasn't interested in that, and would tell people to get back to talking about their abduction experiences. He refused to see a possible link between the experience of abduction and some kind of spiritual or psychic awakening happening in the people to whom experiences occurred."

Asked for his opinion on why Hopkins was refusing to give serious consideration to such testimonies, Strieber said, "He's interested in gaining respectability and legitimacy among mainstream scientists and intellectuals, so he's creating an abduction scenario that they can buy."

For the moment, then, Budd Hopkins has left us with an image that verges on the edge of painting the visitors as cosmic criminals who break into and enter people's homes without the slightest shred of consideration for their victims. Nor does it appear that Hopkins questions the physical reality of the abductions he studies. In his books he makes it clear that there can be no mixture of psychological and physical elements. His intellectual categories are either/or, not both/and. As he expresses his position in *Intruders:*

> I have made the point again and again in these pages that UFO abduction reports, because of their similarity of content and detail, must be accepted one of two ways: Either they represent some new and heretofore unrecognized and universal psychological phenomenon—a theory which does not take into account the accompanying *physical* evidence—or they represent honest attempts to report real events. Obviously, it is absolutely crucial to know if extraterrestrials exist and are, as the reports indicate, experimenting with humankind—or if the reports represent some profoundly radical new mental aberration. [Italics Hopkins's] [27]

In Hopkins's view, the abductions are indeed real events, and the abductors are without doubt extraterrestrials, because he rejects the possibility that so many abduction reports could somehow contain the same elements and represent some kind of "profoundly radical new mental aberration" taking place among thousands of people around the world. In framing the questions as he does, though, it appears that Hopkins sees any and all attempts to obtain a psychological explanation for abductions as a threat to their reality, and in so doing has cut himself off from examining dream patterns of abductees or other psychological dynamics experienced by them. In creating this conflict between the world of the mind (where psychology seems to wait, ready to pounce upon abduction reports and explain them away) and the world of matter (where presumably hard physical evidence exists to convince us of the reality of the abductions), Hopkins may have created a false opposition. Can one cleanly separate that which is physical from that which partakes of the psyche? Perhaps Hopkins has not yet provided us with the kind of unequivocal information that Jacobs would have us applaud.

Toward a Theory of UFO Abductions: The Rogo Hypothesis

There are, of course, numerous other reported cases of abductions that have been recorded in both UFO magazines and a variety of fairly recent anthologies that present the writings of several serious UFO researchers. Some of these books include *Encounter Cases from "Flying Saucer Review,"* edited by Charles Bowen; *UFO Phenomena and the Behavioral Scientist* by Richard F. Haines; and *Science and the UFOs* by Jenny Randles and Peter Warrington.

One popular anthology that gives a fairly representative view of the wide variety of stories associated with the UFO abduction phenomenon has been edited by D. Scott Rogo, a recognized author and researcher of the unexplained, and an editor of *Fate* magazine. His book, *Alien Abductions: True Cases of UFO Kidnappings*, deals with some of the most famous reported cases, which are divided into "waking encounters" (where the abductee is taken while awake and presumably has face-to-face conscious contact with his or her abductor, sometimes remembering what he describes as his experiences without need of hypnosis), "time lapse cases" (where there is an element of missing time in a person's experience, perhaps later explored through hypnosis), and "psychic abductions" (in which the experience of abduction proceeds entirely in a dream-state or other altered state of consciousness, the contents of which are also largely explored through hypnosis).

Among the UFO investigators besides Rogo who contributed to the book are Bill Barry, Ralph and Judy Blum, Jerome Clark, Gordon Creighton, Ann Druffel, Bill Fail, and the late Coral Lorenzen. They represent a wide spectrum of backgrounds, and a considerable amount of experience.

Rogo's book is very useful in that it points out the richness of the abduction phenomenon itself, and Rogo refuses to try to force it onto some kind of procrustean bed by describing the elements of a "classic" abduction in a way that omits or distorts important factors. Descriptions of aliens encountered in the various case histories presented range from the typical dome-headed, black-eyed little men to froglike creatures and jellylike brains encountered on the streets of a southern California suburb! The information the book contains about the sexual elements of abductions (as in the famous Brazilian case of Antonio Villas Boas, who claimed that he made love to a semihuman woman during his abduction aboard a UFO, and was given to understand that she conceived during the experience) and its careful treatment of the psychological (and psychic) factors in such cases, however, point to a new sensitivity to human (as distinct from technological) concerns and questions among some UFO researchers.

Rogo's attempt to find an explanatory hypothesis that could have some predictive value in relation to the abduction experience is worth noting, especially in the light of the personal changes that Strieber said he underwent following his visitor experiences. It may be argued whether Rogo's proposal is an actual theory or still only a hypothesis, but this should not prevent us from looking at what he has to say:

> The theory I have proposed about the nature of the abduction experience is equally predictive. It could be tested in the following way:
>
> *Each time an abduction experience is uncovered, a psychological inquiry into the life of the witness would indicate that he or she was undergoing a life-crisis at the time or was recovering from a psychological trauma.* [Italics Rogo's]

This hypothesis reflects a Rogerian person-centered approach to studying the problem of abductions. As Rogers notes: "Ufologists have, in the past, been more interested in studying *abduction events* than the *people* involved in them. The Andreasson case is an exception" [italics Rogo's].[28]

Noting that a trauma was indeed identifiable in the life of one abductee, Lori Briggs, Rogo speculates that perhaps Betty and Barney Hill suffered from a crisis in their interracial marriage, since their own abduction occurred at a time near the beginning of the American civil rights movement.

Rogo concludes by making a series of recommendations for changes in the manner in which ufologists ask their most basic questions:

First, it seems obvious to me that such incidents [i.e., UFO abductions] should not be studied solely by ufologists. They should be studied by teams of researchers comprised of ufologists, psychologists, and parapsychologists. Second, we should stop focusing our attention on the UFO events surrounding the abduction experience, and begin taking detailed looks at the victims involved. We should try to learn everything about them through psychological and physical examinations. Third, we should realize that the UFO experience is here because *we* have brought it into existence. It is not alien, it is part of us. So perhaps we should start educating the public about how to act when confronting a UFO or a UFO occupant, or when in the face of an abduction experience. The UFO phenomenon is guiding us, and we should seek to understand the message behind the communications UFO abductees deliver to us. They might be vital for our psychological and social survival.

In short, when we confront the UFO abduction phenomenon, we are actually looking at a hidden part of our own minds. Let's do our best to learn from these encounters. (Italics Rogo's)[29]

Rogo's plea for a change in investigative methodology has so far fallen largely on deaf ears. While researchers occasionally work in pairs, there is still a great deal of the "lonesome cowboy" in most ufologists, even some of the most distinguished ones. More significant, though, Rogo's position with respect to the identity of the visitors reveals his conviction that one must look not only to so-called physical evidence, but also at the dynamics of our minds themselves. It is a remarkable statement, for it essentially turns its back on the methods and assumptions of proponents of the "extraterrestrial hypothesis."

Yet Rogo seems to have set up a paradox. While accepting the abduction phenomenon as being real enough to warrant serious study, and accepting that there does occasionally appear to be physical evidence corroborating reported UFO experiences, he nevertheless asserts that it is pointless to try to establish the physical reality of UFO events as the most important framework for the study of abductions. By directing us toward ourselves and our own minds, Rogo would have us examine even our habits of thinking about "abductions" and "aliens" to search for some potential for communicating the *meaning* of abduction experiences.

Chapter 8

The Green Men, the Goddess, and the Fairy Queen

An Analysis of Whitley Strieber's
"Abduction" Experiences in the
Light of the "Fairy Faith"

> Up the airy mountain,
>   Down the rushy glen,
> We daren't go a-hunting
>   For fear of little men;
> Wee folk, good folk,
>   Trooping all together;
> Green jacket, red cap,
>   And white owl's feather!
>
> Down by the rocky shore
>   Some make their home,
> They live on crispy pancakes
>   Of yellow tide-foam;
> Some in the reeds
>   By the black mountain-lake,
> With frogs for their watch-dogs
>   All night awake.

—From "The Fairies," by William Allingham, 1910[1]

There seems to be a curious coincidence at work in the way in which the term "little green men" has slipped so seamlessly into contemporary English slang and parlance. The roots of that coincidence, it appears, lie in the language of Ireland, the Emerald Isle, where what the Irish people themselves have for centuries called "little people" and "green men" occupy a fundamental place in that nation's folklore. While Irish folklorists would have us know that leprechauns were by no means as noble a race as the fairies, the "wee folk" (also known as the "Gentry") were legendary as much for their mischief as for the kindness they showed to simple people, though they had a way of appearing and disappearing very suddenly and frighteningly.

Yet can it be said that there is anything more connecting the "fairies" with "visitors" or "aliens" than a common figure of speech? In making comparisons of this kind, we are limited from the beginning by the fact that we are speaking of entities that may be referred to only through stories and legends. Yet while it might be only the slightest of coincidences, they do have something strange in common.

Both share a reputation for abducting human beings from their homes.

Fairies as abductors of humans have long been the subject of a considerable amount of folklore, most noticeably in the tradition of the "changeling," or the surrogate-human placed by fairies in a crib for the express purpose of deceiving the infant's parents as to the fate of their child. According to Katherine Briggs in her extraordinary work, *Encyclopedia of Fairies:*

> The fairies' normal method was to steal an unchristened child, who had not been given proper protection, out of the cradle and to leave a substitute in its place. This "changeling" was of various kinds. Sometimes it was a stock of wood roughly shaped into the likeness of a child and endowed by glamour with a temporary appearance of life, which soon faded, when the baby would appear to die and the stock would be duly buried. More often a fairy child who did not thrive would be left behind, while the coveted, beautiful human baby was taken.[2]

The majority of fairy "abductions" were traditionally understood to occur with children, but one may easily find stories of fairies taking adults, as well. In that same work, Briggs recounts a story from Shetland, England, known as "Mind [Remember] da Crooked Finger!" In this story, the wife of a Shetland man had just given birth to her first child, whereupon he heard three knocks coming from underground and a voice saying, "Mind da crooked finger." As the man knew his wife to have a crooked finger, he thought that she might be the victim of an attack by little folk known in his parts as the "grey neighbors." As it turned out, he surprised a group of the rascals and flushed them out of a byre by throwing a Bible their way. As Briggs recounts the story:

> They left behind a wooden stock, carved feature by feature and joint by joint in the image of his wife. He lifted it up and carried it in the house. "I've won this from the grey neighbors," he said, "and I'll make it serve my turn." And for years afterwards he used the image as a chopping block, and the wife was never molested by the fairies again.[3]

It may well be argued, of course, that the whole of fairy lore in the Western world is naught but the product of peasants' imaginations, and it has even been observed that the Irish belief in changelings was often associated with a fair amount of child abuse, as children suspected of being of fairy origin were sometimes subjected to torturous "tests" as a means of getting the fairies to return the "real" child. Given such a background, it is hard to separate the idea of belief in fairies from the kind of backward superstitiousness that for many a decade impeded advances in public health and other aspects of general social progress. Yet the image of the fairies was still potent among the educated classes of the British Isles of only one hundred years ago, as may be seen in the works of several noted Irish writers. The fairy abduction motif, in particular, is transparent in the Irish playwright-poet William Butler Yeats's 1886 poem "The Stolen Child":

Away with us he's going
The solemn-eyed:
He'll hear no more the lowing
Of the calves on the warm hillside
Or the kettle on the hob
Sing peace into his breast,
Or see the brown mice bob
Round and round the oatmeal-chest.

For he comes, the human child,
To the waters and the wild
With a faery, hand in hand,
From a world more full of weeping than he can understand.
[Italics Yeats's]⁴

Although they both derive from Germanic rather than Celtic oral traditions, the stories of "Rumplestiltskin" and "The Pied Piper of Hamlin,"⁵ as recorded by the Brothers Grimm, are two additional literary examples of attempted abduction of children by fairylike creatures.

Fairy behavior, as we read of it both in first-person accounts as collected by folklorists and as codified in the classic fairy tales, is characterized, if anything, by elements of absurdity that seem at variance with what would be considered the norms of human behavior. For example, fairies were reputed to have a way of suddenly appearing at doorsteps to ask people for stores of grain such as barley, oatmeal, and buckwheat, and were known to give little cakes of the same to people whom they favored. People who ate the fairy cakes were said to suddenly prosper in all their affairs. Likewise, the fairies were regarded as inhabiting certain round hills or large piles of stones, and were often reported as dancing in circles near such sites. Reports of visits to fairyland at such sites abound in folklore, and such visits were considered dangerous in that sometimes the guest to fairyland would eat a bite of fairy food while on the other side and lose forever the ability to return home. Fairy sites were also considered dangerous to people who would disturb them. People who dared move a rock from a fairy site were, it was held, cursed with constant and debilitating misfortune.

"Green men" who reportedly danced in circles but inspired graphic representations somewhat different from contemporary renderings of "leprechauns" were known in Britain, too, according to some English researchers of Neolithic culture and its surviving forms in medieval art. What were called green men by the local people are still to be seen as carvings in certain churches dating variously from the twelfth to sixteenth centuries in rural England, notably on the church at Kilpeck (Hereford and Worcester) where the green men are depicted as wearing "a foliate mask, often demoniacal in appearance, probably representing the spirit of fertility."⁶ Such green men were associated with the older, pre-Christian fertility cults of the Great Goddess, and represent a mixture of Catholicism and paganism not entirely dissimilar to the blending of traditional European, Native American, and African religious practices and imagery that occurred in Latin America during the Spanish colonial era.

Strieber has clearly stated his interest in the parallels that might be drawn between descriptions of the behavior of "UFO occupants" and stories of fairy antics of old. As a matter of fact, it is one of the first speculations he makes in *Communion* as to the identity of the visitors. Certainly, the fact that both the visitors and the fairies have long been noted to have a penchant for "abducting" humans is striking, but such a coincidence would hardly of itself be sufficient to support an identifying link between fairies and visitors. Most of the stories that would seem to establish such a link are quite dated, too, making them difficult to verify. Yet there is a pattern of consistency in fairy lore itself in the manner in which fairy behavior is described. Remarkably, too, there are a number of contemporary stories that may be pointed to as evidence of a similarity of behavior between that traditionally attributed to fairies and that reported of UFO occupants, as Jacques Vallee does at length in his previously mentioned work, *Dimensions*.

Fairy Food, the "Italians," and the "Gentry"

Vallee's story of the small "cookies" given by a UFO occupant to Joseph Simonton, a sixty-year-old chicken farmer of Eagle River, Wisconsin, in the fall of 1961, is a classic example of such a parallel being noted by a seasoned investigator, despite its "apparent absurdity":

> The time was approximately 11:00 A.M. on April 18, 1961, when Joe Simonton was attracted outside by a peculiar noise similar to "knobby tires on wet pavement." Stepping into his yard, he faced a silvery saucer-shaped object, "brighter than chrome," which appeared to be hovering close to the ground without actually touching it. The object was about twelve feet high and thirty feet from the ground, and Simonton saw three men inside the machine. The occupants were about five feet tall. Smooth shaven, they appeared to "resemble Italians." They

had dark hair and skin and wore outfits with turtleneck tops and knit helmets.

One of them held up a jug apparently made of the same material as the saucer. His motioning to Joe Simonton seemed to indicate that he needed water. Simonton took the jug, went inside the house and filled it. As he returned, he saw that one of the men inside the saucer "was frying food on a flameless grill of some sort." The interior of the ship was black, "the color of wrought iron." Simonton saw several instrument panels and heard a slow whining sound, similar to the hum of a generator. When he made a motion indicating he was interested in the food one of the men, who was also dressed in black but with a narrow red trim along the trousers, handed him three cookies, about three inches in diameter and perforated with small holes.

The whole affair lasted about five minutes. Finally, the man closest the witness attached a kind of belt to a hook in his clothing and closed the hatch in such a way that Simonton could scarcely detect its outline. Then the object rose about twenty feet from the ground before taking off straight south, causing a blast of air that bent some nearby pine trees. . . .

When two deputies sent by Sheriff Schroeder, who had known Simonton for fourteen years, arrived on the scene, they could not find any corroborative evidence. The sheriff stated that the witness obviously believed the truth of what he was saying and talked very sensibly about the incident.[7]

Vallee observes that, in an unusual official follow-up to Simonton's testimony, the cakes were sent for analysis by the Food and Drug Laboratory of U.S. Department of Health, Education and Welfare, where they were found to contain "hydrogenated fat, starch, buckwheat, soya bean hull, wheat bran." The conclusion of the study? The officials determined that the cookie "was an ordinary pancake of terrestrial origin."[8]

While some professional skeptics and even ufologists might take such a conclusion as a condemnation of Simonton's story, Vallee uses it to take his readers in an unanticipated direction. Chiding ufologists for their lack of knowledge of general culture, he suggests that were they better educated "they would know about the Gentry and the food from fairyland." Quoting from Evans-Wentz's *The Fairy Faith in Celtic Countries*, Vallee gives us the story of an Irishman named Pat Feeny, who one day received a little woman who came to his house to ask for a quantity of oatmeal:

> Paddy had so little that he was ashamed to offer it, so he offered her some potatoes instead, but she wanted oatmeal, and then he gave her all that he had. She told him to place it back in the bin till she should return for it. This he did, and the next morning the bin was overflowing with oatmeal. The woman was one of the Gentry.[9]

Then, too, there is the Irish poet William Allingham's mention of "crispy pancakes/Of yellow tide-foam" in his simply titled poem "The Fairies," which Yeats saw fit to include in his anthology *Irish Fairy and Folk Tales*. Allingham, whose poetic output reveals an astonishing familiarity with fairy lore, depicts those "crispy pancakes" as fairy food itself, though I have yet to see another reference to "tide-foam" as being nutritive to the Gentry. While Vallee cites the first two verses of Allingham's poem, he leaves us wondering about the rest, which in the fourth verse curiously enough bears out the theme of human abduction:

> They stole little Bridget
>   For seven years long;
> When she came down again
>   Her friends were all gone.
> They took her lightly back,
>   Between the night and morrow,
> They thought that she was fast asleep,
>   But she was dead with sorrow.
> They have kept her ever since
>   Deep within the lake,
> On a bed of fig leaves,
>   Watching till she wake.[10]

To Vallee, there are so many instances of human-fairy interaction involving the transaction of grain or what he himself came to call "crispy pancakes" that the appearance of such a motif in a UFO story

is worthy of very close attention. While stories such as that of Joe
Simonton far from provide a logical link between reports of UFO occupant behavior and those of the fairies, it must be admitted in fairness that they do tug at a certain part of the mind that finds such
anecdotes to be pleasingly intriguing. Could it be the case that we
have unconsciously come to use the term "little green men" as a synonym for "extraterrestrials" and "aliens" because we have intuitively
sensed a possible relation between the often humorously absurd and
"nonsensical" behavior reported of extraterrestrials and certain customary behavior traits traditionally ascribed to the Gentry?

Green Men, Blue Men:
What Do We Have to Fear?

Of course, we have no way of answering such a highly speculative
question. In regard to Strieber's accounts of visitors in *Communion*,
though, there appears to be a problem in suggesting that his visitors
might bear something of a relation to little green men. After all, Strieber reported that some of his visitors were apparently blue, in that they
wore blue or blue-gray overalls. (These are the ones he also dubbed
"the good army.") Though the line of reasoning might seem ridiculous, one is led to wonder if leprechauns were thought to be green
because they hail from Ireland (where green is the national color), or
because, as can be seen from William Allingham's poem, they are
reputed to wear green jackets. Surely the answer is immaterial, as any
survey of the literature of folklore studies will quickly show that there
exists a plethora of references to "little people" of many descriptions
throughout the world, though of course the documentation most accessible to us comes from Western Europe, and particularly Ireland
and England. If we are to entertain the possibility of the "little men"
as having some existence apart from the human imagination, though,
it might be useful to pay attention to seemingly irrelevant details in
Strieber's and other persons' descriptions of the visitors as they may
yet reveal unsuspected commonalities or differences.

Judging from the usefulness that the term "little green men" has
proven to have for humorists and persons interested in ridiculing others who have been brave enough to report their own encounters with
apparently nonhuman entities, it is clear that the mere thought of

such an encounter actually taking place is loaded with a tremendous emotional charge of fear of ridicule. Yet there is another fear—that high intelligence and self-consciousness could incarnate in a semihuman (or even totally nonhuman) form—which of course provides the basis of much horror fiction and a good deal of science fiction. Just as in ancient magical thought it was assumed that knowing the name of any person or thing gave you a degree of power over it, we continue to have a visceral need for knowing, at least in rudimentary fashion, the identities of the people with whom we have any kind of dealings. If we are to take Strieber at his word and grant that there may be different varieties or types of visitors and that the visitors may bear a relation to the fairies, is there any parallel that we might find in terms of descriptions of reportedly different kinds of "fairy folk"?

Interestingly, such a "list" of differing kinds of "fairies" is to be found in *The Fairy Faith in Celtic Countries*. As Evans-Wentz heard from one of his informants, there are five classes of fairies:

> (1) There are the Gnomes, who are earth-spirits, and who seem to be a sorrowful face [sic]. I once saw some of them distinctly on the side of Ben Bulbin. They had rather round heads and dark, thick-set bodies, and in stature were about two and one-half feet. (2) The Leprechauns are entirely different, being full of mischief, though they, too, are small. . . . (3) A third class are the Little People, who, unlike the Gnomes and Leprechauns, are quite good-looking; and they are very small. (4) The Good People are tall beautiful beings, as tall as ourselves, to judge by those I saw at the rath in Roses Point. They direct the magnetic current of the earth. (5) The Gods are really the Tuatha De Dannan (Sidhe) and they are much taller than our race. . . . (Recorded on October 16, 1910).[11]

There are numerous other references one might cite throughout the length and breadth of fairy literature that describe a wide variety of other creatures ("brownies," "trolls," "the grey neighbors," and so forth), each with its own distinguishing characteristics. What is of particular interest in the above-mentioned passage from Evans-Wentz is the mention of tall, humanlike fairies, even of "gods," for one of the types of aliens or visitors often mentioned in contemporary UFO literature is known generically as "the blonds." Tall, blond people (some of them noticeably lacking a sense of humor) have become a part of modern UFO folklore, as may be seen in George Adamski's account of his meeting with a blond-haired "Venusian."

Of course, objective evidence for the existence of fairies is pretty much limited to what are known as the Cottingley Photographs, a series of glass-plate photographs of what were represented as fairies, taken in Cottingley, Yorkshire, England, in the summer of 1917 by Elsie Wright (then sixteen) and her cousin, Frances Griffiths (ten). While the photographic plates were reportedly examined by contemporary photographic experts and pronounced authentic, the images of different classes of fairies have been subject to a great deal of justifiable skepticism, for they seem to reveal a graphic style reminiscent of professionally rendered illustrations of the period. Robert Sheaffer, author of *The UFO Verdict*, has used the various assertions of Sir Arthur Conan Doyle and other contemporaries (notably prominent Theosophists) to lampoon the rhetoric of "true believers" who would have us accept the photographs as constituting valid, scientific evidence. In his essay "Do Fairies Exist?" Sheaffer recounts Geoffrey L. Hodson's reported "clairvoyant perceptions" of a "water nymph," "wood elves," a "brownie," "fairies," and "goblins" prior to summing up (with tongue firmly planted in cheek) the "overwhelming" case he makes "in favor" of fairies:

"Multiple independent witnesses. A series of photographs. Worldwide sightings. Close encounter cases. Certainly Conan Doyle did not exaggerate when he described the evidence for fairies as 'overwhelming.' "[12]

Sheaffer has a point in questioning the faulty logic used by people who would have us accept a mass of information as "scientific proof" of the existence of any of several anomalous phenomena (Bigfoot and the Loch Ness monster, included). His attitude is certainly reflective of those people who practice the kind of highly intellectual if occasionally irrational skepticism previously mentioned. Belief in fairies, in the technical, industrialized world in which we live, has become almost synonymous with being a simpleton, a peasant, or, in more contemporary terms, a member of that nearly extinct social class known as the hippies.

Still, even if we were disposed to grant that something akin to fairies might possibly exist, it would seem at first glance extremely unlikely that the entities Strieber describes as his visitors bear any relation to leprechauns or fairies. His visitors seem too terrible or frightening, in some ways, to be identified with the same creatures whom Shakespeare depicted as Puck in A *Midsummer Night's Dream*, or whom Walt Disney immortalized in the form of the winged sprite Tinker Bell, whose magic wand always sprinkled stardust over Disneyland at the beginning of his television show, *The Wonderful World of Color*. In the arcane reaches of ufology, as we have seen, there are plenty of alternative hypotheses as to the nature and identity of the visitors, ranging from posing them as extraterrestrial geneticists to fallen-angel entities (e.g., Choronzon) to enlightened philosopher-adventurers from the Pleiades here to show us a new spiritual path. How is one to interpret Strieber's first-person testimony of encounters with visitors in the light of such a plethora of explanations?

Perhaps the simplest way to approach the question is to examine Strieber's descriptions of them, as published in *Communion*. What does Strieber say he saw?

From Bedroom to "Round Room": The Visitors Close Up

Strieber's first mention of a visitor in *Communion* reads as follows:

> No sooner had I settled back than I noticed that one of the double doors leading into our bedroom was moving closed. As they close outward, this meant that the opening was getting smaller, concealing what was behind that door. . . . Then I saw edging around it a compact figure. It was so distinct and yet so astonishing that at first I could not understand it at all. I simply sat there staring, too stunned to move. . . ."
>
> This figure was too small to be a person, unless a child. I have measured the approximate distance that the top of the head was from the ground, based on my memory of the figure's position in the doorway, and I believe that it was roughly three and a half feet tall, altogether smaller and lighter than my son.
>
> I could see perhaps a third of the figure, the part that was bending around the door so that it could see me. It had a smooth, rounded hat on, with an odd, sharp rim that jutted

out easily four inches on the side I could see. Below this was a vague area. I could not see the face, or perhaps I would not see it. A few moments later, when it was close to the bed, I saw two dark holes for eyes and a black downturning line of a mouth that later became an O.

From shoulder to midriff was the visible third of a square plate etched with concentric circles. This plate stretched from just below the chin to the waist area. At the time I thought it looked like some sort of a breastplate, or even an armored vest. Beneath it was a rectangular appliance of the same type, which covered the lower waist to just above the knees. The angle at which the individual was leaning was such that the lower legs were hidden behind the door.[13]

Further on in the book, Strieber relates how, outside his house after being "abducted," he saw

a small individual whom I could see only out of the corner of my eye. This person was wearing a gray-tan body suit and sitting on the ground with knees drawn up and hands clasped around them. There were two dark eyeholes and a round mouth hole. I had the impression of a face mask.

Strieber also saw another person.

Immediately on my right was another figure, this one completely invisible except for an occasional flash of movement. This person was working busily at something that seemed to have to do with the right side of my head. It wore dark-blue coveralls and was extremely fast.[14]

Later, when Strieber was taken to a large, round room that he described as "messy," he encountered a being whom he thought of as being female. Strieber recounted his terrified screaming at being told by the visitors that they proposed to insert a silver-colored needle in his brain. In response to the female's question about what she could do to help him stop screaming, Strieber said he asked (much to his own surprise) to smell her. She complied with his request, proffering him her hand. As he described it:

There was a slight smell of cardboard to it, as if the sleeve of the coverall that was partly pressed against my face were made of some substance like paper. The hand itself had a faint but distinctly organic sourness in its odor. It was not a human smell, but it was unmistakably the smell of something alive. There was a subtle overtone that seemed a little like cinnamon.[15]

Very shortly thereafter in the text, Strieber offers something of a summary of visitors whom he had seen in his initial encounters:

I was aware that I had seen four different types of figures. The first was the small robotlike being that had led the way into my bedroom. He was followed by a large group of short, stocky ones in the dark-blue coveralls. These had wide faces, appearing either dark gray or dark blue in that light, with glittering, deep-set eyes, pug noses and broad, somewhat human mouths. Inside the room, I encountered two types of creature that did not look at all human. The most provocative of these was about five feet tall, very slender and delicate, with extremely prominent and mesmerizing black slanted eyes. This being had an almost vestigial mouth and nose. The huddled figures in the theater were somewhat smaller, with similarly shaped heads but round, black eyes like large buttons.[16]

These descriptions are all presented within the book's preamble, which is entitled "Prelude: The Truth Behind the Curtain."

Although the summary that Strieber gives is useful in enabling the reader to categorize the visitors into different species, so to speak, his descriptions do not go into great detail. Of course, as may be seen in the testimony of Strieber's hypnotic regressions, it appears that obtaining any kind of memory at all of his visitor experiences was a painfully difficult process, in which it would stand to reason that his ability to describe the visitors was initially rather limited.

Sex and Angst in the "Round Room"

While some UFO investigators (notably Budd Hopkins) have gone to great lengths to try to get their interviewees to draw pictures of the visitors or otherwise produce detailed verbal descriptions of them and their behavior, it is worth noting that Strieber does not seem to place so much emphasis on a physical description of the visitors as he does on relating what they did to him and the psychological impact that they had on his life and way of being.

What is also interesting to observe, as I have pointed out before, is that if one compares Strieber's descriptions of his visitors with other accounts published by Hopkins, Vallee, and other UFO researchers (as well as with some descriptions published a generation ago by Charles Fort, the great collector of inexplicable stories), there may be found a number of interesting parallel references to small, stocky fellows in blue coveralls as well as bald, short creatures with large heads and black, slanted eyes.

It should be observed, too, that the image on the cover of *Communion* as described by Strieber corresponds with the above-mentioned description of the five-foot-tall "female" being, with black eyes and vestigial mouth and nose. (According to Strieber, the image was assembled by an artist skilled in the image-composition techniques used by police departments.) This unnamed female being figures very prominently in the book. In fact, she is the predominant personage in Strieber's narrative. From the accounts of Strieber's hypnotic regressions, it appears that he had some kind of traumatic sexual encounter with her, yet he even goes so far as to say he felt some love for her.

This is the first mention that Strieber makes in *Communion* of his sexual encounter, which takes place during the first abduction sequence he describes in the "round room," and at which "she" is present:

> Soon I was in more intimate surroundings once again. There were clothes strewn about, and two of the stocky ones drew my legs apart. The next thing I knew I was being shown an enormous and extremely ugly object, gray and scaly, with a sort of network of wires on the end. It was at least a foot long, narrow, and triangular in structure. They inserted this thing into my rectum. It seemed to swarm into me as if it had a life of its own. Apparently its purpose was to take samples, possibly of fecal matter, but at the time I had the impression that I was being raped, and for the first time I felt anger.
>
> Only when the thing was withdrawn did I see that it was a mechanical device. The individual holding it pointed to a wire

cage on the tip and seemed to warn me about something. But what? I never found out.[17]

Although Strieber rationalizes his experience as possibly having had a sample-collecting purpose, what is important in his account is that he says that he felt he was being raped. It had a sexual meaning to him, irrespective of what it may have been objectively meant to be as far as his visitors were concerned. Nor is his "rape" separable from the experience that immediately preceded it, previously mentioned as the incident in which the visitors said they would insert a needle into his brain.

Strieber recounted the experience as follows, in the same section of the book:

> My memory of the one that came before me next is of a tiny, squat person, crouching as if huddled over something. He had been given the box and now slid it open, revealing an extremely shiny, hair-thin needle mounted on a black surface. This needle glittered when I saw it out of the corner of my eye, but was practically invisible straight on.
>
> I became aware—I think I was told—that they proposed to insert this into my brain.
>
> If I had been afraid before, I now became quite simply crazed with terror. I argued with them. "This place is filthy," I remembered saying. Then "You'll ruin a beautiful mind." I could imagine my family awakening in the morning and finding me a vegetable. A great sadness overtook me.[18]

It was after those protests that Strieber screamed in terror, only to be comforted by the female visitor, whose distinctive smell, Strieber said, was later to be the only "real" memory he could summon of the experience. It was the remembrance of that female visitor's smell, he said, that kept him from losing his mind.

The last thing that Strieber said he remembered of that experience with the visitors involved the letting of some of his blood: "One of them took my right hand and made an incision on my forefinger. There was no pain at all. Abruptly, my memories end. There isn't even blackness, just morning."[19]

How does one interpret these experiences, so central to Strieber's story that he places them at the very beginning of his narrative? Their very bizarreness seems to repel any attempt to look at them closely, and, by themselves, they would seem to be nothing but a series of inexplicable tortures. In order to attempt to understand them better, one simply must have more information. As it turns out, Strieber remembered his visitor experiences in greater detail while under hypnosis, as recorded in the transcripts of Strieber's hypnotic sessions with Donald F. Klein, M.D., at which Budd Hopkins was present.

In the hypnotic regression session of March 5, 1986, Strieber again remembered being in the presence of the female visitor, whom he described as looking "like a little person made out of leather, sort of." The transcript apparently records a conversation with her and subsequent events. Strieber is the speaker:

" 'You know what. I think you are old? Are you old?'

"She says, 'Yes, I am old.'

"She's lookin'—lookin' at me. [Moves head back, then to left and right, as if being held by the chin and examined.] She's lookin' real close. She's got a matchbox. No, it's not a matchbox. (In this exchange, I remembered a deep, basso profundo voice. She then told me that an operation would be performed.) 'Aww, what is it? What do you mean, an operation, an *operation*?' I'm getting real scared again. Real scared. Because I cannot do anything about this. I don't even want to look up at this.

" 'Can we help you stop screaming? Can we help you stop screaming?'

" 'You could let me smell you.' She puts her cheek up by my face. They are here. You have to understand that. They are here. 'I'm not going to let you do an operation.'

" 'We won't hurt you.'

" 'I'm not gonna let you do an operation on me. You have absolutely no right.'

" 'We do have a right.'

"That was it, bang. There was nothing to it. I thought they were gonna cut my whole head open. There was nothing to it."

Dr. Klein: "What happened?"

"Just a bang back behind my head, that's all. Not loud.

Just bang. She's sittin' right in front of me the whole time, just lookin' at me. They're moving around back there. (I could sense them, but I was looking at her. She drew something up from below.) 'Jesus is that your penis?' I thought it was a woman. [Makes a deep, grunting sound.] That goes right in me. [Another grunt.] Punching it in me, punching it in me. I'm gonna throw up on them. [Pause]" [Italics Strieber's] [20]

After the "bang," Strieber said, "I felt like weeping and I remember sinking down into a cradle of tiny arms." [21]

Strieber goes on to say, in the same session, that the visitors told him he was their "chosen one," a designation that he interpreted as a device they were employing to flatter him and mollify him. At a certain point, though, he produced the following hypnotically remembered conversation with the female visitor:

> Voice: "Can you be harder?"
> "Can I be harder? Oh Lord. Didn't know I could be hard like that. No, not with you around I can't be harder."
> Voice: "What would you like me to be?"
> "What would I like you to be? I'd like you to be a dream, is what I'd like you to be."
> Voice: "I can't be that." [22]

Klein asked Strieber to take another, closer look at the female visitor.

> [Klein asked] "What did she mean by saying can you get harder?"
> "I was about half up. Hard. Penis. And she says, 'Can you get harder?' And the truth is, I could not. I didn't even know I was in that state. And with her around there's just no way."
> "Was this natural or somehow induced?"
> "I don't know. No. But you see, that thing stayed in me. I don't even know when it went out. It was almost like it was alive. It was a big, gray thing with what looked like a little cage on the end of it, a little round nubbin about the size of the end of your thumb. And they shoved it into me . . . they showed me afterward . . . so they must have taken it out of me, but I don't remember them doing it. These things happen

sometimes like they're sort of in between. [Pause.] You know, they talk to me, but I can't hear them. [Long pause. Sigh.]"[23]

It is significant that Strieber makes very little comment in *Communion* on the possible significance of his sexual experiences with the female visitor, a fact that stands in marked contrast to Budd Hopkins's focus on experiences that presumably demonstrate what he believes is essentially "alien" genetic experimentation with humans. While the interpretation of his experience is, of course, ultimately up to Strieber himself, the events he describes are so extraordinary—in fact so bizarre and frightening—that one cannot help but wonder about their larger significance. Assuming for the sake of argument that his experience was at least psychically "real," why would the visitors engage in an apparent attack on the integrity of Strieber's mind? Why would they do something to him that made him feel as though he was being raped?

Those questions are subject to a multiplicity of answers, yet upon closer inspection it would seem that Strieber's experiences with the needle and the device that was inserted in his rectum dealt with two of the most primal of all human instincts: power and sex. For Strieber, an intellectual whose livelihood has been gained by use of his mind, brain damage would threaten his entire identity, not merely his professional ability. Likewise, the fear of rape is so widespread throughout society at large that one need hardly emphasize that, for a normal, heterosexual man (as Strieber says he is), the experience of being anally raped would be highly traumatic. After such experiences, anyone would be completely overwhelmed, and very possibly in a period of personal crisis, perhaps feeling compelled to know himself better, to draw on his inner reserves, in order to overcome it.

Fear, Apocalypse, and the "Magic Wand"

There was another aspect to Strieber's initially remembered experiences with the visitors that points to a highly traumatic sequence of internal events, in which they seem to reveal themselves as acting toward Strieber as givers of visions, intense images that Strieber in one case said he felt were prophetic. In the hypnosis session of March 1,

1986, with Klein and Budd Hopkins, Strieber was regressed to October 4, 1985. On that day, Strieber said, he had an experience with a being who was "sticking something in—not into my head, y'understand, but it was like sticking it into my mind." Under deeper hypnosis, Strieber recounted the following passage:

> When he sees I see him he comes over to the bed. He looks *mean*. He's little. Goes up to about the top of the lamp. Looking down at me. Got eyes. Big eyes. Big slanted eyes. A bald head. He's looking down at me. He's got a ruler in his hand. Has a tip of silver. Touches me. I see pictures. [Long pause.] I see pictures of the world blowing up. I see pictures of the whole world just blowing up. I see pictures of the whole world just blowing up when he touches me with this thing. [Weeps.] Jesus. It's a picture of like a whole big blast, and there's a dark red fire in the middle of it and there's white smoke all around it. [Italics Strieber's] [24]

Further on in that same session, after coming out of the hypnosis, Strieber again described the instrument this entity was apparently employing to produce those visions: "He had a little ruler thing that had a silver tip on it and it's dark in the room." [25]

That apocalyptic vision caused Strieber and Hopkins to reflect on its significance, which was particularly powerful to Strieber because he had only a short time before then coauthored *Warday* (with James Kunetka), a novel about a limited nuclear war. As Strieber put it:

> "Maybe if I had not been afraid of nuclear war and perfectly happy, when he touched that thing to my head other images would have come out. See what I mean?"
> Budd Hopkins: "It certainly intersects with—"
> "My own fears. Exactly." [26]

Given his understanding of himself as a writer of horror fiction, it is not at all unlikely that Strieber recognized the challenge to overcome his fears as being potentially very rewarding. In nearly all of his previously published fictional works, he deals with fear and horror in the interest of showing the cathartic and transformative nature of fear—how, in the experience of terror, we wake up to seeing the reality of our lives as they are, not as we would believe them to be, and in the process of that awakening, are empowered and encouraged to deal with our fears, enabled to overcome them. That is precisely the theme of Strieber's short story, "Pain," which he said was the last thing he wrote before fully remembering his visitor experiences.

Strieber has described at length the period of disorientation he underwent after his visitor experiences of late 1985. What is interesting to observe, however, is that in his period of learning to cope with the enormity of his experiences, his mind turned time and again to reflect on the "female visitor." Although there are a few descriptions of the other "beings" throughout the rest of *Communion*, the female is described again on several occasions. While some of the information is repeated, each reference throws additional light onto her as a figure of what could be described as archetypal dimensions.

Strieber Communes with "Her"

The next reference to the female visitor that Strieber makes recounts the memories he derived from hypnosis in greater detail:

> Sitting before me was the most astonishing being I have ever seen in my life, made the more astonishing by the fact that I knew her. I say *her* but I don't know why. To me this was a woman, perhaps because her movements are so graceful, perhaps because she has created states of sexual arousal in me, or maybe it is simply the memory of her hand touching the side of my chest one time, so lightly and yet with such firmness. [Italics Strieber's][27]

Later, Strieber reflects on what this figure came to mean to him:

> That night in the cabin, I found myself thinking about the one I knew, turning her presence over and over in my mind. She had those amazing, electrifying eyes . . . the huge, staring eyes of the old gods. . . . They were featureless, in the sense that I could see neither pupil nor iris. She was seated across from me, her legs drawn up, her hands on her knees. Her hands were wide when placed flat, narrow and long when

dangling at her sides. There was a structure, perhaps of bone, perhaps faintly visible under the skin. And yet other parts of her body seemed almost like a sort of exoskeleton, like an insect would have.

She was undeniably appealing to me. In some sense I thought I might love this being—almost as much as I might love my own anima. I bore toward her the same feelings of terror and fascination that I might toward someone I saw staring back at me from the depths of my unconscious.

There was in her gaze something that is so absolutely implacable that I had other feelings about her, too. In her presence I had no personal freedom at all. I could not speak, I could not move as I wished. [28]

Strieber goes on at some length about this being, describing the psychological effect that she had on him. In doing so, he indirectly introduces his reader to the concept that these beings are deliberately seeking some kind of communion with us, or we with them:

Her gaze seemed capable of entering me deeply, and it was when I had looked into her eyes that I felt my first taste of profound unease. It was as if every vulnerable detail of my self were known to this being. Nobody in the world could know another human soul so well, nor could one man look into the eyes of another so deeply, and to such exact effect. I could feel the presence of that other person within me—which was as disturbing as it was curiously sensual. Their eyes are often described as "limitless," "haunting" and "baring the soul." Can anything other than a part of oneself know one so well. It's possible, certainly. . . .

The realization that something was actually occurring within me because this person was looking at me—that she could apparently look into me—filled me with the deepest longing I can ever remember feeling . . . and with the deepest suspicion. [29]

Strieber returns to speak of this female visitor on several occasions throughout the text of *Communion*, though primarily in terms of his memories of her during hypnosis. It is quite remarkable, though, that in closing his remarks about her and his first remembered "abduction" he makes the following statement:

> I reflected that the abduction to a round room had a long tradition in our culture: There were many such cases in the fairy lore. The story called "Connla and the Fairy Maiden," as collected in Joseph Jacobs' *Celtic Fairy Tales* (Bodley Head, 1894, 1985) could with some changes be a modern tale of the visitors.

As suggestive as this was of the possibly historical roots of the experiences, it was no more definitive of that origin than the whole texture was of the notion of recent visitors.

Maybe the fairy was a real species, for example. Perhaps they now floated around in unidentified flying objects and wielded insight-producing wands because they have enjoyed their own technological revolution. [30]

The Fairy as a "Real Species": "Connla and the Fairy Maiden"

At first glance, it must have struck many a reader as curious that Strieber would direct one's attention to a *fairy tale* as a point of departure for explaining the visitor experience. Such an approach would hardly have been satisfying to readers who would like to have had a more factual and evidential basis for understanding the visitor experience. Even more intriguing is the fact that Strieber makes no remark whatsoever upon the content of that tale. An examination of "Connla and the Fairy Maiden," however, reveals that it is essentially a tale of seduction, in which Connla, son of the Irish king known as Conn of the Hundred Fights, is taken away to another land by a maiden invisible to all but him. Is this theme of seduction, then, what Strieber would have us begin to understand?

In his narration of the tale, Jacobs give the following dialogue for the first meeting between Connla and the fairy maiden:

> "Whence comest thou, maiden?" said Connla.
> "I come from the Plains of the Ever Living," she said, "there where is neither death nor sin. There we keep holiday alway,

nor need we help from any in our joy. And in all our pleasure we have no strife. And because we have our homes in the *round green hills*, men call us the Hill Folk." [Italics added] [31]

The king, able only to hear the maiden's voice, calls for his Druid to banish the maiden, which he does with success. Prior to leaving, though, the maiden throws a magical apple to Connla, which restores itself to full size after each bite he takes of it. Connla pines after the Fairy Maiden, and will take no food but of the apple, and speaks to no one until one day she returns and addresses him, saying:

"The ocean is not so strong as the waves of thy longing. Come with me in my curragh, the gleaming, straight-gliding crystal canoe. Soon can we reach Boadag's realm. I see the bright sun sink, yet far as it is, we can reach it before dark. There is another land, too, worthy of thy journey, and land joyous to all that seek it. Only wives and maidens dwell there. If thou wilt, we can seek it and live there together in joy."

When the maiden ceased to speak, Connla of the Fiery Hair rushed away from his kinsmen and sprang into the curragh, the gleaming, straight-gliding crystal canoe. And then they all, king and court, saw it glide away over the bright sea towards the setting sun, away and away, till eye could see it no longer. So Connla and the Fairy Maiden went forth on the sea, and were no more seen, nor did any know whither they came. [32]

I italicize the phrase "round green hills" to point out the most obvious connection between this fairy tale and Strieber's description of a "round room" motif in his abduction. The "round hill" motif, itself, is a frequent part of Irish fairy lore, with many stories telling of people who went out to rest upon the hills, only to hear the sound of drumming and flutes within—sounds the country people attributed to the fairy folk. The Reverend Robert Kirk, the previously mentioned author of *The Secret Commonwealth of Elves, Fauns and Fairies*, was reputed to have been taken to fairyland by them near a round hill. Then, too, in light of the overpowering "female" whom Strieber says he encountered in the round room, the story of Connla's seduction by an overwhelming young fairy maiden becomes all the more interesting. Are the parallels coincidence, the result of Strieber's having imaginatively structured his narrative so as to include folkloric elements, or are they the result of some objective similarity of the extraordinary experiences attributed to Connla (and found throughout fairy lore) and those described by Whitley Strieber?

Jacobs's notes in regard to "Connla and the Fairy Maiden" are quite interesting in themselves, since it appears that Conn of the Hundred Fights was a historical personage who was the first head king of Ireland, ruling from A.D. 123–157. Curiously, Conn was succeeded by his third son, Art Enear. His eldest son, referred to as Conly and whose death is not recorded in the Annals of Clonmacnoise, "was either slain or disappeared during his father's lifetime," according to Jacobs. He also claims that this story is "the earliest fairy tale of modern Europe."

Strieber's suggestion in *Communion* that a simple fairy tale could throw light on his visitor experiences requires that the reader be open to a metaphorical, rather than a hard-evidence-oriented, mode of understanding the visitor experience. Yet the idea of the fairy as more than a metaphor, as indeed a real species was an idea that was nothing new to Strieber, as can be seen from his depiction of the "little people" in his novel *Cat Magic*.

The Leannan Sidhe, Queen of the Fairies

Cat Magic tells the story of a conflict between violent, intolerant, fundamentalist Christians and a group of sensual, nature-worshiping followers of the Old Religion, also known as Wicca. While Strieber uses the book to depict and dramatize his convictions on authentic versus pathological spirituality, he also expands at length on the subtleties of the traditions still kept alive by Wicca, among them a belief in (or perhaps knowledge of) the "little people." In a moment of psychological crisis, the book's principal character, a beautiful and talented young woman named Amanda Walker, has a fateful encounter with an entity who is no less than the queen of the fairies, known in Gaelic, the ancient language of Ireland, as the Leannan Sidhe. That meeting occurs atop a mountain on the grounds of a Wiccan estate known as the Covenstead. In *Cat Magic*, Strieber depicts the men and women of the Covenstead as aware of the life of the little people around them, and in fact has one character describe them as an actual biological race of people who were systematically hunted and wiped out in Europe during the Middle Ages.

In his description of Amanda Walker's face-to-face meeting with the Leannan Sidhe, Strieber amply displayed his fascination with the little people:

> About the rowan there stood six small men in snow-white coats and breeches. On their feet were white pointed shoes, and on their heads close fitting caps just as Constance had described. . . . These men had sharp faces with pointed noses and large eyes. Perhaps they looked so different precisely because they were so almost-human. But one of them licked his lips, and Mandy got a glimpse of tiny teeth more like a rat's than a man's.
>
> Together they raised bows, and mounted arrows on them made of twigs. There came then on the air the ringing of small bells and a whisper of tiny feet in the snow.
>
> She appeared from behind the stone, all blond, her hair as soft as elder blow, her eyes startlingly dark brown, her body lightly dressed in the very lace Constance had promised. She was wee, not nearly as large as her six guards. On her head was a garland of rowan, berries and stems and leaves. Seeing such beauty, how ineffable, how frail, how strong, Mandy thought she would simply sink away. By comparison she herself was coarse. All delicacy seemed to have concentrated itself in this single small creature. Around her neck there was drawn a silver chain, and at her throat hung a gleaming sickle of a moon.[33]

Nor was the Leannan Sidhe merely a beautiful woman as Strieber would have us know her. She assumes a larger-than-life significance for Amanda Walker, who has a full-blown psychic-symbolic experience with her. It could be said that Strieber had Amanda "commune" with the Leannan Sidhe:

> Mandy instinctively lowered her eyes. It was more bearable this way, just looking at the woman's feet, no more than two

inches long, naked in the snow. Then the feet rose out of her line of sight. She looked up, startled. The girl was floating in the air. Wings flapped and she was gone. A great gray owl hooted from the top of the rowan, its horns darkly silhouetted against the sky. It took flight, racing round and round the rowan. Next hoofs clattered on the stones, and a black mare reared into nothingness, its neighs echoing off to silence.

An ancient woman, drooling, her teeth yellow, one eye put out, her hands fantastic with arthritis, scraped up on a stick.

"O, my God! Can I help you?"

She held out her hands and was as suddenly gone, the maiden spinning forth from her flying gray hair. The girl took Mandy's large hands in her own tiny ones. She was grave now, her eyes limpid—and yet so very *aware*. They were scary. Her lips parted as if she would speak.

Mandy remembered Robin's warning about the whisper. The girl's voice was as much the wind's as her own. "You're trembling," she said.

"I'm cold."

"Come a little way with me."

Mandy started to stand up, but she was stopped by the astonishing sensation of being enclosed in enormous, invisible hands. Woman's hands, immense and strong and soft. They drew her to an invisible breast, clutched her, enfolded her. It was a terrifyingly wrong sensation: there was nobody here, and nobody could ever be so huge. She struggled, she tried to scream, she felt her stomach unmooring with fright.

But she found herself being cuddled in warm perfumed folds that could be felt and smelled and even tasted, so rich they were. All of the tension, the discomfort, the fear in Mandy's body melted away. Then, as she was beginning to enjoy herself, she was set down. She wobbled, she cried out, she flailed at the air.

Never had she felt so thoroughly explored, so—somehow—examined. [Italics Strieber's][34]

Would it be too farfetched to note the similarity of Strieber's description of the Leannan Sidhe (in both physical and psychic terms) with his description of the female visitor? Is there any significance, then, to the fact that the most powerful figure of a visitor in *Communion* is described as being female?

Some of the most salient features of Strieber's comments on the female visitor have been italicized by me for emphasis below:

> Sitting before me was the most *astonishing* being I have ever seen in my life, made the more astonishing by the fact that I knew her. I say *her* but I don't know why. To me this was a woman, perhaps because *her movements are so graceful*, perhaps because she has created states of sexual arousal in me, or maybe it is simply the memory *of her hand touching the side of my chest one time, so lightly and yet with such firmness.*[35]

There is a remarkable and highly obvious similarity of emotion in what Strieber communicates in the statement above and what he has Amanda Walker experience in encountering the Leannan Sidhe: astonishment, an appreciation of her grace (or "delicacy"), and the intimation of strength and fragility, lightness and firmness coexisting with one another in a single being. Strieber's descriptions of how the female visitor entered into his mind and assumed a larger-than-life quality for him have already been quoted, making it clear that Strieber is prepared to think of entities such as what have been called "fairies" and what he calls his "visitors" in much the same way. Besides their both seeming to be possessed of a capability to come and go from this world as they please, they also seem, as Strieber sees them, to have a profound connection with the life of the unconscious mind.

Another interesting parallel between Strieber's description of Amanda's experience with the Leannan Sidhe and his own visitor experience may also be found twice in the text of *Communion*: Both come from his recollections of his experiences in the round room.

After the "bang," Strieber said, "I felt like weeping and I remember sinking down into the cradle of tiny arms.[36]

And again: "When they held me in their arms, I had been as helpless as a baby, crying like a baby, as frightened as a baby."[37]

And here, once again, is how he described Amanda's experience in *Cat Magic*: "Mandy started to stand up, but she was stopped by the astonishing sensation of being enclosed in enormous, invisible hands. Woman's hands, immense and strong and soft."[38]

Similarities such as these in two different texts may well inspire literary critics to argue that Strieber consciously drew upon his *Cat Magic* material in writing *Communion*. While Strieber maintains that his statements in *Communion* are original, he does go so far as to conjecture, in the introduction to his new paperback edition of *Cat Magic*, that the "wee people" he described in that novel were perhaps a foreshadowing in his own mind of the same little men he described in *Communion*. In regard to this particular "coincidence," one simply has to ask of oneself the question about the reason for its occurrence.

Yet there exists a deeper coincidence in this matter of the "fairies" that is of necessity much more significant than the similarities one may find between one piece of text and another. We are led to ask the inevitable question: Does Whitley Strieber in fact regard his "female visitor" as having been the equivalent of what in ancient times was known as the Fairy Queen?

The Goddess, Wicca, and Cuts on the Finger

Questions about the identity of the female visitor as understood in earthly (though mythological) terms take us into dangerous waters. It is impossible, of course, to find some kind of literal label for something that, by its very nature, seems to defy any kind of categorization. How does one speak of such an elusive creature in relation to anything we have ever previously encountered? In the conclusion of *Communion*, though, Strieber reflects at length on the apparent significance of the number 3 in relation to the visitors—as a symbol of the balance they required of him in dealing with his experience of them. It is in this context that Strieber writes in the section of *Communion* entitled "Triad" of the many goddesses throughout history who partook of a triune aspect, as Robert Graves has made amply evident in his classic exploration of the roots of poetry, *The White Goddess*, not to mention the Trinity of Roman Catholicism, the shamrock of Saint Patrick, and other examples of the symbolic importance of the triad as a unifying principle. Perhaps Strieber's speculations on this point may have been difficult for some readers to follow, but one cannot get the gist of his meaning in *Communion* without attempting to follow Strieber's philosophical speculations out to their logical conclusions.

One thing is certain, however, from what Strieber writes in *Com-*

munion: the female visitor speaks to him as would a goddess to a mortal. When Strieber protested that the visitors had no right to conduct an operation on him, she responded by saying, "We do have a right." Strieber was simply thunderstruck by that reply. As he reflected in *Communion:* "Five enormous words. Stunning words. *We do have a right.* Who gave it to them? By what progress of ethics had they arrived at that conclusion? I wondered if it required debate, or seemed so obvious to them that they never questioned it" [italics Strieber's]. [39]

An examination of the role of the female visitor is not by any means out of place in analyzing the question of the identity of Strieber's visitors, and his use of references to aspects of what Evans-Wentz called "the fairy faith" is all the more interesting in the light of the similarity that his experiences related in *Communion* bear to some of the above-mentioned passages in *Cat Magic.* Taking that point of comparison one step further, it may also be observed that "the fairy faith" is inextricably intertwined with the entire history of pre-Christian fertility cults throughout Europe, which were generally characterized by the worship of a great mother goddess in one of many forms. Although there are considerable differences of opinion among scholars about the relationship between the fertility cults and the worship of the Great Horned One (also known as the worship of Pan, later one of the most frequently condemned forms of what has been negatively labeled "witchcraft"), it may generally be said that the subjects of witchcraft and fertility rituals are two elements that bear a very significant tangential relationship to Strieber's story in *Communion.* They bear a particular relationship, too, it seems, through one of the few pieces of physical evidence that remained with Strieber after his first recollected visitor experience: the cut on his finger.

Such parallels, however, should by no means be construed to mean that there is some sort of intrinsic link between UFO phemonena and Satanism, as has often been alleged by the tabloid press, and even law enforcement officials. The allegations made by some sheriffs in the western United States that cattle mutilations associated with UFOs were somehow the work of Satanists have never been proved, leaving the connection between cattle mutilations and UFOs a true mystery. Moreover, it would be a mistake to identify the contemporary practice of Wicca with contemporary UFO cults or what was labeled witchcraft or devil-worship in years past.

As regards the question of the relationship between "witchcraft" and strange marks on the body that occur in relation to UFO "abductions," Vallee made the following observation in *Dimensions:*

> Budd Hopkins and scores of other ufologists carefully examine UFO witnesses for unexplained scars or marks that might indicate they were victims of an abduction (perhaps one they cannot recall consciously). Throughout the Middle Ages priests and inquisitors similarly examined the bodies of people suspected of having attended the sabat of the witches. The proof of such supernatural contact was a scar or a mark. The authorities went to great extremes to find it and were usually successful: what normal individual doesn't have a scar whose origin is forgotten or unexplainable? Many of these alleged witches were tortured and burned at the stake.[40]

Several such cases are documented by Margaret A. Murray in her classic anthropological work, *The God of the Witches.* As Murray relates:

> In Bute in 1662, Margaret NcWilliam [sic] who seemed to have been one of the chief witches there, was marked in three places, one near her left shinbone, another between her shoulders, and the third on the hip, all of them blue marks. Margaret NcLevine [sic] of the same coven, stated that the Devil came to her, "he took her by the middle finger of the right hand which he had almost cut off her, and therewith left her." Her finger was so sorely pained for the space of a month thereafter that there was no pain comparable to it, and also took her by the right leg which was sorely pained likewise also by the Devil.[41]

In Strieber's case, the incision that was made on his finger was, as he recounts it, the last event he remembers before losing consciousness of his first recollected visitor experience.

References to scars by women accused of worshiping the devil, of course, may be scoffed at as "inadmissible evidence" by some observers, since the women themselves may be judged unreliable witnesses. What accounts, though, for the frequency of such reports in the literature of witchcraft? Were women in different places at different times all inflicting the same kinds of wounds on themselves? While such a possibility is not inconceivable, the psychological motivation for such extensive self-mutilation would have to be explained.

In regard to Strieber's incision, we may question whether he included it in his narrative as another invented detail of his experience, since he had already gained extensive familiarity with the literature of witchcraft. Yet here Strieber's wife, Anne, may testify as to the physical reality of the finger wound that refused to heal. It seems a small detail, but one that opens up a vast field of resonances within a great unknown realm of experience.

Strieber's sexual excitation in relation to the female visitor, curiously, was another rather interesting detail of his experiences that he mentioned but hardly developed in the course of his story. One may understand Strieber's reluctance (if such was the case) to explore that area of his experience in a public way, but it is all the more intriguing in the light of all the other indirect references that Strieber makes to the old fertility cults. Did Strieber go through a transformation in his sexuality as a result of his visitor experiences? Did he become more aware of the feminine principle at work not only in sexuality but in Nature herself? Strieber does not explicitly say so in *Communion*, but he does describe his visitors as being highly concerned about the future fertility of the earth. They reportedly gave him information about the degeneration of the planet's ozone layer, a matter of great concern to Strieber.

Yet such parallels to the old nature religion may only whet one's appetite to understand the deeper psychological aspects of Strieber's visitor experiences. In this light, the female visitor plays a central role, too. Strieber states in *Communion* that he suspects the female visitor has an ability to see into the very depths of his unconscious mind, to commune with him at depths he hardly knows himself.

The Female Visitor as Anima

In describing the female visitor in such a manner, Strieber broke completely with standard conventions in UFO abduction research, which, as we have seen, has remained primarily concerned with verifiable events and hard evidence that can be found in the outer, testable world, rather than what has been considered the unreal psyche. Evidence such as scars, blood left behind from the alleged insertion of probes in "abductees' " bodies, marks on the ground where craft presumably landed, and so forth has been collected and interpreted by numerous investigators for years. Yet with the exception of the great analytical psychologist C. G. Jung and some of his followers (not to mention the writings of Jacques Vallee), almost no serious writer has truly explored the mythological and psychological depths of UFO experience. Certainly Strieber was the first writer who knew how to communicate with a popular audience to produce a narrative that approached the UFO abduction scenario in such an inner-directed manner.

In mentioning the "anima," and saying that he could love his female visitor as much as his own anima, Strieber reveals his ability to think of his visitor-related experiences as in some way connected to the deeper realms of his own psyche. As developed by Jung, the concept of the anima represents the feminine, or shadow, side of the personality, the "animus" being the masculine, or light, side. In each of us, Jung said, either anima or animus predominates, and the less-developed side gradually makes its needs for fulfillment known by impinging into consciousness in a variety of ways, most forcefully (and intelligibly) through dreams.

Yet for Strieber his encounter with the female visitor took on the numinous quality of a religious experience, something we have seen in another context with Betty Andreasson's ecstatic experience after seeing the phoenix she reported under hypnosis. For Strieber, the outcome of his experiences with the visitors was that state of communion that inspired the title of his book, a state in which opposites meet to transform themselves into a third entity that resolves the opposites' contradictions and establishes harmony. Strieber's speculations upon the spiritual significance of his experience are also outlined at length in the previously mentioned penultimate chapter of *Communion*, entitled "Triad."

Although Carl Jung's book, *Flying Saucers: A Modern Myth of Things Seen in the Sky*, is suspect among some ufologists for its alleged tendency to psychologically explain away UFO phenomena, it would seem that Jung had a framework in which to understand the kind of experience that Strieber reported with the female visitor.

As Jung put it:

If we try to define the psychological structure of the religious experience which saves, heals, and makes whole, the
simplest formula we can find would seem to be the following:
*in religious experience man comes face to face with a psychically
overwhelming Other.* As to the existence of this power we have
only assertions to go on, but no physical or logical proofs. It
comes upon man in psychic guise. We cannot explain it as
exclusively spiritual, for experience would immediately compel
us to retract such a judgment, since the vision, according to
the psychic disposition of the individual, often assumes the form
of sexuality or of some other unspiritual impulse. [Italics
Jung's].[42]

In Strieber's case, the coincidence of his encounter with the female visitor and an experience of what he responded to emotionally
as an anal rape was no doubt profoundly disturbing to him. Perhaps
the mere mention of the incident may have been disturbing, even
offensive, to many readers. Yet, for Strieber, that coincidence does
seem to confirm Jung's remark that the vision of the Other "often
assumes the form of sexuality or of some other unspiritual impulse."
Jung believes, however, that there is a purpose for the intrusion of
something "unspiritual" in this category of religious experience. He
goes on to say:

Only something overwhelming, no matter what form of
expression it uses, can challenge the whole man and force him
to react as a whole. It cannot be proved that such things happen or that they must occur, nor is there any proof that they
are anything more than psychic (neither is there any proof that
they are only psychic!) since the evidence for them rests solely
on personal statements and avowals.[43]

Jung may seem to many readers to be straddling a fence in referring to this sort of experience as having an ambiguous physicality. He
suggests that some experiences in this category may seem to have a
physical quality, but does not develop the idea. Nevertheless, his comment is intriguing in the light of the very nature of Strieber's experience and all classic abduction narratives, in which elements both psychic
and physical seem inextricably intertwined. Jung is aware, too, that

his contention that "unspiritual" influences such as sexuality may serve as catalysts to religious experiences could well offend religious purists. He continues:

> This, in view of the crass undervaluation of the psyche in our predominantly materialistic and statistical age, sounds like a condemnation of religious experience. Consequently, the average intelligence takes refuge either in belief or in credulity, for to it the psyche is no more than a miserable wisp of vapour. Either there are hard-and-fast facts, or else it is nothing but an illusion begotten by repressed sexuality or an over-compensated inferiority complex. As against this I have urged that the psyche be recognized as having its own peculiar reality.[44]

While we may have to forgive Jung his apparent intellectual snobbery in referring to "the average intelligence," his final comments in this passage represent a particularly trenchant (though of course unintended) criticism of Budd Hopkins's mode of thinking in insisting that UFO abduction stories prove that UFOs represent "real, hard-and-fast facts" and not "an illusion." In order to understand Jung's point of view, it is necessary to consider for a moment that he is asking us to accept the possibility that the psyche (which includes both conscious and unconscious levels of mind, including the entire racial memory of humanity) is indeed capable of manifesting in ways that are real but not physical, at least in the sense of the kind of definite materiality we usually associate with the term. In short, Jung is asking us to regard the psyche itself as being *real*, just as we think of our bodies, though they will die, as being real. It is really a modern plea for consideration of the existence of the soul.

Jung, in a famous 1958 letter to Major Donald Keyhoe, former director of NICAP, expressed his own position as regards UFOs by saying, "Things are seen, but one does not know what." He did, however, spend a great deal of time analyzing the dreams of people who saw images of flying saucers while asleep, something that virtually no major psychologist and certainly no ufologist has subsequently done with any comparable degree of thoroughness. Unfortunately, as far as we know Jung did not have the opportunity to analyze an account of an abduction experience. I believe it unlikely that if Jung could have been presented with information now becoming available about the incidence of this phenomenon, and if he had enjoyed the opportunity to speak firsthand with abductees, he would have explained it away. Jung's well-documented interest in Western occultism and Eastern mysticism attest to his profound respect for and lifelong interest in truly anomalous phenomena and their relation to the mind.

If we choose to regard the psyche as having "its own peculiar reality," though, we are in a position to develop a way of looking at the UFO abduction experience as not merely limited to the events that presumably take place when human beings are "taken aboard" UFOs, but also as experiences that continue onward in time and that can be described in terms of personal changes witnessed in the abductee. Jung regards the psyche itself as changing, dynamic, and working toward its own transformation, which he described in many works (notably *Aion: Researchers into the Phenomenology of the Self*) in language drawn from the literature of Western laboratory alchemy. Jung compared the development of the personality to a process of *solve et coagula*, a breaking down and reorganization of the self, which in alchemy was seen as a process of purification of matter, raising it from a lower to a higher state. Following Jung's line of thinking, then, an overwhelming encounter with the "Other" leads to an "alchemical transmutation" of the personality.

Jung's assertion that the psyche has "its own peculiar reality" is, in itself, only that: a statement by a respected observer and healer of the human mind. Yet, in a larger sense, his description of religious experience as an overwhelming, face-to-face encounter with the Other seems to be a model into which Strieber's experience with the female visitor would tentatively fit. By suggesting a possible relation between his female visitor and his anima, Strieber was alluding to his belief that, though she appeared to be external to him in every way, she nevertheless partook of some of the same, mysterious qualities that our minds present to us in the form of dream life, where the actions of dream people often have more psychological impact on the dreamer than do those of people whom we know in the real, waking world.

But What About the "Great Mother"?

In writing of his "female visitor" in such a manner, Strieber was also touching in a highly original way upon a theme that has been developed to a great extent by other writers and commentators on UFO phenomena: the figure of the Great Mother, regarded by Jung as an "archetypal figure" and also referred to by some more contemporary writers as "the feminine principle." Some commentators have gone so far as to hypothesize that the appearances of UFO-related phenomena in conjunction with reported apparitions of the Blessed Virgin Mary at Lourdes, France, and Fatima, Portugal, are manifestations of the feminine principle at work in the mass human psyche. Such manifestations, it is maintained, are indications of the need for humanity to abandon its patriarchal, exploitative, rape-the-earth ways and search for a new order closer to that enjoyed in Neolithic times, when the Great Mother held sway in nature-worshiping religions. Although there exist competing explanations of UFO phenomena in relation to the Virgin, in *Communion* Strieber does not in any way engage in speculation of this sort. He prefers to relate his experiences as best he remembers them, and in this lies much of the strength of his narrative.

Indeed, generalizations about UFO phemonena as manifestations of the feminine principle may well be overgeneralizations. An alternate hypothesis about the apparent connection between UFO phemonena and apparitions of the Blessed Virgin Mary holds that the majority of such cases are examples of the manipulation of mass human consciousness by entities capable of producing visual and auditory displays that are specifically designed to lead worshipers to the Virgin to believe that the displays are, in fact, the Virgin herself. The motivation for this deception, according to Salvador Freixedo, a Spanish ex-Jesuit priest who does not blush at proposing hypotheses that would give the tabloid press a field day, is the entities' desire to psychically feed upon the mass emotions of agony and ecstasy that are only observed in miraculous shrines. Freixedo goes so far as to hypothesize that we are literally preyed upon by certain classes of entities who create UFO phenomena in the interest of feeding off of our religious emotions, in a manner analogous to the way in which blood has been found entirely removed from cattle that have been found strangely mutilated in UFO-related events throughout the world.

Freixedo's two books on UFO phenomena, *Defendamonos de los Dioses!* (*Let Us Defend Ourselves from the Gods!*) and *Las Apariciones Marianas* (*The Marian Apparitions*), are as yet unavailable in English, having only been published in Spanish by Editorial Diana of Mexico City.

Clearly, unfounded speculation about the Blessed Virgin Mary and the feminine principle could draw one into a labyrinth that might well have no exit. Nevertheless, by drawing the reader's attention to his mode of psychological introspection into his own experiences, and by revealing his inclination to speculate that perhaps his "visitors" were the same things that have elsewhere been called "fairies," Strieber makes it clear that he feels such approaches will have a more productive outcome (at least for himself) than attempts to elucidate what happened to him from psychological tests or an examination of physical evidence alone. Indeed, apart from the two triangular scars that he said appeared on his left forearm, the previously mentioned slow-to-heal cut on a finger and a small scab on the back of his head, Strieber had precious little physical evidence to work with. He had a memory of something having been inserted up his nasal cavity, but no proof of there being any physical object lodged within, at least at the time that he wrote *Communion*.

As mentioned, Strieber has subsequently taken a magnetic resonance imaging test of his cranium, in which the examining specialist remarked upon the presence of several "unknown bright objects" in the image taken of his brain.

How would one describe Strieber's visitors, then? Certainly, they seem to partake of the qualities of Jung's archetypes, in the sense that they are an "unknown psychic force," but they are also, it seems, an unknown physical force. Are they some kind of sadomasochistic cosmic goon squad that seems to get satisfaction from subjecting innocent people to horrifying experiences, or are they the practitioners of a highly developed, technologically sophisticated system for accelerating the evolution of human consciousness? Are the "tortures" that Whitley Strieber experienced at their hands designed to make him bow his knee to their overwhelming power, or are they intended to awaken him to a level of awareness and strength he previously never knew?

It would seem that, for both sets of questions, Strieber would have us see the visitors not as goons but as testers and liberators. The potential represented by the visitor experience, he would have us know, is nothing less than a major self-transformation.

To Whitley Strieber, the visitors are in essence agents of change, catalysts to personal evolution, alchemists of the soul. In a word, they are "transformers."

The Politics of "Cosmic Seduction"

Standing on its own, Strieber's speculation about the possible relation between his visitors and members of the "fairy kingdom" is admittedly subject to accusations of being the product of literary fancy. Without a larger framework of investigation and carefully constructed hypotheses, *Communion* remains testimony and speculation, though it may yet prove valuable to the development of UFO research. Such a framework, however, is not entirely lacking, in that some ufologists have become increasingly critical of the "extraterrestrial hypothesis" in recent years, and have begun to develop alternative hypotheses that, though apparently even more "far-out" than the idea that spaceships carrying aliens have been studying us, are based on a very thorough examination of evidence often neglected by other researchers.

The leader of this still-nascent movement (if it can be called a movement) is Jacques Vallee, who has yet to receive the adulation of the UFO community for producing a number of books that have systematically attempted to uncover whatever deeper phenomena—social, psychological, psychic, and physical—might underlie the UFO phenomenon. Vallee's *Messengers of Deception*, for example, was the first serious work to be published that examined the development of UFO cults, and was posed as a warning against the forces of irrationality in society that would have us reject scientific rationality on the grounds of a new revelation from UFO-nauts. Vallee is also quite different from the majority of American ufologists in that he has attempted to view the development of the UFO phenomenon from a historical point of view, and has done considerable research in that regard.

With the publication of Vallee's *Dimensions: A Casebook of Alien Contact*, the general reader and anyone seriously interested in exploring the subtleties of the UFO phenomenon now have what is probably the most exhaustive single volume elucidating what could be an entirely revolutionary investigative approach. In it, the author reworks elements of two of his earlier books, *Passport to Magonia: From Folklore to Flying Saucers* and *The Invisible College*, which explored the possibility that UFO phenomena were not an exclusively twentieth-century phenomenon). In *Dimensions*, Vallee castigates what he considers the "intellectual naiveté" of the proponents of the "extraterrestrial hypothesis," with whom he seems to be losing some of his patience. While there is little that is fundamentally new in *Dimensions*, Vallee has richly developed his arguments and reemphasized his evaluation of UFO phenomena as partaking of an essentially psychic nature that must be understood on its own terms. Vallee has been making the argument for years that the UFO phenomenon is not all that it seems to be, but has been something of a voice crying in the wilderness as far as the UFO community was concerned. Nevertheless, given the recent increase of available information about UFO abductions and a correspondingly greater degree of public interest, his time to make an impact may finally have come. Vallee's work could well provide us with the most useful frame of reference yet advanced by any serious researcher for discovering whatever lies behind the curtain of the abduction phenomenon.

After opening his introduction to *Dimensions* with a description of what he sees as the gap between academic interest in UFO phenomena and the increasing public appetite for such information, Vallee states his central thesis:

> This book is an attempt to close the gap by examining the evidence for the existence of UFOs, not only in our time, but in earlier ages as well.
>
> Such a historical perspective . . . is entertaining and often captivating. But more importantly, it is critical to a full understanding of the problem. If these objects have been seen from time immemorial, as I will show, and if their occupants have always performed similar actions along similar lines of behavior, then it is not reasonable to assume that they are "simply" extraterrestrial visitors. They may be something more.
>
> Perhaps they have always been here. On earth. With us.
>
> In my view, the widespread belief among researchers of the field in the literal truth of the "abductions" is only a very crude approximation of a much more complex tapestry. Another reality is involved here. A reality characterized by cosmic seduction, strange signs in heaven, and paranormal events that present a rich panoply of psychic phenomena.[45]

Vallee's use of the term "cosmic seduction" is quite interesting in the light of Strieber's descriptions of his sexual interactions with and feelings of love for the visitor whom he described as female. It is even more curious in the light of the content of the fairy tale "Connla and the Fairy Maiden," which Strieber recommended as a sort of paradigm for approaching an understanding of the abduction phenomenon. What does Vallee precisely mean by "cosmic seduction"?

Although Vallee does not specifically define that term, he does enumerate a series of five propositions that he believes express certain salient features of the UFO phenomenon. In the fifth proposition, Vallee states:

> Contact between human percipients and the UFO phenomenon always occurs *under conditions controlled by the latter*. Its characteristic feature is a factor of absurdity that leads to a rejection of the story by the upper layers of the target society and an absorption at a deep unconscious level of the symbols conveyed by the encounter. The mechanism of this resonance between the UFO symbol and the archetypes of the human unconscious has been abundantly demonstrated by Carl Jung, whose book *Flying Saucers* makes many references to the age-old significance of the signs in the sky. [Italics added][46]

In this sense, Vallee does not emphasize a sexual nature for the "seduction," though he does not deny that there are many reports of human-visitor interaction that seem to be characterized by a sexual quality. What is of importance here is Vallee's observation that in human-UFO contacts, it is the "UFO phenomenon" that is in control, not the human percipient, a situation analogous to that of the power imbalance that makes sexual seduction possible. It seems to be Vallee's implication that our fundamental experience of the UFO phenomenon, abductions included, is an initial *powerlessness*. It is in response to our powerlessness, then, that we begin to "close the gap" in our experience by projecting certain patterns of belief onto aerial and abduction phenomena that we cannot rationally explain. These beliefs, in turn, change over time as our perceptions of ourselves and our cultures change. Indeed, it is Vallee's contention that what we are witnessing in the UFO phenomenon is nothing less than the intervention of a "control system" that functions to affect changes in our beliefs at significant historical junctures.

Vallee writes:

I propose that there is a spiritual control system for human consciousness and that paranormal phenomena like UFOs are one of its manifestations. I cannot tell whether this control is natural and spontaneous; whether it is explicable in terms of genetics, of social psychology, or of ordinary phenomena—or if it is artificial in nature, under the power of some superhuman will. It may be entirely determined by laws that we have not yet discovered.

I am led to this idea by the fact that, in every instance of the UFO phenomenon I have been able to study in depth, I have found as many rational elements as absurd ones, as many that I could call friendly as I could call hostile. This is what tells me that we are working on the wrong level.[47]

Vallee's comment about "working on the wrong level" refers to his ongoing critique of researchers who accept the phenomenon at face value, who actually suppose that because abductees report having been taken aboard spacecraft, such events did in fact occur as described.

Clearly, Vallee is no more a believer in fairies than he is in extraterrestrials, for the "control system" he postulates goes far beyond any one category of understanding, any label ascribed to anomalous beings from any particular historical period. Nevertheless, he goes to great pains to analyze stories of reported human interactions with "sylphs" and "fairies," which he has uncovered with an impressive degree of investigative prowess.

Bringing History to Bear: Ignore the Psyche at Your Own Risk

Of particular interest are passages of Vallee's that are drawn from Jerome Cardan's *De Subtilitate* (quoted in the previous chapter) and from the autobiography of the German poet Goethe. In the first instance, Cardan described beings who appeared as the result of a ritual invocation; in the second, the poet described a group of aerial lights he had perceived while traveling to the University of Leipzig in 1768. Both instances document the fact that the subjects of strange lights in the sky and encounters with nonhuman beings were matters of considerable interest to men of unquestionably great intellect. Yet Vallee's historical accounts are composed of far more than first-person accounts by distinguished men of the past. They record as well the persecution suffered by witnesses to strange events in the sky, the accusations of witchcraft and ghastly punishments leveled against those who reported experiences of encounters with "fairies," experiences that today might well be interpreted, he points out, as "UFO abductions."

A historical view of the UFO phenomenon may ultimately throw little light on the question of the "identity" of our visitors in the manner in which we conventionally understand the concept, but it does establish one single, overriding fact: Mankind's fascination and reported encounters with nonhuman entities and anomalous aerial phenomena is of a long-standing nature, and not a recent cultural phenomenon. In tandem with that point, Vallee makes a very strong case for recognizing that, in conducting any kind of UFO research, we cannot separate the psychic, or inner, component of the UFO phenomenon from its apparent outer, or physical, aspects. If such a postulate ever became an axiom of UFO research, we would probably see an entirely new emphasis on understanding the symbolic content of the apparently absurd communications we receive from the "visitors."

Lastly, as an antidote to our tendency to see our own experiences as being unique and the result of some kind of "progress," Vallee asserts that the manner in which we have perceived the UFO phenomenon and the visitor experience has changed over time, as our cultural frame of reference has changed. As Strieber himself says in his foreword to *Dimensions*:

> He [Vallee] reveals an appalling truth: the phenomenon has been with us throughout history, and never have we been able to deal sensibly with it. Whatever it is, it changes with our ability to perceive it. The fifteenth century saw the visitors as fairies. The tenth century saw them as sylphs. The Romans saw them as wood-nymphs and sprites. And so it goes, back into time.[48]

In approaching the question of who these visitors are, then, it appears we must confront a complex but interrelated series of questions that takes us on a seemingly endless journey through labyrinthine passages of the past, of folklore, of our own minds. At every turn, we seem to encounter an image that is recognizable, but only for a fleeting instant. Ultimately, and most disturbingly, it appears that in asking who might be these evanescent entities who break the laws of physics and defy normal forms of identification, we are led to one question that is even more difficult to answer.

It is a question so basic and obvious it is often completely overlooked by all of us once we are safely past the rocky shores of adolescence.

Who, after all, are *we?*

Chapter 9

Beyond the "Boggle Threshold"

Examining the Ultimate Implications
of the "Visitors"

Whether he likes it or not, Whitley Strieber is engaged in an ongoing trial. It is a trial that still involves both the question of his personal credibility and, even more significantly, the objective truth of his story. That trial is taking place in the court of public opinion, which, for better or worse, is not always as well-informed as it could be. Yet we would be shortchanging ourselves if we did not have confidence in our ability to come to a fair conclusion regarding many aspects of Strieber's "abduction" story. It is by far more challenging to try to make sense of the phenomenon of UFO abduction as reported throughout the world, but an honest attempt to understand some of the dynamics of this one case may prove beneficial toward reaching an understanding of the phenomenon in general.

That, at least, has been the reasoning I have employed in the writing of this book, knowing from the first that it was impossible to use physical evidence to "prove" that Strieber was "telling the truth." And what if I had somehow found a piece of an alien alloy in the backyard of his old home on Elizabeth Road? Would that enable us to understand the meaning of his narrative? Of course not, for that meaning is specific to Whitley Strieber. It may apply to others as well, but that is a matter that concerns those who say they have had experiences such as his. My aim has been to try to convey whatever shreds of meaning, both individual and social, I have found in the threads of his stories, both of the "visitors," and of his objective personal history.

There is obviously a social problem involved in dealing with the stories of abduction we are told by Whitley Strieber. If we might someday find out (through some sort of public action taken by the visitors) that they (and the stories told by other "abductees") are objectively true, then we as a species would be confronted with an extraordinary situation. We would have to surrender our precious status of being alone in the universe. In the modern age, when the Judeo-Christian "God" has died a thousand deaths, our status as lonely heroes, defiantly challenging fate, has even acquired its measure of existential glamour. Living as we do in times where historical memory is at a minimum, though, we tend to think that a public recognition of "alien" life on earth would be an unprecedented event, perhaps evoking panic. Yet what did the ancient Hebrew people think of the "pillar of fire" that led them out of Egypt, if indeed such a phenomenon was an objective fact? Whether or not the events described in the Book of Exodus are objectively true, it is certainly a fact that the response of the Jewish people to the mere concept of a nonearthly force intervening in their life was the development of a vibrant culture and a strong intellectual tradition.

The concept of a public panic following upon the heels of a public recognition of alien life has become a cliché in popular discussions about UFOs. Some persons, in fact, seem to delight in the concept of a crisis even more profound than the various sorts of public panic elicited by Orson Welles's 1938 broadcast of H. G. Wells's *War of the Worlds*. Yet it would be a mistake to immediately assume that "the public" would necessarily run amok under such circumstances. Worldwide response to such news would no doubt vary, assuming that the news itself could somehow find its way more or less intact through the world's various news services, many of which are completely state-controlled. There are alternative visions, as Arthur C. Clarke posited in his novel *Childhood's End*, and in the story of the film *2001: A Space Odyssey*. The aliens could even turn out to be just the latest in a long line of cosmic refugees, as I observed in Chapter 5 in referring to the film *Alien Nation*.

As Timothy Good points out in *Above Top Secret*, the world has learned to live with the constant threat of nuclear destruction. What could be worse than that? One might add to Good's observation that in many parts of the world where the problems of starvation, war, progressive environmental collapse, and political tyranny are particularly grave, many people would be far too preoccupied with their immediate, personal survival to attach much importance to any official declarations about the existence of alien beings. In a country like Brazil, where spiritist religions have long been a part of the fabric of daily life, a public announcement to the effect that the government of the United States had recognized the real existence of aliens might be greeted with a simple shrug of the shoulders, and perhaps the addition of a new god to the spiritist pantheon.

For those of us who participate in the special mythologies of technological societies, however, the problems involved in granting any credence whatever to the hypothesis that human beings are being abducted by aliens or visitors are manifold. For one thing, the acceptance of such a hypothesis would seem to open a Pandora's box of competing explanations. Moreover, many might argue, there appears to be no compelling reason to even begin to do so. The standard skeptical argument, that abductions are a delusion often reinforced by amateur hypnosis, might seem to many people to be an effective bulwark against superstitious belief in aliens. Such an argument, however, would be regarded as absurd by people who have had to personally deal with the problems of having an abduction-type experience occur to them or someone whom they love. In such cases (and no one can deny that such cases do exist in numbers yet to be told, but certainly in the thousands in the United States alone), the witnesses to such abduction experiences have an objective need for answers and therapy that respect their freedom and dignity as autonomous human beings.

Skepticism is warranted in approaching any kind of paranormal experience, but the most useful form of skeptical thinking is a radical doubt that is willing even to question the framework of established cultural and social values that form the bedrock of our lives. Like science itself, skeptical doubt is not, in and of itself, a value-free tool independent of the people who use it. As individuals with perceived self-interests and differing stakes in the social orders in which we live, we all tend to direct our doubts in different places. The Soviet Union questions whether AIDS is the result of biological warfare research in the United States, while the United States is skeptical of recent Soviet proposals to reduce troops in Eastern Europe. In the case of the debate over alien abductions, a critical thinker has to question whether vociferous UFO skeptics such as Philip J. Klass are not motivated by what they perceive to be a threat to a social order based on the idea that international security can be gained forever through the use of the nuclear arsenal (an order in which Klass, as an editor of *Aviation Week and Space Technology* magazine, would probably not be ashamed to say he has something of a vested interest and sincere belief). Likewise, the UFO community's "skepticism" of Klass and his colleagues appears to be motivated by an agenda intent upon forcing open the clam shell of United States government secrecy about UFOs and alien abductions, leading to their ultimate vindication through official recognition of the reality of UFOs.

There are serious problems with both approaches. Mainstream UFO skepticism, as expounded by Klass and company, is essentially based on an a priori denial of the possibility that there could be any validity at all to the UFO phenomenon. It is one big, long, "No!" Moreover, their response to the suffering of people who experience abductions— that they should seek the aid of a psychiatrist—is inadequate. Modern psychiatry, which in its present state would treat abduction accounts as psychotic fantasies, could condemn people with abduction experiences to lifetimes of dependency on antipsychotic drugs or even periods of involuntary incarceration in mental hospitals where electroshock therapy and other harsh measures could be practiced upon them. Despite the advances that have been made in many sectors of medical practice, people who seek or are forced to receive psychiatric care are still stigmatized by society as being somehow defective and unreliable. Science may have progressed, but society is slow to change.

The pronouncements of the UFO community and even many of its most prestigious members, though, are less than reliable guides to understanding the full extent of the UFO phenomenon. Behaving in a manner reminiscent of many minority groups who feel persecuted, the community tends to waste its energies in internecine fighting, forcing many of the best available minds away from research and public dialogue about the phenomenon. There are numerous problems with the formation of support groups for UFO abductees, as well, for such groups are subject to the same kinds of social pathologies that have afflicted initially well-meaning efforts to help alcoholics and drug addicts. Once again, the problem of stigmatization rears its head, as many people tend to shy away from support groups of any kind owing to fear of ridicule and perhaps even the loss of professional and community standing. The recent upsurge in popularity for support groups dealing with the problems of codependent relationships, however, may be a very positive factor that could stimulate the acceptability of abductee support groups.

Is there any middle ground between these two extremes, in which one might accept Klass's warnings about cultism in the UFO community, and yet at the same time take the abduction phenomenon seriously? Is it even necessary to try to do so? What does it matter, after all, if Whitley Strieber was actually abducted? Perhaps such alien interventions have been going on for all time, and the world has still had to suffer its miserable history of poverty and bloodshed, no?

I believe that a middle ground is possible, but it has to be constructed individually by each person who is willing to seriously examine the UFO phenomenon in its totality. The problem of finding a balanced approach does not lie, moreover, in whether we are smart enough to comprehend how truly anomalous UFOs are. We are smart enough to learn, and who can say what our limits really are? In my view, as with most problems in society, the question is whether we can handle the complex emotions that occur when we encounter things that challenge our cherished views of ourselves and our world.

It is an undeniable fact that the subject of aliens has been exploited in innumerable ways by movie directors by playing upon public fears. Yet the intense public excitement that accompanied the early days of what was called the "space race," not to mention the Buck Rogers-style science fiction culture that had preceded it in the 1930s and 1940s, served to remind us of the fact that part of us yearns to break free of the earth. In the last decade, however, plans for exploring Mars and other planets have been scrapped in favor of the militarization and industrializing of orbital space around the earth. It may be argued that public interest in UFO phenomena in industrialized nations has increased as a not indirect result of the turn in public policy away from planetary exploration. Denied a "legitimate" form of expression, it turned to the scientifically condemned area of UFOs.

Now that many people are seriously willing to consider the possibility that UFOs are real, however, we are seemingly paralyzed by the implications of what we are being told by the UFO researchers. There are still people, of course, who may choose to become anesthetized by the "space brothers" gospels of Ruth Norman and the Aetherius Society, but the fact remains that intelligent people are pleading for a public hearing on what has been found from years of patient inquiry into the stories told by UFO abductees.

Given the groundwork already done by ufologists who tell us that alien abductions are primarily a genetic experiment performed by extraterrestrials, it would seem inevitable that our society will eventually have to make an attempt to evaluate the legitimacy of that claim. If the research seemed valid (which has by no means yet been determined), we would have to consider the motivations of the apparent aliens for taking sperm and ova samples, for presumably taking fetuses from women's wombs before they complete their first trimester. The legitimization of such a scenario would be particularly challenging in that it would imply that human beings are indeed some kind of prey for beings against which we have no known defense. Such a prospect, as horrifying as it is, is precisely the proposition being advanced by Budd Hopkins.

No less horrifying, perhaps, to many people, is Whitley Strieber's proposition that the visitors, as terrifying as they seem to be in and of themselves (irrespective of any genetic considerations), are nevertheless pushing, prodding, indeed hounding us, into a higher level of consciousness. We are familiar enough with the concept of the "hounds of hell," but somehow the idea of the visitors as "hounds of heaven" is at a rather far remove from our normal way of thinking about spirituality itself. We are rather habituated to thinking of pleasure as good and fear as evil, and many of us recoil from the thought of spiritual influence coming anywhere save from recognized, culturally identifiable sources. While we say we admire people who conquer their fears, we tend to ridicule or pity people who say they have conquered fears of things that we might ordinarily regard as fantasies. To the skeptic who denies any possibility that Strieber's visitors have any reality, Strieber's claims to have learned how to deal with his fears of them— and that he has gained precious insights into himself from doing so— must seem pathetic. Yet is that a fair assessment of how the man has kept himself and his family together through a time of extraordinary stress?

One has to wonder, too, whether Strieber's understanding of the rewards of confronting personal fears is comprehended by Hopkins, who seems rather oblivious to considerations of the unconscious psychological dynamics of abductees. His "therapy" for them seems to consist in a posthypnotic suggestion that they will be able to deal with their problems, as well as the discussions of his support group, which have yet to be publicly subjected to analysis of their group dynamics by anyone clinically trained in group therapy. Is this response adequate to the fear that a literal acceptance of Hopkins's interpretations of the abduction experience could engender?

Complicating consideration of both propositions, of course, is the understandable human tendency to deny any reality or seriousness to reports of phenomena as strange and bizarre as those represented by alien abduction. Yet, in the face of continuing reports of alien abduction, and barring any change in the increasing social trend toward breaking down taboos that once prevented public discussion of "certain" areas (homosexuality, child abuse, etc.), it appears that we are being drawn into making a choice in terms of the public attitude we adopt toward abduction witnesses: Either we accept them as credible, sane people (assuming they are otherwise generally responsible) or we choose to ignore them. Hopefully, we will not be overcome by our fears and persecute them. Perhaps we may try to learn more about ourselves through them.

One of the most difficult areas of Strieber's writings for most people to accept has been its prophetic side. His statements about having seen in a vision a nuclear reactor accident, not very long before the Chernobyl disaster in the Soviet Union, and his vision of seeing the moon explode (both related in *Transformation*) are the two best-known examples of this feature of the man and his beliefs about himself. It would be easy and rather glib for me to say that Strieber is not the first person who has reported UFO-type experiences to have made prophetic utterances. Such a statement could be interpreted two ways, and I do not mean to be ambiguous. The phenomenon of "prophecy" is a subject unto itself, and history gives us many remarkable examples, not the least of which are the sayings of Nostradamus, or the pronouncements of Joan of Arc.

I am unable, as a reporter, to evaluate Strieber's precognitive abilities. All I can do is report that he has told me: that, on more than one occasion in his life, he has been able to make statements that, in retrospect, indicated to him that he somehow had access to information he would not ordinarily have. Strieber gave me the name of an old friend from his London days who may have heard him say one such statement, but I was unable to contact him, never finding him at home.

As I was nearing the end of this book, however, Strieber called me up and read to me a personal letter that I include here, for what it is worth. Apart from its connection to Strieber's vision of seeing the moon exploding, the information it contains should be of intrinsic interest. Strieber introduced the letter by saying, "This is a letter from Dennis W. Chamberland, safety specialist, space vehicle operations, from the NASA base at Cape Kennedy. It is dated January seventh, 1989. He writes in reference to the vision of the moon exploding in *Transformation*. This is not the whole letter because it is quite long":

> The Star Wars technology seeks to develop so-called kinetic kill weapons. These are weapons not made out of atomic isotopes but a simple mass moving at very high speeds. It doesn't matter what. Just as a fifty-five-gallon drum filled with high explosive and nails is one of the most deadly and terrifying weapons ever constructed, so is the kinetic kill weapon.
>
> And now the connection. It has been widely speculated that such mass drivers on the moon could do much more than deliver raw materials to space colonies. Each one of those buckets of material weighing tons becomes a multikiloton weapon if aimed at the earth. The capacity to direct to a given orbital coordinate immediately implies the ability to boost it out of the moon's gravitational influence and into that of the earth. All it needs is greater than one-mile-per-hour velocity in the gravitational airspace. These would amount to kinetic kill weapons which could destroy whole cities and be launched by the thousands off the moon and directed to any point on the earth spinning under its gravity well. For you see the velocity to get the bucket into orbit is not related to the velocity of impact on the earth. The atmospheric entry velocity is exactly 25,000 miles per hour, which is a function of the gravitational attraction of the earth on any freely falling body prior to reentry. It is precisely this interchange of such tremendous kinetic energy that causes the devastation.
>
> It is widely suspected today that the Tunguska explosion of 30/2/1908 was caused by a once-in-three-century natural event, a one-million-ton, one-hundred-meter-across meteor that had the equivalent destructive capacity of twelve million tons of

TNT when it disintegrated in the atmosphere.

The ground damage is dependent on the angle of approach, and velocity of composition, both factors of which are controllable with mass drivers. If someone on the moon decided to adjust the orbital parameters of the mass drivers, a bucket of moon rocks, "gigantic boulders sailing off the edge of the moon" [quoting Strieber] in this distant mechanical manner, would do as much damage as nuclear weapons. So, you see, the vision you had takes on whole new dimensions. If one was interested in calculating these events, if they were originated by human technology, then one can calculate the earliest possible date of such an occurrence, about fifty to seventy-five years from now.

If any nation were intent upon destroying another from space, only this approach makes any sense. No nuclear fallout would be left to contaminate the vanquished nation. A space-based defense system of today's tactical design is a look-down system to counter an earth-based threat. The incoming velocity of a moon meteor would be far and again greater than any earth-launched weapon and therefore much more difficult to detect and destroy. Much of the technology being designed for the Star Wars defense system is based on interference with command and control and disruption of electronic guidance and propulsion systems. A rock incoming from the moon is immune to any of these. A massive direct nuclear hit wouldn't make any difference to these weapons.

The weapons are free. Only the launch system will cost. Destruction of the moon launcher would take four or five days after impact of the first meteor. Even if a retaliatory strike were launched, the war would long be over before the launcher could be destroyed. What your vision has described, Mr. Strieber, is the apparent evolution of weapons in the technological future of the next century. It is also of some note that Albert Einstein said that the next world war would be fought with nuclear weapons, and the one following with stones. He obviously meant something else, but its credible prophecy is extraordinary.

I leave the reader to draw his own conclusions from that letter. Whatever one may think of Strieber's prophetic pronouncements, it is certainly a fact that few contemporary authors have exhibited such an

intense and well-informed ability to visualize scenarios in the immediate future based upon well-known trends in technology and society.
Both *Warday* and *Nature's End*, which he coauthored with James
Kunetka, reveal the authors' capacity for extrapolating from those trends
to an extraordinary degree. In particular, the phenomena of ecological
destruction described in *Nature's End* take on a greater immediacy as
reports about the deterioration of the atmosphere become more frequent, authoritative, and grave in their implications.

While it may appear that Strieber is quite pessimistic about the
fate of the earth, he is actually far from pessimistic when talking about
the future of humanity as a whole. This attitude, it has become clear
to me from many discussions with him, stems from the fact that he
feels we are being inevitably drawn closer to one another, for we are
being driven closer to God. It may seem ironic to some readers that
he feels this way in the face of encounters with "visitors" by whom he
was initially terrified. Yet there is more to it than meets the eye, according to Strieber.

Perhaps one of the reasons why we have such a difficult time in
even thinking about "alien abductions" may derive from the fact that
we consider the aliens to be exactly that: completely other from us,
unrelated in any way. How is it, though, that Whitley Strieber has
gotten to the point that he says he no longer experiences the fear and
terror that once filled him from head to foot during his visitor experiences? Perhaps the answer is simpler than might be expected.

In an interview Strieber gave me in early December 1988, he put
forth his own ideas of who he thinks the visitors really are.

To paraphrase Pogo, he has met the visitors, and the visitors are *us*.

The key to understanding Strieber's idea, moreover, lies in the
biological phenomenon of *neoteny*. It is best to let Strieber describe
this concept in his own words. And, as is appropriate in this particular
instance, I will let Whitley Strieber have the last word.

CONROY: How did you get the idea, Whitley, that the visitors
are neonates of us?

STRIEBER: Beings who need breathing apparatus are seldom
encountered. It seems to me that they are quite at home here.
In addition to which, I've seen beings that were clearly, to my
eyes at least, partially, if not completely human. I find it difficult to believe that they're some sort of mix between us and

some so-called alien species, and I think I know what is happening.

One of the apparent evolutionary processes is neoteny. Here is an example. If you take the human and the chimpanzee, there is a ninety-five-plus percent parallel between the genetic structure of the two species, and yet they're radically different. At a certain point in the growth of a chimp fetus, the chimp has many of the characteristics of a fully grown human being. If you were able to extract the fetus of a chimpanzee at that stage of its growth and bring it to full sexual maturity, without causing it to mature in other ways, in other words to mature without fully gestating, you would have something like a human being. Now, oddly enough, the visitors most commonly described often look like a fetus that has emerged at about the end of the first trimester of a human pregnancy, and been brought to maturity in just this way, with something having been done to their eyes, such as a covering of some sort placed over them. There is a tradition in the context of the visitor experience, a great deal of material about the stealing of fetuses after the end of the first trimester. This is something that goes back a long time in folk tradition. Budd Hopkins comments on it in his books, as does E. S. Hartland in his book about fairy lore, *The Science of Fairy Tales*. He says, "By the belief in changelings, I mean the belief that fairies and other imaginary beings are on the watch for young children, and they carry them off, and leave in their place one of them."

CONROY: Now this idea of aliens seizing human beings is very old.

STRIEBER: So, whatever it is, it's been going on for a long time. It may be that the human species is the womb of the angels. If that is the case, it's no wonder that we're so important to them. It could be that what they are is a sort of next step in evolution, in part artificially emerging by some means that is presently unknown to us. Then we would literally be the receptacle out of which the future was flowing. But it would also explain why I and so many other witnesses feel or are told that we are with members of our families when we go and are with the visitors. Certainly I think of the ones that I've been with as my family—absolutely do. That's a commonplace feeling.

CONROY: This is a feeling that has gradually evolved, or that you even felt in the terror of being in the round room?

STRIEBER: Yeah, I did. I had the impression that one of the beings involved was my mother and another was my sister. I did have that impression, even though I don't mean my human mother and sister. I didn't say anything about it at the time because it sounded so bizarre, but now it's beginning to make a little more sense. What the agency that started this whole process was I don't know. However, I can only repeat what I've said before many times, that what we may be witness to is what the process of evolution looks like when it is applied to the conscious mind. The universe may not be an immensely intricate unconscious organism, but rather at some level consciousness may append to matter—even to energy—in ways that we have not understood except figuratively and mythologically. I refer to the concept of God. For example, if consciousness has a plasmic form, as I think it does, then many of these lights that people see and the balls of light that come into their bedrooms at night, and so forth, are literally projections of this plasma. Then it's probable, also, that this plasma is extremely old, and it may even predate matter, that it could literally be the oldest thing in the universe. What I'm talking about is a description of God which is not abstract, but which rather is comprehensible. I'm suggesting that there may ultimately be consciousness which may be measurable and directly accessible to communication, using the right technology, and this consciousness may be completely indistinguishable from what we now call God. It may be that this consciousness is responsible for what is happening to us. I think that the visitors literally are us, and I wouldn't be surprised if some of these beings that I've seen that look like half-visitor and half-human aren't the progeny—they are what happens when one of the pure neonates is somehow crossed with a fully mature human being, and the fetus is then removed, also in the first trimester, or even done in vitro, and you might very well end up with something quite like some of the beings I've seen, and in fact very like the one on the cover of *Communion*.

Another startling thing about all of these beings is that they do not look like they have skulls under their skins. Like fetuses, their heads are soft, and it fascinates me to think that perhaps the skull is what isolates us in ourselves from a consciousness that very well might pervade the whole universe, and thus be immediately present on the other side of the barrier of bone. This would be that plasmic consciousness—which leads me to ask myself, what about all of the trepanning that went on in the past? Was it to let the evil spirits out, or to let the good ones in?

CONROY: This would explain also their extraordinary mental powers, their telepathic powers?

STRIEBER: Yes.

CONROY: Their ability to break the laws of physics, to move between physical barriers?

STRIEBER: Well, the ability to pass through physical barriers is a technology. They've said to many people, "We rearrange atoms," which is an extremely important statement, because anyone who can do that has really gotten control over the nature of matter. They could literally form and reform matter in patterns unimaginable to us. What's interesting, though, is that this isn't such an obscure technology. Within a hundred years, we'll be able to do it, too. We're already well on our way in that direction.

It means, by the way, absolutely extraordinary control over the nature of experience, and the capacity to create materials which are fundamentally different from anything that now exists outside of the mind. It may be that we'll be able to create anything that we can conceive.

CONROY: Which appears to be the modus operandi behind the various types of ships which appear in the sky. It's often been observed by ufologists that they seem to have almost a direct connection with ideas about design at different times. In the late 1890s, they looked like dirigibles, which were just emerging into the human imagination with the work of Jules Verne, *Master of the World.*

STRIEBER: A characteristic of the visitor experience in modern times is that not only the design of implements and so forth that are seen, but also what the visitors do and say are always just a few years ahead of what's going on in the world around them. In some cases this has been startling, such as the ob-

vious use of amniocentesis by the visitors in the 1960s before
it had been invented. In the case of Betty Hill and a few others, this process was reported before it was invented.

CONROY: So they seem to be precursors of our technological
development.

STRIEBER: I think of mankind as being the projection into
the physical universe of something else from another realm. It
has created us because in its nonphysical state it has no access
to temporal mystery. It isn't in sequential time, but extratem-
poral. It has literally projected itself into matter in order to
partake of the mystery of time. In that it exists outside of time,
it is therefore incapable of changing itself, and of evolving,
growing, unless it projects its consciousness into sequential time
and has spontaneous experiences in sequential time. That may
be what life is about, that the process of living itself is what is
important, not how it is done at all, that something is changing
and being energized by the process of life. The physical universe may be largely a side-effect of another kind of activity
which is much more important, much more extensive and much
more conscious. It may have created and entered the physical
universe in order to experience time. If living planets are extremely rare, or if there is only one, then every single thing
that happens here must be incredibly important. Increasingly
as we go on with this experience I get the feeling that we are
all but alone. I'm losing my ability to believe that there are
many, many other planets, and that they are all somehow in
contact with us and all somehow hanging back. I have a feeling that there may be only a few in the universe, and perhaps
only one or two others where we are known. I think that conscious species must be extremely rare.

CONROY: What are your thoughts, then, about how the visitors get around, assuming that they do indeed travel in their
ships?

STRIEBER: There was a paper in the *Physical Review Letters*,
Volume 61, Number 13, called "Wormholes, Time Machines, and the Weak Energy Condition." This is an important paper, in that for the first time the idea that extremely
large space-time curvatures could be generated has been
broached. Such holes would be governed by the laws of quan-

tum gravity. If you can imagine the universe as a curved surface, a wormhole would take two opposite points on that surface and press them together in a sort of hyperspace between the two, and all of a sudden, two places that had been millions of light-years apart would be right next to one another. If a civilization existed that was capable of engineering such a thing to classic size, that is to say to large size, then it would explain much of what has happened and what has been described. For example, Betty Andreasson has described on a number of occasions being taken aboard a vessel which apparently flies a short distance, and it opens up and she steps down a tunnel to another world. That is exactly what it would be like to go through a wormhole, I'm sure. I had an experience in 1968—an apparent journey to another world. I've viewed it as possibly hallucinatory, but a wormhole could have been involved. I seemed to go to a university[1] of some sort in another world, a place of sun and deserts.

CONROY: You weren't totally in a normal state of consciousness?

STRIEBER: I wasn't in a normal state of consciousness during this experience, absolutely. I would say this: I don't think that a final answer is accessible. I think that like every carefully observed visitor experience, there are always three possibilities. Possibility number one is that it emerged out of an unusual version of perfectly ordinary psychophysiological phenomena, in other words an intense hallucinatory dream. Possibility number two is that it was done by human beings using a variety of unusual and little-known technologies, a synergy between hypnosis and hallucinogenic drugs. Possibility number three is that real aliens in metal spaceships came from the dark reaches of space and carried me away. These are the three possibilities, and nothing anyone can say or do will make one of these possibilities lead over the other two. There is always something you can bring forth to promote one or the other of these theories.

CONROY: Yet now you have reached a critical mass of understanding?

STRIEBER: It is necessary to think in a new way to understand this material—to abandon determinism once and for all. It is possible to conceive of real, physical beings emerging out of nonphysical experiences, and to relate to those beings as if they were entirely valid—and then to throw it all into question. Once highly organized but indeterministic modes of thought are adopted, one becomes much more effective at the difficult task of thinking clearly about the nature of the visitors and relationship with them. Once you cross the barrier into their world, you're very much as ordinary as you are in this world, only you have access to a different set of memories, a different past— your life with them. But when you cross the barrier again, it's as if your memories of that world are turned off and your familiar memories are turned on, and you can no longer access the exotic ones. But I can access them to a degree, and one of the things that I remember from the visitor experience is that there are lots of people involved, and they take this as a perfectly ordinary part of their lives when they are with the visitors, but when they are back there is absolutely nothing they remember about it. They have extensive personal involvement, virtually without knowing it. They live indeterministically, but they hide this from themselves.

When I'm with the visitors I feel as if I'm in the presence of human beings, but I also feel, interestingly enough, that they're more animallike than we are, they don't seem to have any enculturation at all, or at least there isn't any enculturation that I can recognize. They are an aspect of humanity that has dispensed with history and returned to the spontaneous reality of the forest. They are conscious animals. The future.

CONROY: They don't have the sexual repressions that we do?

STRIEBER: No, they don't have the enculturation that we do. They don't, for example, wear clothes like we do. They all wear exactly the same thing. Sometimes I felt that souls at their level may be able to have more than one body, because I've seen them moving together in lockstep, almost as if a group of three or four were being directed by a single mind.

CONROY: There's your "English empire" story, where you saw the little bodies wrapped in plastic cellophane. . .

STRIEBER: And I've seen them also in another situation stacked like cordwood, and I've seen them being brought to life.

CONROY: One has to wonder, well, when they're not in their

bodies, where are they? What are they doing—zipping around as little plasmic balls somewhere, perhaps?

STRIEBER: If you knew everything and were eternal, you would be absolutely desperate. You would have to be extremely creative if you expected to remain sane. You would be in a state of extraordinary terror, because you would be so alone and so unable to change anything. You would be desperate for a companion. I think that's probably what the motive is behind the physical universe. I think that the plasmic being—God—is attempting to create a companion. That's what we will one day become. The companion of God.

CONROY: And that is why love is so important to us.

STRIEBER: Yes, of course. This extraordinary being can't afford to fail. Therefore it goes on and on and on, trying and trying and trying. It must succeed in this. We assume, by the way, that there's only one universe. But why even make that assumption? What if there is an infinity of universes, if it never stops, no end to the expression of matter, the material, the plasma, goes on forever, ceaseless. It fills nothing, because it is everything. Then the fact that we are finite would make us one of the most remarkable things in the whole creation. Because of this we would have a specialness about us, rather than this endlessly repeated story, unchanging, empty, predictable. There would be this one place where things could not be predicted, and all of a sudden this eternal presence would find in the universe a little dust mote that was interesting.

I suspect that's why I feel as if God was staring me in the face every moment that I'm alive. I think it's literally true. We are, if you will, a very sacred and special form of entertainment. I guess what these thoughts have given me is the idea that mankind is very valuable, that we devaluate ourselves.

People are all very interested if I say that I think that we're dealing with aliens, but when I say I think we may be dealing with something that in essence comes out of the mind, they lose interest and they say, "Well it's only the mind." I say, "Only the mind—my God, you're talking about the most extraordinary thing we know, and the greatest unknown." The mind is more unknown than the depths of the sea, or the reaches of space, for goodness sake. It is by far the richest thing that we can come into contact with. It is much more interesting, frankly, than the firmament as we really see it—blank and endlessly repeated phenomena of the same sort, stretching over light-years upon light-years. The mind is a much, much richer field, for I have the feeling that we are the doors into another universe that is far more fully expressed and conscious than this one is. We literally are God—are God in the physical form. And suddenly there is no guilt, there is no evil, there are no demons, there is only life itself, experience, the richness of search. And it's all fundamentally theatrical.

I have a feeling we're in the process of discovering that the world around us is, in effect, a cardboard backdrop. The reason I think this is that I just don't see certain things. You know Fermi's paradox? If there are civilizations older than we, millions of years older than we, then where are they? Where are their remnants, where is their electromagnetic debris? The answer is it doesn't exist, we can't find it at all! The universe is extremely quiet, and I suspect it's because there's not a lot out there. I do think there are other planets on which there is life, but simple life. In the few places that you find intelligent life, you're going to find enigmatic forms such as mankind and the visitors, one emerging from the other, a situation expressing in physical reality the quantum indeterminism of plasmic consciousness. And I suspect that the second form, being composed almost of thought, may not be able to reproduce in a physical context. Maybe this is one reason for the neoteny. Perhaps hybrids between us and our second selves—our "visitors"—are produced. Some of these may be able to bear infants, others not. This would explain, for example, the Villas Boas experience in Brazil, and also would explain numerous of my own experiences, because sex with such a being has been one of the primary secrets of my life.

CONROY: Was this woman the inspiration for Miriam Blaylock?

STRIEBER: Of course, and for the woman in "Pain." She is also the visitor on the cover of *Communion*. I have been involved with this woman for most of my adult life, and in addition to that, she is the one I remember from all of my childhood. It's always been this woman. She is also the one who confronted Bruce Lee in the bookstore. She was with a man then, and also when I met them in the backseat of a car, a few months ago when I was making an attempt to take pictures of them. She was with him, and I felt a tremendous sense of jealousy, and an extraordinary sense of relief, because I have my own wife, and I was glad to find that she had a husband.

If you want to ask who has created *Communion*, she did it. It's her thing, she created it, she brought it forth. This particular individual. I'm not talking about faceless aliens, I'm talking about a specific person, and in my opinion if you were to fingerprint her, you'd find she has fingerprints. If you were to look at her genetic material, you'd find that she was ninety-eight to ninety-nine percent just like us. She is a human being, like all of her kind. But she is of the next level of man. What we call "unconscious" is among her kind full of light. I would like to take her away, for my own self.

CONROY: Because you love her and long for her so much?

STRIEBER: If I had that sort of sentiment I think she would be extremely annoyed. She's already nearly always extremely annoyed with me, which is fine. I don't mind that. I got used to it years ago. She told Bruce Lee that *Communion* was all wrong. Typical of her. She is very hard on me. Sometimes she's very friendly and she has the capacity to become almost totally innocent. She can be as innocent as a baby and as sensual as a fox. She's absolutely amazing in that respect. Normally, she is very, very emotionally open. When you're angry, it's like she's physically being hurt, and you have to reach into the depths of yourself to find a level of serenity that is deep enough to enable her to be calm in your presence. And when her passion comes on her, she appears out of the night. It's absolutely amazing. I'm afraid that my succubus is quite real. And I am sharing her with many other people. Maybe that's because our incubi and succubi have always been real, that they represent a level of human life that is very real, but which we are afraid to acknowledge. And we don't acknowledge them for a very simple and straightforward and practical reason, and that is because of their access, so to speak, to the group mind or to God, or to the conscious plasma, whatever you want to call it. They are, for all practical purposes, without will. And our essence is to have will. So we preserve our isolation with a fury. This is why people don't want to remember their visitor experiences, why they're so frightened of remembering them. We preserve that isolation from the deity with absolute fury. The essence of our reason for existence is that we have extracted ourselves, as it were, from heaven, and gone on this adventure in order to have experiences of chance, to face a real, genuine unknown. Opening our minds to the visitors is like raising the curtain, going too close to the cardboard backdrop. If we do that we destroy our reason for living, and we may have waited a long, long time to have this experience. If we return too soon to God, we will be an unworthy companion. To be God's companion, our will must first grow as strong as His.

We protect ourselves from remembering our relationship with the visitors, and we do it in order to preserve our individuality, in order to stay inside the time stream where we can continue to grow, both as individuals and as a species.

CONROY: It seems to me, then, that what you are saying is that for individuals to integrate these experiences into their personalities is something new.

STRIEBER: Something completely new. The ability to have a separate relationship with deity—that does not interrupt the spontaneity of one's existence, but rather enhances it—that is quite new. We are at last, some of us, learning how to become conscious companions of God, which is what this species is all about. That's what man has been striving for since the beginning. We seek to become such a companion of God that he's not something incredible, not a bearded man in the sky, or a great awesomeness before which we prostrate ourselves, but a friend, as ordinary as you or me—a dear friend. This is what is being looked for by those of us who are in this process of demythologizing the emergence of sacred consciousness into the physical world. The visitor experience is a part of this effort, in my opinion.

Epilogue

Dealing with Traces of the "Visitors"

In the course of discussing this book with friends and acquaintances, I've had to deal many times with one inevitable question.

"Has something like what happened to Whitley ever happened to you?"

Many times, I've had to answer yes.

That one admission, as simple as it is, has served to put me through some of the most agonizing periods of self-reflection I've every experienced. I even considered dropping my plan to write a book on Strieber and the "visitors," since I had to consider the thought that perhaps my capacity for objectivity had somehow been violated. After all, few people who write about UFOs from an investigative angle ever mention having had anomalous personal experiences. To do so might well seem to one's readers that one had somehow become contaminated by the subject.

Yet, despite my initial fears, I have come to see that, far from impeding my investigation, my visitorlike experiences have served to deepen my capacity to relate to the strange events that make up the narratives of *Communion* and *Transformation*. I have come to see myself as not only an investigative reporter, but also a participant-observer in the style long adopted by anthropologists who study tribal peoples. In that regard, I now think that it is far better for me to share even the subjective side of my investigation than to regard it as a secret. To not share it would mean that I would have to publicly deny having had any such experiences, even though I have been reluctant to deal with discussing them in public. I dislike lying, and I refuse to subject myself to the negative psychological effects that would result from making a secret of this material. "Objectivity" that does not honestly deal with subjective elements isn't worth much to anyone, I think.

Prior to recounting the events that have served as a personal backdrop to my investigation of Whitley Strieber, I should say that I have still reached no final conclusions about them. I cannot responsibly say that I know I have been in touch with "extraterrestrials." I have no test for determining extraterrestriality in anyone. I do know, however, that I have been in touch with some kind of phenomenon that, as far as I am able to tell, acts in a manner indistinguishable from the kind of intelligence one would expect from other beings, other individuals. Am I experiencing what Whitley Strieber experienced? I do not know. Some of my experiences, though, are remarkably similar to those I have heard reported by him and other people.

I am aware that it will be argued that none of the material I set forth here has any relevance to the matter under investigation, which is the subject of alleged "UFO abductions" that presumably occurred in the life of Whitley Strieber. My experience, it will no doubt be said, is purely the result of my own fascination with my subject matter.

I must reiterate, however, that I did not consciously seek to encounter all of the extraordinary experiences that have occurred since the beginning of my inquiry, and while it will be argued that they were entirely subjective, I will advance reliable testimony from witnesses to some of the incidents I describe. I am fully aware that in writing this Epilogue I am placing my personal and professional reputation on the line. It is only through doing so, however, that I may be able to convey an adequate feeling for the unexpected influences that came to bear upon this book.

The event that first shattered my conceptions about visitor experiences occurred on a night in early July 1987. (I failed to record the exact date because I was not keeping a diary at the time.) Sometime in what seemed like the predawn hours, I suddenly found myself sitting bolt-upright in bed, completely awake, alarmed at what I strongly sensed was a presence in the adjoining room of my apartment. The thought of there being someone present in my apartment was especially disturbing because of its improbability. I live on the sixth floor of a building with electronic security. My solid hardwood front door is secured, moreover, with a heavy deadbolt. My only thought was for the defense of myself and my wife, Lucila, who was sleeping next to me. The only weapon available to me was a heavy piece of wood, a back massager known as a Ma Roller, which lay next to the bed. I moved to grasp it with my left hand.

The next thing I knew it was early morning, and light streamed through the venetian blinds. Instead of sitting upright, I was lying on my stomach, my face buried in the pillow. Arising, I was startled to see a four-inch-diameter splotch of blood on my pillowcase, and a similarly sized red stain on the white sheet below me. Even more odd, my right sinus ached dully, and when I went into the bathroom to look at myself in the mirror, I noticed a small amount of dried blood at the edge of my right nostril.

My first thought was, "Well, they did it to *you*." My second, "This can't really be happening."

By using the term "they," I was jokingly referring to my concept of the "beings" of whom I had read in *Communion* and *Intruders*. By the time of this incident I was familiar with descriptions of insertions of nasal probes by nocturnal visitors, often reportedly accompanied by nosebleeds. My immediate denial of that first thought, as I see it now in retrospect, was an attempt on my part to try to slow myself down and approach this occurence in a rational way. On the emotional level, though, it was clearly an attempt to control the fear and alarm I felt at the memory of the events of the previous night.

The sight of blood on my pillowcase and bedsheet was especially disturbing in that I have no memory of ever having had a spontaneous nosebleed in my life. Upon questioning, my mother told me that she likewise had no recollection of my having had any nosebleed at all in my childhood. For me, this was a new and unique occurrence.

More disturbing to me than the nosebleed incident, however, was Lucila's condition. As she entered the shower, I noticed she bore two heavy bruises—one on her left buttock, and another just below it on the back of her left thigh—which she had not had upon going to sleep. While the most "rational" way in which to explain those bruises would be to say that I gave them to her, I certainly have no memory of having done so, nor did Lucila accuse me of having hit her in the middle of the night. (I never once punched her in the course of our six-year relationship.) She was as mystified as I was at their appearance. She did not, however, think it was funny when I quipped that perhaps we had been abducted.

I am aware that some readers will immediately presume that I unconsciously beat my wife that night, but I am including this detail in my narrative in the interest of rendering a complete version of the facts.

Shortly after that incident, I met Whitley and Anne Strieber in New York, as I have described in the introduction to this book.

The months that followed that meeting were difficult ones for me. My father died suddenly two days after I met the Striebers, requiring me to immediately return home to San Antonio. Lucila and I decided to divorce about a month later, ending a relationship that we had tried to keep going for a long time despite conflicting personal desires and needs. It is a decision I accepted with regret, but also with relief. How much did the "nosebleed" incident and my growing interest in Strieber have to do with the end of our relationship? I cannot objectively say.

It has often been observed by therapists and counselors that people in times of transition are especially vulnerable to new influences and often have "conversion experiences" or otherwise adopt new belief systems. As I was going through the grief I felt over the loss of both my father and my wife, I reminded myself of my vulnerability and endeavored to maintain an even keel with my responsibilities as a critic and feature writer for the *San Antonio Express-News*. My sister, Mary Furness, was a great help to me and served as the best therapist I believe I could have found during that difficult time. No further nighttime incidents comparable to that of the "bloody nose" recurred during that time, although my curiosity was piqued and I began to read as much abduction-related information as I could find.

My investigation of Whitley Strieber's background deepened as fall and winter drew 1987 to a close, and I obtained the benefit of many people's opinions and impressions of the man. Over the Christmas holidays, however, I took a vacation with my mother to visit my sister and brother-in-law at their home in California's Napa Valley. After a pleasant week spent skiiing near Lake Tahoe, California, I paid what proved to be a rather dramatic visit to my friends Neil and Naomi Kantor at their home in San Francisco on New Year's Day, 1988.

Neil, a certified acupuncturist now practicing in Mill Valley, California, had been one of my closest friends when I lived in San Francisco during the 1970s. As I was in the business of importing acupuncture supplies and medicinal herbs from China and Japan at that time, we shared a deep interest in oriental medicine and other therapies. During our visit, though, our conversation turned to the subject of my research into Strieber, and the question of extraterrestrial contact in general.

As we conversed at the dinner table, looking out at the Kantors' garden through a magnificent plate-glass window with sliding doors, Neil suddenly stopped eating and sat for a moment in a daze. He excused himself and left the table for a moment. When he returned, he said he had just remembered an incident that was greatly disturbing him even as he recalled it.

Neil proceeded to recount that, on a fairly recent night, he had been awakened by sensing an unusual light in the house. He and Naomi had been sleeping on a sofa bed in the living room, having decided to stay there and enjoy the fire they had kindled in the hearth. Since the dining room directly adjoins the living room, the plate-glass window was visible from Neil's position in bed. The glow that awoke him, Neil said, appeared to be a shaft of coherent light of about twelve inches in diameter, seemingly being projected down onto the window at an angle from a position on the hill above the Kantors' garden. Neil remembered getting up from the bed and going to the dining area to observe the light. Neil said he thought, "Oh, it's just a bunch of kids playing with a laser," and, returning to bed, went back to sleep.

What was disturbing Neil at that moment of recollection, however, was the memory of the width of the beam, and the realization that no neighborhood teenager could possibly have obtained access to technology required to produce a twelve-inch-diameter shaft of laser-like light. Moreover, Neil said, what was especially strange was the additional memory of seeing that shaft of light break up as it passed through the glass into a multitude of serpentine wavelets that splayed across the surface of the floor, walls, and ceiling in a stunning display that totally begged comprehension. On top of that, there was a small pool of light that had settled by the edge of the sofa bed, seemingly without direct source.

Needless to say, Naomi and I were somewhat taken aback by this sudden confession on Neil's part, and were unable to say much except to ask questions about the details of what Neil said he remembered. I could see, too, that Neil was having a hard time believing what he was saying. He pointed to a house on the hill behind the garden and said he had believed the beam was emanating from it. He even said he now intended to go outside and look at the house to see whether any kind of apparatus was attached to it. On reflection, though, he admitted that, if his memory of the beam was faithful to his experience of it, then there was obviously no way it could have come from a window of that house since it would have assuredly required a large building for the apparatus and the generation of the power required.

Neil continued having a hard time accepting what he was remembering (he even took a bath to relax), but we passed a pleasant evening playing the piano, joking, and watching a tape of *Indiana Jones and the Temple of Doom*. I stayed with Neil and Naomi until around midnight, and would have stayed overnight were it not for a date the next day to go bicycle riding with another friend in Marin County.

As it turned out, rain prevented that ride and I stayed at my sister's house in Napa. I was surprised, then, to receive a call that very next day from Neil in which he described having been awakened in the middle of the night by the sound of three loud notes being played on his piano. The interval was a third, from G down to E, as I recall him describing it, with the rhythm having been a heavy downbeat on the first note with a sharp attack, followed after a beat by the two E's in rapid succession. The sound awoke both Neil and Naomi, and while they were debating whether it had been made by their cat jumping onto the keyboard, the same sequence of notes was repeated, in exactly the same manner. Neil said he also heard floor boards creaking as though someone were walking around in the living room.

In the light of the evening's discussion, it would be fair to say that Neil and Naomi were doubly terrified by what occured to them. However, the phenomenon restricted itself to the piano, Neil said, and he and Naomi eventually returned to sleep.

That incident, though, seems to have had a catalytic effect on both Neil and myself, in that afterward we both began to experience a series of more or less "classical" nighttime visitor experiences. Neil's experiences, in retrospect, were far more spectacular and far-reaching than my own, including a sighting (also witnessed by Naomi) of a triangle-shaped UFO that flew above San Francisco and later enveloped itself in a cloud of some kind of vapor that apparently emanated from the UFO.

Neil sought hypnotherapy with David Cheek, M.D., past president of the American Society of Clinical Hypnotists and a close associate of the late Milton Erickson, generally regarded as the father of modern hypnotherapy. He told me that during his hypnotic sessions, although he remembered what appeared to be experiences of having been aboard flying saucer-like craft, he did not feel that those memories were faithful to what had really happened during those experiences. Neil told me he felt that his abduction memories were themselves a screen behind which other memories of the true experiences lingered, impervious to recollection even under hypnosis.

I decided not to pursue hypnotherapy as a means of dealing with my experiences, as I was sensitive to allegations to the effect that the hypnotist could possibly impose his own interpretation on information revealed during the hypnotherapy session. Neil's comment also made me ponder whether hypnosis could ever be a tool for discovering the truth of my own experiences.

It was against this backdrop of increasing communication with Neil about his experiences, then, that my 1988 began. I stayed in touch with Neil, discussing his experiences and mine for several months, until Neil reached a point where, although we remained on friendly terms, he was no longer comfortable speaking of them. For me, however, the year proved to bring with it a number of anomalous incidents that challenged the fragile peace I was endeavoring to restore to my life.

On January 16, 1988, I had brunch with a young San Antonio woman who had reported to me a number of visitorlike incidents in her life, some of which we discussed that morning in general terms. That afternoon, while raking leaves in the front yard of my mother's house in a northside San Antonio neighborhood, I was surprised to see a Bell 47-style helicopter pass immediately overhead at an altitude only just above the tops of the tallest trees. While it was curious enough to see a helicopter flying at such an altitude in a residential area, it was even more remarkable to see the manner in which it shined a spotlight, mounted in front just below the cockpit bubble, in my general direction. I looked at my watch and noted the time: exactly 4:00 P.M. The helicopter bore no markings of belonging to any organization such as the San Antonio Police Department or any local radio or television station. I did not see any identifying numbers on it, though I will admit I would not have known where to look for them at that time.

My mother emerged from the house as the helicopter was flying away, and though she did not see it, she remarked on the noise it was making. She also said that it was the first time she had ever heard a helicopter flying over the house, and thought it was odd. (My mother has resided in the same house for over twenty years.)

For my part, I simply filed that experience away in my mind. It was not long afterward, in the month of February 1988, that I began to go through a period of awakening at precisely 4:00 A.M. under a variety of curious subjective and objective circumstances. The subjective aspect of many of the experiences was the feeling of someone touching the back of my head, as though my head were being put down upon my pillow. On occasion, too, I had a number of extremely vivid dreams, in which visitorlike entities were among the dramatis personae. The objective aspect of such experiences was awakening at that hour to find myself feeling very hot, in fact almost sweating. Upon checking the thermometer on the thermostat for my central heating unit, I noticed with surprise on more than one occasion that the temperature was higher than that which I had set the thermostat to maintain. While I usually set the thermostat at 68 degrees Fahrenheit, it read up to 80 degrees in a room that had partially opened windows with an outside temperature that was often around 40 degrees Fahrenheit.

Another aspect of the experience, which is hard to classify as either objective or subjective, was a kind of crackling and pinging sound that I heard emanating from the walls of my room upon awakening from these experiences. The pings were extremely delicate and high-pitched in nature, and the crackling was likewise low-key but continuous. The two kinds of sound occurred simultaneously and intermittently, lasting for as much as a half hour after such an experience of early awakening.

I did not experience immediate anxiety upon having these experiences, but rather an immense sense of curiosity at what was happening to me. On one occasion, however, I perceived something quite extraordinary. Sitting on a pile of large pillows against one wall of the bedroom was what appeared to be a kind of shadow man, completely black, poised in the classical pose of Rodin's "The Thinker."

I perceived this "entity" immediately upon awakening in one of these early-morning incidents, and remember being somewhat amused by it. No sooner was I fully conscious, though, than the image seemed to spring up and fly over my head, only to disappear into the wall behind me.

These experiences were mystifying and somewhat unsettling to me, as well they might be to anyone. I hesitated to draw any definitive conclusions from them, not only because they were so decidedly evanescent, but because it seemed too early to do so. There did seem to be some sort of periodicity to them, and I reasoned that they might be building up toward some experience that might prove to be less fragmentary, more complete, than the wisps of occurrences I had experienced previously. However, they did have one definite effect upon my general psychological orientation toward self-observation, in that I became greatly interested in the nuances of my dreams and subjective experiences in general.

I also began to pay a great deal more attention to details in my ordinary life. It was just as well that I did so, for I soon had a new phenomenon to deal with, equally mysterious but apparently much more objective that my shadow man.

On a morning in early March 1987, I was momentarily distracted from my work by the sight of a Bell 47-model helicopter outside my window. The building in which I work is a seven-story structure located in the middle of downtown San Antonio, and I had been working there for well over a year without seeing any downtown air traffic except for an occasional Army Huey-style helicopter landing atop a local hospital, a few military transport planes, and an occasional civilian single-engine plane. I certainly had never seen anything like the maneuvers I witnessed on that occasion.

The first feature of the helicopter that drew my attention was the fact that its nose was equipped with a searchlight that, curiously enough for that daytime hour, was shining brightly. In addition, the helicopter was painted so that the fuselage was blue and the metal enclosing the transparent bubble cockpit was white. I perceived no identifying numbers on it, even though I had an opportunity to observe it for about fifteen minutes. What was remarkable about this particular helicopter was the inordinate amount of attention it seemed to be paying to my building, in that it was passing by my windows at a distance of less than fifty yards, and even went so far as to shine its searchlight in my direction. After making a pass by my building, the helicopter would make a circle of the immediate area between two local buildings (the Nix Hospital and the Tower Life Building) and return to make another close pass. It made at least eight tight circles before making what I believe were four larger circles that took the helicopter further out to the western edge of downtown, whereupon it would return. On one such larger circuit, the final one of the sequence, the helicopter came directly toward my building, in a straight line that enabled it, before passing directly overhead, to shine its light straight into my main office windows.

I would have ignored this occurrence had it not been for the repeated buzzings and circlings that seemed quite out of the ordinary. In fact, I was trying to get back to work when, only about a half hour after the helicopter's final fly-by, I was startled to see it again outside my window, this time flying parallel to the building and closer than ever before, searchlight shining. After making another circuit of the immediate area, it flew behind the Nix Hospital, out of immediate sight. Immediately afterward, though, there appeared a jet-black, military-looking helicopter of a type I had never previously seen, completely unmarked, which flew out of the western horizon directly toward my building. Once above my building, the helicopter lingered there for nearly a minute, during which time it made a tremendous sound. I opened my window and attempted to see it by looking upward, but could not do so. The sound eventually diminished, only to be followed by another appearance of the small Bell 47, which after a brief circuit of the area, flew away to the north.

Curious, I phoned the local Federal Aviation Administration office and described the antics I had just beheld to one of their officials. He said to me that the kind of flying I described was, in his words, "definitely not kosher," and asked if I had seen any identifying numbers on the helicopters. When I replied in the negative, he said that was understandable since in some cases such numerals are only painted to a maximum height of two inches. Nevertheless, he urged me to call him again if I saw a repetition of such an incident.

It was not long before the blue-and-white Bell 47, complete with blazing searchlight, again appeared during the daylight hours outside my office window. I made another call to FAA to report the incident, but as I had not been successful in seeing any identifying numbers on the vehicle, there was little the polite and helpful gentleman on the other end of the line could do to clarify the matter. I was satisfied, however, that it was not a police helicopter, as I had made a point of looking at the police helicopters that land atop a downtown garage building and noted that they are of a different design and color scheme.

Thus began a remarkable presence of anomalous helicopters in my life. During the spring and summer of 1988, it seemed that I could hardly go anywhere in San Antonio without seeing a helicopter beside or above my car, or even above my bicycle when I would take recreational rides. The Bell 47-style helicopters were soon joined by Chinook-style helicopters—one type painted red, blue, and white and another painted brown with a horizontal red strip running through the cabin down the tail—which likewise began to buzz about my area. I began to even notice searchlight-bearing helicopters in other areas of town. One Huey-style helicopter with a searchlight even buzzed a pool party at a friend's house three times in a row on a late summer afternoon in 1988.

One of the stranger aspects of the downtown helicopter incidents is that many appeared over my building at exactly 4:00 P.M., the same hour at which I had seen the first all-white Bell 47 helicopter above my mother's house in January 1988. Sometimes three black, apparently unmarked helicopters would fly by, one following the other, Indian-file at that hour or (curiously enough) at precisely 3:33 P.M. I once saw three such helicopters fly by in a triangular formation, at very close range to one another.

I have had witnesses for some of these phenomena. On one occasion it occurred to me to borrow a pair of binoculars from a neighbor in the building, Pilar Wellbaum. I explained what was occurring to Pilar, who is an old and dear friend, and while she listened the same helicopter that I had seen flying by my window now appeared hovering outside her window. Pilar noted it with casual interest, and said that she regretted no longer having binoculars in the apartment—her husband, Bill, had taken them to his office. Shortly after that, a good friend who had also seen some of these helicopters gave me some binoculars for my birthday.

I should add that I had more at hand than my binoculars to help give me more information on these helicopters. In particular, I had read the chapter on "mystery helicopters" in Fawcett and Greenwood's *Clear Intent*[1] as long ago as six years before, and was familiar with their as yet unexplained role in UFO-related cattle mutilation reports and other UFO reports, such as the famous Cash-Landrum affair. I had read the excellent accounts of black helicopters published by Tom Adams of Paris, Texas, in his newsletters *Crux* and *Stigmata*.[2] I had heard of accounts from UFO witnesses who had seen mystery helicopters "shape shift" into classical silvery, disc-shaped UFOs, and vice versa. Yet some of the accounts I had read gave no doubt that the mystery helicopters (often black and unmarked) that had appeared in some cases had been independently seen by reliable witnesses. (In the Cash-Landrum sighting the UFO and about twenty black unmarked helicopters following it were observed by a Texas highway patrolman.)

I also read an interesting passage in Timothy Good's *Above Top Secret*, which opens as follows:

> Official investigation into unidentified flying objects in comparatively recent times began in 1933 when, according to contemporary newspaper reports, mysterious aircraft appeared over Scandinavia and, to a lesser extent, the US and Britain. Often seen flying in hazardous weather conditions which would have grounded conventional aircraft of the period, the "ghost aircraft" (as they were called) *frequently circled low, projecting powerful searchlights on to the ground.* Another puzzling feature was that although engine noises accompanied the sightings, the aircraft sometimes described low-level maneuvers in complete silence.[3]

That reference, combined with some I had read of the appearance at the end of the nineteenth century of great, cigar-shaped airships which reportedly bore searchlights (years before the construction of the first dirigible), certainly piqued my interest and led me to wonder if what I was beholding was a purely ordinary aerial phenomenon—or perhaps something quite out of the ordinary.

Since that period of time, I have seen some truly extraordinary helicopter "apparitions," which have completely challenged my conception of their behavior as normal aircraft. I saw one helicopter fly behind the rather narrow Tower Life Building—and not appear on the other side. I still have a hard time believing I saw that. Yet the occurrence that finally put the icing on the cake, so to speak, was a fly-over in late August 1988 made by two Chinook-style helicopters, one with blue fuselage and white cab, the other painted brown with a red horizontal stripe, which flew out of the western horizon in perfect tandem, so close to one another that their blades must have been meshing as though they were eggbeaters. I got a good, long look at them through my binoculars as they flew over downtown San Antonio in a north-easterly direction, as did my upstairs neighbor, Linda Winchester, who commented to me as I was returning to my apartment from my perch on the building's fire escape that she was wondering why she hadn't seen a wreck of those two helicopters.

Whitley Strieber also told me he had seen those helicopters from street level outside my building, as he, Anne, and Andrew had just paid me a visit and were leaving the building. Whitley later told me he was astounded by what he had seen, as mystery helicopters had not been a component of his experiences.

As the summer of 1988 passed into spring, I noticed that there was also an uncanny apparent connection between my telephone conversations and the appearance of the helicopters. On more than one occasion when I had entered into a conversation regarding the subject of UFOs and/or the visitors, a helicopter flew into view. A small Bell 47-type helicopter also appeared out my window immediately after the telephone conversation with my agent in which I accepted the terms for the contract for this book. Curiously, after I got my binoculars, I was never able to get a good look at the occupants of these helicopters, as they kept a greater distance than in their original appearances. Even when they had originally appeared, I had only been able to see the outline of a human frame in the cockpits—never a recognizable face.[4]

As if strange helicopters weren't enough, unusual events also began to occur with my telephone answering machine. After a trip to New York in June of 1988 to visit with the Striebers, I returned home to find that my answering machine message had been changed. Since my apartment bore no sign of anyone having broken into it, it seemed reasonable to assume that it had been done from a remote location. The message's content had been changed from a somewhat lengthy text to a simple "Hi, this is Ed. Please leave your message after the beep." Oddly, the voice had a rather mechanical tone to it. A few weeks later, the message changed again, and while the message stayed essentially the same, the voice was now clearly more human, and it had a youthful, almost boyish quality to it. Its juvenile aspect led me to laugh it off as some kind of prankster-hacker's trick.

Upon returning to San Antonio in September after a trip to Los Angeles, I was startled, though, to hear my message changed once again. On this occasion, though, its implications were somewhat more ominous. The message said, "Hi, Ed. This is Whitley. It's about ten o'clock in the evening, August 24. I just had an experience I wanted to tell you about. Please call me in the next half hour or give me a call in the morning." The audio quality of the message was mediocre, with a great deal of static in the background, but Whitley's voice was quite distinct and recognizable. A tape of that recording is in my possession.

The astounding feature of that message was that it was obviously derived from a tape of an actual message that Whitley had left for me on my answering machine that day. The call originated from his house in the country, and I remembered it well. Since I had been using the same incoming message tape in the answering machine for the past month, the original message that I had received had long since been taped over by another incoming message. The only conclusion that I could draw from the presence of that message on my outgoing message tape was that, at least on that particular night, my telephone was tapped, and that someone had recorded the message from the tap. (I had, incidentally, been noticing unusual clicking noises on my telephone line for months prior to that time.) That person or group was then able later to break the code for replacing the outgoing message on my answering machine and inserted the message onto the outgoing message tape, most probably from a remote location. It is possible, of course, that Strieber himself staged this event, as a prank, but if he did he has not owned up to doing so. I think it unlikely. Certainly, the possibility of a prankster involved with my telephones didn't explain the anomalous helicopter events I was witnessing.

With helicopters buzzing my office and a sequence of messages indicating that my telephone conversations were of interest to someone unknown, I proceeded with my research work feeling very much like a goldfish in a glass bowl. Two messages I received on the telephone answering machine were particularly strange: They were an unrecognizable series of sounds like a human voice uttering unrecognizable syllables against a background of static. I mention them because I received one of them only a few days before visiting with another UFO researcher in another state who had received a similar call just a day before my arrival. He played his message for me from his answering machine, and I found it to be essentially similar in its strange audio quality. Throughout these telephone experiences I was aware, moreover, that such phenomena have been recorded by such investigators as John Keel (who in particular had numerous "Men in Black"

experiences and mystery callers)[5] and Budd Hopkins (who has noted
that some of the abductees he has studied have reported similar calls).[6]

In retrospect, while at first many of the anomalous events that
occurred in my life were decidedly evanescent and dreamlike, the appearance of mystery helicopters and strange telephone messages added
a very strange, "hard," technological aspect to these occurrences that
made them difficult to rationally discount as being entirely subjective,
simply the product of an overheated imagination. Throughout it all,
moreover, there lingered the memory of that original nosebleed and
the dull ache in my head that followed—a leitmotif, perhaps, for much
of what followed.

It would be inaccurate for me to write about my experiences, however, as though they had occurred in isolation from other people. Remarkably, other persons whom I know—some of them close, personal
friends—began to report having nighttime experiences with entities,
balls and flashes of light, and other anomalous phenomena during the
winter months of 1987–88. One friend, David Catacalos, who recorded his experience in detail, later became my research assistant and
secretary for this book, and developed a profound interest in Jungian
psychology that was extremely helpful in formulating some of the interpretive aspects of Chapter 8. Other friends who have told me of
their experiences have chosen to remain anonymous and exhibit no
desire whatsoever for publicity, and I have respected their wishes in
the course of my investigation. One such person has known Ron McAtee
for years and has told me of experiences she has had since childhood.
She lives only a few blocks away from the old Strieber home in Alamo
Heights.

I have also been in communication with a number of people around
the country who have in one way or another expressed an interest in
speaking with me on the telephone about visitorlike experiences. Some
of these people have been referred to me by Whitley, while others
have come to speak with me through mutual friends. I have spoken
with these people as a human being with an experience to share, not
as a clinically minded investigator, since any real investigation of their
experiences was outside my scope as a researcher. I realize that some
criticism may be leveled at me for having done so, yet no one with
whom I have spoken has yet wished to be formally studied. I have
taken notes on what they have told me of their experiences, and I
have related what I have of my own to them. I can say these conver-

sations have shown me ways we can learn to cope with experiences that may totally deprive us of any feeling of living in the "real" world we knew before their occurrence. In some cases, the people with whom I was speaking simply needed to be reassured that they were by no means alone in having the experiences they were reporting. That simple reassurance was not always easy to give, but it was often quite an effective means of enabling these people to get some grip on their turbulent emotions in the wake of a recent visitor experience.

I have endeavored, also, to get to know people who were in touch with Strieber and had reported visitor experiences. One such effort took the form of a visit to the Striebers' country home in the company of eight people who all said they had had such experiences. The group was composed of people from around the country, and was fairly diverse in composition. Two of the people in the group were also journalists, and we struck up lively conversations with one another.

The express purpose of that weekend gathering was to see if we, as individuals and as a group, could literally "call" the visitors. As a journalist, I had no objection to doing so. After all, if I could meet the visitors, why not?

My experience of being with the group was rather simple and enjoyable. One night, while gathered with the others at a stone circle behind the cabin, I looked up in the sky and saw an orange ball moving in an undulating fashion. It had the apparent size of a golf ball and moved just above the line of the tops of the tall pine trees. It started moving in the pattern of a sine wave before disappearing behind the trees.

One woman in the group, Lorie Barnes, told me she had seen the ball, too. Had I seen an extraterrestrial craft? I don't know. What I saw was indeed quite unusual.

That night, while dreaming, I thought that I heard rain falling outside. I dreamed that I went out onto the deck behind the house, carrying an umbrella to keep myself dry. I was greeted by a pleasant young woman who seemed to have the air of a stewardess and was standing next to a sporty white Toyota (!), holding the door open for me. I got into the driver's seat, she closed the door, and the car flew deep into the night sky.

I enjoyed that dream.

The next night, some of the people sleeping in the front room described being awakened by light pouring into the windows in the wee hours of the morning. Another person described being jostled in his bed by unseen hands. Others reported strange noises—a froglike croaking sound that we had heard coming out of the dark the night before, while seated in the circle.

Some of us were very excited. I savored the memory of my dream— or was it a dream?

As a result of the relationships that I have developed here in San Antonio and with other people who have reported visitorlike events in their lives, I have come to deal with the subject matter of my investigation not merely as a question of "What in the world is happening with Whitley Strieber?" but also as one of "What in the world is happening to me and to my friends?" While some UFO researchers might think that such an attitude may have "contaminated" my inquiry, or that my friends with visitor experiences are now no longer in possession of "pure" accounts of their experiences since they have talked with one another about them, I can only say that the kind of clinical objectivity such an attitude is apparently striving to obtain is not an appropriate response to the immediacy of the visitor experience. The appropriate response to someone who is asking for help in the middle of the night is to listen to him or her, provide as much information and reassurance as is possible, and try to help bring the person back into a state of personal equilibrium. I've inadvertently found myself spending a good deal of time simply being called upon to listen to people who felt they couldn't even talk about their experiences with their spouses or doctors.

At the outset of my inquiry, I had something of a tendency to regard Whitley's experiences as quite bizarre and very individual. Now, well over a year since I began to inquire into this matter, I have come to see that, in relation to the experiences reported by many other people, Whitley Strieber's experiences are neither totally bizarre nor totally unique. I do not mean to suggest that all UFO abduction experiences follow a predictable template. I do not believe that they do so, and any suggestion to that effect, in my opinion, is a rather hasty overgeneralization. Moreover, I have come to think that there may be a social element to the visitor experience that has been rather overlooked in many abduction investigations. One person's experience can be a catalyst, perhaps, for those of others. Perhaps there are other, hidden relationships we have yet to discover, too. In the course of constructing an informal network of people who have reported visitor experiences, I have been witness to some rather extraordinary stories and events from people who, curiously, seem to lead lives impinging in one way or another on Whitley's story of life with the visitors.

My friendship with Ron McAtee has been particularly fruitful in that regard. McAtee and I live in such different worlds that it is unlikely we would have ever met under ordinary circumstances. I made a point, however, of following up what I could of McAtee's story and going with him to places in the Olmos Basin where he remembers having had anomalous experiences in his boyhood. One place, of particular beauty, is an old quarry near the headwaters of the San Antonio River where stone for the Alamo and the early missions was cut. There is an old mill nearby, which McAtee found interesting since Strieber had mentioned a memory of an "old mill" near the site of his "children's circle" meetings. I returned to that site on numerous occasions, simply to meditate on the curiousness of my inquiry.

McAtee continues to report visitor experiences to me, and his are quite personal, sometimes even involving awakening with strange bruises on his body. My experiences are less direct, these days, although I must admit that my dream life has changed radically and that occasional visitor figures appear to me in my dream state.

Of course, it will be argued that my mind has taken me on a joyride. Yet, even when I have wondered about all this to myself, there have remained the helicopters—and their appearance at extraordinary times—as a strange question mark hovering above the whole complex of this experience. These experiences have even intruded into my journalistic work.

In September of 1988 I had a series of interesting helicopter sightings in the company of Ron McAtee and Craig Phelon, previously mentioned as a staff writer for the *San Antonio Express-News Sunday Magazine*. I had signed a contract with Ben King, editor of the *Sunday Magazine*, to serve as a consultant for an article on UFOs in San Antonio, with a heavy emphasis on Strieber. King was also interested in seeing if McAtee would be willing to be mentioned in the article. When I sounded him out on the idea, McAtee agreed, and before long Phelon and I met him at the playground near Cambridge Elementary School. (I should note that a small Bell 47 helicopter flew by our side for a while on the freeway while we were en route to meet McAtee.)

Shortly after McAtee described his sighting to Phelon, we all noticed a large, Sikorsky-style helicopter flying over some houses at the top of a nearby hill. McAtee said, "There's one of your helicopters, Ed!" jokingly, and we paid it no more heed.

We next drove to a parking lot adjoining the wooded area near the quarry and old mill in Olmos Basin. When we got out of our cars, we noticed the same helicopter, flying at a low elevation, not more than one hundred yards from us. It was, curiously, painted pastel blue.

When we found our way to the site of the old mill (which happened at that time of the year to have been under a great deal of foliage cover from large surrounding oak trees), I began to explain to Phelan that this was a site that McAtee thought might have some relationship to Strieber's "children's circle" experiences. At that moment, we heard the sound of a low-flying helicopter and looked up to see what appeared to be the same large, pastel-blue Sikorsky fly directly over our heads.

How about that for timing?

I must admit I have become rather blasé about this whole aspect of the phenomenon. If my telephone has been tapped, I have nothing to hide. I have spoken with one young man in California named Ron Rodriguez, as a matter of fact, who has told me that not only has he seen UFOs and strange black limousines following him, but he experiences voices in his head who communicate with him twenty-four hours a day. He says he has been checked out by his local psychiatrist and found to be fine, and has learned to live with his voices. So, I would conjecture, did Joan of Arc.

So, too, I have learned to live with what appears like a tremendous amount of surveillance.

Call it "UFO researcher's disease" or what have you. The complex of experiences I have had, in their general outline, is well known in the UFO community. I will admit to having experienced a fair amount of initial fear in dealing with what seemed like an invasion of my privacy. In the end, though, I have come to see that there is a degree of legitimate personal power in communicating one's own experiences.

Moreover, I have come to see extraordinary similarities between anomalous events reported by Strieber and those objectively reported in the outside world. These similarities have forced me to hypothesize that some real, objective force is at work here. For example, in the final weeks of writing this book, I received a call from Strieber telling me about an article he had just read in the November 1988 issue of the *UFO Newsclipping Service.*

As I had just gotten my copy of that same issue, I opened it and read along.

What I saw was rather astonishing. At the top of an article entitled "The Otherwordly Obsession of Dr. Leo Sprinkle" from the Denver *Rocky Mountain News* dated August 7, 1988, I saw a sidebar headlined "Aliens Knocking at Town Door?" Reporter Matthew Soergel wrote:

> Linda Martin's dogs normally bark at any noise. But they hid and whimpered when the nine knocks—in three sets of three knocks—sounded on the walls of Martin's mobile home early in the morning of Feb. 27.
>
> "All three of my dogs went and hid under my bed," says Martin, a resident of Glenrock, Wyo. "Oh yeah, there was no doubt, they were scared to death."
>
> They weren't the only ones. The strange knocking was heard all over Glenrock that morning, mystifying residents and police.

The rest of the sidebar relates a sighting of a strange light over Glenrock, a report from one local person of seeing a "spaceship" on his lawn, and a comment from Carol Tober, the Glenrock police dispatcher, that maybe half the town of seventeen hundred people heard the knocks.

I phoned Mathew Soergel at the *Rocky Mountain News* and talked to him about this story. He told me Carol Tober told him she had received over forty-five calls from Glenrock residents. He gave me Linda Martin's telephone number, but my call did not go through. An operator came on and asked me what number I had been dialing. When I told her, I got a recording. The telephone company recording I listened to stated that the number had been disconnected "and no further information is available."

Did Soergel realize that Whitley Strieber had written in *Transformation* about having heard nine knocks on the wall of his house—"in three sets of three knocks"—long before this event occurred? I asked him that question, and he replied that he didn't even realize that Strieber had recounted such an incident in *Transformation.* I told Soergel that I knew Strieber had written his story months before the occurrence in

Glenrock, as I had read an early manuscript of *Transformation*.

The occurrence that Strieber describes came, he said, after reading a line from an essay by Dr. John Gliedman that stated, "The mind is not the playwright of reality." I quote Strieber:

> At that moment there came a knocking on the side of the house. This was a substantial noise, very regular and sharp. The knocks were so exactly spaced that they sounded like they were being produced by a machine. Both cats were riveted with terror. They stared at the wall. The knocks went on, nine of them in three groups of three, followed by a tenth lighter double-knock that communicated an impression of finality.[7]

Strieber adds that his cats were so terrorized they ran from the room and hid, one staying in a cupboard for hours.

What does it all mean? I am still working on that question, myself. I have come to have an operating hypothesis, though, that this phenomenon, whatever it is, has a direct link with human consciousness. It is indeed tricksterlike, here one moment, gone the next, dazzling us with amazing shows and feats of derring-do. Has it served any purpose to benefit me—or has it been some kind of demonic interference in my life? While my initial response to much of it was alarm, I have come to see this trickster phenomenon as a friend in one sense: It has kept me on my toes and made me keenly aware of details in ordinary life that I might not normally perceive.

And that, for now, is enough.

Appendix

This Is No Dream

Chapter I   Incident of the 50's
by Ron McAtee

As best I can remember it was winter, when the blue tint of the sky takes on a cold appearance. Whether there was much cloudcover I cannot recollect, but I remember the afternoon sun.

It was my first year at school and I was at recess. There were no organized games for first graders like myself then; we were just a young mob let loose on a playground. There were swings and slides for us loners while the joiners played games.

The fabulous 50's so longed for today were in full swing: the songs, the cars, the art deco look. But I was too young to appreciate all that; too young to sense the magic of that decade. But if I lost the clear memories of those years I did not forget what happened next.

There was no way possible I could ever forget the following moments, no matter how much I may have wanted to later. For that memory differs from others in the way a steel etching differs from a written page. It was as if a pall of eeriness had descended over the entire playground; like something that did not belong to this world was getting very near. I cannot recollect what made me look up into the sky. Perhaps when I was young I was used to it or perhaps it was just a destiny being acted upon.

If it was destiny then what a destiny it was and is, for I beheld in

the sky—not directly overhead but northward in the immediate horizon—a spectacle the likes of which I had never seen before nor have I seen anything even close to it since. It was a rocket-powered flying ship to be sure, and that was the only certainty. As clear and vivid as it was, I still could not believe it was really there and thought I must be looking into the sun and hallucinating. It was just too weird for me to believe.

I turned my head towards the sun, which was in the other side of the sky. I turned back straight ahead and the ship was still there. It was real! If there was one earthly word to describe it, it was eerie. It was eerie as hell itself and even though apparently made of metal, even the color of the metal had a dark eerie shade to it like nothing I had ever seen. The ship was powered by six rockets and the heat waves flowing from the orange-yellow flame of each rocket distorted the sky. The central sphere in which the occupants rode was easy to see. The ship was completely silent, yet there was an awful symmetry to the configuration of the ship, like it did not belong at all here. And yet there was a magnificent beauty to it all, actually beholding the art of another world.

I stood there on the playground in a motionless state with my eyes transfixed on the ship, and suddenly a thought wave seemed to come from one of the ship's occupants. It entered my head in a low masculine sort of tone. The thought was:

WE ARE BEING WATCHED.

Then after a brief pause another thought came forth from apparently another entity on board the ship. This tone of thought was slightly lower and more authoritative than the first:

WE ARE NOT TO BE SEEN.

WE MUST LEAVE.

At that point the rotor began to rotate around the sphere of the ship faster and faster until the ship just seemed to shrink and disappear.

The memories I have since that incident are rather hazy, but I remember telling my mother of what had happened and drawing a picture of the ship. Whether I did this right after the sighting or a year or two later I cannot recall. In the fourth grade a classmate described the ship as he had apparently seen it too. I know I discussed what had happened with my mother and tried to figure out how the ship worked. The years passed and the incident was put aside, and only occasionally entered into conversation. But what had happened was never completely forgotten and paths that cross seem to cross again—and so it was destined to be with me and those associated with the ship.

Notes

Chapter 1

1. Robert Graves, *The White Goddess* (New York: Farrar, Straus and Giroux, 1966), p. 17, reprint of 1948 edition.

2. Thomas Bulfinch, *Bulfinch's Mythology* (New York: Thomas Y. Crowell Company, 1947), pp. 185–188.

3. André Fraigneau, *Cocteau on the Film* (New York: Roy Publishers, 1954), pp. 101–102.

4. Edward Beecher Claflin, "When Is a True Story True?" *Publishers Weekly*, August 14, 1987.

5. Philip J. Klass, *UFO-Abductions: A Dangerous Game* (Buffalo: Prometheus Books, 1988), pp. 133–139.

6. Thomas Silverberg, M.D., Strieber said, has been his personal physician for over twelve years and was the first person to whom Strieber confided the story of his December 26, 1985, "abduction."

7. Whitley Strieber, *Communion: A True Story* (New York: Morrow/Beech Tree Books, 1987), pp. 129–130.

8. Steve Hassan, a former Unification Church leader now specializing in counseling people in cults and former cult members, has expressed to me

his concern that Gurdjieff-related groups may practice harmful mind control techniques upon their members. Hassan is the author of *Combatting Cult Mind Control* (Rochester, Vt.: Park Street Press, 1988).

9. I refer to Strieber's account of experiencing something being inserted up his nose one night, as recounted in *Communion*, pp. 127–128.

Chapter 2

1. Mary Strieber was referring here to Leon and Lanette Glasscock.

2. Craig Phelon, "They're Here! They're There! They're Everywhere! The Latest UFO Craze Is Focusing San Antonio," *San Antonio Express-News Sunday Magazine*, October 30, 1988.

3. Timothy Good, *Above Top Secret: The Worldwide UFO Coverup* (New York: William Morrow and Company, 1988), p. 263.

4. Ibid.

5. Donald Keyhoe, *The Flying Saucers Are Real* (New York: Fawcett Publications, 1950).

6. I have failed to find such a direct statement by Keyhoe in *The Flying Saucers Are Real*. It appears that he did not report the actual condition of or retrieval of Mantell's body, though he mentioned it was rumored that the body had been riddled with bullets. See ibid., p. 37.

7. According to Strieber, the film was *The Owl and the Pussycat*.

8. Whitley Strieber, *Transformation: The Breakthrough* (New York: Morrow/ Beech Tree Books, 1988), pp. 125–126.

9. Whitley Strieber, *The Hunger* (New York: William Morrow and Company, 1981), p. 84.

10. Whitley Strieber, *Cat Magic* (New York: Tom Doherty Associates, 1986), p. 145.

11. Luminous owls and flying fireballs in conjunction with one another have been reported in a most curious manner by Charles Fort in Chapter 10 of his book, *Lo!* See *The Books of Charles Fort* (New York: Henry Holt and Company, 1941), pp. 624–628.

12. Strieber, *Cat Magic*, p. 316.

13. Dennis Etchison, eds., *Cutting Edge: Brave New Horror Stories* (New York: Doubleday, 1986).

14. Ibid., p. 267.

15. Ibid., p. 273.

16. Ibid., p. 287.

17. Douglas E. Winter, ed., *Prime Evil, New Stories by the Masters of Modern Horror* (New York: New American Library, 1988).

18. Ibid., p. 259.

19. Ibid., p. 264.

Chapter 3

1. Transcript of *The Phil Donahue Show*, February 23, 1987.

2. Ibid.

3. Transcript of *The Larry King Show*, March 25, 1987.

4. Transcript of *Nightwatch*, April 1, 1987.

5. Ibid.

6. Ibid.

7. Transcript of *Good Morning America*, September 7, 1988.

8. Transcript of *The Late Show*, September 16, 1988.

Chapter 4

1. Hopkins, a noted visual artist working in the abstract expressionist mode, has works exhibited in the collections of the Guggenheim and Whitney museums, and has been investigating UFO "abductions" for over twelve years. He has developed the hypothesis that UFO "abductions" are related to an ongoing genetic experiment between extraterrestrial life-forms and the human race.

2. Jacques Vallee, *Messengers of Deception: UFO Contacts and Cults* (Berkeley: And/Or Press, 1979), pp. 221–223.

3. For a description of life in certain UFO groups that seem to justify suspicion of mind control activities in association with them, see Douglas Curran's account of a visit to the home of two young members of the Unarius Educational Foundation, in *In Advance of the Landing* (New York: Abbeville Press, 1985), p. 37. His account of his visit to the Aetherius Society in Los Angeles, is also instructive in this regard; see ibid., pp. 63–69.

4. See Steven Hassan's *Combating Cult Mind Control* (Rochester, Vt.: Park

Street Press, 1988), pp. 195–197, on dangers of cultism in the New Age movement.

5. For a remarkable case study of the social dynamics of a UFO cult that survived despite events that cast doubt on the "channeled" information of its leader, I direct the reader to the classic work by Leon Festinger, Henry W. Riecken, and Stanley Schachter, *When Prophecy Fails: A Social and Psychological Study of a Modern Group That Predicted the Destruction of the World* (New York: Harper and Row, 1956).

6. Jacques Vallee makes reference to this situation in the introduction to his most recent book, *Dimensions: A Casebook of Alien Contact* (Chicago: Contemporary Books, 1988). See also Budd Hopkins's final chapter in *Intruders: The Incredible Visitations at Copley Woods* (New York: Random House, 1987) and Timothy Good's information on alleged CIA infiltration of NICAP in *Above Top Secret: The Worldwide UFO Coverup* (New York: William Morrow and Company, 1988).

7. McKenna is coauthor, with his brother Dennis J. McKenna, of *The Invisible Landscape: Mind Hallucinogens and the I Ching* (New York: Seabury Press, 1975).

8. Strieber refers here to a series of sightings that occurred in 1988 in Gulf Breeze, Florida, and gained considerable national publicity as a result of a remarkable series of Polaroid and 35-millimeter photographs and a video tape of what appeared to be aerial craft that hovered above the town. A responsible local businessman who chose to be known simply as "Mr. Ed" was the chief source of these reports, which, according to Strieber, also involved "Mr. Ed" in some "abduction" experiences.

9. The disc jockey questioning Randles had commented earlier that there had been a story of UFO "abduction" even on the American television show *Dynasty*.

10. "MJ-12 information" is identified in the UFO community with the efforts of independent researchers Stanton Friedman, William Moore, and Jaime Shandera. According to them, they have been clandestinely given copies of purportedly authentic United States government documents dating from 1947 that outline the formation and command structure of "MJ-12."

11. Leo Sprinkle, Ph.D., is a psychologist on the faculty of the University of Wyoming, Laramie, who has investigated many noted UFO "abduction" cases.

12. Held November 21–22, 1987.

13. Vallee is referring to his book *Passport to Magonia: From Folklore to Flying Saucers* (Chicago: Henry Regnery Company, 1969), which was the

first attempt by a serious UFO researcher to relate UFO phenomena to historical reports of "fairy"-human interaction and other aspects of paranormal aerial phenomena from antiquity. "Magonia" was a mystical land inhabited by the fairy.

14. The "Lonnie Zamora case," a report on an April 24, 1964, incident in Socorro, New Mexico, became the first generally recognized American instance of alleged human-"alien" contact. Zamora, a police officer, was apparently regarded as a reliable witness. See D. Scott Rogo's account of this case in *Alien Abductions: True Cases of UFO Kidnappings* (New York: NAL/Penguin, 1980), p. 2.

15. Vallee here refers to "waves" of sightings, in that UFO reports have been observed to flow in a periodic fashion, leading to the casual use of the terms "waves" or, especially in the popular press, "flaps," to denote such times of apparently high UFO activity.

16. Vallee is referring to the Lexington Broadcast Systems television show *UFO Cover Up? . . . Live* by Seligman Productions, broadcast on the Fox Network on October 14, 1988. While it was applauded by Walt Andrus, president of the Mutual UFO Network, the show was widely criticized in other UFO circles as being a "video tabloid" and unprofessional in its presentation of information on sightings, close encounters, and purported secret government documents and witnesses dealing with alleged official knowledge of alien presence on earth. One curious aspect of the show was the inclusion of telephone numbers audience members could call to report "close encounter" experiences with UFOs and/or "aliens." No mention was made of to whom this information would be given.

Chapter 5

1. *Close Encounters of the Third Kind*, released in 1977, starred Richard Dreyfuss, François Truffaut, and Teri Garr. Steven Spielberg both directed the film and wrote its screenplay.

2. The remake of *Invasion of the Body Snatchers* hit American movie theaters in 1978, starring Donald Sutherland, Brooke Adams, and Leonard Nimoy. It was directed by Philip Kaufman from a screenplay written by D. W. Richter. The original *Invasion of the Body Snatchers* was a 1956 release starring Kevin McCarthy, directed by Don Siegel. The film was adapted from the novel *The Body Snatchers*, by Jack Finney.

3. The widely reported American "abduction" story of Betty and Barney Hill was dramatized for television by the National Broadcasting Company. *The UFO Incident*, which starred James Earl Jones as Barney Hill and Estelle

Parsons as his wife, Betty, was first shown on October 20, 1975. See Philip J. Klass, *UFO-Abductions: A Dangerous Game* (Buffalo: Prometheus Books, 1987) p. 39.

4. This phenomenon was recorded on film during a nighttime helicopter shot of the New York skyline. I saw the film at the same time as did Strieber and Mora, during the screening of film shot the previous day. When the strange light appeared and began moving toward center screen, Strieber let out a huge guffaw. The light resembled ball lightning, appearing to be just less than a foot in diameter, glowing with a very high degree of constant intensity.

5. I discuss my own experience of sleeping at Strieber's cabin in the Epilogue to this book.

6. I direct the reader to the numerous statements made on Geller by James Randi ("the Amazing Randi") in his book *Flim-Flam!* (Buffalo: Prometheus Books, 1987).

7. David Swanson, "Identification of the Antagonistic Relationship Between Science Fiction Readers and People with Psychic and Occult Experiences," *Journal of Occult Studies*, Vol. 1, No. 1, publication of the University of Rhode Island Extension and Occult Studies Foundation, Providence, May 1977).

8. Ibid., p. 86.

9. Douglas Curran, *In Advance of the Landing: Folk Concepts of Outer Space* (New York: Abbeville Press, 1985).

10. Ibid., p. 115.

11. *Hombre Mirando al Sudeste (Man Facing Southeast)*, a 1987 release, was written and directed by Eliseo Subiola, and features Hugo Soto as Rantes.

Chapter 6

1. *UFOs: The Public Deceived* (Buffalo: Prometheus Books, 1985) and *UFO Abductions: A Dangerous Game* (Buffalo: Prometheus Books, 1988).

2. *Webster's Third New International Dictionary* (Springfield, Mass.: Merriam-Webster, 1981), p. 2132.

3. Robert Sheaffer, *The UFO Verdict: Examining the Evidence* (Buffalo: Prometheus Books, 1986), pp. 34–35.

4. Klass, *UFO-Abductions*, p. 138.

Chapter 7

1. W. Y. Evans-Wentz, *The Fairy Faith in Celtic Countries* (New York: University Press, 1966), pp. 85–86.

2. John A. Keel, "The Man Who Invented Flying Saucers," *The Whole Earth Review* (Fall 1986), p. 58.

3. Martin Gardner also recounts his version of the "Shaver hoax" in *The New Age: Notes of a Fringe Watcher* (Buffalo: Prometheus Books, 1988); see Chapter 30, "Who Was Ray Palmer?," pp. 209–222.

4. Whitley Strieber, *Communion: A True Story* (New York: Morrow/Beech Tree Books, 1987), p. 30.

5. D. R. McAnally, *Irish Wonders: Popular Tales as Told by the People* (New York: Weathervane Books, 1988), pp. 92–93.

6. Carl Gustav Jung, *Archetypes of the Collective Unconscious* (Princeton, N.J.: Princeton University Press, 1968), pp. 3–4.

7. Marie Louise von Franz, *Interpretation of Fairy Tales* (Dallas: Spring Publications, 1978), p. 1.

8. Ibid., p. 1.

9. Ibid., p. 2.

10. Brad Steiger, *The Fellowship: Spiritual Contact Between Humans and Outer Space Beings* (New York: Dolphin/Doubleday, 1988), p. 4.

11. Kenneth Grant, *Outside the Circles of Time* (London: Frederick Müller, 1980), p. 1.

12. Ibid., p. 110.

13. Francis King, *The Magical World of Aleister Crowley* (New York: Coward, McCann & Geoghegan, 1978), p. 57.

14. Ibid., p. 58.

15. Ibid. p. 59.

16. Ibid. p. 59.

17. Reproduced in a facsimile edition by Stephen Skinner under the imprint of Askin Publishers (London: 1976).

18. George C. Andrews, *Extra-Terrestrials Among Us* (St. Paul: Llewellyn Publications, 1987), pp. 67–68.

19. Ibid., p. 68.

20. Jacques Vallee, *Dimensions: A Casebook of Alien Contact* (Chicago: Contemporary Books, 1988), pp. 20–21.

21. Ibid. p. 89.

22. W. Y. Evans-Wentz, op. cit, p. 85.

23. Hilary Evans, *Visions, Apparitions, Alien Visitors: A Comparative Study of the Entity Enigma* (Wellingborough, Eng.: Aquarian Press, 1984), pp. 304–305.

24. Raymond E. Fowler, *The Andreasson Affair* (New York, Bantam Books, 1980), p. 87.

25. Ibid., cover, paperback edition, 1987.

26. Michael Grosso, "Transcending the 'ET Hypothesis,' " *UFO*, Vol. 3, No. 1 (1988).

27. Budd Hopkins, *Intruders: The Incredible Visitations at Copley Woods* (New York: Random House, 1987), p. 193.

28. D. Scott Rogo, *Alien Abductions: True Cases of UFO Kidnappings* (New York: NAL/Penguin 1980), p. 239.

29. Ibid., p. 240.

Chapter 8

1. *Irish Folk and Fairy Tales*, William Butler Yeats, ed. (New York: Dorset Press, 1986), p. 13; quoted in Jacques Vallee, *Dimensions: A Casebook of Alien Contact* (Chicago: Contemporary Books, 1988), pp. 72–73.

2. Katherine Briggs, *Encyclopedia of Fairies* (New York: Pantheon/Random House, 1976), p. 70.

3. Ibid., p. 71.

4. Yeats, op. cit., pp. 78–79.

5. See the chapter "Phantom Clowns" in Loren Coleman's *Mysterious America* (Winchester, Mass.: Faber and Faber, 1983), pp. 211–217.

6. See Janet and Colin Bord, *The Secret Country: An Intrepretation of the Folklore of Ancient Sites in the British Isles* (New York: Walker and Company, 1976).

7. Jacques Vallee, *Dimensions: A Casebook of Alien Contact* (Chicago: Contemporary Books, 1988), pp. 50–51.

8. Ibid., p. 51.

9. Ibid., p. 49.

10. Yeats, op. cit., pp. 13–14.

11. W. Y. Evans-Wentz, *The Fairy Faith in Celtic Countries* (New York: University Press, 1966), pp. 11–12.

12. Kendrick Frazier, ed. *Paranormal Borderlands of Science* (Buffalo: Prometheus Books, 1981), p. 73.

13. Whitley Strieber, *Communion: A True Story* (New York: Morrow/Beech Tree Books, 1987), p. 22.

14. Ibid., p. 25.

15. Ibid., p. 29.

16. Ibid., pp. 29–30.

17. Ibid., p. 30.

18. Ibid., p. 28.

19. Ibid., p. 30.

20. Ibid., pp. 82–83.

21. Ibid., p. 29.

22. Ibid., p. 84.

23. Ibid., p. 85.

24. Ibid., p. 64.

25. Ibid., p. 66.

26. Ibid., p. 67.

27. Ibid., pp. 104–105.

28. Ibid., pp. 105–106.

29. Ibid., pp. 106–107.

30. Ibid., p. 110.

31. Joseph Jacobs, *Celtic Folk and Fairy Tales* (New York: G. P. Putnam's Sons, 1968), p. 1.

32. Ibid., pp. 1, 4.

33. Whitley Strieber and Jonathan Barry, *Cat Magic* (New York: Tom Doherty Associates, 1986), p. 144.

34. Ibid., pp. 144–146.

35. Strieber, *Communion*, p. 104.

36. Ibid., p. 29.

37. Ibid., p. 106.

38. Strieber and Barry, *Cat Magic*, p. 146.

39. Strieber, *Communion*, p. 104.

40. Vallee, op. cit., pp. 41–42.

41. Margaret A. Murray, *The God of the Witches* (New York: Oxford University Press, 1970), pp. 101–102.

42. Carl Gustav Jung, *Flying Saucers: A Modern Myth of Things Seen in the Sky* (Princeton, N.J.: Princeton University Press, 1978), pp. 39–40.

43. Ibid., p. 40.

44. Ibid., p. 40.

45. Vallee, op. cit., pp. x–xi.

46. Ibid., p. 179.

47. Ibid., p. 272.

48. Ibid., p. vi–vii.

Chapter 9

1. Strieber is referring to a trip he described in *Transformation*, pp. 109–114.

Epilogue

1. Lawrence Fawcett and Barry J. Greenwood, *Clear Intent: The Government Cover-Up of the UFO Experience* (Englewood Cliffs, N.J.: Prentice Hall, 1984), pp. 99–111.

2. See also Tom Adams's *The Choppers and the Choppers: Mystery Helicopters and Animal Mutilations* (Paris, Tex.: Project Stigmata, 1980).

3. Timothy Good, *Above Top Secret: The Worldwide UFO Coverup* (New York: William Morrow and Company, 1988), p. 13.

4. Strange helicopters formed a good deal of the experience of noted UFO abductee Betty Andreasson, and photos of some of the ones she and her husband have reported seeing are reproduced in Raymond Fowler, *The Andreasson Affair, Phase Two* (Englewood Cliffs, N.J.: Prentice Hall, 1982).

5. John A. Keel, *Why UFOs?: Operation Trojan Horse* (New York: Manor Books, 1976).

6. "Kathie Davis," of whom Hopkins writes in *Intruders*, has reported such strange calls to him. When I spoke with Mrs. "Davis" on the telephone to hear her story of having had an unpleasant lunch with Strieber, there was a tremendous amount of static on the line. "Kathie Davis" said to me that problems with her telephone were commonplace at her home. At that point the line simply went dead—with no dial tone. I listened to the headset for over a minute and noted no return of the dial tone. Only after I replaced the headset and then lifted it up again did I obtain a dial tone.

7. Whitley Strieber, *Transformation: The Breakthrough* (New York: Morrow/Beech Tree Books, 1988), p. 129.

Bibliography

Abell, George O., and Barry Singer, eds. *Science and the Paranormal: Probing the Existence of the Supernatural.* New York: Charles Scribner's Sons, 1981.

Adamski, George, with Desmond Leslie. *Flying Saucers Have Landed.* New York: Werner Laurie, 1953.

Adler, Margot, *Drawing Down the Moon: Witches, Druids, Goddess Worshippers, and Other Pagans in America Today.* Boston: Beacon Press, 1986.

Andrews, George C. *Extra-Terrestrials Among Us.* St. Paul: Llewellyn Publications, 1987.

Ballester Olmos, Vicente-Juan, and Miguel Guasp. *Los Ovnis y La Ciencia.* Barcelona: Plaza & Janes, 1981.

Bearden, Thomas E. *The Excalibur Briefing: Explaining Paranormal Phenomena.* San Francisco: Strawberry Hill Press, 1980.

Bender, Albert K. *Flying Saucers and the Three Men.* New York: Paperback Library, 1968.

Bergier, Jacques. *Extraterrestrial Intervention: The Evidence.* Chicago: Henry Regnery Company, 1974.

Berlitz, Charles, and William L. Moore. *The Roswell Incident.* New York: Berkley Books, 1980.

Bloecher, Ted, with Aphrodite Clamar, Budd Hopkins, and Elizabeth Slater.

Final Report on the Psychological Testing of UFO "Abductees." Mt. Rainier, Md.: The Fund for UFO Research, 1987.

Blum, Ralph, and Judy Blum. *Beyond Earth: Man's Contact with UFOs.* New York: Bantam Books, 1974.

Bord, Janet, and Colin Bord. *The Secret Country: An Interpretation of the Folklore of Ancient Sites in the British Isles.* New York: Walker and Company, 1976.

Bowen, Charles, ed. *Encounter Cases From Flying Saucer Review,* New York: Signet/NAL, 1977.

Briggs, Katherine. *Encyclopedia of Fairies,* New York: Pantheon/Random House, 1976.

Bulfinch, Thomas, *Bulfinch's Mythology.* New York: Thomas Y. Crowell Company, 1947.

Bullard, Thomas E., Ph.D. *On Stolen Time: A Summary of the Comparative Study of the UFO Abduction Mystery.* Mt. Rainier, Md.: The Fund for UFO Research, 1987.

———. *UFO Abductions: The Measure of the Mystery, Vols. I and II.* Mt. Rainier, Md.: The Fund for UFO Research, 1987.

Campbell, Joseph, *The Hero with a Thousand Faces.* Princeton, N.J.: Princeton University Press, 1968.

Carey, Ken. *Return of the Bird Tribes.* Kansas City, Mo.: Uni-Sun, 1988.

Chambers, Howard V. *The Facts on the Flying Saucer Controversy.* New York: Grosset & Dunlap, 1968.

Christian, James L., ed. *Extra-Terrestrial Intelligence: The First Encounter.* Buffalo: Prometheus Books, 1976.

Clarke, Arthur C. *Childhood's End.* New York: Random House, 1953.

Coleman, Loren. *Mysterious America.* Winchester, Mass.: Faber & Faber, 1983.

Crowe, Catherine. *The Night Side of Nature Or, Ghosts and Ghost-Jeerers.* Wellingborough, Eng.: Aquarian Press, 1986.

Crowley, Aleister. *Liber 220 (AL: The Book of the Law).* London: Ordo Templi Orientis, 1938.

Curran, Douglas. *In Advance of the Landing: Folk Concepts of Outer Space.* New York: Abbeville Press, 1985.

David, Jay. *The Flying Saucer Reader.* New York: New American Library, 1967.

Davis, Lorraine. "A Comparison of UFO and Near Death Experiences," *Journal of Near Death Studies,* Vol. 6, No. 4 (1988).

Edwards, Frank. *Flying Saucers—Serious Business*. Secaucus, N.J.: Citadel Press, 1966.

Emenegger, Robert. *UFOs, Past, Present and Future*. New York: Ballantine Books, 1974.

Etchison, Dennis, ed. *Cutting Edge: Brave New Horror Stories by Peter Straub, Whitley Strieber, Clive Barker, and Others*. New York: Doubleday and Company, 1986.

Evans, Hilary. *Gods, Spirits, Cosmic Guardians: Encounters with Non-Human Beings*. Wellingborough, Eng.: Aquarian Press, 1987.

————. *Visions, Apparitions, Alien Visitors: A Comparative Study of the Entity Enigma*. Wellingborough, Eng.: Aquarian Press, 1984.

Evans-Wentz, W. Y. *The Fairy Faith in Celtic Countries*, New York: University Press, 1966.

Fawcett, Lawrence, and Barry J. Greenwood. *Clear Intent: The Government Cover-Up of the UFO Experience*. Englewood Cliffs, N.J.: Prentice-Hall, 1984.

Festinger, Leon, with Henry W. Riecken and Stanley Schachter. *When Prophecy Fails: A Social and Psychological Study of a Modern Group That Predicted the Destruction of the World*. New York: Harper and Row, 1956.

Fitzgerald, Randall. *The Complete Book of Extraterrestrial Encounters*. New York: Macmillan Publishing Company, 1979.

Flammonde, Paris. *UFO Exist!* New York: Ballantine Books, 1976.

Fort, Charles. *The Books of Charles Fort*. New York: Henry Holt and Company, 1941.

Foster, Alan Dean. *Alien Nation*. New York: Warner Books, 1988.

Fowler, Raymond E. *The Andreasson Affair*. Englewood Cliffs, N.J.: Prentice-Hall, 1980.

————. *The Andreasson Affair, Phase Two*. Englewood Cliffs, N.J.: Prentice-Hall, 1982.

————. *Casebook of a UFO Investigator*. Englewood Cliffs, N.J.: Prentice-Hall, 1981.

————. *UFOs: Interplanetary Visitors*. Jericho, N.Y.: Exposition Press, 1974.

Fowles, John. *A Maggot*. New York: NAL Books, 1985.

Fraigneau, André. *Cocteau on the Film*. New York: Roy Publishers, 1954.

Frazier, Kendrick, ed., *Paranormal Borderlands of Science*. Buffalo: Prometheus Books, 1981.

Freixedo, Salvador. *Las Apariciones Marianas*. Madrid: Editorial Posada, 1985.

————. *¡Defendamonos de los Dioses!* Madrid: Editorial Algar, 1985.

Fry, Daniel W. *The White Sands Incident*. Louisville, Ky.: Best Book Company, 1966.

Fuller, John G. *Aliens in the Skies: The New UFO Battle of the Scientists*. New York: G. P. Putnam's Sons, 1969.

———. *Incident at Exeter: Unidentified Flying Objects Over America Now*. New York: G. P. Putnam's Sons, 1966.

———. *The Interrupted Journey; Two Lost Hours Aboard a Flying Saucer*. New York: Dial Press, 1966.

Gardner, Martin. *The New Age: Notes of a Fringe-Watcher*. Buffalo: Prometheus Books, 1988.

Geller, Uri, and Guy Lyon Playfair. *The Geller Effect*. New York: Henry Holt and Company, 1986.

Gooch, Stan. *Creatures from Inner Space*. London: Rider, 1984.

———. *Uri Geller: My Story*. New York: Praeger Publishers, 1975.

Good, Timothy. *Above Top Secret: The Worldwide UFO Cover-Up*. New York: William Morrow and Company, 1988.

Grant, Kenneth. *Outside the Circles of Time*. London: Frederick Müller Ltd., 1980.

Graves, Robert. *The White Goddess: A Historical Grammar of Poetic Myth*. New York: The Noonday Press/Farrar, Strauss and Giroux, 1948, 1969.

Greenberg, Marian. *An Extraterrestrial Conspiracy: A Case Study*. Phoenix: Falcon Press, 1986.

Haines, Richard F., ed. *UFO Phenomena and the Behavioral Scientist*. Metuchen, N.J.: Scarecrow Press, 1979.

Hall, Richard. *Uninvited Guests: A Documentary History of UFO Sightings, Alien Encounters and Coverups*. Santa Fe, N.M.: Aurora Press, 1988.

Hartland, E. S. *English Fairy and Folk Tales*, London: Walter Scott, 1893.

———. *The Science of Fairy Tales: An Inquiry into Fairy Mythology*. Walter Scott, London, 1891.

Hassan, Steven. *Combatting Cult Mind Control*. Rochester, Vt.: Park Street Press, 1988.

Hasted, John. *The Metal Benders*. Boston: Routledge & Kegan Paul, 1981.

Hickson, Charles, and William Mendez. *UFO Contact at Pascagoula*. Tucson: Wendelle C. Stevens, 1983.

Hoagland, Richard C. *The Monuments of Mars: A City on the Edge of Forever*, Berkeley, Calif.: North Atlantic Books, 1987.

Holzer, Hans, *The UFONAUTS*. New York: Fawcett Gold Medal Books, 1976.

Hopkins, Budd. *Intruders: The Incredible Visitations at Copley Woods.* New York: Random House, 1987.

———. *Missing Time: A Documented Study of UFO Abductions.* New York: Richard Marek Publishers, 1981.

Hufford, David J. *The Terror That Comes in the Night.* Philadelphia: University of Pennsylvania Press, 1982.

Hurtak, James J. *An Introduction to the Keys of Enoch: The Preparation for the Brotherhood of Light.* Los Gatos, Calif.: The Academy of Future Science, 1975.

Hynek, J. Allen. *The UFO Experience: A Scientific Inquiry.* Chicago: Henry Regnery Company, 1972.

———, and Philip J. Imbrogno with Bob Pratt. *Night Siege: The Hudson Valley UFO Sightings.* New York: Random House, 1987.

———, and Jacques Vallee, *The Edge of Reality: A Progress Report on Unidentified Flying Objects.* Chicago: Henry Regnery Company, 1975.

Jacobs, David Michael. *The UFO Controversy in America.* Bloomington, Ind., Indiana University Press, 1975.

Jacobs, Joseph. *Celtic Folk and Fairy Tales,* New York: G. P. Putnam's Sons, 1968.

Jung, Carl Gustav. *Aion: Researches into the Phenomenology of the Self.* Princeton, N.J.: Princeton University Press, 1951.

———. *Archetypes of the Collective Unconscious.* Princeton, N.J.: Princeton University Press, 1968.

———. *Flying Saucers: A Modern Myth of Things Seen in the Sky.* Princeton, N.J.: Princeton University Press, 1958, 1978.

Keel, John A. *Disneyland of the Gods.* New York: Amok Press, 1988.

———. "The Man Who Invented Flying Saucers," *Whole Earth Review,* No. 52, Sausalito, Calif. (1986).

———. *Why UFOs?: Operation Trojan Horse.* New York: Manor Books, 1981.

Keyhoe, Major Donald E. *Aliens from Space . . . The Real Story of Unidentified Flying Objects.* New York: Doubleday and Company, 1973.

———. *Flying Saucers: Top Secret.* New York: G. P. Putnam's Sons, 1960.

———. *The Flying Saucers Are Real.* New York: Fawcett Publications, 1950.

Kinder, Gary. *Light Years: An Investigation into the Extraterrestrial Experiences of Eduard Meier.* New York: Atlantic Monthly Press, 1987.

King, Francis. *The Magical World of Aleister Crowley.* New York: Coward, McCann & Geoghegan, 1978.

Kirk, Robert. *The Secret Commonwealth of Elves, Fauns and Fairies.* Stirling, Eng.: Mackay, 1933.

Klass, Philip J. *UFO-Abductions: A Dangerous Game.* Buffalo: Prometheus Books, 1988.

———. *UFOs: The Public Deceived.* Buffalo: Prometheus Books, 1983.

Koch, Howard. *The Panic Broadcast.* New York: Avon Books, 1967.

Kunetka, James. *Shadow Man.* New York: Warner Books, 1988.

Landsbury, Alan, and Sally Landsbury. *The Outer Space Connection.* New York: Bantam Books, 1975.

Loosely, William Robert, with David Langford, ed. *An Account of a Meeting with Denizens of Another World 1871.* New York: St. Martin's Press, 1980.

Lorenzen, Coral, and Jim Lorenzen. *Abducted: Confrontations with Beings from Outer Space.* New York: Berkley Publishing Corporation, 1977.

McAnally, D. R., Jr., *Irish Wonders: Popular Tales as Told by the People.* New York: Weathervane Books, 1988.

Maccabee, Bruce, Ph.D. *Documents and Supporting Information Relating to Crashed Flying Saucers and Operation Majestic Twelve.* Mt. Rainier, Md.: The Fund for UFO Research, 1987.

MacGregor-Mathers, S. L., ed. (authorship ascribed to "Abraham the Jew") *The Book of the Sacred Magic of Abra-Melin the Mage.* New York: Causeway Books, 1974.

McKenna, Terence K, and Dennis J. McKenna. *The Invisible Landscape: Mind, Hallucinogens, and the I Ching.* New York: Seabury Press, 1975.

Montgomery, Ruth. *Aliens Among Us.* New York: Fawcett Crest, 1985.

Murray, Margaret A. *The God of the Witches.* New York: Oxford University Press, 1970.

Oberg, James. *UFOs and Outer Space Mysteries: A Sympathetic Skeptic's Report.* Norfolk, Va.: Donning Company Publishers, 1982.

Puharich, Andrija. *Uri: A Journal of the Mystery of Uri Geller.* Garden City, N.Y.: Anchor Press, 1974.

Randles, Jenny. *The UFO Conspiracy.* Poole, Eng.: Blandford Press, 1987.

———, and Peter Warrington. *Science and the UFOs.* New York: Basil Blackwell, 1985.

———, and Paul Whetnall. *Alien Contact: Window on Another World.* London: Hodder & Stoughton, 1983.

Redfinn, Michael. *Being,* New York: Leisure Books, 1988.

Redgrove, Peter. *The Black Goddess and the Unseen Real: Our Unconscious Senses and Their Uncommon Sense.* New York: Grove Press, 1987.

Regis, Edward, Jr. *Extraterrestrials: Science and Alien Intelligence*. New York: Cambridge University Press, 1985.

Ring, Kenneth. *Heading Towards Omega: In Search of the Meaning of the Near-Death Experience*. New York: William Morrow and Company, 1984, 1985.

Rogo, D. Scott, ed. *Alien Abduction: True Cases of UFO Kidnapping*. New York: NAL/Penguin, 1980.

Rojcewicz, Peter M. " 'Men in Black' Experiences: Analogues of the Traditional Devil Encounter," *Fortean Times*, Issue No. 50, London (1986).

Ruppelt, Edward J. *The Report on Unidentified Flying Objects*. New York: Fieldcrest Publishing Company, 1966.

Sagan, Carl, and Thornton Page, eds. *UFO's—a Scientific Debate*. New York: W. W. Norton and Company, 1972.

Sheaffer, Robert. *The UFO Verdict: Examining the Evidence*. Buffalo: Prometheus Books, 1986.

Skinner, Stephen. *A True Relation of What Passed for Many Years Between John Dee and Some Spirits (as edited by Meric Causabon, 1659)*. London: Askin Publishers, 1976.

Smith, Marcia S. *The UFO Enigma*. Washington, D.C.: Library of Congress, Congressional Research Service, 1983.

Spencer, John, and Hilary Evans. *Phenomenon: Forty Years of Flying Saucers*. New York: Avon Books, 1988.

Steiger, Brad. *The Fellowship: Spiritual Contact Between Humans and Outer Space Beings*. New York: Dolphin/Doubleday, 1988.

————. *Mysteries of Time and Space*. New York: Confucian Press, 1973.

————. *The UFO Abductors*. New York; Berkley Publishing Corporation, 1988.

————, ed. *Project Blue Book: The Top Secret UFO Findings Revealed*. New York: Ballantine Books, 1981.

————, and Francie Steiger. *The Star People*. New York: Berkley Publishing Corporation, 1981.

Stemman, Roy. *Visitors from Outer Space*. London: Aldus Books, 1976.

Stevens, Wendelle C., and William J. Herrman. *UFO . . . Contact from Reticulum: A Report of the Investigation*. Tucson: Wendelle C. Stevens, 1981.

Story, Ronald D., *The Encyclopedia of UFOs*. Garden City, N.Y.: Dolphin Books/Doubleday and Company, 1980.

————. ed. *UFOs and the Limits of Science*. New York: William Morrow and Company, 1981.

Stott, Murray. *Aliens over Antipodes*. Sydney: Space-Time Press, Australia, 1984.

Strieber, Whitley. *Black Magic*. New York: William Morrow and Company, 1982.

————. *Communion: A True Story*. New York: Morrow/Beech Tree Books, 1987.

————. *The Hunger*. New York: William Morrow and Company, 1981.

————. *The Night Church*. New York: Simon and Schuster, 1983.

————. *Transformation: The Breakthrough*. New York: Morrow/Beech Tree Books, 1988.

————. *The Wolfen*. New York: William Morrow and Compay, 1978.

————. *Wolf of Shadows*. New York: Fawcett Crest, 1985.

———— and Jonathan Barry. *Cat Magic*. New York: Tom Doherty Associates, 1986.

———— and James Kunetka. *Nature's End*. New York: Warner Books, 1986.

———— and James Kunetka. *Warday*. New York: Holt, Rinehart & Winston, 1984.

Sullivan, Walter. *We Are Not Alone*. New York: McGraw-Hill, 1964.

Swanson, David. "Identification of the Antagonistic Relationship Between Science Fiction Readers and People with Psychic and Occult Experiences," *Journal of Occult Studies*, Vol. 1, No. 1 (1977).

Temple, Robert G. K. *The Sirius Mystery*. New York: St. Martin's Press, 1976.

Vallee, Jacques. *Dimensions: A Casebook of Alien Contact*. Chicago: Contemporary Books, 1988.

————. *The Invisible College: What a Group of Scientists Has Discovered About UFO Influences on the Human Race*. New York: E. P. Dutton and Company, 1975.

————. *Messengers of Deception: UFO Contacts and Cults*. Berkeley, Calif.: And/Or Press, 1979.

————. *Passport to Magonia: From Folklore to Flying Saucers*. Chicago: Henry Regnery Company, 1969.

————. *UFOs in Space: Anatomy of a Phenomenon*. Chicago: Henry Regnery Company, 1965.

von Däniken, Erich. *Chariots of the Gods?* New York: G. P. Putnam's Sons, 1970.

von Franz, Marie Louise. *Interpretation of Fairy Tales*. Dallas: Spring Publications, 1978.

Walton, Travis. *The Walton Experience*. New York: Berkley Publishing Corporation, 1978.

Weldon, John, with Zola Levitt. *UFOs; What on Earth Is Happening?* Irvine, Calif.: Harvest House, 1975.

Williamson, George Hunt. *Other Tongues—Other Flesh*. London: Neville Spearman, 1965.

Wilson, Dr. Clifford. *The Alien Agenda*. New York: NAL/Penguin, 1974.

Wilson, Colin. *The Geller Phenomenon*. London: Danbury Press, 1976.

Wilson, Robert Anton. *The Cosmic Trigger: Final Secret of the Illuminati*. Berkeley, Calif.: And/Or Press, 1977.

Winter, Douglas E., ed. *Prime Evil: New Stories by the Masters of Modern Horror*. New York: NAL Books, 1988.

Yeats, W. B. *Irish Fairy and Folk Tales*. New York: Dorset Press, 1986.

Zaleski, Carol. *Otherworld Journeys: Accounts of Near-Death Experience in Medieval and Modern Times*. New York: Oxford University Press, 1987.

Index

Grateful acknowledgment is made for permission to use the following:

Excerpt from Robert Graves, *The White Goddess*. Copyright © 1948, 1966 by Robert Graves. Reprinted by permission of Farrar, Straus and Giroux, Inc.

Excerpt from Andre Fraigneau, *Cocteau on Film: A Conversation Recorded by Andre Fraigneau*. Copyright 1954 by Roy Publishers, New York, New York.

Excerpt from Craig Phelan, "They're Here! They're Here! They're Everywhere! The Latest UFO Craze Is Focusing on San Antonio," *San Antonio Express-News Sunday Magazine* (October 31, 1987).

Excerpt from Edward Beecher Claflin, "When Is a True Story True?" *Publishers Weekly* (August 14, 1987).

Letter to Whitley Strieber from William Mebane. Reprinted by permission of the author.

Excerpts from Timothy Good, *Above Top Secret: The Worldwide UFO Cover-up*. Copyright © 1988 by Timothy Good. Reprinted by permission of William Morrow and Company, Inc.

Excerpts from Whitley Strieber, *Transformation: The Breakthrough*. Copyright © 1988 by Whitley Strieber. Reprinted by permission of William Morrow and Company, Inc.

Excerpts from Whitley Strieber, *The Hunger*. Copyright © 1981 by Whitley Strieber. Reprinted by permission of William Morrow and Company, Inc.

Excerpts from Whitley Strieber, *Cat Magic*. Copyright © 1986 by Wilson & Neff, Inc. Used by permission of Tor Books, 49 West 24th Street, New York, New York 10010.

Excerpt from Whitley Strieber, "Pain." Reprinted by permission of the author.

Excerpt from Whitley Strieber, "The Pool." Reprinted by permission of the author.

Excerpt from Marie-Louise von Franz, *An Introduction to the Interpretation of Fairy Tales* (Dallas: Spring Publications, 1970). Copyright © 1970 by Marie-Louise von Franz. Reprinted by permission of Spring Publications.

Excerpt from Brad Steiger, *The Fellowship: Spiritual Contact Between Humans and Outer Space Beings*. Copyright © 1988.

Excerpt from Kenneth Grant, *Outside the Circles of Time* (London: Frederick Muller). Copyright © 1980.

Excerpts from Francis King, *The Magical World of Aleister Crowley*. Copyright © 1978 by Francis King. Reprinted by permission of the Putnam Publishing Group.

Excerpt from George C. Andrews, *Extra-Terrestrials Among Us*. Copyright © 1987. Reprinted by permission of Llewellyn Publications.

Excerpt from Jacques Vallee, *Dimensions: A Casebook of Alien Contact*. Copyright © 1988. Reprinted by permission of Contemporary Books, Inc.

Excerpt from Hilary Evans, *Visions, Apparitions, Alien Visitors: A Comparative Study of the Entity Enigma*. Copyright © 1984. Reprinted by permission of Aquarian Press Ltd.

Excerpt from Michael Grosso, "Transcending the 'ET Hypothesis,'" *UFO*, Vol. 3, No. 1 (1988).

Excerpt from Budd Hopkins, *Intruders: The Incredible Visitations at Copley Woods*. Copyright © 1987. Reprinted by permission of Random House, Inc.

Excerpt from D. Scott Rogo, ed., *Alien Abductions: True Cases of UFO Kidnappings*. Copyright © 1980 by D. Scott Rogo. Reprinted by permission of New American Library, a division of Penguin Books USA, Inc.

Excerpt from William Allingham, "The Fairies" from *Irish Folk and Fairy Tales*, edited by W. B. Yates. Copyright © 1986. Reprinted by permission of Dorset Press.

Excerpt from the transcript of *The Donahue Show* (February 23, 1987). Reprinted by permission of Whitley Strieber.